The Chinese Reassessment of Socialism, 1976–1992

The Chinese Reassessment of Socialism, 1976–1992

Yan Sun

PRINCETON UNIVERSITY PRESS

PRINCETON, NEW JERSEY

Copyright © 1995 by Princeton University Press
Published by Princeton University Press, 41 William Street,
Princeton, New Jersey 08540
In the United Kingdom: Princeton University Press,
Chichester, West Sussex

Library of Congress Cataloging-in-Publication Data

Sun, Yan, 1959–
The Chinese reassessment of socialism, 1976–1992 / Yan Sun.
    p.   cm.
Includes bibliographical references and index.
ISBN 0-691-02999-7 (alk. paper). — ISBN 0-691-02998-9 (pbk. : alk. paper)
    1. Communism—China.   2. Socialism—China.   3. China—Economic
policy—1976– .   4. China—Politics and government—1976– .   I. Title.
HX418.5.S87   1995
335.43′45—dc20   95-6349
CIP

This book has been composed in Adobe Galliard

Princeton University Press books are printed
on acid-free paper and meet the guidelines
for permanence and durability of the Committee
on Production Guidelines for Book Longevity
of the Council on Library Resources

Printed in the United States of America by Princeton Academic Press

10   9   8   7   6   5   4   3   2   1

10   9   8   7   6   5   4   3   2   1
(Pbk.)

To my parents

Contents

Preface

MY FORMER classmates and mentors at the School of Foreign Affairs in Beijing will be quite surprised that I have written a book on Chinese politics and socialism. While studying there I was known for having little interest or capability in the required politics classes. One politics instructor even admonished me that if I could not master Marxist analytical tools, I would never be able to write analytical reports on world affairs. She insisted that I would see the empirical relevance of such tools once I left school.

Their relevance actually became apparent to me, however, even before I left that school. In 1984, during a special political report session, a report by Deng Liqun was read to us. The report criticized a couple of little-known graduate students who had presented papers challenging Marx's theory of cognition at a recent academic conference in Guilin. The gist of their challenge was that whereas Marx would say that the moon existed before and without one's seeing it, they argued that the moon did not exist for them if they could not see it or if they chose to close their eyes. Deng warned us that graduate students, with their typical active minds, should guard against such dangerous discussions. Deng's report seemed to me to be focusing on a ridiculous piece of trivia, but it also set me thinking: Why was an obscure argument taken so seriously?

The campaign against spiritual pollution also occurred while I was attending that school. While I and most of my classmates barely noticed the campaign, our Canadian instructor took it rather badly, to our puzzlement. Even though we assured her that we were used to such irrelevant campaigns and did not take them seriously, our instructor decided to return home. When another political campaign swept China in late 1986, I was studying at Johns Hopkins University. Even from a distance, this time I could not help but notice it. The question again came to my mind: Why were those "bourgeois liberals" and their ideas taken so seriously? After all, most people would not even notice them if they were not singled out in campaign criticisms.

But what finally set my mind on the topic of this study was an article that I read for a course for which I was serving as a teaching assistant at Johns Hopkins. Discussing post-Mao Chinese pragmatism, the article flatly says that even China's foremost thinkers and writers only complain about the problems of their system; they do not analyze or know how to analyze the deeper causes. Because they do no soul searching, they do not truly learn from the past. Having just witnessed the flourishing of ideas and debates about reform in China in 1986, I was of course surprised and disappointed by such arguments. I realized that there were few systematic studies of Chinese analyses in or outside China, and that this was a void that should be filled.

The result is the present book, which emphasizes what Chinese have actually said about the sources of the problems in their system. My primary objective is a systematic and comprehensive account of the diversity and complexity of post-Mao Chinese analyses about the socialist system, supported by an overwhelming body of evidence. My analytical concerns focus on the relationship between socialism and the system, and between socialism and reform; the interaction between official and unofficial analyses; and the evolving dynamics and politics of those analyses. The research has been greatly aided by the abundance of post-Mao discourse and, as evidenced by the reference list, by the birth and flourishing of a great variety of periodicals across sectors, regions, and even ideological leanings. At least three of the listed periodicals (*Shijie jingji daobao, Jingjixue zhoukan*, and *Jingjixue zhoubao*) stopped circulation after mid-1989 for political reasons.

Of the periodicals, emphasis has been given to articles and views reprinted or excerpted in three leading national publications: *The People's University Digest of Newspapers and Journals, Xinhua wenzhai*, and *Renmin ribao*. Although authoritative, these publications do not just report the officially acceptable discourse. In fact, the first two often offer good indices of the divergent views on prominent issues from different forums and circles. *Renmin ribao* includes both the domestic and overseas editions. Articles dated after 1986 are mostly from the overseas edition, whereas those prior to that year are all from the domestic edition. Chinese periodicals listed in the reference section include only those published in the People's Republic of China.

Because of the abundance of material cited in this work, all article titles and chapter titles from Chinese sources are given in English translation only. Titles of Chinese books and documents are given in both languages at their first appearance in the notes, then in short Chinese titles subsequently. Central documents published since the Third Plenum are identified by their titles in the notes, since they have all been compiled by the CCP Central Committee's Document Research Office. The titles of a few familiar periodicals are abbreviated in the notes: *Renmin ribao* (*RMRB*), *Guangming ribao* (*GMRB*), *Jiefangjun bao* (*JFJB*), *Hongqi* (*HQ*), *Qiushi* (*QS*), and *Shijie jingji daobao* (*Daobao*).

This project began in late 1989 when one socialist regime after another was literally collapsing before our eyes. But as I wrote and completed it, developments in China and elsewhere only reinforced the themes and significance of this study. For this work to have evolved and endured through such an unprecedented transitional period, I must first thank the foresight, guidance, and support of Dr. Germaine A. Hoston, my dissertation adviser. Her strong belief in taking seriously the ideas and statements of the participants whose actions one is studying, her firm background in political philosophy and Marxist theory, and her critical insights have been of much inspiration throughout my endeavor. I am also particularly grateful to Dr. William T. Rowe, who served as both an adviser and a teacher. It was in his classes that I first became interested in various ways of studying China, and he has been a wealth of enlightenment and inspiration ever since. Especially appreciated is the unfailing enthusiasm and graciousness with which he has supported my research efforts. Both mentors have also encouraged me to publish this work. My personal and intellectual debt to them goes far beyond what I can express here.

I owe a special debt to Dr. Bruce Parrott of the Paul Nietz School of Advanced International Studies, who served initially as a dissertation adviser and who offered useful suggestions on the conceptualization and scope of the project. My thanks also go to other members of political science department at Johns Hopkins: to Drs. Norma Krigger and Steven David for their interest in and support for my work, to Junling Ma and Mark Rush for their encouragement and friendship, and to Evelyn Stoller and Esther Abe for their valuable administrative assistance. I am also grateful to the department for its financial support, which made my years of fruitful study there possible.

The other members of my dissertation committee, Drs. John Pocock, Christopher Chase-Dunn, and Steve Breckler, helped me improve my work with thoughtful questions and comments. Joseph Fewsmith, Maurice Meisner, and George Totten provided thorough and insightful readings of the manuscript. They offered many useful suggestions for revising and clarifying and helped sharpen many important points throughout the study.

To my colleagues at Queens College of the City University of New York, whom I joined in September 1991, I express my appreciation. In particular I thank Drs. Burton Zwiebach, Andrew Hacker, I. L. Markovitz, and John Bowman for their interest, guidance, and support. Dr. Zwiebach and Dr. Patricia Rachal made generous course arrangements that allowed me more time to complete and revise the manuscript.

I am deeply indebted to the psychological, intellectual, and other invaluable support of my family. My parents made it possible for me to have access to the libraries and copying facilities of their host institution in China and sent me many valuable primary materials over the years. My husband Gang Xiao returned from trips to China with useful books and other materials. To their unremitting support I owe my ability and endurance to bring this work to completion.

The Chinese Reassessment of Socialism,
1976–1992

CHAPTER ONE

The Affirmation, Development, and Negation of Marxism

THE YEAR 1989 witnessed both the forceful suppression of the Tiananmen demonstrators in China and the swift collapse of communism in Eastern Europe. These events were followed in 1991 by the demise of the birthplace of the October Revolution. The disparities among these dramatic and almost concurrent events have raised important questions about the sources of the divergent outcomes in these systems. Why was the Chinese leadership able to cling successfully to the intrasystem, reformist approach, whereas Mikhail Gorbachev presided over a revolution that led to the demise of the Soviet Communist party and state? In the Soviet case, Gorbachev's relentless efforts to promote "new thinking" clearly helped to open the path for substantial reforms that eventually heralded the collapse of the entire Stalinist edifice. By contrast, Deng Xiaoping's simultaneous promotion of "rethinking socialism" and the Four Fundamental Principles (i.e., adherence to the leadership of the party, to Marxism-Leninism and Mao Zedong Thought, to the socialist road, and to the people's democratic dictatorship) has both stimulated the kind of revolutionary dynamism displayed by the Tiananmen demonstrators and brought about its suppression.

The rethinking of established socialism that accompanied both the Chinese and the Soviet reform processes preceding the dramatic events of 1989 had a direct link to the character and outcome of the reforms undertaken in these communist societies. This was particularly manifest from the reaction of the Chinese Communist party (CCP) to the events in China and in other communist systems. After the traumatic ending of the mass demonstrations in China in mid-1989, the conservative-dominated official rhetoric immediately turned to pinpoint a "small handful" of instigators who had allegedly exploited the good intentions of the masses by attempting to stage the overthrow of the socialist system and the Communist party. The accused instigators, as they came to be identified in official accounts, included mainly reform theorists and intellectuals prominently associated with advocating the "rethinking" of socialism and capitalism. The direction in which this reconceptualization had developed was now said to have approached the negation of socialism and the advocacy of bourgeois liberalism. It is this ideological position of the "counterrevolutionaries" on which post–June 4 official attacks centered. It allegedly represented a recent intellectual and political trend that advocated renouncing China's socialist framework politically, economically, and ideologically. Thus official rhetoric depicted the events of mid-1989 as in essence a battle between socialism and capitalism and posited the crackdown as the struggle for the survival of the 1949 Revolution.

The flourishing of these bourgeois liberalization trends, moreover, was attributed to the influence of a heterodox approach to socialism within the party leadership. The former general secretary of the party, Zhao Ziyang, in particular was held responsible for the spread of "bourgeois liberal" tendencies. His tolerance of proponents of "bourgeois liberalization," his promotion of some of them as his brain trust, and his own indifferent attitudes toward socialism were said to have encouraged the ideological climate that contributed to the "counterrevolutionary" riot of 1989. Thus the roots of the so-called battle between socialism and capitalism were traced to the reform program of Zhao and his brain trust since the mid-1980s. As one *Renmin ribao* editorial claimed, bourgeois liberal forces "have covered their anti-socialist views in the name of reform and in this way have created considerable ideological confusion. More seriously, they have obtained support from within the party."[1] Wang Renzhi, head of the CCP Central Committee's Department of Propaganda (CDP), called the crisis of 1989 "a struggle between reform of a socialist nature or reform of a capitalist nature." The reform program of Zhao and the bourgeois liberals, he charged, "amounts to . . . replacing the socialist system and installing the capitalist system." Therefore, the protests of 1989 and the subsequent crackdown symbolized "a class struggle in the ideological arena." At the same time, the social basis of the protests of 1989 was attributed to the consequences of Zhao's deviation from socialism. That is, Zhao's "unrestrained" market reforms were blamed for creating widespread economic corruption and social inequality, which were the initial causes of the popular protests.[2]

After the disintegration of the Soviet Communist party and the Soviet Union in late 1991, the CCP also attributed the "peaceful dissolution" of the birthplace of the October Revolution to Gorbachev's infidelity to and betrayal of socialism. His promotion of "new thinking" and "humanistic and democratic socialism" and his gradual "desertion and negation of socialism" during his six years in office were said to have directly eroded the socialist ethos and yielded ground to antisocialist forces in and outside the party. To avoid experiencing the fate of socialism in Eastern Europe and the Soviet Union, the CCP has issued internal documents among official strata and workplaces to strengthen "socialist education" and criticize the Soviet reassessment of socialism.[3]

The CCP's characterization of an ideological battle between socialist and "bourgeois liberal" forces within and outside the party was not just political propaganda to provide a post facto legitimation for the suppression of the protest movement or for the dismissal of the victims in the power struggle among the elites. Rather, it epitomized the explosion of a deep-seated conflict between the so-called conservative and radical reformers over the nature of socialism (see table 1). Over the last decade, this conflict permeated the politics of reform at the top. Radical reformers, mostly the younger generation of leaders, placed priority on adapting established socialism to the requirements of reform and on "developing" Marxism under contemporary conditions. They encouraged a critical reassessment of established theory and practice and permitted this effort to extend to China's entire experience with Marxism. These efforts have been so transformative that they have brought revolutionary changes in Chinese thinking about socialism. More orthodox reformers, mostly veteran revolutionaries, placed priority on reform within the basic confines of socialism and on "upholding" Marxism. Referred to by the dissident intellectual Guo Luoji as "Marxist fundamentalists," members of this group have clung to their political and moral ground by appealing to the continuing orthodoxy of the Four Fundamental Principles.[4] The parallel existence of a growing iconoclasm and a confining doctrine has generated much tension and contradiction in Chinese politics.

Indeed, according to Yan Jiaqi, former director of the Institute of Political Science at the Chinese Academy of Social Sciences (CASS) and a key member of the CCP Commission on Political Structural Reform, the lack of a strong ideological backing was one of the main reasons for the eventual collapse of Zhao's reform program and of the reform leader himself.[5] Reform threatened the foundation of the system and had itself to be defended on doctrinal grounds. Such grounds are needed not only to promote reform but also to sustain it during difficult periods. In late 1988 in particular, the crisis of economic reform reached such unprecedented severity that it put the legitimacy of Zhao's entire program into question. In part, this was because the crisis was precipitated by Zhao's attempt that summer to bring about a more thorough transition to the market and by his neglect of traditional strongholds of socialist economy, such as macroeconomic balance, the rural economy, and state enterprises. The negative consequences of Zhao's policies (double-digit inflation, financial panic, a runaway economy, agricultural decline, a squeezed state sector, and, above all, cadre racketeering) were all attributed to his deliberate erosion of two leading economic mechanisms of socialism, namely, planning and public ownership. The failures of Zhao's reforms, therefore, exposed him both to policy criticisms and to charges of ideological deviation.

On a more personal level, Zhao's ideological persuasiveness was crucial to sustaining his reform agenda because he lacked Deng's prestige and

TABLE 1
The Post-Mao Ideological Spectrum: Political Elites

Groups	Representatives	Marxism and Mao Zedong Thought	Political Reform	Economic Reform
Ultra-Left (1977–1981)	Hua Guofeng, Wang Dongxing, Chen Yonggui,	Completely upholding	Completely opposing	Completely opposing
	Petroleum group	Upholding	Opposing	Opposing esp. reform of the heavy industrial model
Left (1978–present)	Chen Yun, Peng Zheng, Wang Zhen, Bo Yibo, Li Xiannian, Deng Liqun, Hu Qiaomu, Li Peng, Yao Yilin	Upholding then developing	Reform of the Maoist model; priority of stability and party leadership; opposing bourgeois liberalization	Reform of the Maoist model; reform of the heavy industrial model; partial reform of the planned model; dominance of socialist economy
Middle (1978–present)	Deng Xiaoping	Developing	Reform of Maoist and Soviet models; priority of stability and party leadership; opposing bourgeois liberalization	Reform of Maoist and Soviet models; partial reform of the Marxist model; most efficient mechanisms
Right (1978–present)	Zhao Ziyang, Hu Yaobang, Hu Qili, Wan Li	Developing	Reform of Maoist and Soviet models; priority of reform; tolerance for bourgeois liberalization	Reform of Maoist and Soviet models; partial reform of the Marxist model; most efficient mechanisms

power base. A weak ideological standing would mean the deprivation of a powerful means of legitimation in an ideologically conscious political party. Yet despite the throngs of intellectuals and theorists rallying for him, Zhao's ideological standing was precarious in 1988.[6] Earlier reforms were partial accommodations to the capitalist mode of production, justifiable within the frame of "socialism with Chinese characteristics." But the question in 1988 was of a different nature. It was no longer one of what and how much of nonsocialist modes of production to introduce. Zhao's attempts to bring about a full transition to the market and an overhaul of state ownership entailed the abandonment of what was left of the socialist components of the economy. Despite Zhao's efforts to devise a new theory of socialism for China, neither the notion of the "primary stage of socialism" nor that of "socialist commodity economy" was sufficient to defend himself or his policies from charges of ideological deviation. In the end, his ideological standing was branded as closer to that of "bourgeois liberals" than to the Four Fundamental Principles (see table 2). Many criticisms of established socialism made under Zhao were now seen as attacks on socialism. The showdown over the direction of reform in mid-1989—between radical and conservative reformers, on the one hand, and the liberal intellectuals and the state, on the other—has once again shown the centrality of the ideological question in Chinese politics. The essence of the battle among these contending forces in and outside the party is symbolized respectively in the "upholding," "development," and "negation" of Marxism. "Affirmers" and "negators," in opposite ways, have both raised the question of the validity of Marxism as the source of truth and rectitude, and as the basis of social development for China. While the former insist on Marxism as the sole valid source, the latter oppose it. "Developers," on the other hand, have taken the middle road of building socialism with Chinese characteristics and the primary stage of socialism. Except for the dramatic turn of events in mid-1989 and shortly after, the developers' platform dominated the official forum and provided the basis upon which to reappraise and rectify China's socialist path. Dodging challenges from the so-called Left and Right, it sought to accommodate within socialism exogenous values and practices necessitated by or arising out of reform. And it has represented a new approach to and understanding of socialism.

This study is an investigation of the incremental reassessment and reformulation of socialism in post-Mao China. It is also an analysis of how and why these efforts became a focal point of political contention within the party and a catalyst of bourgeois liberalization outside it. Finally, through a comparison of the Chinese discourse with its Soviet counterpart in the final chapter, the study offers an interpretation linking these discourses to the divergent outcomes of reform and revolution in the two countries.

TABLE 2
The Post-Mao Ideological Spectrum: Social Forces

Groups	Representatives	Marxism	Political Reform	Economic Reform
Antisystem	Abolitionists (Wei Jingsheng, underground writers), Fang Lizhi, Wang Ruowang, Liu Xiaobo	Negating; opposing one unified ideology; choice of beliefs	Systemic change; Western-style democracy; individual rights; negating proletarian dictatorship	Capitalist road; free market; private ownership; market-based distribution
Intrasystem	Socialist democrats (Li Yizhe), Su Shaozhi, Wang Ruoshui, Yan Jiaqi, Hu Jiwei	Developing and transcending; equality of diverse beliefs	Non-class-based democracy; humanistic goals; rule of law; expression of diverse opinions	Multilinear routes; dominant market; diverse ownership and distribution forms

SOCIALISM AND REFORM

The Chinese reassessment of socialism is an important and yet little studied subject. The empirical aspect of the post-Mao reforms has attracted much attention academically and journalistically. So has the recent demise of socialism globally. But amid the attention, not to mention celebration, important questions concerning how the elites and people of former and reforming socialist countries themselves have thought about the idea and track record of socialism, and the impact of this thinking on reforms, have apparently been neglected. For example, if established socialism had failed as a design of social order and model of development, how do members of those countries think about what went wrong, and why? What remedies should there be in the light of the diagnosed and perceived problems? How have different political and social groups reacted to these questions? And what has been the impact of their analyses on empirical changes and the future?

The lack of appreciation for the connection between indigenous reassessment of socialism and empirical reforms seems to have stemmed from two latent assumptions. One is that the question of socialism is irrelevant or that it does not genuinely exist. As noted by Arif Dirlik and Maurice Meisner, "what is absent from much of the discussion on China today, expert or nonexpert, is a sense of a problematic of Chinese socialism and its historical context, which must provide a framework for all evaluations of current developments in Chinese society."[7] Instead, socialism is perceived as irrelevant because it seems either an "ideological disguise" for a national quest for "power and wealth"[8] or a camouflage of factional politics.[9] Or ideological concerns are supposedly superseded by a new "pragmatism"[10] or by uncontrollable bureaucratic and local interests.[11] More generally, socialism is simply assumed to have been abandoned.[12]

Another underlying assumption, derived from earlier analyses of Communist regimes, is that the cognitive function of Communist doctrine is often negligible, at least less pertinent than its imperative function. That is, the use of ideology as a normative guide is less important than its use as a mechanism of social control. In the observation of one analyst, Communist doctrine in the hands of party leaders was "a means of influencing the masses, a means of mobilizing classes and social strata for attaining aims whose real meaning remains obscure to the masses." As such, it served as the "most important linkage" in the system of control over the behavior of individuals, groups, institutions, and society. Seen in this way, the content of ideology is significant only to the extent that it serves the purpose of control. Therefore, "not only ideas, but also information on facts that do not conform to communist ideology, are perverted or distorted, and only that is passed on which does not contradict the Teaching."[13] Since the fundamental goal of the doctrine is to induce desired behavior and minimize resistance to the system, ideology simply has the effect of "replacing terror as the chief buttress of the party's power."[14] Thus viewed, the cognitive function of Communist doctrine only serves its imperative function: it is useful to the extent that it maintains social stability without threatening those in power.[15] Consequently, leaders and the masses alike were all too ready and adept at renouncing Maoism for Dengism in accordance with changed political circumstances.[16]

In demonstrating the relevance of socialism in post-Mao political development, several considerations are in order. The first is the ideological premise of the post-Mao reforms. The starting point of the post-Mao reform leadership was not the abandonment of socialism but its rectification. The change of leadership at the end of the Mao era was an intragenerational rather than intergenerational transition. As veterans of the Chinese Revolution, the leaders' ideological commitment must be emphasized because the Chinese Revolution was the result of conscious struggle by indigenous groups. Moreover, the concern with political doctrine and ideological legacy is a peculiarly eminent feature of the Chinese Communist party, as Tang Tsou has noted.[17] No matter how socialism is defined, it has remained meaningful to the Chinese leadership. To Chen Yun, it may denote an economy based on central planning, public ownership, and equitable distribution. To Hu Yaobang, it may denote a political order devoted to the masses' interests and popular rule. And to Deng Xiaoping, it may denote a path of development that will not make China a dependency of strong powers.[18] All these necessitated that socialism be reoriented, rather than abandoned, for the purpose of reform. It is only by appreciating this premise that one can comprehend the motives and concerns of post-Mao reformers, their views of the system to be rectified, the context of their choices and constraints, and the meaning and nature of their break with the past.

The reappraisal of socialism is an important part of post-Mao developments not just because Chinese leaders made it a premise of their reform program; it would be an important issue even in a reforming or former socialist regime where socialism did not come about indigenously. For serious analyses of what has gone wrong with the old system form a crucial basis for finding appropriate remedies. That the post-Mao leadership proceeded from the premise of intrasystem reforms does not render such analyses superficial, because the directions of reappraisal they permitted or opposed reveal much about the nature of those analyses. Moreover, the interplay between official and unofficial analyses, between intrasystem and antisystem analyses, will shed light on such key issues as whether the symptoms of past wrongs have been taken as the causes, whether the right lessons have been learned, whether simple solutions have been sought, and whether an enduring new order may be built on the repudiation of the old. Those divergent analyses will offer insights into debates about contending models of reform and why a particular model prevailed while the others did not. In the Chinese case, the shaping of a reform model in which economic changes preceded political ones deserves special attention in the light of the difficulty of Russia's model of political before economic reforms.

The discrepancy between the practical goals of reform and the fundamental principles of socialism is necessarily a source of political conflict, and an analysis of this discrepancy is necessary to a complete understanding of post-Mao political developments. The drastic course of change in post-Mao China has often led to the neglect of the facts that there have been serious struggles over the nature and goals of reform and that a particular course of change has only occurred as an outcome of such struggles. Moreover, these struggles and outcomes are by no means settled, as has been demonstrated by the zigzag course of post-Mao politics. Integral to those struggles has been a disagreement over the ideological direction of policy change, which is characteristic of politicians of a revolutionary movement. In his study of Soviet ideology from the beginning of bolshevism to the height of Stalinism, Barrington Moore has observed several kinds of elite resistance to change in the political doctrine of the revolutionary movement. One is the tendency for various groups within the movement to develop emotional attachments to its doctrine. Another is the tendency for some leaders to take official doctrine seriously, as in the case of N. I. Bukharin, so that compromising or adapting becomes very difficult for them.[19] Martin Seliger has also noted different responses of politicians to ideological change: "Purists and diehards are normally bothered by dissonance between cherished and applied principles, and, in return, they worry the leadership with their rather articulate misgivings—which at least part of the leadership may share but choose to ignore."[20] For true believers and emotional adherents, political conflict over policy change has a fundamental value dimension. Insofar as reform threatens certain features and goals of socialism, control over ideology influences the reform agenda to be pursued.

The question is also more than that of the difficulty of some politicians to part with cherished ideals. The convictions of veteran revolutionaries are deeply rooted in history and in the issues that motivated their pursuit of the Chinese Revolution in the first place. The qualms that these veteran revolutionaries have felt over certain changes reflect a general Chinese qualm, as Arif Dirlik notes, about joining the "capitalist stream of history" and abandoning certain national goals embodied in the Chinese Revolution.[21] Most of all, this qualm reflects concerns about national independence and memories of semicolonialism and imperialism. In this context, socialism becomes a source of conflict over the direction of reform between politicians who are able to compromise under political exigencies and those who find it more difficult to do so. It is this content of leaders' cherished beliefs, more than the force of their habitual attachments, that has made elite conflicts impassioned and sustained. In this sense, Dirlik has a point in objecting to the labeling of veteran leaders as "conservatives."[22]

The rethinking of the socialist system is also more than a function of elite conflict and reform politics. The acceptance of socialism in modern China was the corollary of the breakdown of traditional Confucianism and disillusionment with Western liberalism in the early twentieth century. Thus the rethinking of the socialist path of national development is an object of contention not merely by policymakers, but also by the entire nation. As Li Honglin, one of the leaders of the Chinese reappraisal, puts it, the rethinking efforts of the post-Mao era date back more than a hundred years to when China was first forced to realize the need to build a strong, modern country.[23] Or, as Joseph Fewsmith demonstrates, "although the Dengist reforms represent a reaction against the Cultural Revolution and the 'leftist' traditions within the CCP, they also are forced to confront the very dilemma that produced the communist movement and revolution in the first place."[24] Yet socialism is not a mere "ideological disguise" for the quest for "wealth and power," because the Chinese concern with it has involved fundamental questions of the type of modern country to be built and the means of building it. The current rethinking, therefore, has been a continuation of the historical search for the nation's choice of guiding values, its path of modernization, and the desirable form of society. In this broader context, the officially sponsored rethinking of socialism has eventually evolved into unofficial challenges to the very place of socialism as a source of value and a path of development for China.

At the other end of the political spectrum, the so-called conservative reformers associate the defense of socialism with patriotism, which was an original goal of the Chinese Revolution. They equate certain reforms with capitalism, against which the revolution was partly motivated. Most of all, they see the wholesale acceptance of the Western-type economic and political system as "wholesale Westernization," which all reform movements in modern China have tended to oppose. These designations are more than mere polemic; they reflect both the genuine concern of these leaders for certain social goals and the difficulty of China as a nation to deal with Western civilization, including capitalism. To the extent that more reform-minded leaders have responded to such misgivings seriously and sometimes sympathetically, those conservative sentiments indeed echo a general Chinese concern with that part of national history and self-image associated with the quest for socialism. In this context, the post-Mao rethinking, of whatever ideological leaning, has not been a mere rationale for retreat from socialism. It must be seen as part of the effort to search for China's own path of modernization on its "own terms."[25]

The crisis of Marxism also contains an internal dynamic for the rethinking of socialism. Changes abroad and pressures at home have raised questions about the sagacity of classic teachings. The opening to the outside has intensified the realization of the gap between reality and doctrine. College textbooks on the political economy of socialism have been updated at least five times within the past decade. Classic teachings on capitalist political economy have posed greater difficulties: written by the classic masters, they cannot be updated randomly. The strenuous efforts of the political economy instructor to struggle through a class with a doubting audience are a reflection of this deep dilemma. If the basic precepts of socialism are based on the critique of its historical predecessor over a century ago, reality has cast many shadows on them. The loftiness of socialist ideals has also lost much appeal, as popular fervor has been exhausted by excessive ideologizing. As different groups have different diagnoses and remedies for these problems, there inevitably are conflicts over what to do about the crisis of faith.

In short, the elaborate efforts to reexamine socialism in the post-Mao period and the persisting disagreements among major groups over the nature and severity of the problems and their import for the direction of socialism in China have demonstrated the important link between the rethinking of socialism and empirical reforms. They have also raised an array of interesting questions about the relationship between socialism and Chinese practice, between socialism and problems of the Chinese system, and between rethinking and empirical reforms. An important objective of this study is to elucidate the post-Mao rethinking as a response to these questions.

Existing studies of post-Mao ideological developments have dealt mostly with the first few years of Deng's ascendancy, when ideological shifts were most dramatic.[26] More recently a few works have assessed the import of post-Mao reforms for Chinese socialism.[27] The only work that gives full attention to the question of socialism in the context of post-Mao reforms is *Marxism and the Chinese Experience*, edited by Arif Dirlik and Maurice Meisner. The authors address the meaning of the definition and direction that Mao's successors have given to socialism from a metahistorical point of view. Meisner observes that the post-Mao course of de-radicalization has reduced socialism to an "ideology of modernization."[28] Dirlik characterizes the post-Mao course of policy and ideology as "post-socialism," in which capitalism is accommodated but socialism is retained as a future option.[29] However, because both are concerned with issues of historical and theoretical import involving broad generalizations, they tend to emphasize the "unsocialist" nature of post-Mao politics. In doing so, they neglect the presence of divergent interpretations of socialism, elite consensus on a basic socialist discourse, the hegemony of the normative and analytical framework of Marxism, and the accommodation of capitalist practices without full acceptance of the underlying values of capitalism. In short, a systematic study has yet to be made that will account for these phenomena and look closely into the substance of the post-Mao discourse on socialism.

The Reassessment of Socialism and the "Rationality" Model

Kenneth Lieberthal and Michel Oksenberg have characterized three major models in English-language studies of Chinese politics: the rationality model, the power model, and the bureaucratic model.[30] The first model emphasizes the importance of policy preferences and value conflicts in policy processes. The second stresses the role of personal and factional power motives of participants in policy processes. The third underscores the constraints of bureaucratic and local interests in policy processes. The present study reflects a conceptual focus on the role of ideas and choices in political change and thus falls into the "rationality" model. The underlying assumptions of this model about coherent groups in policy disputes, different leaders' distinctive values and preferences, reasoned diagnoses of problems and rational debates over perceived problems, the inner logic and coherence of each viewpoint in a particular policy debate, and the evaluation of choices are also the premises upon which this study is built.[31]

In this context, it is pertinent to consider the limitations of the other two models, which dismiss the relevance of value conflicts and policy preferences in Chinese politics. The power paradigm, deriving from factional politics, views power politics and factional concerns as the primary basis for elite conflicts in Chinese politics and depicts policy and ideological disputes as a symbolic expression of factional alignment.[32] The dismissal of the substantive significance of value conflicts is problematic on several accounts. The assumption that politics is a mere contest for power and selfish quests is above all one-sided. It ignores the basic fact that politics is often a struggle between different views of how society should be organized, resources distributed, and authority exercised.[33] To deny the influence of values is also problematic epistemologically, for this fails to recognize politicians' need for affective and analytical categories. Individuals, not least of all politicians, rely on these tools to "make sense of complex social and political reality." And in a long-established socialist regime, Marxism-Leninism alone furnishes leaders with a conceptual framework for organizing their understanding of the world.[34] Even a cynical observer of Soviet ideology concedes that there is a basic Marxist component in the operative ideology of Soviet politicians, which is no other than their coherent vision of the world in Marxist perspectives and categories.[35] The same is true of Chinese revolutionary leaders. Some key Marxist notions, such as the central role of material conditions in determining the forms of superstructure, the paradigm of the forces of production versus social relations of production, and the relationship between base and superstructure, have influenced the basic way of thinking of the Chinese leadership—reformers and conservatives.

On the empirical side, factionalism cannot satisfactorily explain the conflict between the radical and conservative reformers in post-Mao China. Zhao Ziyang is known to be wary of cultivating factions and *guanxi* (interpersonal connections), and Chen Yun is reputedly not keen on such dealings.[36] The assumption about the reducibility of power motives is not only ill-founded but may itself be culturally biased, as it seems to be based on one's observation of political behavior in one's own cultural context. Not surprisingly, leading Chinese participants and observers of post-Mao politics almost uniformly agree that power struggles and factionalism among Chinese elites often originate from ideological cleavages rather than the other way around. Group clingings develop because of shared perspectives, and interpersonal animosity accumulates because of divergent outlooks.[37] Deng Liqun may be the only leader who can clearly be said to cultivate his personal political circle (conservative theoreticians and literary figures under the CDP and the Secretariat of the Central Committee) and pursue personal ambitions under an ideological bandwagon. But even here, ideological affinity is the essential denominator.[38]

The bureaucratic paradigm, deriving from bureaucratic politics and policy implementation, points to the constraints of bureaucratic and local interests that can overshadow value conflicts or policy preferences of the center.[39] Several factors weigh against this argument.[40] The center initiates and engineers reforms, while the bureaucracy can only adapt or distort them. The center determines the overall policy direction and makes concentrated policy efforts while local efforts and influences are fragmented and unsystematic. The center also has the power and capacity to react to the problems in policy implementation. In short, "a strong and skillful leadership" can overcome bureaucratic impediments to reform.[41] Finally, the size and scope of changes in post-Mao China have demonstrated the dominant role of the central leadership.[42] Although policies that are technical in nature (for example, energy or the Three Gorges Dam) do not lend themselves to ideological disputes, broad policies that affect how society will be organized, resources distributed, and authority exercised certainly do.

In addition to these models, the cultural analysis also plays down ideological issues by asserting a Chinese capacity for pragmatism and inability to hold strong beliefs.[43] In this depiction, the Chinese tend to abandon past commitments unemotionally and swing in any direction with little psychological constraints. Since leaders and masses feel free to accept all manners of change with no capacity to appreciate "cognitive dissonance," there are no such things as "inertia, friction, or tension" in the post-Mao reform process. Such cultural traits make ideological transition smooth and fuel pragmatic politics. This thesis ignores many problems that have been constant concerns of the post-Mao leadership, such as "public disillusionment," "faith crisis," and "conservative inertia." Efforts to conduct the "emancipation of the mind," "conceptual adaptation," or "cultural transformation" have marked important phases of the Chinese reform process. Different social groups, generations, and regions have also reacted differently to change. The assumption of a nation of "pragmatic" leaders and followers cannot explain the protracted ideological battles in Chinese politics. It also obscures much of the fire and passion that has fueled post-Mao political developments.

In pointing out the limitations of these various models, however, I do not pretend that my approach is superior or that the factors emphasized in the other models do not matter. Rather, my focus on ideas is intended to offer a unique viewpoint from which to observe what may be obscured in other analytical perspectives. In so doing, I seek to demonstrate that the ideological factor cannot be excluded in any fruitful discussion of post-Mao politics. This focus is also of great utility in the Chinese case because, as one student of East Asian regimes notes, "the plausibility of ideological arguments for policy choice increases with the degree of autonomy of political elites from societal or international constraints . . . when political elites are autonomous, their ideological visions and 'projects' weigh more heavily on the course of policy."[44] At the very least, ideology should not be dismissed without a serious investigation. It is ironic that while Western analyses of Chinese politics tend to dismiss ideological arguments as naive and simplistic, leading Chinese analysts tend to use the same labels to describe arguments that emphasize power motives, bureaucratic interests, and factionalism.[45]

Several reasons underlie this study's conceptual focus on value conflicts and policy preferences. First, because the old Chinese system was based on a set of explicitly articulated ideas, its reassessment offers a mirror into the motivating force and the nature of reforms being undertaken. As one scholar notes, change of ideology is the decisive criterion for determining the degree of empirical change under way. If ideology is constrained by considerations that run counter to its basic principles and yet undergoes little substantive change, then there is no fundamental change in the basis of the system.[46] In this sense, ideological change is a measure of the flexibility or limitation of change for the system as a whole.[47]

Second, a significant portion of post-Mao politics has involved ideological disputes. Although these disputes stemmed initially from power struggles over post-Mao succession, subsequent contentions between conservative and radical reformers have focused on issues of a fundamental value dimension, such as the priority of development versus upholding of Marxism, the scope of the plan versus the market, public versus nonpublic ownership, and collectivism versus "individualism" (geren zhuyi). The misgivings of conservative reformers over nonsocialist reform measures can be attributed largely to their preference for planned and regulated development, much as the propensity of radical reformers for a greater market can be ascribed to their preference for growth-geared development.[48] If leaders make a difference on the type of reform, the "source of their reform ideas and determination are a crucial variable in explaining the nature of their reform program."[49] At the least, the zigzag course of Chinese politics during the past decade, as Schram notes, "must be explained in substantial part by the interplay of influence and ideas within the leadership."[50]

The role of official doctrine in political change also acquires special significance because of the "consummatory" nature of the Chinese system, a system that integrates all spheres of life under a common rectitude upheld by a central authority. According to modernization theorists, a consummatory system is likely to resist all change (change in one sphere is threatening because it affects everything else), or when it changes, it changes totally and rapidly. It may thus either break down or reappear in revolutionary forms.[51] Post-Mao reforms have posed the second major challenge to the "consummatory" nature of the Chinese state in modern history. The first occurred more than a century ago when the traditional Confucian state came into confrontation with the European civilization.[52] Its response to the challenge of change was typical of a "consummatory" system: "It sought to reaffirm or restore the old Confucian system rather than to modernize it. The Chinese Restorationists' ideal society was one of static harmony among all closely integrated values, not of dynamic, segmented growth. After its failure and the deposition of the emperor, the political system decayed into praetorianism. Lacking the traditional ideology and ceremonial sanctions of the Son of Heaven, and not having developed modern sanctions, the successors of the Chinese empire had to rely increasingly on military force."[53] The initial resistance resulted in decay: As the Qing court failed to reform, the traditional order disintegrated into the chaos of warlord politics. This led eventually to the rejection of the Confucian order in the May Fourth Movement and its total replacement by a new "consummatory" system. "The inability to engage in instrumental, syncretic change leads to resistance and often to breakdown. It can also lead to radical, drastic change, as it did in China . . . , and to the establishment of a new consummatory system."[54] In post-Mao China, however, the so-called consummatory system has avoided total change or breakdown. This has been possible, arguably, because political leaders have made conscious efforts to adjust it incrementally. In some areas this system has been accommodating to change, while in other areas it remains inflexible. This interesting fact must necessarily be an important part of the post-Mao reform course that we need to understand.

The role of ideology in political change is particularly interesting when the outcome of reform in China is contrasted with that in other Soviet-type regimes, especially the former Soviet Union. What is the role of a doctrinal reassessment in the reformism of China and the revolution of the former Soviet Union? What is its role in the maintenance of the Chinese system and the demise of the others? Finally, what is its role in the successful economic transition of China and the strenuous transition of Russia? Ideology is relevant here because, as one scholar points out, "the Soviet Union's recent experience with 'de-ideologization' of political debates and the concurrent meltdown of its central political institutions have pointed to the potential cause-effect relationship between these two phenomena and the centrality of ideology to a system of this kind."[55] In the

Chinese case, guided ideological change has served to sustain an ideological hegemony, which has in turn contributed to political and social stability. Systemic maintenance and stability, finally, have contributed to a smoother economic transformation.

The central importance that the Chinese generally and historically attach to the role of thinking on political action also lends justification the conceptual focus of this study. This has been due to the Confucian exaltation of doctrine, the related cultural emphasis on the primacy of ideas,[56] the CCP tradition of the command of correct ideas, and the legacy of Mao. Other factors include the effects of long-time ideologization, the integration of moral and political authority in the state, and the political and cultural need for moral guidance. In particular, cultural tradition entails that ideas play a more important role in Chinese politics than in other Communist societies. Even the reputed pragmatist Deng Xiaoping declared at the outset of post-Mao reforms that the "emancipation of the mind" was a precondition for reform. The underlying assumption, ironically, was that the very need to deradicalize ideology demanded that ideology itself be called upon to justify it. Equally ironically, the frequent complaint of Chinese reformers and intellectuals about "rule by ideology" has also led them to emphasize the priority of conceptual change. Thus they see the lack of a conceptual revolution among the conservative forces as the main obstacle to reform. As *Renmin ribao* remarked in 1987, "Structural reform has met with a variety of unanticipated difficulties from the very beginning. Here, the fundamental barriers did not lie in the design of reform programs, the choice of reform strategy, or the implementation of policy. Rather, these barriers stemmed from ideological confusion, outdated concepts, and one-sided thinking, and most of all, the lack of clear theoretical guidance."[57] In this context the rethinking of socialism became an opportunity to cast old faith that amounted to, as CASS Vice President Zhao Fusan put it, an attitudinal revolution to provide a basis for empirical reform.[58] Or as Su Shaozhi, director of the CASS Institute of Marxism, stated, when China's Marxist intellectuals reconsidered the mistakes that had been made during the Cultural Revolution, they realized the importance of the "requisite of independence of thought" to challenge party doctrines and decisions.[59]

Finally, the Chinese concern for ideological and conceptual adaptation is related to the national search for identity and resurrection that has faced the nation since its confrontation with the West in the last century. Not incidentally, the reconception of socialism is frequently linked with the question of "cultural reconstruction"—the reconstruction of Chinese cultural values—in academic and political discussions.[60] Such concerns lend further support to a basic assumption of this study: that both the Chinese elite and the public have taken the rethinking of socialism seriously. If we see little concern with such larger questions in other culturally Confucian countries, it is perhaps because China remains a "consummatory" system and the cradle of the Confucian civilization upon which the burden of history is more keenly felt. It is little wonder that China is the only Confucian society that inherited the traditional "consummatory" system in revolutionary forms and is now faced with the task of reappraisal.

A few words are in order about why we should take the Chinese discourse seriously. There seems no better way to justify this than quoting Tsou: "an outside observer must take seriously the ideas, viewpoints, perceptions and pronouncements of the participants whose actions he is studying."[61] Failure to do so entails at least two pitfalls. One is to dismiss those statements on no grounds. Another is to make analysis on the basis of limited facts. One assertion that resulted from such approaches is that the Chinese are incapable of undertaking the critical examination of the past that is necessary for true learning and soul searching and therefore do not confront the deeper question of what caused the past failures of which they complain so much—were they due to personal failings, political culture, or Chinese Marxism?[62] By presenting what the Chinese have actually said, my study will offer an overwhelming body of evidence to the contrary.

RESEARCH DESIGN AND SOURCES

The nature of this work as a comprehensive and systematic study of post-Mao rethinking on socialism makes its interpretative framework inherently complex. On one level, the study deals with controversies over the meaning and relevance of socialism as part and parcel of the reform policy-making process, especially elite conflicts over policies. On another level, it traces debates as part of a genuine intellectual effort to come to grip with basic issues of China's social and economic development. Intertwining the two levels is the question of the relationship between them. On the one hand, the two levels are closely related because the political context sets a policy agenda and the boundaries of intellectual discourse even while many intellectuals contribute to debates in support of particular policies and leaders as individuals or through institutional or informal ties to the official strata. On the other hand, intellectuals and other social critics do have their independent agenda and pursue independent analyses even while they elicit official responses that form part of the discourse at the political level. Out of this web of relationship emerge two additional sets of conflict: that among political elites within the state and that between the state and society. This study sets out to examine both levels of post-Mao rethinking while attempting to clarify the interactions and conflicts among them.[63]

The scope of the work as a study of both political development and political theory also makes its organizational framework rather complex. I have chosen a chronological ordering of empirical processes in a given period, followed by a thematic ordering of theoretical developments in that period. The chronology is intended to lay out the political and intellectual context in which debates and issues have arisen, while the thematic discussion is to explicate their substance and theoretical import. Thus chapter 2 deals with the process and the content of the repudiation of Mao's legacy in 1976–1980. Chapters 3 and 4, respectively, discuss the politics and the content of reappraising the socialist economy from 1978 to 1992. In the same order, chapters 5 and 6 examine the rethinking of the socialist political system from 1978 and 1992. Chapter 7 analyzes the process and content of the rethinking on Marxism as a theory and on socialism as a model of development. Chapter 8 looks at official responses to discussions outside the officially sanctioned framework of political and intellectual discourse.

The discussion of the Chinese rethinking ends with a comparison of the Chinese discourse with its Soviet counterpart under Gorbachev. This comparison will serve three useful purposes: to shed sharper light on the characteristics of the Chinese discourse; to illuminate the function and impact of ideological rethinking in reforming socialist societies by linking the discourse of the two cases to their divergent outcomes of reform and revolution; and, finally, to elucidate certain generic problems of theory and practice in socialist movements. This comparison will also help to fill a void in the literature.[64] The former Soviet Union provides an ideal case for comparison because both regimes came to power through a hard-won indigenous revolution and both undertook serious reappraisals of socialism during their recent reform courses. The dramatic turn of events in China in mid-1989 and in the Soviet Union in late 1991 prompts one to ask why the socialist ethos survived in the former but not the latter, and what role ideological reorientation played in these divergent outcomes. These questions are discussed in chapter 9. The study concludes with a discussion of the implications of the Chinese reassessment for China's socialist experience and the future.

The study draws data from a wide range of primary sources. It makes use of official, quasi-official, and unofficial sources; national and local presses; journalistic, academic, and interview sources. Dramatic developments in China over the past decade, such as the relaxation of control on publication, the decentralization and multiplication of publishing facilities, the flourishing of journalistic and academic publications, the autonomy of special economic zones, the rise of the profit ethic, and the exile of leading dissidents, have all contributed to greater access to primary sources that reflect a wide spectrum of opinion and information.

Official sources include both openly and internally circulated materials from party plenums, congresses, government conventions, central work conferences, special plenary sessions, ministerial meetings, and other official forums. Quasi-official sources include elite statements on informal occasions and analyses of official materials by party theoreticians, especially those published by the Central Party School, *Hongqi*, and the People's Publishing House, all of which provide useful elaboration and contextual information. Also useful are the publications backed by different wings of political leadership, such as the reformer-backed *Shijie jingji daobao*, which was closed down after mid-1989.

Materials and views of unofficial capacity are mostly found in local and academic publications. For example, *Jingji yanjiu* first published Su Shaozhi's analysis of "undeveloped socialism" and later many discussions and debates on economic reform. Publications along the southern coast face little central control. *Guangzhou yuekan*, for instance, published many provocative articles by liberal intellectuals in the late 1980s. Institutionally and independently based journals have also expressed more independent voices: Chunqiu Publishing House, for example, published a series of books on political reform in the 1980s. *Jingjixue zhoubao* was edited by Wang Juntao and Chen Ziming, both imprisoned after June 4. Finally, the Tiananmen crackdown has made it possible to interview leading government advisers, reform theorists, and liberal intellectuals now in exile in the West.

CHAPTER TWO

From the Whatever to the Dialectical Materialist Approach

ONE MAJOR legacy of the Mao era was ideological absolutization. The claim of official doctrine to total truth gave grounding to constant imperative appeals to correct behavior and thinking. These appeals recurred in official efforts in ideological education, media promulgation, and political campaigns. The "two whatevers" expounded by Hua Guofeng and Wang Dongxing upon Mao's death reflected the state of rigidity in Mao's late years.

It is hardly surprising that a debate on the criterion of truth was the first issue of serious political contention in immediate post-Mao China. This was a controversy between a "whatever" (*fanshi*) faction that insisted on the total truth of existing ideology and a "practice" (*shijian*) faction that counterposed practice as the "sole criterion of truth." Questions of legitimacy and the political environment at the time necessitated that the issue at stake was not whether or not to continue Mao Zedong Thought but how. Thus, of the many issues disputed in this debate, the most important concerned what constituted the correct approach to upholding Mao Zedong Thought. The fact that the debate was politically motivated did not trivialize its substantive aspects. On the contrary, precisely because the debate arose out of political contention, its content was not limited to theoretical questions but involved the important political question of how to gauge the correctness of past political leaders and their policies. In particular, because the debate touched on basic issues of methodology and epistemology, it has had a lasting impact on post-Mao China by shaping the pattern and direction of ideological reorientation.[1]

Earlier analysts of the debate have been reluctant to give credit to the novel approaches developed by the practice faction during the debate. Instead, they emphasize this group's underlying continuity with Mao's empiricism and its circular reasoning in using Mao against Mao.[2] This chapter will examine the truth controversy as an effort of one political group to repudiate an alleged erroneous approach of another group to Marxism-Leninism and Mao Zedong Thought and as an effort to develop a new approach. I will first review the evolution of this controversy and then elaborate on the dimensions of the new approach.

Aside from the controversy over the criterion of truth, a number of specific tenets of Mao Zedong Thought were involved in the debate. They buttressed a line of policy that the whatever faction insisted on continuing but the practice faction insisted on discarding. This aspect of the truth debate will also be documented in this chapter. Together, the epistemological and substantive aspects of the truth debate led to the negation of the theory and practice of socialism associated with the late Chairman Mao.

THE ORIGIN OF THE CONTROVERSY

What came to be known as the "two whatevers" (*liangge fanshi*) in Chinese political vocabulary represented a classic example of dogmatism: "Whatever policies Mao has made we will resolutely safeguard and whatever instructions Mao has given we will forever follow." Not only the content but the manner in which the slogan was publicized was characteristic of the arbitrary style of the Cultural Revolution. The phrase first appeared in January 1977 in a speech drafted for Hua Guofeng, the new party chairman who had been handpicked by Mao as his heir apparent.[3] The speech was prepared on the basis of Hua's ideas, but its content was determined by Wang Dongxing, head of the CDP and chief of the late chairman's security forces. On February 7 the two whatevers were publicized in a joint editorial of the three major propaganda organs under the title "Study Documents and Grasp the Key Link."[4] The editorial was published at Wang Dongxing's order and without the prior knowledge of other officials in charge of propaganda work. The "key link" referred to a quotation from Mao that delineated the "gradual resolution of the contradiction between socialism and capitalism" as the "key link" of the party's agenda in the socialist period.

The crux of the two whatevers was to justify the continuation of the political line of Mao's late years aimed at combating the so-called capitalist line and capitalist roaders. Hua and other core members of the whatever group, Wang Dongxing, Chen Yonggui, Chen Xilian, and Wu De (known as the "little Gang of Four"), were beneficiaries of this radical line, while veteran revolutionaries were its primary victims. In ideology, therefore, the Hua regime pledged commitment to "continuing the revolution," "class struggle as key link," and other key slogans of the Cultural Revolution.[5] In economic policy, he endorsed a new, high-speed, high-growth "Great Leap Forward" strategy. To implement it, he exalted the Dazhai model of ideological exhortation, moral incentives, and class consciousness.[6] The most serious manifestations of the two whatevers, however, were centered on the political platform. Citing Mao's opposition to "capitalist roaders" and to the "rightist wind of rehabilitation," the Hua group resisted the return of Deng Xiaoping and other victims of the Cultural Revolution to political office. "If we let Deng return to work immediately," Wang asked, "where would Chairman Mao be placed? Would Mao's instructions be carried out or not?" On similar grounds, the Hua group resisted public appeals for the reversal of the party's and Mao's verdicts on the Tiananmen incident of 1976.[7] When a collection of verses written by participants in the movement was published on its first anniversary, Wang issued orders to investigate all those involved in the publication.[8] By refusing to revise Mao's verdict on the movement, the whatever group posed a major obstacle to Deng's return to power.

Because the appeals to reverse the verdicts and policies of Mao's late years implied a call to repudiate the Cultural Revolution, the whatever group also obstructed linking the campaign against the Gang of Four to a criticism of the Cultural Revolution. Thus, to avoid attributing the excesses of the Gang to Mao's emphasis on class struggle, Hua referred to the Gang of Four as "pseudo-left" in form but "true-right" in nature. Thereupon the campaign against the Gang of Four became a struggle against "ultra-rightists."[9] This orientation legitimated continuing the "left" line and excluding the "right" liners, that is, the "capitalist roaders." The designation of the Gang as "ultra-rightists" also enabled Hua to avoid pinpointing the real social basis of the Gang, who consisted mostly of the beneficiaries of the Cultural Revolution to whom Hua belonged. Instead, Hua identified the Gang's social basis in traditional "class enemies" such as old landlords, rich peasants, and the old and new bourgeois classes.[10] In this way, he found further grounds to resist the return of "right liners." Such a policy of "whateverism," as CDP deputy head Geng Biao stated at the time, meant that "the Gang of Four was not ousted at all" because "nothing can be changed."[11] This whateverism was also a "tricky subject" in 1977, as the party theoretician Wu Jiang wrote later, because "nobody dares to touch it."[12] Consequently, it became the focus of contention between the two groups of political leaders.

The First Phase: March 1977–May 1978

In March 1977 Hua reiterated the two whatevers at a work conference of the CCP Central Committee. This finally prompted Deng, who was not yet rehabilitated from his second purge, to write to the party's Central Committee, which was headed by Hua and Ye Jianying. In his letter, Deng proposed "treating Mao Zedong Thought accurately and comprehensively as a scientific system." This call was not exactly new, for Deng had also made it in 1975 during his second rise to power.[13] But it was now counterposed against the two whatevers. By "accurately and comprehensively," Deng castigated the whatever approach for treating Mao's words "isolatedly and one-sidedly." By "scientific system," he disparaged the whatever way of reading Mao's individual statements regardless of his essential thought.[14] With the support of Ye and other veteran revolutionaries still in power, the Central Committee endorsed Deng's letter by issuing it as an internal document.

After Deng returned to power in July 1977, he continued to espouse and refine his approach to Mao. In a speech at the very Central Committee plenum in which he was formally rehabilitated, Deng drew a distinction between an essential component of Mao's thought that was of fundamental significance and a specific content that was restricted by time, place, and subject context. To the former he designated Mao's concepts of *shishi qiushi* and the mass line.[15] *Shisi qiushi*, as originally interpreted by Mao, means that "the objective world requires our study of its inherent relationships and laws." More commonly the phrase is rendered as "seeking truth from facts." By ascribing *shishi qiushi* to the essential component of Mao's thought, Deng argued that certain individual, nonessential aspects of Mao's thought might be discarded.

These initial efforts by Deng failed to make Hua disavow the Cultural Revolution line. During the drafting of the political report to the Eleventh Party Congress, to be held in August 1977, Deng personally objected to Hua about the report's affirmation of such notions as "capitalist roaders" and "dictatorship of the proletariat in all cultural fronts" and the disparaging of the "unique importance of production forces." Hua refused to delete such references and even inserted other radical concepts, such as "basic contradictions between capitalist and socialist forces," "class struggle as the key link," "continuing the revolution," and "perfection of socialist superstructure and production relations." During the congress, Hua refused to accept some delegates' criticism of the complete affirmation of the Cultural Revolution in his political report.[16]

The conflict surrounding the Eleventh Party Congress led many veteran leaders to join Deng in the battle against the two whatevers after the congress. Despite barriers created by Wang Dongxing, who presided over propaganda work, senior leaders such as Chen Yun, Nie Rongzhen, Xu Xianqian, and Zhang Dingcheng published articles to enunciate the idea of "seeking truth from facts." Their articles came through usually after the direct intervention of Deng Xiaoping or Hu Yaobang. Emboldened by these leaders, the media began to carry articles in the remaining months of 1977 on the subjects of science and democracy, personality cult, and Marxist epistemology. The period is known as the beginning of "setting wrongs to right on the ideological front" and the prelude to the debate on the criterion of truth.[17] During the period, Hu Yaobang, as the new head of the Central Party School (which trained cadres and usually groomed them for promotion), initiated a discussion of "practice is the sole criterion of truth" at the school. By the end of the year, Hu proposed two principles to cadres under training there regarding the evaluation of the party's recent history. Both of these echoed Deng's recent statements but were more pointedly directed at Mao's legacies: First, Mao's relevant instructions should be viewed "accurately and comprehensively"; second, "practice" (*shijian*) should be used as the criterion to gauge the right and wrong of the party's political lines.[18] In this context the theoretical and media circles began to prepare for a debate against the two whatevers in late 1977.[19]

The clash between the practice coalition and the whatever group extended to the policy arena beginning in early 1978 and was frequently seen in public exchanges of rhetoric. The practice faction scored victory in January by issuing two central documents to encourage material incentives in rural communes.[20] One month later, at the first session of the Fifth People's Congress, Hua countered with exaltation of "major efforts to criticize revisionism and capitalism," even while paying lip service to "respect for objective laws" and "material interests of the people."[21] A few weeks later Deng devoted his speech at the national science conference to the theme of the development of production forces, the four modernizations, and the importance of "experts." Then in March Wan Li, one of the two provincial heads recently appointed to experiment with rural reforms,[22] wrote in *Renmin ribao* on self-government and ownership rights of production teams, peasants' material interests, and distribution according to labor.[23]

In response to the surge of such discussions, a *Renmin ribao* editorial appeared in mid-April to exalt Mao's idea of "a simultaneous grasp of class struggle, production struggle, and scientific experiment."[24] It emphasized class struggle as the guarantee of the other two causes. A few days later, practice advocates responded with a two-page commentator's article in the same paper to affirm "distribution according to labor," a forgotten socialist tenet now recovered to defend material incentives. The article was drafted by Deng's think tank, the Political Research Office at the State Council, and read by Deng before its publication.[25] Such public debates were possible because neither political group was in full control of the propaganda apparatus at the CDP, at the State Council, or at the major media organs. For example, while *Renmin ribao* director Wu Lengxi and *Hongqi* chief editor Hu Sheng supported the whatever group, Hu Jiwei, chief editor of *Renmin ribao*, and Zeng Tao, head of the Xinhua News Agency, backed the practice group.

The State Council's article enraged Wang Dongxing, who denounced it as an attack on Mao Zedong Thought and questioned "which central party committee" it represented. Chen Yonggui, former head of the Dazhai brigade and now a vice prime minister in charge of agriculture, was particularly dismayed by rural reform experiments being undertaken in Anhui and Sichuan. He criticized media reports on rural reforms for promulgating "individual economy" and "free market" and running counter to Mao's lines.[26] These were serious charges in the political climate of early 1978, when the cult of Mao was still intact. As the whatever group's high ground rested on its role as the guardian of Mao's word, it became clear from the exchanges of rhetoric that the fundamental question that must be resolved was indeed the one raised by Deng: how should Mao Zedong Thought be upheld?

The Second Phase: May–November 1978

Against this background, Hu Yaobang instructed members of the Theoretical Research Office at the Central Party School to prepare a rebuttal of the two whatevers on the basis of his two recently laid principles. Around the same time, the "Theoretical Column" at *Guangming ribao* received an independently submitted article from Professor Hu Fuming of Nanjing University, under the title "Practice Is the Criterion of Truth." The column editor felt that the topic was of such importance that it should be given more widespread attention. He sent the article to the Theoretical Research Office at the Central Party School for revision, where a similar article was being drafted. On the basis of Hu Fuming's contribution and the ideas of many theoreticians (both inside and outside the Central Party School), Sun Changjiang, deputy director of the Theory Research Office, wrote up the article that came to be known as "Practice Is the Sole Criterion of Truth." Hu Yaobang edited and approved the final draft and added a key word, "sole," to Hu Fuming's original title.[27]

Because of the political environment at the time, the article first had to be published in the internally distributed *Lilun dongtai* (Theoretical trends) on May 9 before it appeared in *Guangming ribao* on May 11.[28] *Lilun dongtai*, a theoretical journal recently created under Hu Yaobang's sponsorship at the Central Party School, carried views that were considered bold and fresh in 1978 and was already influential among cadres. The journal would shoulder the responsibility for what was bound to be a politically explosive article. Indeed, although the article eventually became better known in association with *Guangming ribao*, that newspaper had to reprint it under the name of a "special commentator," a practice specially coined by Hu Yaobang for the purpose of this article and later frequently used by reformers to avoid the censorship of the CDP.[29] Besides Sun Changjiang, Wu Jiang (director of the Theory Research Office at the Central Party School), Ruan Ming (deputy director), and Zheng Bijian (Hu Yaobang's assistant) were involved in writing many of the special commentator articles subsequently published in this period. These articles were not only under Hu Yaobang's auspices but often edited by him. Political leadership thus played a decisive role in initiating ideological debates and reformulation at this juncture.

The May 11 article immediately caught widespread attention. The Xinhua News Agency broadcast it on the very afternoon of its appearance in *Guangming ribao*. *Renmin ribao* and the majority of other national and local papers reprinted it the next day. The article marked a turning point in the dispute over how to handle Mao's legacy. Until then, most of the discussions on "seeking truth from facts" only putatively defended the postulate as a fundamental tenet of Marxism–Leninism–Mao Zedong Thought and as a fine tradition of the CCP. By contrast, the *Guangming ribao* article defended "Practice is the sole criterion of truth" as the most fundamental principle on a philosophical ground, that is, on Marx's dialectical materialist epistemology. In so doing, the article sought to weaken the ideological ground of the two whatevers. The political importance of such a ground was evident because the very publication of the article had to be backed by Hu Yaobang.

The whatever group was infuriated by the article. Apart from Hua and the "little Gang of Four," some heads of the party's major ideological organs were leading opponents: CDP deputy director Zhang Baihua, *Hongqi* chief editor Hu Sheng and deputy editor Xiong Fu, and *Renmin ribao* director Wu Lengxi (chief editor, 1957–1966). They tried a variety of ways to suppress the article. First they criticized Zeng Tao at the Xinhua News Agency and Hu Jiwei at *Renmin ribao*, who had decided on their own to carry the *Guangming ribao* article. In his telephone call to Hu Jiwei at 11 P.M. on May 12, Wu Lengxi called the article "very bad, very bad" theoretically and politically.[30] On May 17 Wang Dongxing told a small gathering of propaganda officials that the spearhead of the article was "directed at the Chairman's thought" and that investigation must be made to find out who was behind it. "Our Party newspapers must not do things like this!" he declared. "Which Central Committee do these views represent?"[31] Faced with growing pressure for a public discussion of the issues raised by the *Guangming ribao* article, Wang laid down a policy of "three don'ts": "Don't cut down the banner," "Don't give up the weapon," and "Don't make a 180-degree turn."[32] On May 18, in an address to a gathering of provincial officials responsible for ideological work, Zhang Baihua encouraged them to criticize the article.[33] Hua and Wang also forbade *Hongqi* to reprint it, instructed provincial leaders not to express support for it, and threatened reprisals against those who did. The party's most authoritative media organ, *Hongqi*, indeed did not reprint the article. As the original author, Hu Fuming and his work unit Nanjing University also came under censure but together resisted the pressure from above.

At the theoretical level, central propaganda officials raised three key objections to the article. First, it made no distinction between "revisionism" and "dogmatism," because it impugned the two whatevers for dogmatism but failed to acknowledge its own revisionism. That is, the article only criticized the inflexible approach of the two whatevers and failed to recognize its own doctrinal deviation (a more severe blunder). Second, the article showed a one-sided understanding of Mao's theory of practice, for it only stressed that theory originated from practice but ignored that theory also guided practice. Third, the article encouraged the public to "doubt everything" and to question which part of Mao's thought was correct or incorrect. In the final analysis, the article "declared a war" on Marxism and Mao Zedong Thought.[34]

These reactions of the whatever group led Deng to respond by publicly endorsing the article at the All-Army Conference on Political Work on June 2.[35] While Hua's and Ye's speeches at the conference were filled with clichés and references to "politics in command,"[36] Deng devoted half of his speech to expounding on the criterion of truth. In the same way that the *Guangming ribao* article placed "seeking truth from facts" as the essence of Marxist philosophy, Deng now called the postulate the "most fundamental component" of Mao's thought. Adherence to it was "genuine fidelity," he declared, because there were two kinds of fidelity: one to Mao's fundamental thought and one to "whatever" he said. By affirming the former, Deng allowed a partial negation of Mao without discrediting the whole.[37] But to maintain some distance from the debate, Deng did not use the phrase "Practice is the sole criterion of truth" in his speech.[38]

Political calculations were obviously involved in Deng's move to turn an intraelite dispute into a public debate.[39] For one thing, Deng was not strong enough politically to defeat the other group at this time. Thus he needed the ideological fallout of a public debate to strengthen both his political and his ideological position. This was especially necessary because the political strength of the whateverists rested in part upon their high ground as the guardian of Mao's words. Moreover, the ideologization of the Mao era did leave a considerable "mass base" for Hua's whateverism. This social base could be better eroded with a public debate than with a high-handed pronouncement by a new leadership.

Deng's speech intensified the resistance of the whatever group. On June 7 Hua used the occasion of the conference on learning from Dazhai and Daqing to warn against "deviation from correct political direction" and reiterated the "superiority of socialist production relations."[40] On June 15, at a meeting of leading personnel from major media organs, Wang Dongxing called for a criticism of the *Guangming ribao* article and other articles advocating reform policies. Raising the issue as one of the media's "party spirit" (*dangxing*) versus its "individual spirit" (*gexing*), Wang criticized the media's subordination of the former to the latter, thus asserting the party's authority over intellectual authority. Wang also expressed disapproval of the title used in media reports of Deng's speech at the army conference—"Vice-Chairman Deng Eloquently Enunciates Mao's Idea of Seeking Truth from Facts"—because this played down Hua's and Ye's statements on the subject. Wang further disparaged recent media articles on distribution according to labor, material incentives, and the reversal of verdicts on the victims of past political campaigns. He even criticized several leaders of the practice group by name. But Wang generated passive responses at the meeting.[41] Failing at these efforts, Wang and Hua simply forbade any nationwide discussion of the truth criterion, on the claim that "practice is the sole criterion of truth" amounted to the denigration of Mao.[42]

To counter this seemingly forceful claim, Hu Yaobang found it necessary to respond with a second article. But he could no longer participate in its preparation because of the intense pressure to which he was subject after the publication of the first article. Similarly, the three papers that first carried the *Guangming ribao* article could not get involved. Hu Yaobang obtained help from the army paper *Jiefangjun bao* (Liberation Army daily) and from Luo Ruiqing, general secretary of the Central Military Committee and a veteran revolutionary. Drafted primarily by Wu Jiang, the second article was laboriously edited by the ailing Luo practically in the last few weeks of his life. On June 23 the article appeared, again in the name of a special commentator, in *Jiefangjun bao*, under the title "A Most Basic Principle of Marxism." The article deepened the debate over the criterion of truth by addressing the distinction between the teachings of revolutionary leaders and the criterion of truth. For the first time in the debate, the article advanced the argument that political leaders' teachings were not equivalent to the criterion of truth and that leaders and their political lines were not above the criterion of truth, that is, practice.[43] This article put the military openly on Deng's side. After its publication, the debate over the criterion of truth, otherwise known as the campaign to "emancipate the mind," began to spread nationwide.[44]

Despite continued objections from the whatever group, many national, local, and academic papers and journals joined the discussion of the truth criterion in the latter half of 1978. Among the veteran leaders not yet openly committed to the criterion, Li Xiannian expressed his public endorsement in July, whereas Ye Jianying still failed to do so. Except in a few strongholds of radicals, most regional and army officials expressed their support for the practice criterion. The pledge of public support was not out of mere political calculation, for the outcome of the power struggle at the top was still uncertain for much of the period, and *Hongqi* did not publish anything on the subject until December 1978, when an article by the veteran leader Tan Zhenlin appeared. Even in this case, Tan's article went into print only after the intervention of Deng Xiaoping and Li Xiannian.[45]

By and large, it was a deeply felt recognition of the destruction that the ultra-left line had done to the country that led many regional cadres to take a stand on the issue. Many drew on the lessons of the Cultural Revolution and local conditions to demonstrate how important it was for the country to face the grim realities of its recent past and to reverse Mao's ultra-leftist policies. Frequently they warned that at this juncture of Chinese history, the "emancipation of the mind" determined the "success or failure" of China's socialist course and the "life or death" of the country. Discussions were also held among social scientists and philosophers who lent intellectual support to the practice criterion. For this group, too, expression of public support was not without fear or political cost: When the renowned writer Zhou Yang spoke of the truth debate as a matter affecting the "future of our party and country," he was reprimanded by Wang Dongxing personally. Such dogged political resistance led Deng to admit later how critical it was to discard dogmatism immediately.

> The more one looks at the progress of the debate, the more one comes to see how important it is. If a political party, a state, a nation does everything according to the books, its thinking is ossified, and it allows superstition to prevail, then it will not move forward. Its life will stop, and the party and country will perish.[46]

Deng was hardly exaggerating. Dogmatism, whether due to Hua's blind loyalty or Wang's power calculations, provided the ideological basis for policy continuity that could be countered only by a demystification of dogmas from a higher ideological plateau. The debate over the criterion of truth served this function by addressing the basic questions of epistemology and methodology.

The Third Phase: November 1978–February 1980

Once the debate had created a favorable political and ideological climate for Deng, he felt that the moment had arrived for policy changes. In September he proposed shifting the party's priority from the campaign against the Gang of Four to economic modernization.[47] However, because the truth debate sought to discredit only dogmatism and not the content of radical lines, the whatever group soon added a new twist to their opposition.

Shortly after Deng made his proposal, *Renmin ribao* published a Special Commentator's article to urge continuing the campaign against the

Gang of Four as the "absolutely necessary precondition for the four modernizations." The article also indirectly attacked Deng by criticizing the Gang's "pseudo-left, genuine-right" revisionism that distorted many of Mao's "concrete policies."[48] On October 1 *Renmin ribao*'s National Day editorial reiterated Hua's high-speed, heavy-industrial economic strategy and Mao's axiom of using class struggle to promote production. From early October the truth debate took on a new dimension by turning to Mao's radical policies. On October 6 *Renmin ribao* published Hu Qiaomu's article "Act According to Objective Laws," a speech drafted under the State Council's political research office and delivered internally in July.[49]

By early November the Central Committee accepted Deng's suggestion to convene a work conference on shifting national priority to economic development. But the conference had to devote some discussions to the rationale for the shift before touching on the substantive issues of agriculture and economy. After all, there was not yet a consensus on this shift within the leadership. As part of the initial discussions, Chen Yun went beyond the conference agenda to raise many political questions that were still taboo at the time, for example, the political mistakes of the Cultural Revolution and the wrong verdicts imposed upon officials and individuals during previous political campaigns. Chen's speech changed the tone of the conference but inadvertently contributed to the smooth adoption of Deng's economic agenda.[50] After his speech, many participants were emboldened to speak out, often directly confronting members of the whatever group. Most of their criticisms were leveled at the two whatevers and the resistance to the practice criterion. Now that many officials took the courage to defy them, the whatever group could no longer intimidate participants by acting as the guardians of Mao's lines. This atmosphere enabled the practice coalition to emerge victoriously from the thirty-day work conference, which in turn cleared the way for the convening of the historic Third Plenum of the Eleventh Party Congress in mid-December. In his closing speech at the conference, Deng pronounced the dialectical materialist approach the new "thought line" of the party. The Third Plenum formally affirmed this new line and the shift of the party's priority to economic development.

Although the Third Plenum drew a de facto conclusion of the debate on the truth criterion, it did not resolve the controversy over some key tenets of Mao Zedong Thought. At Ye Jianying's suggestion, the CCP convened a conference on theoretical work to "debate the issues democratically." Originally planned for about one month, the conference lasted nearly three months, from mid-January to early April. Sponsored by the CDP and the Central Committee, the meeting was attended by ideological officials from central to local levels and leading political theorists and social scientists. Many of the latter were recently rehabilitated intellectuals.[51] As it progressed, the conference became a forum to criticize openly and heatedly the followers of the two whatevers and their credos. In particular, the leading discussions sought to discredit the theoretical foundations of the Cultural Revolution model of socialist development, such as Mao's concepts of the principal contradiction of Chinese society, "class struggle as the key link" and "continuing the revolution." These efforts set the momentum for a public criticism of the fundamental tenets of the radical line nationwide. The criticism of the Gang of Four also entered a new phase against this background. For the first time since their downfall, the Gang came to be criticized as "ultra-leftists," whose policy and ideological linkage with Mao was no longer a forbidden zone of discussion in the national media.

But intellectuals also went beyond the official agenda at the theory conference, especially during the first half of the meeting, to explore the *sources* of Mao's misguided policies and ideology. This coincided with similar discussions at the height of the Democracy Wall movement in the spring of 1979, which are treated in chapter 5. The significance of these intellectual and social insurgencies was their immediate impact on ideological discourse. It was in response to these insurgencies that Deng, in a closing speech at the theory conference on March 30, pronounced the Four Fundamental Principles to which all political discussions must accord. These were emphatically spelled out to give warning to the intellectual participants at the conference and to justify Deng's imminent crackdown on the Democracy Wall activists. This swing backward immediately caused a brief "relapse into ultra-leftism" in the spring of 1979. At the CCP work conference in early April, convened to discuss Chen Yun's proposed adjustment policies, members of the whatever group actively opposed everything that had happened since the Third Plenum. They subordinated the truth criterion to the Four Principles, reiterated Mao's slogan "Never forget class struggle," and blamed the insurgency of the Democracy Wall activists and intellectuals on the policy of emancipating the mind. For a moment, the two whatevers could no longer be criticized. Rather, the target of official and media attention became the forces on the Right.[52]

The counterattack of the whatever group led Deng and Hu Yaobang to view leftism as a greater danger and see the need to continue the debate on the criterion of truth. In particular, further consolidation of his own position and the restoration of his veteran supporters to power after the Third Plenum allowed Deng to shift direction again less than two months after his "Four Principles" speech. Again at the instruction of Hu Yaobang,

Guangming ribao published a two-page special commentator's article on the anniversary of the original practice article to mark the return to the Emancipation of the Mind.[53] *Hongqi* soon followed suit to support the second debate by calling on the nation to "make up for the missed lessons" of the debate of 1978 and by making a self-criticism of its stand on the matter during the first debate.[54] *Hongqi*'s change of stand was in part pressured by the recent theory conference, at which its heads were compelled to make self-criticisms for their stance on the truth criterion and were challenged to publish articles to show their change of faith.[55] In contrast to the epistemological focus of the first debate, the second debate focused on the concrete issue of whether recent economic reforms had deviated from Mao's thought. The debate lasted until February 1980, when the "little Gang of Four" was ousted at the second session of the Fifth National People's Congress (NPC). A central party document cited "the opinions of many in and outside the party" as the basis for this decision.[56]

In sum, an elite controversy over the policy of two whatevers led to a debate over the appropriate attitude toward Mao's legacy, resulting in a repudiation of an allegedly mistaken approach to established theory and practice and of the substance of a radical ideology. Leadership, particularly that of Hu Yaobang and Deng Xiaoping, was crucial in initiating and protecting these efforts. Theoreticians at the Central Party School played a major role in articulating arguments for the practice leadership, due both to Hu's presidency of the school and to their semiofficial status as party theoreticians. Intellectuals and the public, on the other hand, largely followed and supported the officially led debate.

DIMENSIONS OF THE DIALECTICAL MATERIALIST APPROACH

Mao Zedong Thought as a "Scientific System"

The first aspect of the new approach to ideology was to treat Mao Zedong Thought as a "scientific system." This designation may seem dubious,[57] but its usage in 1978 was meaningfully counterposed to the whatever claim to the total truth of Mao, a claim vividly expressed in popular precepts like "every word [of Mao] is truth" or "every sentence [of Mao] should be followed." By "scientific system," Deng did not directly challenge the whatever claim to total truth. Rather, he stressed the connections between Mao's words and the specific contexts in which they were uttered.

As Deng wrote in his letter to the Central Committee, "Comrade Mao's remarks on a given subject are correct under a particular time and condition, and are correct on the same subject under another time and condition. But his words on the same subject can differ in variance with time and condition, in emphasis, perspective, and even in wording." So it was not enough to understand Mao Zedong Thought "from his individual sentences," but rather, "from the entire system of Mao Zedong Thought."[58] Song Zhenting, an ideological official from Heilongjiang who would soon be promoted to the Central Party School, put it more clearly by defining the "scientific system" as one in which "different principles are interconnected and reflect the relationship among different aspects of the objective reality, with each specific principle connected with specific historical conditions." To treat every word of Mao as truth regardless of context, Song suggested, was to quote Mao like "a collection of unconnected fables or a box of unrelated index cards with a truth written on each one of them."[59]

The emphasis on the connection between Mao's teachings and their special contexts was to suggest that the whatever approach was arbitrary, mechanistic, and "unscientific" because it amounted to an inaccurate and one-sided understanding. By ignoring the connections between Mao's words and their contexts, Deng suggested, whateverism ran counter to dialectical materialism and was guilty of "metaphysical idealism." The latter was characterized by its placing cognition above existence and its neglect of interaction among things. In Marxist terminology, "cognition" refers to the human perception and conception of the material world, whereas "existence" refers to the material world. According to dialectical materialism, existence precedes cognition, though the two interact. The whatever approach was also found to distort Mao's thought through isolated use of Mao's words. For example, Mao talked about both "red" and "expert," politics and economy, revolution and production, but the whateverists emphasized red over expert, politics over economy, and revolution over production—although, unlike the Gang of Four, they did not treat the paired concepts as if they were unrelated. The consequence was said to be a skewing toward a one-sided policy and political line.[60]

The concept of a "scientific system," however, did not suggest discarding any specific principles of Mao. It only purported to balance some of Mao's words against those of others. But in cases where this balancing could not be achieved, as in the notion of "class struggle as the key link," it became problematic to apply the "scientific system" argument. In response to this difficulty, a new conception of classic teachings began to emerge after the *Guangming ribao* article first located the ideological base of the practice criterion in Marxist philosophy. This new conception distinguished between two levels within Marxism–Leninism–Mao Zedong Thought: the level of *jiben yuanli* (fundamental principles), which were universal and indispensable, and the level of *gebie yuanli* (specific principles), which changed with time and context. The distinction provided not only the basis for a purportedly new approach to official doctrine but also a more coherent repudiation of the whatever approach.

The Integration of Fundamental and Specific Principles

Although Deng had previously referred to "seeking truth from facts" as one of the fundamentals of Mao's thought, he spoke of it as the most fundamental component in his June 2 speech at the army conference. The notion of the "fundamental component" differed from that of the "scientific system" in that it emphasized different types of components that existed within classic teachings. The fundamental ones were essential, but the specific ones were not. Thus, while Deng continued to use the term "scientific system," he modified it to denote only the fundamental principles: "What we should uphold and use as a guide to action are the fundamental principles of Marxism–Leninism–Mao Zedong Thought, in other words, the scientific system consisting of these fundamental principles. As to the specific conclusions, neither Marx, Lenin, nor Mao can avoid making this or that error. These do not belong to the scientific system formed by the fundamental principles."[61]

This bifurcation is structurally similar to but semantically different from Franz Schurmann's distinction between "pure" and "practical" ideology. In Schurmann's scheme, only Marxism-Leninism belongs to the universal "pure ideology." The constantly developing Mao Zedong Thought serves as the "practical ideology" of Chinese revolutionaries.[62] In the Chinese bifurcation developed during the 1978 debate, both Marxism-Leninism and Mao Zedong Thought contained universal "fundamental principles" and transient "specific principles." The relationship between the two was not *Marxist-Leninist* versus *Chinese* but methodological versus derivative. In other words, specific principles were the products of applying fundamental principles to concrete situations. As a *Renmin ribao* special commentator put it, fundamental principles "have the significance of universal laws" whereas specific principles and conclusions arrived at on their basis "concern the problems of specific revolutionary experiences under different historical conditions." Further, the fundamental principles of Marx included his philosophy of dialectical and historical materialism, while those of Mao were founded on his philosophical treatises, which "inherited, defended, and developed" Marxism (i.e., *On Practice, On Contradiction*, and *On Correctly Handling the Contradictions among the People*).[63] In other words, the emphasis was on treating classic teachings as an epistemology and methodology that could be creatively applied and developed as empirical situations changed. The logical corollary of the bifurcation was that true fidelity would entail being faithful to fundamental principles only.

Within the so-called fundamental principles, however, dialectical materialism was given an almost exclusive emphasis. The slighting of historical materialism was both deliberate and convenient. Politically, the practice group tried to focus the debate on epistemology and methodology rather on world view. Thus, although the essence of Marxism was summarized as the duality of its "empirical" and "class" (*jieji*) nature, emphasis was given to the "empirical" aspect in the special commentator articles.[64] The theory of class struggle—the fulcrum of social development central to historical materialism as well as to Mao Zedong Thought—was something that practice proponents wanted to avoid at this time. Since Mao Zedong Thought was itself a product of integrating Marxism with China's realities, they argued, its essence was its empirical approach. Moreover, Mao's works on dialectical materialism constituted the philosophical basis of his entire thought. Finally, the philosophical foundation of Marxism lay in dialectical materialism, from which derived historical materialism as Marx's analysis of history and society.[65] With these arguments, the leftist exaggerations of the "class" nature of Marxism were rebuked for obscuring its "empirical" nature and for allowing leftist leaders to impose their personal will as the criterion of truth in the name of "class will."[66]

In response to a charge from the whatever group that the bifurcation of classic doctrines amounted to "abstract affirmation" and "concrete negation," the special commentators responded that it was dogmatism that had actually resulted in "abstract affirmation and concrete negation" of Marxism.[67] This dogmatism was shown to manifest a series of epistemological fallacies, many of which pertained to the divorce of theory from practice. One fallacy was to neglect the empirical context in which certain classic theories were formulated and to which they should be applied, thereby exaggerating the universality of theory. Another was to disregard the particularity of reality. Rather than seeking the particular manifestations of a theory in an empirical context, the dogmatists substituted theory for reality by assuming that the general superseded the particular. This was now judged as philosophically unsound, because it violated the dialectical principle of the unity and contradiction between the general and the particular. These fallacies contributed to "abstract affirmation and concrete negation," practice advocates argued, by distorting the essence of original theories and damaging their credibility.[68]

In the final analysis, the whatever approach of absolutizing theory and disregarding reality was said to have constituted a "metaphysical-idealist" line of cognition common to both the Gang of Four and Mao in his later years.[69] In this sense, practice advocates saw the significance of the debate on the truth criterion as far beyond the struggle against the two whatevers.

The Guide to Action versus the Criterion of Truth

Another critique of the whatever approach concerned the role of Marxism–Leninism–Mao Zedong Thought as the guide to action rather than the criterion of truth. This critique was formulated in response to the complaint that the elevation of practice lowered the authority of Mao Zedong Thought. In fact, Wang Dongxing accused the practice criterion of "de-Maoization."[70] The same misgivings were echoed among the general public. In their letters to *Renmin ribao*, some readers questioned that if practice was the sole criterion of truth, where would Mao's place be? Others suggested that theory and practice should both serve as the criterion of truth. Still others found the elevation of practice an insult to the revolutionary masters.[71] The question raised here about the role of theory versus practice was addressed in the *Jiefangjun bao* article and in a response to *Renmin ribao* readers by Xing Fensi, head of the CASS Institute of Philosophy.[72]

Confusion about the role of Marxist theory, both articles contended, arose from equating theory as a guide to practice with theory as the criterion of truth. This equation was refuted on several grounds. First, as generalized conclusions from practice, classic teachings could only serve as a guide to practice, in which case "theory reacts on practice" rather than acting in its stead. That is, the role of theory was to provide analytical insights into universal features and laws, which, when applied to reality, would help to discern the specific manifestations of those features and laws.[73] Against this light, the whateverists were criticized for relying on theory for authoritative answers to all situations. "In judging whether something is right or wrong," noted a *Renmin ribao* special commentator's article, "they ignore the after-effects of practice and consult the books as the only authority. . . . They invariably think that there is something wrong about a thing, a policy, a measure, or a certain statement, if it was not said in the books or was not phrased in exactly the same way as in the books."[74]

In attributing the authority of truth to practice, the practice criterion in effect challenged a fundamental feature of the socialist regime as what Western social scientists call a "consummatory" system. Typical of such a system, the "consummatory" ideology serves as the ultimate source of value for most spheres of life. The practice criterion, however, renounced the use of ideology as the authoritative source of value. But ambiguity remained because the fundamental principles were still upheld as "irrefutable truths" that could never be violated. The dilemma was partly resolved by the designation of the analytical methods of Marxism as fundamental principles, thus lending support to the use of Marxism as a guide to action. Still, the designation dodged the question of what should be the criterion for testing the fundamental principles of Marxism themselves. This left unanswered the question of what was the source of legitimacy of a centrally sanctioned Marxism. It would prove problematic for later debates and especially for those who wished to challenge the fundamental principles.

A second source of confusion over the role of theory was attributed to a dogmatic view of the nature of theory. That is, the claim to the absolute supremacy of theory entailed the final and eternal truth of theory. It was on this claim, Deng complained, that whateverist proponents opposed any policies that were negated or not effected under Mao.[75] This treatment of theory was shown to exaggerate the role of theory by misconstruing its origin, that is, a failure to recognize an ongoing process of change internal to theoretical formation. The *Jiefangjun bao* article even added that neither fundamental nor specific principles were immutable or above reality.[76] Pragmatists also invoked dialectical materialism to make the case for the changing nature of theory. That is, as the material world changed, human cognition—being a reflection of that world—must change accordingly.[77] If this observation were pushed to its logical conclusion, Li Honglin wrote, "nothing in the world is eternal except the eternally moving material world and its inherent dialectical laws," and this "applies to Marxism itself."[78]

This discussion of the role of theory touched on another fundamental question in a "consummatory" system, namely, the authority for determining the "consummatory" rectitude. In essence, the two groups in the truth debate battled over the use of ideology or practice as the source of truth. Yet because the practice criterion was as much politically determined as the two whatevers, the debate failed to address the issue of how practice could be objectively determined and by whose authority.

In their speeches at the theory conference of 1979, both Deng and Hu Yaobang spoke of democracy as an important condition for emancipating the mind. Hu even admitted that the struggle with the two whatevers was at heart a struggle against the monopoly of truth, and that the CCP's mistakes in the past had resulted mainly from this monopoly. As Hu recalled, Mao himself conceded in 1965 that Peng Dehuai, his bitter critic during the Great Leap, may have held the truth after all. "You should look forward," Mao was said to have told Peng. "Let your problem be judged by history. Perhaps truth was on your side." Shortly after the launching of the Cultural Revolution in 1968, Hu also recalled, Mao showed remorse over its outbreak. Yet in both cases, Mao's monopoly on truth failed to prevent the occurrence or an early termination of the tragic events. In the same speech, Hu Yaobang characterized the leading ideologues of the radical line—Chen Boda, Kang Sheng, Zhang Chunqiao, and Yao Wenyuan—as "theoretical bullies" whose major weapon was a monopoly on truth. "They monopolized Marxism–Leninism–Mao Zedong Thought so that they can distort and twist them at will while others are not allowed to creatively study them," Hu observed.[79] In short, Hu recognized that the domination of truth by power was a more basic problem than the content of a criterion of truth. This recognition also became one of the reasons for Hu's and Deng's concern over political reform and democratization, then and later.

Still, neither Hu's statements nor the official discourse during the truth debate developed into an inquiry into the deeper causes of why the monopoly of truth had occurred repeatedly. Instead, the discussions emphasized the subjective errors on the part of the offenders. Thus Hua Guofeng's dogmatism was blamed on his "blind faith," "confused thinking," and "low level of ability." For Wang Dongxing, it was a combination of "personal interests," "dictatorial style," and "dogmatic thinking."[80] Mao's subjective tendencies in his late years were blamed on his increased divorce from the masses, his neglect of empirical investigation, and his personal arbitrariness.[81] Only the Gang of Four's cognitive line was blamed on causes of a more serious nature: deliberate manipulation of theory so that "all kinds of contraband entirely different from the essentials of Marxism–Leninism–Mao Zedong Thought" could be smuggled. As such, their "metaphysical-idealist" cognitive line became the "ideological basis of their counterrevolutionary line."[82]

The conclusion drawn from these analyses, thus, was not that it was necessary to overcome the monopoly of truth, but rather that it was important to ensure the dialectical materialist approach. That is, once the party guaranteed the proper integration of theory and practice, it could avoid the dogmatism of Hua's two whatevers, the subjectivism of Mao's later years, and the distortions of the Gang of Four. In short, because the debate on the criterion of truth was politically dictated, the problem of the monopoly of truth by the opposing side rather than the problem of monopoly per se was a target of criticism. The monopoly of Deng's own practice criterion was above discussion.

Not surprisingly, the debate of 1978 fell short of resolving the issue of how to guarantee the objectivity of the practice criterion. At the theory conference, Hu Yaobang remarked, in reference to the Democracy Wall movement, that the "emancipation of the mind" should not go beyond the "universal principles of Marxism, the party's leadership, or the socialist system."[83] Similarly, in outlining the Four Fundamental Principles, Deng spelled out the boundaries of the criterion of truth. Hu also came to define Emancipation of the Mind as the use of Marxist methodology to "study new situations and solve new problem" appropriate to economic reform.[84] Initiated as a battle against radical policies and ideology, the truth debate thus came to serve Deng's economic agenda and the political and intellectual liberalization necessary for this purpose.

The establishment of a new ideological line, in sum, reflected the perception of its proponents that the problems of a mistaken political line had originated from an erroneous ideological line. It also reflected their perception of the necessary political function of an ideological debate. Both perceptions resulted in certain limitations of the truth debate. Despite the conflict between the two political groups, both still upheld one authoritative body of truth. The real differences were over the scope of official doctrine to be deemed as truth and the methods of application. These differences contributed to a divergence in perspective and approach within a broad value scheme. The similarity between the two groups prevented one from addressing the question of what allowed the other to assert the total truth in the first place.

On substantive levels, the repudiation of the two whatevers led the pragmatists to apply their new ideological line to sorting out the key areas of radical ideology and politics that needed to be discarded. Here three major tenets of the past were criticized: the pursuit of "class struggle as the key link," the constant promotion of production relations to be more socialist, and the exaltation of politics in command. These three tenets were later identified as the core components of the leftist line from 1958 to 1978 in the Resolution on CCP History.[85] Their repudiation was linked to the affirmation of the new ideological line because the two whatevers were aimed at continuing them. Moreover, as those tenets were seen as the basis of the ultra-leftist model of socialism since 1958, their repudiation became necessary to justify the discarding of that model.

The Misconception of the Principal Contradiction of Society

The central argument against the tenet of "class struggle as the key link" was that a misconception of the principal contradiction in Chinese society had contributed to a misplacement of the party's priority since 1958.

The thesis of a principal contradiction between production relations and production forces in a given social mode was basic to Marx's idea of historical development as a series of progressive stages. Class struggle, generated by that contradiction, becomes the motive force of social development in a given historical period, when revolution ensues from the rise of new progressive classes that challenge and eventually overthrow those who dominate the old production forces, thereby resolving the contradiction.[86] Hence, for Marxists, the diagnosis of class contradictions in a given historical period provides the basis for formulating the tasks of society. The adequacy of this diagnosis, therefore, is crucial to adequate political decision making. But Marx did not provide a clear answer to a key question here: If class struggle is the motive force of development in the pre-socialist stages of history, what would be the motive force during the socialist phase, when the basic class contradiction has been resolved?

It is here that post-Mao critics located the source of Mao's misdiagnosis since 1958. According to them, the party correctly diagnosed the basic contradiction of Chinese society at the Eighth Congress in 1956, when it pronounced the end of the principal contradiction between the proletarian and bourgeois classes after the completion of the transformation of private ownership. In early 1957 Mao himself twice remarked that the principal contradiction of Chinese society had shifted from that between two antagonistic forces to that between production relations and production forces. The fundamental task of the party, proclaimed both Mao and the Eighth Congress, was no longer one of liberating production forces from the old order but one of developing them under new production relations.[87] However, a series of events since 1957 led Mao to redefine the state of class contradiction in China. The first was the unexpected surge of the so-called rightists during the "blooming of one hundred flowers" drive of 1957, which led Mao to reaffirm the conflict between the proletarian and bourgeois classes as the principal contradiction in China. Following this change, Mao began to apply the class analysis to the critics of his Great Leap Forward within the party. At the Lushan conference in 1959, Mao declared his conflict with Peng Dehuai a "class struggle," setting the precedent of labeling intraparty disputes as class struggle. The worsening of the political environment in the early 1960s contributed further to Mao's indiscriminate emphasis on class. Externally, the Sino-Soviet rift and the Sino-Indian border war strained China's international relations. At home, private farming and cadre corruption increased in the wake of the "three difficult years."

Against this background of domestic and international pressures, Mao's thinking underwent a further change. In 1962 he extended the idea of the principal contradiction between two hostile classes to the entire historical phase of socialism, pinpointing it as the possible cause of the restoration of capitalism in China as well as the source of revisionism within the party and the international Communist movement. As the theoretical basis for policy, this new identification set the stage for incessant political campaigns since 1958 keyed to the theme of class struggle, culminating in the theory of "continuing the revolution" that materialized in the Cultural Revolution.[88] It also led to the notion of "class struggle as the key link," which served to shift the party's agenda away from economic modernization. On the same rationale, Hua Guofeng continued to insist on class struggle as an "absolutely necessary political precondition" of the Four Modernizations.

Prior to the theory conference of 1979, efforts to modify the concept of class struggle did not challenge its theoretical basis, even though the modifications were made by special commentators or other powerful authors.[89] They simply sought to redefine the purpose of class struggle in terms of material benefits of the people, basing the argument on the Marxist thesis that all class struggles stemmed from conflicts over material interests. Judged by this redefinition, the kind of class struggle waged in the Mao era did not serve the proletariat because it had decreased rather than increased their material interests. But this redefinition of class struggle fell short of removing the theoretical basis of the key link thesis, that is, the designation of basic contradictions. Without a complete repudiation of its theoretical basis, the post-Mao shift away from class struggle created considerable misgivings among some cadres and masses about deviation from Mao's thought.

Party theoretician Hu Qiaomu was the first official to question the underlying assumptions of the key link thesis. At a CDP conference in January 1979, he asked whether the concept was appropriate after the proletarian revolution and socialist transformation: In what scope and conditions do class struggles still exist? Do they continue to be a motive force of social development? What role do they play in propelling social development, as opposed to the role of production activities and technology? More fundamentally, should the conflict between the working and bourgeois classes remain the principal contradiction? Can any residual class struggle in socialist society function as the motive force of social development? Mao's misconceptions on these issues, Hu concluded, had led to the overexpansion of class struggle since 1958.[90] These analyses were endorsed by Hu Yaobang at the theory conference shortly after, where he introduced them in his keynote speech.[91] In his closing speech at the theory conference, Deng also endorsed the conclusion reached at the conference that as a socialist society, China no longer possessed the conditions for nurturing exploitation and exploitative classes.[92] This reassessment was formally adopted in the government report of the second session of the Fifth NPC in July 1979.

These official initiatives paved the way for a more thorough rethinking nationwide in 1979–81. Based on the dialectical materialist approach, this rethinking identified three major causes of Mao's misconception of the principal contradiction. The first was Mao's failure to characterize correctly the nature of the transitional period between the presocialist and socialist stage as well as the nature of the socialist stage.[93] In this analysis, Mao applied his view of class relations during the transitional period to the entire socialist stage. He ignored the fact that by 1956, after the transformation of private ownership, the transition to socialism had been completed, thereby eliminating the sources of the fundamental conflict between major economic classes. Any residual class conflicts—arising from remnants of former class enemies or overseas forces—could not function as the motive force of social development. In other words, the empirical context of class struggle no longer existed. In continuing to focus on class struggle, the theory and practice of the key link resulted in "artificially engineered" political campaigns and misguided policy priorities.[94]

A deeper source of the neglect of changed social conditions was attributed to the special experience of the CCP, which changed from being a party out of power to a party in power. That is, the CCP was more familiar with the destruction of the old order than with the building of the new. As admitted in the party's 1981 Resolution on CCP History, "some of the laws governing the development of socialist society are relatively clear, but many more need to be explored. Our party had long existed in circumstances of war and fierce class struggle and was not prepared, either ideologically or in terms of scientific study, for the swift advent of the newborn socialist society." Consequently, the CCP was prone to extending its wartime perspective and strategy to the postrevolutionary period. "Even after the basic completion of socialist transformation, we were liable . . . to continue to regard issues unrelated to class struggle as its manifestation."[95]

A one-sided understanding of Marxist theory was also said to have given rise to the overestimation of class contradictions in socialist society. For example, Marx envisioned the idea of distribution according to labor for socialist society, even though he admitted that it reflected the concept of "bourgeois right." Mao, however, understood this to mean that any recognition of material interests would give rise to a new bourgeois class, even under socialism.[96] Similarly, Lenin once made the observation that small-scale production would give rise to bourgeois forces during the transitional period of the Bolshevik revolution. Yet, well after the consolidation of China's transition to socialism, Mao still followed Lenin's precept. Because these classic masters were misunderstood or dogmatically interpreted, says the Resolution on CCP History, the party's "subjective thinking" found a false "theoretical basis" in the writings of Marx, Engels, Lenin, and Stalin.

> For instance, it was thought that equal right, . . . or "bourgeois right" as it was designated by Marx, should be restricted and criticized, and so the principle of "to each according to his work" and that of material interest should be restricted and criticized; that small production would continue to engender capitalism and the bourgeoisie daily and hourly on a large scale even after

the basic completion of socialist transformation, and so a series of "left" economic policies and policies on class struggle in urban and rural areas were formulated; that all ideological differences inside the party were reflections of class struggle in society, and so frequent and acute inner-party struggles were conducted. All this led us to regard the error in broadening the scope of class struggle as an act in defense of the purity of Marxism.[97]

The ultimate criticism of Mao's idea of the principal contradiction was thus directed at his disregard for Chinese reality, on the one hand, and his misunderstanding of theory, on the other.

To bring the conception of the principal contradiction closer to reality, the party formally announced a return to a formulation of the Eighth Party Congress of 1956. That is, the principal contradiction of Chinese society after the completion of socialist transformation had become that between the low level of production forces and the increasing material and cultural needs of the people. Resurrection of the definition was found justifiable in both theory and reality. The theoretical basis was Stalin's basic law of socialist society on which the 1956 definition was based,[98] while the empirical basis was the discrepancy between the level of production forces and the material needs of society that existed in China.[99]

Yet this discrepancy also led a few heretics to find the principal contradiction in Chinese society in the conflict between its "advanced production relations" and "backward production forces." Su Shaozhi, a leading student of Marxism, for one, openly raised questions about the official restoration of the 1956 formula in an article in July 1979.[100] For example, if existing production relations were indeed "advanced," as the new official tenet alleged, then Deng's proposed reforms would be poorly justified. If existing production forces were "backward" in relation to production relations, as the new official formula asserted, then the soundness of those relations became questionable. Official sources quickly discouraged this view for fear of its implications.[101] The reformulation of the principal contradiction, then, was as politically dictated as the practice criterion, set forth in accordance with the party's new economic priority. Although less divorced from reality, it was nonetheless "subjective."

The One-sided Elevation of Production Relations

The second radical credo that came under attack was the constant transformation of production relations to more socialist forms. In Marxist terminology, production relations refer to the relations of the ownership of the means of production, management, and distribution in the production process. Production forces denote the factors of production, both human and material. It is a basic tenet of historical materialism that production relations must conform to production forces. The Marxist rationale for transforming repressive production relations is that they have become hindrances to the release of potential production forces.

This rationale, in turn, became the basis for pursuing "higher" forms of production relations during much of the Mao era. Although twice in 1957 Mao acknowledged the imperfect conformity between production relations and production forces under socialism, he did not identify its causes.[102] With the intensification of class struggle since 1958, Mao became preoccupied with protecting and purifying socialist production relations against possible erosion by the so-called enemy forces, resorting to political measures such as mass campaigns and class struggle to achieve that objective. These methods were reflected in the Great Leap Forward of 1958, the socialist education movement of 1964, the Cultural Revolution of 1966–76, the move against the "rightist wind of rehabilitation" of 1975–76, and the constant interim efforts to restrict private production and material incentives. In the process, socialist production relations became sacred and their superiority absolute. The heated exchanges between the practice and whatever groups over material interests, the "struggle between two roads," and "learning from Dazhai" all centered on the relevance of socialist production relations.

The assumption of the superiority of socialist production relations per se was first questioned by Deng. He alluded to the question in an address to the National Science Conference in March 1978, and then in a speech in July.[103] By September he spoke about it more directly: "From the viewpoint of historical materialism, correct political leadership in the end should manifest itself in the growth of the production forces of society and the improvement of the growing material and cultural needs of the people." Deng went on to ask, "If in a long historical period, the rate of the growth of production forces in the socialist country is slower than that in capitalist countries, where is the superiority of which we talk?"[104] Here, Deng raised the question of whether the superiority of socialist structures was a matter of subjective supposition or whether it should be judged by empirical criteria.

Following this line of reasoning, the special commentators, party theoreticians such as Xue Muqiao and Hu Qiaomu, and economists from the CASS Economic Research Institute began to reexamine radical theories and practices concerning production relations. Again, the principal fallacies were found in a mistaken approach to theory and practice. With regard to theory, the blame was placed on a misunderstanding of the nature of scientific socialism. On the faulty assumption that socialism was the inevitable product of the contradiction between production forces and outdated capitalist production relations, policy makers had taken the superiority of socialist institutions for granted. There was a neglect of the Marxist premise that old capitalist relations were made obsolete not by the nature of those relations but by the expansion of production forces. Socialist relations replaced capitalist ones only to accommodate the expansive productive demands, rather than to display some imaginative superiority. Along this line, post-Mao critics concluded that once socialist relations were established, they should be used to promote production forces rather than normative goals (e.g., promoting the proletarian viewpoint or expressing indignation at capitalist relations). In short, scientific socialism was "scientific," not "utopian," precisely because of its material premise.[105]

The one-sided emphasis on production relations was also attributed to a misunderstanding of Marx's idea of the conformity between production relations and production forces. Here, the problem was not so much the neglect of production forces vis-à-vis production relations. After all, the Great Leap Forward of Mao and the new Leap Forward of Hua were both aimed at increasing production. Rather, the problem lay in the assumption that "conformity" between production relations and production forces entailed that the former automatically guaranteed the constant increase of the latter. According to this assumption, once the socialist system was established, the only way to advance economic development was to promote socialist institutions. Difficulties in economic development were traced not to problems in those institutions, but to their insufficient promotion. As a result, the incessant efforts to promote socialist relations only led to a downward spiral of economic growth and a constant restriction of exogenous economic institutions that may conform more to reality.[106] In short, the mistake of the one-sided promotion boiled down to a methodological one: The positive role of advanced socialist institutions was affirmed without regard for the context of the original theory.

In practice, the post-1958 political leadership was criticized for disregarding the empirical context to which socialist relations should be applied. Insofar as the low and uneven level of development in China did not reach the level envisioned in Marx's socialist society, the transition to higher forms of economic structures had been pushed despite this discrepancy. Critics such as Xue Muqiao and the economist Xu Dixin argued not that socialist transformation should not be made, but that it should not have been made so completely, hastily, and indiscriminately. On the issue of ownership, for example, past policies assumed that the more public and the larger the scale, the more superior the ownership form. Hence, the transition to state ownership was carried out without regard for the material base or its capacity for production of social scale. "Lower" forms of ownership that conformed to reality, such as private plots, family side-line production, market fairs, and individual business, were treated as "capitalist tails" that must be discarded.[107] The result was called a "transition in poverty," or a transition without an adequate material base. The endeavor was seen not only as impossible but also as obstructive to socialist development.[108]

Objective Laws versus Subjective Will

The third radical credo that came to be repudiated was politics in command. Central to this effort was the counterposing of the credo to a new tenet, "respect for objective laws." Tang Tsou has described the post-Mao affirmation of objective laws as a "sociological postulate" that emphasizes the autonomy of the socioeconomic sphere and the retreat of the state from policy making.[109] In actuality, the affirmation of objective laws was directed not so much at the penetrative role of the state as at how the state's role should be played. Politics in command was criticized for advocating that politics and elite volition should play a key role in policy making and implementation. This "subjective" role of the state allegedly resulted in "blind command" and "arbitrary will," "unrealistic economic targets and speed," and exaggeration of "the unique importance of subjective will." By contrast, the "objective" role of the state, entailed in respect for objective laws, would mean "planned and proportionate development," "scientific attitude" and "realistic spirit," and "seeking truth from facts." The dispute over politics in command stemmed originally from Hua's new Great Leap and his exaltation of politics in command to accomplish it, a dispute made most notably by Hu Qiaomu's article on observing objective laws in October 1978. Because the dispute touched on a key ingredient of the radical line of which Hua was but a follower, it became part of the larger debate over the criterion of truth.

The focus of the critique against politics in command was again its sources in theory and practice. One theoretical source was attributed to the assumption that the "socialistness" of political orientation could substitute for objective laws. This assumption in turn was traced to a distorted understanding of socialism: Because Marx envisioned the replacement of capitalism by socialism, the latter's superior power was automatically assumed. The problem here was a failure to understand the basis of socialism's superior power, which in turn led to exaggerations of its capacity. As Xu Dixin noted, the strength of socialism derived from its conformity with objective laws rather than its replacement of them.[110] Hu Qiaomu put it this way:

The socialist system itself does not automatically guarantee that we act in accordance with objective laws; and therefore it does not automatically guarantee that our economy always develop in a proportionate and rapid manner. The socialist system has provided the *possibility* for us to act in accordance with objective economic laws. This is its superiority, an impossible feature in the historical scope of national economic development under the capitalist system. But to transfer that *possibility* into *reality* still requires great efforts.[111]

In other words, politics in command did not have its proclaimed high ground because it equated the possibility of a superior system with actuality and placed this system above objective laws.[112] Interestingly, these criticisms echoed those raised by Peng Dehuai in his critique of Mao's Great Leap Forward the late 1950s.[113]

Another theoretical source of politics in command was found in the CCP's frequent claim that truth had a "class nature." Under the justification that "class stand" should assume priority in the observation and interpretation of reality, Xing Fensi pointed out, "class will" replaced scientific study and empirical investigation.[114] Thus Hua's high-growth strategy was criticized for following such absurd notions as "how courageous humans can be, how huge the harvest will be" and "better leftist adventurism than rightist conservatism."[115] For practice advocates, the role of class will was one not of enabling the proletariat to bypass objective laws, but of making them conform better to them. As one special commentator put it, "the socialist system makes it possible for leadership organs to plan correctly socialist production," but this did not mean that "our annual plan and five-year plans completely reflect objective economic laws."[116] In this respect, several areas of objective laws were given particular emphasis in 1978–79 in response to Hua's new Leap strategy— for example, the basic law of socialist production (satisfaction of the material and cultural needs of society), the law of planned and proportionate development, the conformity of production relations to production forces, distribution according to labor, and the law of value.

In practice, the emphasis on political volition was criticized for detachment from reality and the people. Because such volition often reflected the will of political leaders or of agents of the state apparatus, policy decisions were based neither on scientific studies or popular opinions. Yet because subjective volition was legitimated by class will, the neglect of objective laws became justified. As a result, Hu Qiaomu concluded, various types of subjective will—social, governmental, elitist—became economic laws that could be changed randomly according to political needs.[117]

In sum, the reassessment of Mao's ideological legacy during the debates of 1978–79 involved repudiating three key ideological patterns of the Mao era: excessive expansion of class struggle that underlaid the *policy priorities* of the prereform regime; one-sided promotion of production relations that underlaid the *structures* of the prereform economy and the neglect of objective laws that underlaid the *manner* of prereform political leadership.

CONCLUSION

The reassessment of socialism in the immediate post-Mao period addressed the mistakes of one group of political leaders in their understanding of established theory and their approach to the practice of the late Chairman Mao. These mistakes were held as responsible for the leaders' refusal to renounce an erroneous line of policy and ideology, which was in turn symptomatic of mistaken conceptions of and approaches to socialism responsible for serious disasters in China's socialist development.

These mistaken understandings and approaches were summarily assessed as guilty of a "metaphysical idealist" line toward the theory and practice of Marxism-Leninism and Mao Zedong Thought. In regard to understanding of theory, carriers of this line were said to have misconceived the role, context, and relativity of theory by exaggerating its universality. In regard to application of theory, they were said to have disregarded the primacy, specificity, and dynamics of reality by ignoring its particularity. These mistakes had allegedly led to a set of policy priorities, economic structures, and leadership methods unsuited to Chinese realities and thus responsible for past failures of Chinese socialism. This radical line was characterized as guilty of "ultra-leftism" because of its alleged universalism, subjectivism, and dogmatism with regard to theory and practice of socialism.

The perceived need for change as well as continuity in the immediate post-Mao period led the other group of Chinese leaders to affirm an allegedly correct approach to theory and practice, which they labeled the "dialectical materialist" line. The crux of the new line was an assertion of the primacy of reality, a bifurcation of theory into fundamental and specific principles, and an emphasis on the integration of fundamental principles with changing realities. The use of official doctrine to justify the new line allowed this group to claim true fidelity while renouncing the specific policies and ideology of the past. Nonetheless, the critiques against the radical tenets all placed the blame on mistaken understandings and application of socialism, not on socialism itself. In this sense, it was the "specific principles" of Maoist socialism that were negated in this period.

The affirmation of the dialectical materialist approach and the negation of key radical tenets of the past set the stage for post-Mao reforms. The questions raised during the truth debate concerning fundamental and specific principles, universality and particularity, and adherence to and development of Marxism would recur throughout the post-Mao reassessment. But the patterns of reassessment in this early period were in many ways time-specific: Political leaders directly initiated ideological debates and intervened to have certain viewpoints published; political leaders participated directly in the preparation and drafting of certain articles; and public discussions supported and observed the frame of official discourse—with the exception of the Democracy Wall movement and parts of the 1979 theory conference. These patterns would soon weaken as reformist leaders consolidated their political position and the ideological climate gradually eased for the general public, allowing more independent explorations.

CHAPTER THREE

Competing Models of the Socialist Economy

DURING the dispute with the whatever group, the veteran leaders—most of whom were victims of the Cultural Revolution—joined forces as a reformist coalition. When these victors of the truth debate turned to proposing ways to redress past wrongs, they began to diverge in perspective and approach. Though unanimous about the priority of economic modernization and respect for objective laws, they disagreed on the types of objective laws that should be emphasized. The more radical of the reform leaders, represented by Deng Xiaoping, Hu Yaobang, and Zhao Ziyang, paid attention to the laws concerning production relations. A more orthodox group, linked to Chen Yun, Li Xiannian, and many other veteran leaders, placed priority on the laws governing the objectives, proportions, and rates of economic development. In attempting to correct ultra-leftist errors, each group was increasingly forced to face the larger question of building socialism in China. For however deviant the radical excesses, they occurred within the broad framework of socialism. In the process of searching for viable reform policies, divergent perspectives on the theory and practice of socialism unfolded among the post-Mao political leadership.

The orthodox economic system of socialism, as developed in the Soviet Union under Stalin, involves a number of basic structural features in the ownership of the means of production, allocation of resources, operation of enterprises, administration of employment and distribution, and exchange of products.[1] Although there were degrees of variability in its variants, the essential features that define the Soviet-type economy may be summed up in three elements: (1) centralization of economic decision making and management, (2) state and collective ownership of the means of production, and (3) relatively level income distribution.[2] These basic features have sometimes been taken as deriving from the Soviet experience of the 1930s, but they are respectively based on Marx's ideas of a product economy, cooperative ownership of the means of production, and distribution according to labor.[3] A product economy denotes an economy that produces goods not as tradable commodities with market values but as nontradable products for planned distribution in a society under a common ownership. Thus its opposite is a commodity economy, a Marxist term for a market economy. Whether or not those patterns of the Soviet-type economy approximated Marx's visions, they were copied as the sole legitimate model of socialism elsewhere. They form the core elements of the Soviet model of socialism, as opposed to the classic model of Marx and Engels.

Aside from these institutional features, one can identify a peculiar Soviet pattern of economic development. This involves macro decisions over the ordering of components of the economy, such as heavy industry over light industry, accumulation over consumption, and quantitative over qualitative growth targets. Stalin summed up this macro arrangement of economic sectors as the socialist road of industrialization. For analytical purposes it may be referred to as the Soviet model of sectoral arrangement. This model was also copied by China in the early 1950s. Although by 1956 Mao came to recognize the problems of this lopsided strategy, his subsequent Great Leap set the momentum for greater one-sidedness in certain areas (e.g., emphasis on accumulation, growth targets, and steel industry) than in the original Soviet model, according to Xue Muqiao.[4] This excess, along with his emphasis on socialist production relations and politics in command, formed the core of the Maoist model of economic development. The Chinese economy on the eve of post-Mao reforms was a mix of all of the above models.

This chapter traces the evolution of the post-Mao reassessment of socialism in the economic arena. The focus of this chronological review is on how each economic model became a center of controversy over the analysis of what was wrong with the Chinese economy and how it should be rectified. The account begins with the Third Plenum of 1978 and ends with the resumption of reform after Deng Xiaoping's spring tour of 1992. The period may be subdivided into three phases, during each of which a particular model of socialist economy was the focus of reappraisal.

READJUSTMENT OF THE SOVIET ROAD
OF DEVELOPMENT

Post-Mao economic reforms began in rural areas immediately after the Third Plenum. They involved devolving production and distribution powers to production teams, raising the price of agricultural products sold to the state, and encouraging distribution according to labor.[5] These "retreats" from the Maoist model were based on the repudiation—made during the truth debate—of the overextension of class struggle against the restoration of capitalism in the countryside, the imbalance between production relations and production forces, and the neglect of objective laws.

A Chinese Model of Sectoral Designs and Planned Management

After the Third Plenum, reform officials began to go beyond the Maoist excesses to locate deeper sources of China's economic problems. Chen Yun began to question the theoretical premises of the Chinese economy even before the Third Plenum. At the work conference of November–December 1978, he expressed concern about the Soviet model of sectoral arrangement by criticizing what he saw as sectoral imbalances in the economy. Though this did not become an issue at the Third Plenum, Chen more actively pursued this line of critique afterward. In March 1979 he formally proposed a readjustment of the Soviet model of sectoral designs in a letter to the Central Committee.[6]

In response, a central work conference was convened in April at which Chen enunciated the reasons for readjustment. Using what he called a true dialectical materialist approach, he spoke of readjustment as a matter of "seeking truth from facts." The "facts" of Chinese reality, he argued, defied the rationale behind the heavy industrial model adopted from the Soviet Union. One key fact was the existence of a large, poor, agrarian population in China that made agriculture and the people's livelihood the priority of its economic development. Another fact was China's limited ability to concentrate on heavy industrial modernization, because the bulk of its population and economy existed outside the heavy industrial sector. A Chinese road of modernization, in his view, must take prior account of the bulk of the population in the rural sector and the improvement of their livelihood. In this context Chen cited imbalances in the economy between agriculture and industry, light and heavy industry, and accumulation and consumption.[7] The identification of these imbalances was made on the basis of Stalin's basic law of socialist economy, namely, the need to satisfy the material and cultural needs of society. The sectoral designs of the Chinese economy were wrong, then, because it had failed to satisfy those needs.

From this adjuster's perspective, Chen presented a coherent critique of the economy and a proposal for its reform. For him, economic imbalances were caused not by the irrationalities of the plan but by the failure of planned development on the basis of Chinese reality. The emphasis on planned development was specifically directed at Hua Guofeng's ambitious heavy industrial targets of 1977–78. To change such a strategy, Chen argued, constituted the key instance of "integrating Marxism with Chinese reality" at present. At the same meeting, readjustment cosponsor Li Xiannian, a major leader during Hua's Leap Forward years, now called for a return to "proportionate development" by "taking primary account of agriculture and reorienting the economy accordingly," and a return to "planned development" by "setting realistic speed and targets."[8] With these proposals the "Chinese road of modernization" became a central thesis in public discourse in early 1979. From the earlier exhortation of "seeking truths from facts," the emphasis was now on seeking specific "facts" about China and the ways to conform to them. Before long Deng also endorsed the "Chinese road of modernization," concurring that China must follow its own path in both its economic system and its sectoral design.[9] The April work conference altered the Third Plenum line by placing readjustment above reform for at least three years.[10] But readjustment was not seriously implemented, at least in Chen Yun's opinion, until after the central work conference in December 1980, thanks especially to resistance by supporters of heavy and defense industries.

Adjusters were also concerned, but secondarily, with the structures of the economy. In fact, it was Chen Yun who initiated a reform of central planning in March 1979. While basically affirming the product economy, he criticized the rigidity of planning and proposed the use of the market for a small, nonessential portion of the economy. His idea was summed up in the phrase "a leading role of the plan and a supplementary role of the market."[11] At the level of production units, Chen and like-minded officials advocated administrative decentralization, namely, devolution of central authority, but not economic decentralization, namely, devolution of regulation to the market.[12] At both macro and micro levels, therefore, these officials were concerned with the scope of the central role rather than the nature of central planning itself. Deng Liqun, a leading ideological official, proposed devolution of power to the enterprise that would go beyond past efforts at intrastate decentralization.[13] Fang Weizhong, an official at the State Planning Commission, advocated "enterprise autonomy" to replace central and regional regulation.[14] Li Xiannian saw a "consensus among all parties" over enterprise autonomy.[15] The emphasis on enterprise autonomy by these adjusters, it is important to note, was directed at the excessive centralization of the Mao era and was thus time specific. The same officials would later advocate tightening central control in response to the decentralizing efforts of more radical reformers.[16] Because adjusters advocated partial reforms in addition to readjustment, they also came to be known as "conservative reformers."

The other group of reformers, who came to be known as "radical reformers," were primarily concerned with problems of economic institutions, that is, structures of planning, ownership, and distribution. Each of these was singled out as the focus of reexamination beginning in 1978.[17] Many reform theorists and intellectuals offered their own analyses within the framework of the overall orientation of the more radical reform leadership. In contrast to the Central Party School theoreticians of the previous period, now economists—especially those from the CASS Economic Research Institute—began to play a more important in public discussions on economic reform. As early as January 1979, the institute's Dong Fureng made the controversial argument that the root problem of the economy lay in state ownership, which must be the starting point of reform.[18] Xue Muqiao, a senior economist and adviser at the State Planning Commission, saw the principal fault in the command economy. Casting it as a Soviet model, he found that its key features, namely, centralized revenues and expenditures, assigned purchase and marketing, and guaranteed employment, were products of wartime exigencies of the Stalin era rather than systemic requirements of socialism. Those practices were untenable in China, he argued, because of its diverse territories and population size. Hence the idea of a Chinese road to modernization should also apply to the economic system.[19] Yu Guangyuan, vice president of CASS, even disputed Chen Yun's vision of planned development and a limited market as capable of reforming the economy.[20] The noted economists Sun Shangqing and Liu Guoguang, both from CASS, also favored reforming the planning mechanism.[21]

In addition, reformers began to question the mutual exclusiveness of the plan and the market as stipulated in teachings of Marx, Engels, and Stalin. As party secretary in Sichuan at the time, Zhao Ziyang encouraged local researchers to make "theoretical breakthroughs" on this question. In a symposium with economists in March 1979, he led one of the first open forums in the post-Mao period to explore the hitherto forbidden issue of the relation between the plan and the market. The forum concluded that the integration of these two mechanisms was a more urgent problem than the provision of enterprise autonomy, for integration would address the problem of chronic gaps between production and demand.[22] At a national conference of economists held in Wuxi in April, the issue was also discussed as a priority topic, followed by many provincial meetings and extensive academic and media discussions. The prevailing view that emerged was that the plan and the market could be mutually compatible if the notion of the product economy was not interpreted dogmatically. By late 1979 Zhao omitted "planned economy" from his definition of socialism.[23] With this reformulation, these reformers sought to go beyond the conservative reform program.

The Chinese road to modernization, proposed by adjusters and reformers, met with a brief thrust of opposition from the Left coalition during the "relapse of leftism" in spring 1979. The April work conference on readjustment was held just a few days after Deng's declaration of the Four Fundamental Principles. The occasion offered an immediate opportunity for the Left coalition to make use of the ideological retightening to voice dissent. This coalition, which may be called "conservers," was made up of the whatever faction and a "petroleum" faction.[24] The latter group included ministerial and military backers of heavy industry such as Marshal Xu Xiangqian, influential protector of the group and defender of defense industry; Yu Qiuli, head of the State Planning Commission and principal backer of heavy industry; and Kang Shi'en, vice premier responsible for the Petroleum Ministry.[25] While the whatever group opposed both reform and readjustment, the petroleum group objected particularly to readjustment. Citing the Four Fundamental Principles, the conservers castigated recent policy shifts as illegitimate "reform after the completion of socialist revolution," destruction of the party's leadership through the expansion of team and enterprise autonomy, "profits in command" through material incentives, and "Westernization" through foreign trade and imports. Along these lines, they defended excessive production speed and growth as permissible "policy errors" and attacked economic retreat as serious "line errors."[26] The surge of ultra-leftism did complicate policy-making and implementation. The Fourth Plenum of the Eleventh Congress, which was to adopt measures on rural reform and industrial readjustment, was postponed. As the media sent out conflicting messages on key ideological and policy issues, local cadres became apprehensive about implementing rural reforms.[27] Rural cadres in Anhui were able to continue with reform under the sanctuary of Wan Li, but others slowed it down for fear of another political campaign.[28]

Politically, the leftist relapse dealt a fatal blow to the whatever group, when several of its members were demoted at the second session of the Fifth NPC in February 1980. Ideologically, the episode had an impact on reformist thinking in two ways. First, the controversy over readjustment prompted a public debate on the Soviet sectoral model. Second, the dispute over rural reform led to a public debate on the nature of rural reform.

Objective Laws Governing Sectoral Arrangement under Socialism

The debate on the sectoral arrangement of the economy started shortly before the Fourth Plenum of the Eleventh Party Congress in September 1979, as an effort to build up support and legitimation for adjusters at the plenum. It was intensified after the contentious but, for adjusters, successful plenum. Adjusters were unequivocal about why a policy dispute had to be resolved through an ideological debate. They traced the roots of misplaced economic priorities to a faulty "guiding ideology." The ideological aspect of the dispute stemmed also from the use of doctrine by the petroleum group to back their arguments. Adjusters were aligned with reformers in this debate, though tensions existed between them. Led by leaders of adjustment in the form of officially sponsored symposiums, special commentator articles, and other front-page articles,[29] the debate also gained contributions from intellectual supporters of both adjustment and reform, such as Wu Jiang, Xue Muqiao, Yu Guangyuan, Wu Jinglian, and Zhou Shulian—the latter two economists from CASS.

The debate over readjustment touched on three key doctrines of economic development under socialism: the basic law of socialist economy, the law of the prior development of the producer sector, and the law of planned and proportional development.

The basic law of socialist economy addresses the purpose of production and the basis for determining the goals of the economy. That is, what is the starting point of central planning? Being the "basic law," it had been debated twice before in the People's Republic, first in the mid-1950s amid the drive to copy the Soviet Union and then in the early 1960s after the failure of the Great Leap. In both debates, moderates accepted Stalin's definition of the basic law, that is, the "satisfaction of the increasing material and cultural needs of the society." On this basis, they distinguished between consumption and production as the end versus the means of socialist production. Both debates led to policy modifications, for example, lower investment rates and higher consumption rates as shares of the GNP. In the debate of 1979–80, the distinction between the ends and the means again drew focal attention. Following this distinction, the adjusters' side claimed that China's sectoral model, patterned after the Soviet Union, encouraged "production for production's sake," rather than the satisfaction of social needs. For the starting point of central planners had invariably been steel output and other heavy industrial targets, around which the rest of central planning was then oriented.[30] According to Xue Muqiao, China's rate of accumulation exceeded the appropriate mark of 25 percent in most of the past five five-year plans: 40 percent between 1959 and 1960, 26 percent between 1963 and 1965 (under adjustment policies), an average of 33 percent between 1970 and 1978, and 36 percent in 1978. In early 1979 Deng suggested reducing the rate to 25 percent, but he was opposed by planning agencies, which regarded an annual rate below 25 percent as potentially harmful to growth.[31]

In analyzing why blind production should happen, however, adjusters were less forthcoming. If Marx saw blind production as a systemic flaw of capitalism and attributed its cause to the profit orientation and anarchy of the market,[32] adjusters denied any systemic cause of "production for production's sake" under socialism. Wu Jiang blamed the abnormality mainly on the historical and psychological pressures under which a backward country like China had to undertake belated modernization. In his analysis, the determination of policymakers to catch up with advanced countries led them to put growth rates above the people's livelihood, and production above producers. Yet in stressing immediate sacrifices, policymakers lost sight of the link between production and the needs of society, resulting in "production for production's sake."[33]

The diagnosis of a cycle of "production for production's sake" in the economy in turn led to the reexamination of the law of prior development of the heavy industrial sector. One aspect of this law, derived from Marx's theory of expanded production, states that when the "organic composition" of the means of production is improved by technological advances, "producer goods" (e.g., machinery) should increase prior to consumer goods.[34] For adjusters and reformers, Marx's emphasis on the means of production here was dogmatically and wrongly understood in the past. Rather than seeing Marx's premise of technological advance and its impact on production, policymakers used Marx to justify the absolute priority of heavy industry and capital construction. The resultant large-scale heavy industrial sector in turn forced investment and production to focus on it. The conclusion, therefore, was that Marx's theory of expanded production should be followed in proper perspective. The production of producer goods should be coordinated with that of consumer goods, and the increase of the former should be defined by the needs of the latter. Further, because of China's objective conditions, that is, a massive demand for consumer goods by a large population, exceptions must be made to Marx's theory of expanded production.[35]

Another component of the law of prior development of the producer sector was attributed to Stalin. It stipulated that the prior development of heavy industry constituted the socialist path to industrialization, as opposed to the capitalist path, which began with light industry. One justification for this assertion was that prior development of light industry occurred under capitalism because the lower investment required enabled capitalists to extract larger profit returns. In the Chinese debate, Stalin's thesis was now dismissed by reform theorists Zhou Shulian, Wu Jinglian, and others on the ground that a peculiar sequence of industrialization was determined not by the systemic features of an economy but by historical conditions. England and France first began to industrialize in the textile sector because of the wool trade and the spinning machine, whereas the Soviet Union started with heavy industry, including defense industry, because of the hostile international environment in the 1920s and 1930s. Agriculture was the main source of accumulation there because Russia's meager light industry did not allow extraction of surpluses. Thus the core features of the Soviet model of sectoral alignment were all found to be peculiarly Soviet in nature.[36] For Wu Jiang, the Soviet imposition of that model on other countries and China's failure to break fully with it in the past had stemmed from a lack of recognition of the particularity of the Soviet model. In the Chinese case, although the Soviet road was criticized and revised in the mid-1950s, the leadership reverted to it after agriculture and light industry were successfully developed in the first five-year plan.[37]

Adjusters faulted the violation of still another objective law for the problems of the economy: the law of planned and proportionate development. For adjusters, the heavy industrial model was premised not on this law but on a belief in the capacity of socialism for higher growth and of heavy industry for ensuring such growth. Under this belief, the centralized character of the economy was misused to pursue recklessly one-sided, often politically determined growth targets. In the process, there resulted a violation of the very premise on which socialism's higher growth was supposed to depend, that is, planned and proportionate development.[38]

From the adjusters' viewpoint, in short, the problems of the economy resulted from a failure to maintain a comprehensive balance. The misallocation of the proportions and priorities of the components of the economy caused serious irrationalities. Remedies, therefore, were to be prescribed on the basis of correctly diagnosed "realities." But these arguments, though helping to discredit the Soviet sectoral model in theory, failed to persuade the backers of heavy industry to scale down their branches. Progress in readjustment was minimal in 1979–80, and the petroleum faction practically halted the debate by early 1980. This group became Deng's chief concern after the demotion of the whatever group in the February session of the NPC in 1980. But he managed to maneuver their eclipse at the NPC's August session that year: Xu Xiangqian was retired; Yu Qiuli was replaced by the adjuster Yao Yilin; and Kang Shi'en was demoted for the Bohai erhao incident.[39] Adjusters launched another offensive to adjust the economy at the end of 1980.

Multiple Forms of Collective Economy

Concurrent with the preceding debate was a controversy over the nature of rural household production. The issue originated from rural reforms introduced after the Third Plenum. Although those reforms amounted mainly to decentralization within the commune, they still caused uproars during the resurgence of ultra-leftism. In response, reform officials formally adopted the trial decree on rural reform at the Fourth Plenum in September 1979.[40] This eased the mind of rural cadres wary of class struggle and political reprisals, but it did not resolve the fundamental question of the socialist nature of recent reforms. When more innovative practices emerged in the course of 1979, controversy resurged on a greater level of intensity, contributing to the debate over rural reforms in 1980.

The debate arose over two forms of household production secretly practiced by a few production teams after the introduction of rural reforms in late 1978. One was called *baochan daohu* (contracting production to the household) and the other *baogan daohu* (contracting output to the household). Known together as "double *bao*," both practices were still forbidden in 1979. Even Zhao Ziyang ruled them out as acceptable forms of rural reform in at this time.[41] But Xiaogang, a production team in Anhui Province, took the risk to contract production to the household in late 1978. Most of the twenty households in Xiaogang had been reduced to begging in the past. Anhui as a whole was also known for its high proportion of poor peasants. But within a year of household production, Xiaogang's grain output in 1979 equaled that of the collective team from 1967 to 1970. The output of vegetable oil that year exceeded the total of twenty years since collectivization. Sideline income was also higher than that for the rest of the commune.[42] Elsewhere, rural teams that tried household contract production also reaped remarkable output increases. These stories spread quickly and were warmly received in neighboring teams.

The reemergence of double *bao* set off a controversy between those who saw "an erosion of the collective economy" and those who saw an effective form of collective economy.[43] At a People's Liberation Army (PLA) political work conference in April 1980, Hua Guofeng and Wei Guoqing, the latter director of the PLA's General Political Department, attacked material incentives and warned of the need to continue the struggle between "two roads."[44] Other leftist leaders blamed "leadership encouragement" and "one-sided ideological orientation," leading some local cadres to reverse those "capitalist tendencies."[45] The dispute was more than symbolic, because household production had been much criticized in the past, and public apprehension was deep-seated. The outcome of the dispute would affect its fate in the current reform, as similar debates in the 1950s and 1960s testified.[46]

But leadership made a decisive difference in 1980. At the height of the controversy in May 1980, Deng met with leading ideological officials Deng Liqun and Hu Qiaomu to talk about the "good results and quick changes" effected by *baochan daohu*. He dismissed misgivings about the erosion of the collective economy and affirmed the legitimacy of diversity within a collective economy. In this context, Deng raised the larger question of the legitimacy of divergent indigenous paths across socialist countries and criticized the Soviet Union for denying this legitimacy in the past.[47] In June Zhao Ziyang wrote to central authorities urging "stabilization" of *baochan daohu* through a formal policy, without which local officials were already trying to ban such practices.[48] Wan Li played a key role in providing a haven for double *bao* in Anhui.

The debate went beyond the usual round of official incitement and media elaboration. Following the emphasis on "objective conditions," researchers were sent to provinces to investigate various new practices in the countryside. In July the media launched criticisms of the Dazhai model to cast the debate as one over diverse models within socialism: While the Dazhai model stressed ideological exhortation and class consciousness to motivate producers, double *bao* emphasized distribution based on labor and the law of value. In August Shanxi Province made a critical report on the Dazhai model to the Central Committee. Then, at the NPC session in September, localities were encouraged to explore new methods that suited local conditions.[49] The session also stripped Hua Guofeng and Chen Yonggui, two leading defenders of the radical model of collective economy, of their government duties.

In the same month the Central Committee gathered provincial leaders to discuss policies toward double *bao*. Despite the recent demise of the whatever group, delegates remained divided over the ideological nature of double *bao*. The meeting also discussed but failed to affirm the "integration of the plan and market" in industry. But reform leaders appealed to the practice criterion to bypass the question of ideological soundness. The meeting agreed to leave the issue unresolved and let "practice" test the best economic forms.[50] Document 75, adopted at the conference, refrained from sanctioning double *bao* in general but endorsed its application in remote and poor regions. That is, in areas where it was difficult to socialize farm work and where basic food was of primary concern, production units could break down to the household and distribution could be tangibly accorded with labor.[51] The document in effect legalized a long-time illegitimate practice. By November the CCP issued a document to repudiate the singular promotion of the Dazhai model.[52]

Following this breakthrough, journalists and scholars began to explore the question of socialism and its diverse forms of application, and the criteria for choosing a particular form of application. It was in this period that the notion developed that whether a specific form promoted "production forces" should be the criterion of its soundness.[53] In the next central resolution on rural reform, adopted in December 1981, double *bao* was fully recognized as a legitimate socialist practice of general applicability, not just an expedient measure for poverty-ridden areas. From Document 75 to the 1981 resolution, the scope of the implementation of the household contract responsibility system jumped from 15 percent of all production teams nationwide in November 1980 to 67 percent by June 1982, expanding to 97 percent of all production teams by the end of 1983.[54] Under this practice, households were assigned state output quotas but were free to dispose of above-quota output. Similar urban reforms underwent experiment in the early 1980s, under which some state enterprises could sell part of their above-plan output at market prices and retain a share of the profits.

In sum, Chinese rethinking on the socialist road in this period pointed in two directions, one critical of the Soviet sectoral model and the other of the Soviet economic model. For proponents of each direction, China's past equation of imported models with the sole legitimate form of socialism must be replaced by a new approach that would heed China's objective conditions. In their judgment, conservers carried imported models to extremes and believed in the singularity of the economic forms that China must adopt.

REFORM OF THE SOVIET MODEL OF SOCIALISM

As conservers lost political influence in late 1980, the difference between adjusters and reformers became central in elite politics. While reformers' vision would require rethinking the defining principles of socialism, the adjusters' program hardly went beyond Stalin's treatise on socialist economy.[55] Insofar as the latter program was aimed mainly at improved decisions on the priorities and growth rates of major components of the economy, it amounted only to policy change, in contrast to systemic change that would involve economic institutions and methods.[56] The competition between the two approaches led to a deeper reassessment of the socialist road between 1982 and 1986.

The Struggle over Policy versus Systemic Change

The prelude to the second phase of reassessment was an increasing controversy between adjusters and reformers over the conflict between readjustment and reform. Chen Yun raised this issue in several speeches between early 1981 and early 1982, in which he criticized the general decline of the plan since reform began in 1979.[57] For it had become clear in the course of the past three years that while readjustment aimed at lower investment and greater balance among sectors, reform had the opposite effects: As central control declined and local rights increased, mandatory output shrank, state revenues diminished, deficits worsened, local investment expanded, and regional economic blockades grew.[58] Chen's talks led not only to policy shifts to strengthen readjustment from late 1980 to 1982 but also to a public debate on the desirability of readjustment versus reform. The focus was on the root cause of the imbalances in the economy.

The diagnosis of each group was affected by their basic assessment of the planned economy. Whereas one side found it to be fundamentally sound, the other saw it as basically faulty. As the CASS economists Wang Jiye and Wu Kaitai argued on behalf of the adjusters, the plan worked successfully under the first five-year plan between 1953 and 1957. Later failures were caused mainly by ultra-leftist deviations from planned development. Improved macro control of the economy was thus of prior importance and should precede the introduction of micro flexibility (i.e., reform).[59] But Wu Jinglian and Zhou Shulian, also economists at CASS, now arguing on behalf of the reformers, emphasized a deeper, institutional cause of economic imbalances. For them, China's economic decision making failed to reflect societal needs mainly because of the nature of the command economy. At the top, the concentration of power in the hands of a few leaders and party organs offered few channels to voice popular demands. At the intermediate level, administrative stratification destroyed natural links among enterprises by organizing the economy along territorial or sectoral lines rather than economic lines. At the grass roots, central allocation of resources and distribution of products discouraged enterprises from showing concern for economic results. In short, such structural impediments were mainly responsible for the delayed correction of ultra-leftism in economic development.[60]

Because of Chen Yun's stature as an economic leader and reformers' inability as yet to question central planning, adjusters dominated the debate initially. Throughout 1981 Chen Yun was given national attention as the party's theoretical authority on economic policy. His economic works from the 1950s and 1960s were published in collections, to be rivaled only by those of Deng Xiaoping. Promoted as study guides for cadres, Chen's works were presented as offering a coherent model of socialist economy. As summarized by Dong Fureng, Chen's model consisted of an economic system with a leading role for public ownership and the plan, and a subsidiary role for individual ownership and the market. It also comprised a sectoral arrangement with a balance between the people's livelihood and production, supply and demand, consumption and investment, and revenue and expenditure.[61] As such this model preserved the basic tenets of the old economy and emphasized the use of command methods to restore economic balance. It was incorporated into the Resolution of the Sixth Plenum of the Eleventh Congress in July 1981.[62]

In response, reformers began to move the debate to the principles underlying China's economic institutions. Zhao Ziyang, who replaced Hua Guofeng as premier at the NPC session in September 1981, called for a "study and discussion of the theoretical basis of reform" in his first government report in November 1981. Contrary to Chen's call for retreat from reform, Zhao sought to expand reform in the urban sector. While reform theorists enthusiastically received Zhao's call, it was halted by Chen Yun's renewed criticism of the erosion of the plan. At a meeting of provincial leaders in December 1981, Chen Yun, noting peasants' short-term self-interested decisions that threatened the interests of the overall economy, reiterated the leading role of the plan in agriculture. On January 25, 1982, Chinese New Year's Day, he summoned leading state planners to his home to discuss, as the occasion symbolized, something of utmost importance: safeguarding the dominant role of the plan.[63] The theoretical exploration urged by Zhao was not launched until May 1982, when two reform "think tanks" for the State Council under Zhao—the Commission on the Reform of the Economic System and the Center for Economic Research—sponsored a symposium.

Sponsors Zhou Taihe and Xue Muqiao admitted that public discussions were necessary because consensus had yet to be reached among "theoreticians and engineers" of reform on key "theoretical issues," in particular, the issue of whether the plan was an inherent feature of socialism and whether the market was compatible with it.[64] In his keynote speech, Xue Muqiao underscored the importance of the ideological conflict when he tried to mollify the apprehension of reform theorists about a public criticism of their views in the light of Chen Yun's recent talks. Stressing that a discussion of the plan and the market was about the larger question of "what kind of socialism" to build in China, he argued that such a basic issue required a "thorough and wide-ranging discussion among many people," not just a few leaders. Marx and Engels could not have conceived all the features of socialist society; nor could Lenin or Stalin have perfected socialist theory. Putting the task to contemporary Chinese, Xue suggested that the views of the founding fathers and those of Chen Yun might all be open to debate.[65]

The symposium was met with a vigorous response from conservative reformers, suggesting the intensity of intraparty cleavage on the issue. In contrast to members of Zhao's economic think tanks and the CASS Economic Research Institute, who usually spoke on behalf or in favor of reform, members of the State Planning Commission and the department of economics at People's University usually defended the conservative economic platform in public. Fang Weizhong, deputy director of the State Planning Commission and present at Chen Yun's Chinese New Year's Day talk, wrote in *Hongqi* to expound on Chen's teachings, under the title "An Unshakable Fundamental Principle."[66] *Guangming ribao* carried a lengthy front-page article by Xue Xin and Ma Piao, associated with the Finance Committee of the State Council headed by Chen Yun and Li Xiannian, under the title "Upholding the Socialist Road Requires Planned Economy," to refute views that indulged a pervasive "invisible hand" under socialism.[67] In a contest to influence the policy agenda of the Twelfth Congress, scheduled for September, contributions to the debate flooded newspapers and journals. But at this early stage of the post-Mao period, more people still saw the dominance of the plan as a non-negotiable issue.[68]

Most deeply, conservatives were concerned with the troubling question, already raised by some scholars who went beyond the reform leaders' agenda, as to whether it was possible or desirable for China to adopt central planning at all, given China's level of economic development and socialized production and the past failures to implement planning.[69] For all its associated social evils, one scholar went so far as to say, the market economy was preferable to an "egalitarian socialism of common poverty" and a "fascist socialism of pervasive official privileges and complete bureaucratism."[70] Although leading reform theorists like Xue Muqiao, Yu Guoguang, and Liu Guoguang disavowed an outright negation of the product economy at this time,[71] conservatives found the raising of the question alarming enough to represent a dangerous trend.[72] They took the rebuttal of this trend seriously in their 1981–82 offensive to reassert the plan, for fear that it would lead to its total negation.

The combination of political and ideological factors led the more conservative platform to prevail at the Twelfth Party Congress. The congress report retained Chen's "leading role of the plan and the supplementary role of the market." It expanded the scope of guided planning for industrial enterprises but did not endorse the less restrictive formula "the integration of the plan and the market," which had become widely used in the media.[73] Politically, Chen Yun's stronger position vis-à-vis the new premier, Zhao Ziyang, and Deng Xiaoping's need to seek political compromise at the congress[74] played an important part. Ideologically, Zhao's offensive was not enough to change a whole way of thinking about the operation of the economy, owing partly to the still rigid ideological atmosphere of this period and partly to the logic of the conservative fear over the total negation of planning.

Showdown over the "Fixed" Model

Hu Yaobang signaled his resolve to continue the fight in his report to the Twelfth Congress. He urged that ideological exploration must continue because the founding fathers could not have resolved the problem of how to build a socialist society in a backward country. He added that such exploration was "preferable" to a return to the Cultural Revolution and the period before it.[75] This was an implicit reply to conservative reformers who believed in the "golden age" of the 1950s. After the congress, reform theorists seized on a thesis put forth by Deng at the congress to redefine the ideological climate. This thesis distinguished between socialism and its Chinese variant by calling for "socialism with Chinese characteristics." This bifurcation set the stage for a more radical discourse. By early 1983 Zhao began to talk about discarding a "fixed" model and to experiment with urban reform, including efforts to reduce the scope of mandatory planning, increase enterprise autonomy, replace state quotas with a profit tax, reform the wage system, decentralize foreign trade decision making, and open port cities along the southern coast.

The new phase of reform was accompanied by a more radical reappraisal of the economic system, necessitated partly by intraparty disputes over the content of urban reform. Unlike the piecemeal rural reform, urban reform would involve the entire system of central planning, pricing, trading, distribution, and regulation of enterprises. These went beyond the adjusters' platform of a limited market and administrative decentralization. Intraparty disputes intensified in 1984 after Zhao made announcements to accelerate urban reform at an NPC session in May and the State Council issued a series of trial documents in the summer.[76] The stake for both sides was high because urban reform threatened to shake the foundation of the planned economy, or what conservative reformers such as Bo Yibo, Fang Weizhong, and He Jianzhang called the "cornerstone of socialist economy."[77]

The most critical struggle came in the summer of 1984, when top leaders took their annual trip to Beidaihe. There they were to discuss the draft resolution on urban reform and face a "trial of strength." The battle line was drawn between veteran leaders Li Xiannian, Peng Zhen, Wang Zhen, Bo Yibo, and Deng Liqun under the leadership of Chen Yun, and younger leaders Hu Yaobang, Zhao Ziyang, Wan Li, and Hu Qili, with Deng typically refraining from taking sides in such close battles. Though the ostensible disagreement between the two groups was over the scope and speed of reform, the focus of debate remained the "leading role" of the plan versus that the market. With a political balance between the two groups, ideological legitimation provided a major recourse for each side. The veteran leaders cited classic teachings on socialist economy, especially from Stalin, to defend the plan as basic to socialism. They phrased their objection to radical reform in the language of orthodox socialism, saying that the expansion of the market was likely to "engender capitalism," "weaken public ownership," and "cause social polarization." Chen Yun, who had been resting in the resort city of Hangzhou due to unhappiness about the chaos created by recent reforms, circulated opinions among top officials stressing the leading role of the plan. Reformers could hardly ignore the question of ideology. At different junctures of the debate, Hu Yaobang and Hu Qili called on reform theorists to develop the "theoretical basis" of radical reform, especially on the experience of the countryside.[78]

From the preparatory stage in late 1983 to the final passage of the resolution on urban reform in October 1984, a heated discussion went on in the media and academic circles. Central to the debate were the two core ingredients of the planned economy, namely, mandatory planning and state management of enterprises through planning. Conservative officials and theorists opposed their "unconditional" repudiation on two major accounts. First, if mandatory planning was replaced by noncompulsory mechanisms, public control of the economy could not be guaranteed. Second, if the state were to lose management of enterprises except for the levying of a profit tax, public ownership would exist in name only. Reform theorists, on the other hand, sought to redefine planning and what they saw as the "state" (not public) ownership of enterprises. In their view, the plan need not mean mandatory planning, nor did public ownership mean state ownership. The lesson of the rural contract system, they argued, was precisely that diverse forms of relationship between the state and the production unit may be developed.

The recent bifurcation of "socialism" and "Chinese characteristics" contributed usefully to reformers' arguments. From late 1983 to early 1984, a CASS research group headed by Liu Guoguang studied the schematic relationship among past and existing models of socialist economy. Their findings suggested five major "models": (1) the supply system of war communism; (2) the orthodox command economy of the Soviet Union; (3) the improved command economy of Chen Yun; (4) the integration of the plan and the market of Chinese reformers; and (5) the market socialism of Yugoslavia. On the basis of this classification, the research concluded that conservative reformers equated the "orthodox command economy" with socialism, because Chen's "improved" model sought only to repudiate the irrationalities and radical abuses of the Soviet command economy.[79] In insisting on planned and state management of the economy, an article in *Jiefangjun bao* argued in mid-July, conservative reformers defended the essentials of a "borrowed" model.[80] In short, since the Soviet model was only one of several possible models, the analysis implied, the Chinese reformers' model would be just as legitimate.

The depiction of radical reform as a new model of socialism was warmly embraced by reform leaders. In June, when the intraparty debate on the draft resolution was most heated, *Hongqi* carried two commentators' articles to expound on the philosophical basis of replacing dated forms of socialism. The first article appealed to the dialectic materialist epistemology and elevated to first priority the "rethinking" (*chongxin renshi*) of socialism under new conditions. The second article pointed out a basic contradiction between production forces and production relations in China. For the first time in the post-Mao era, the article explicitly blamed backward production forces on the "command" features of the superstructure and production relations.[81]

In the same month Deng endorsed this line of argument with an unorthodox exposition of socialism in a speech titled "Building Socialism with Chinese Characteristics":

What is socialism, what is Marxism? Our understanding of these has not been entirely clear in the past. Marxism places highest priority on the development of production forces. We believe in communism but what does communism mean? It means a high level of production forces and enormous abundance of material wealth in society. Hence the most basic task of the socialist stage is to develop production forces. The superiority of socialism lies in its higher and more rapid development of production forces than capitalism. . . . Poverty is not socialism, even less communism.[82]

By September the idea of a Chinese model of socialism became the "theoretical basis" of a summary report of the draft resolution on urban reform, prepared by Zhao for other key members of the Central Commmittee— Deng Xiaoping, Hu Yaobang, Chen Yun, and Li Xiannian. Calling for the rejection of a "fixed" model, Zhao proposed abolishing the formula "the leading role of the plan." In its place, he suggested "a planned commodity economy," distinct from both the Soviet model and the capitalist market economy. Although a compromise, the new formula did put the market on a par with the plan for the first time in the history of the People's Republic. As for the other element under debate, that is, the relation between the state and enterprise, Zhao proposed that state ownership did not necessarily require state management. Rather, the two may be separated. In another letter to the Standing Committee of the Politburo, Zhao addressed the specific reforms envisioned under his planned commodity economy: a concurrent and coordinated transformation of planning, pricing, and economic functions of the state.[83]

Although they never fully accepted the reformist arguments, conservative leaders were weakened in the final round of elite contention on the subject in the fall of that year. The political and ideological context had by now changed for them from that in the early 1980s. The strength of the veteran revolutionaries waned vis-à-vis that of younger leaders of the reform period, thanks in part to the gradual retirement of the former and the ascendancy of the latter through practical involvement in daily affairs of the state. The negative fallout of the anti–spiritual pollution campaign of late 1983 to early 1984 further strengthened the reform leaders. Under the platform of "socialism with Chinese characteristics" and the "rethinking of socialism," the discussion of ideological issues had also become both more open and more sophisticated. Thus not only Deng but also lower-ranking officials whose opinions were solicited during the course of the summer found the ideological stance of the draft resolution acceptable.[84] In October the final resolution adopted Zhao's two formulas of "a planned commodity economy" and "separation between state ownership and state management."[85] The former allowed a drastic reduction of mandatory planning, while the latter allowed state enterprises more autonomy and would later even permit the contract responsibility system and lease system. Reforms that followed in late 1984 and 1985 granted enterprises more autonomy in production decisions, management forms, pricing and sale of above-plan goods, and sharing and distribution of profits. The scope of mandatory planning was also further reduced.

Deng highlighted the ideological breakthrough made in the resolution of 1984 when he spoke about the document to a gathering of veteran leaders. "The best achievement" of the document, he remarked, was its "unprecedented elucidation" of the meaning of socialism, an elucidation that would not have been possible in the past, and even less so its passage at a party plenum.[86]

Relapse into Conservatism

The implementation of urban reform in 1984–85 soon raised new issues concerning the sanctity of the planned commodity economy. Reduced planning, increased autonomy of state enterprises, decentralization of foreign trade authority, establishment of special economic zones, expansion of money supply, and wage reforms caused an overheating of the economy, with a series of negative consequences. Most notable were the excessive growth rates, runaway investment, random wage increases, price hikes and inflation, import surge, trade imbalances, and production dislocations.[87] Conservative officials were typically concerned about such "economic chaos."

Another unpopular consequence of reform, arising from the household responsibility system in the countryside and the reintroduction of private enterprise in the city, also became apparent in the mid-1980s: the widening of income gaps across and within social groups. Unusually high income levels were largely associated with (1) the "ten thousand *yuan*" rural households, (2) urban private entrepreneurs, and (3) the so-called shady and dubious, consisting of (a) private entrepreneurs who abused laws to profiteer (through activities such as smuggling, bribing, tax evasion, and counterfeiting) and (b) corrupt officials who took advantage of loopholes created by reform (through activities such as reselling of state-priced goods, monopoly of supply, bribe taking, and smuggling). Although most complaints were directed at the third group, public discontent was widespread about the problem of "a minority of people getting rich first."

Intraelite disagreement on the causes of these problems led to renewed controversies over the planned economy in the remainder of 1984 and 1985. As before, conservative leaders attributed the overheated economy to the dislocation of macro control mechanisms: As the state reduced its direct control, enterprises became concerned only with immediate profits and worker benefits, rather than with the needs of society or the long-term interests of enterprises or the national economy. As they had warned, the removal of central planning seemed to be undermining the overall economy. Alarmed by the dislocations, the party and the State Council quickly held a conference of provincial leaders in February 1985 to implement contingency measures. Chen Yun lost no time in raising the larger issue of what guiding principles should be used to direct the economy at the CCP National Conference in September. Blaming recent chaos on the erosion of central planning, he reaffirmed the "leading role of the plan," which, he insisted, was not "outdated." Characterizing the market as "blind" and responsible for recent problems, he asserted that the plan must still be based on mandatory planning.[88] That a disciplined member of the party such as Chen would openly challenge a recent party line suggested the depth of the ideological cleavage among the leaders.

Pressures exerted by conservatives led to a cooling down of reform in early and mid-1986. Investment was slashed, money supply slowed, production quotas tightened, imports limited, and open cities restricted in contacts with foreign firms. Because he differed with conservative reformers over the causes of recent economic chaos, Zhao Ziyang favored "soft landing" rather than administrative controls to reduce the overheated economy.

Likewise, reform theorists responded to recent problems by looking deeper into the economic mechanisms. If their major concern was central planning and state management in 1983–84, now some turned attention to public ownership to analyze the short-term behavior of enterprises. Managers and workers did not show concern for the long-term interests of enterprises and society, they found, primarily because they did not feel any real stake in their enterprises. This in turn was attributed to the fact that enterprises did not have real ownership. Separation of state ownership and management was insufficient if the nature of state ownership was not changed.[89] Consequently, in 1985–86 some reformers began to explore new forms of public ownership that would link the interests of enterprises with those of the state. They made efforts to draft an enterprise law to spell out the autonomy of enterprises and rationalize enterprise behavior by allowing bankruptcy. The most prominent advocate of ownership reform was Professor Li Yining of Beijing University, who argued that only such a reform would touch on fundamental questions of economic interests, responsibility, and incentive. He proposed a joint-stock system—the most dramatic of ownership reforms so far—to transform state ownership into stock shares to be jointly owned by the state and enterprises.[90] The idea was endorsed by reform officials such as Tong Dalin, deputy director of the Commission on the Reform of the Economic System.[91] Another prominent reform economist, Zhou Shulian, arguing that ownership was a prerequisite for an enterprise to act as a commodity producer, proposed granting enterprises a "relative" property right while the state retained an "absolute right."[92]

But other reformers made an equally forceful case that a variety of factors other than ownership—such as price disorder and other problems of the economic environment—contributed to the irrational behavior of enterprises. Economists Wu Jinglian and Shi Shangsong, for example, opposed further devolution of state rights and interests to the micro level (i.e., the enterprise), arguing that only the macrolevel reform of pricing and the tax system would make enterprises behave "rationally" according to market forces. Instead of ownership reform, they favored the priority of price reform.[93] Thanks partly to such arguments, the proposed enterprise law failed to pass the NPC in 1986.

On recent problems of social distribution, conservative leaders also adopted a more traditional approach. While unequivocal about the legitimate income of family and individual enterprises, they blamed the emergence of "unhealthy tendencies" on the waning of socialist ideals. In particular, they blamed the influence of selfish and bourgeois values, the neglect of collective and social interests, and lapses in ideological education. To cope with these problems, they went back to the practice of moral exhortation. Throughout 1984 and 1985, Chen Yun and other veteran leaders called on the party and its cadres not to lose sight of "spiritual civilization" in the pursuit of "material civilization."[94] At their initiative, a campaign was launched in 1985 to oppose "unhealthy tendencies" and strengthen "socialist education" of cadres by studying classic works of Marxism.

Reform leaders, meanwhile, still saw the elimination of egalitarianism rather than the building of "socialist civilization" as a more urgent task. Thus they made more efforts to espouse a new sense of equality that legitimated disparities arising from distribution according to labor. In June 1984 and March 1985, Deng twice enunciated that income differences resulting from distribution according to labor would lead not to "social polarization," but rather eventually to "common prosperity." The resolution on urban reform spelled out that "common prosperity" would "absolutely not" mean "complete egalitarianism" or "concurrent prosperity."[95] Encouraged by these lines, the media devoted much attention to repudiating egalitarianism and legitimating income differences under socialism.

By the same token, some reformers felt that the nurturing of a legitimate sense of "self-interest" was more important than a reassertion of collective and social interests at present. For them, corrupt activities should be dealt with legally rather than ideologically. In the midst of the liberal climate in September 1986, the paper *Shehui bao* (Social news) even published an article criticizing the long-held slogan *da gong wu si* (displaying the spirit of public concern and unselfishness). It affirmed "selfish desires" as human nature that could facilitate economic development and called for a halt to their suppression.[96] The article was given national attention when it appeared in the overseas edition of *Renmin ribao*.

Amid the relapse of conservatism, reformist initiatives were resumed toward the latter half of 1986 thanks to the political liberalization of that year. A new labor system was created that introduced labor contracts, thus ending life employment for those hired thereafter. Price controls on more manufactured consumer goods were relaxed so that they could fluctuate in response to market conditions. The draft law on enterprise bankruptcy was adopted. Some cities experimented with capital markets, and other enterprises issued shares of stocks. Some state and collective enterprises were leased to individuals or groups of workers, and others formed boards of directors to supervise management.

But the end of 1986 also witnessed the campaign against bourgeois liberalization following the student protests in December 1986. Urban reforms since late 1984 came under a comprehensive attack during the campaign. As the focus of the attack was the ideological orientation of recent reforms, the radical reassessment of the economy developed in the preceding period was largely negated. In private circles, senior leaders criticized the general direction of reform as having deviated from socialism. They faulted the "commodity economy" for adopting capitalism, the household contract system for "eroding the collective economy," industrial contract and lease systems for "retreat into private ownership," and the manager responsibility system for "rejection of the party's leadership." A statement linked to Deng Lijun implicitly labeled reform leaders "practicers of bourgeois liberalization" by asserting that while advocates of bourgeois liberalization were criticized in the campaign, those who actually carried it out were not.[97]

Efforts were also made to change the direction of public discourse. In a front-page editorial, *Renmin ribao* made a self-criticism for reprinting *Shehui bao*'s article on "selfishness" and renounced its content.[98] In normal circumstances the incident might have just quieted down, since *Renmin ribao* did earlier try to counterbalance the article by publishing two critical letters from readers, including one by the Nobel laureate Dr. Y. T. Lee of the University of California, Berkeley. The "unconditional" promotion of the joint-stock system was also criticized in *Renmin ribao* by the conservative reform theorist Wu Shuqing of the department of economics at People's University.[99] An associate professor at the time, Wu was soon promoted to full professorship for his active role during the 1987 antiliberal campaign. At the height of the campaign in January, rhetoric in the media suggested a return to the command economy: a retightening of central planning and a slowdown of enterprise reform.

The campaign led to economic retrenchment and consolidation in early 1987. Efforts were made to reduce consumer spending, boost production, practice economy, increase revenue, and cut expenditure. Price reform, off the agenda by fall 1986, was further postponed, so that there would be no increase in the number of goods whose prices could be relaxed.

In sum, during the rethinking in the mid-1980s, conservative and reformist leaders contended over the causes of and remedies for the economic problems of past decades. Their different evaluations in turn revealed divergent assessments of the economy. Conservative reformers equated the basics of the Soviet system with socialism, so that its reform became a threat to socialism. Reformers distinguished socialism from the Soviet model and purported to discard the latter.

REORIENTATION OF THE MARXIST MODEL OF SOCIALISM

The period from the second half of 1987 to the first half of 1989 was marked by radical reformers' efforts to move to the last bastion of socialist economy, Marx's original theory. Conservative attacks on economic reform during the recent antiliberal campaign had alerted them to the fact that the reappraisal of the Soviet model did not provide a sufficient rationale for the stage of reform now reached. To their realization, the fundamental components of the Soviet model were ultimately linked to Marx, and so to challenge those components required confronting Marx himself. This was exactly what Zhao Ziyang set out to do upon replacing Hu Yaobang as party general secretary in January 1987.

After a successful attempt to prevent the conservative backlash from encroaching upon the economic domain in early 1987, Zhao sought to redefine the ideological context of national discourse. Such a context would not only reduce reformers' vulnerability to ideological attacks but also play a key role in the political maneuvering in preparation for the Thirteenth Congress, scheduled for October.[100] For these purposes, Zhao turned to the idea of the primary stage of socialism, originally a heretic concept that had increasingly gained intellectual force and party acceptance.[101] The tide began to turn for reformers in April when Deng endorsed the concept. In the next few weeks, Zhao gave a series of speeches to refute the imputation of bourgeois liberal tendencies to economic reform. Numerous media and academic discussions followed in the summer and fall of 1987 on the primary stage of socialism. Eventually adopted at the Thirteenth Congress in October, the theory of the primary stage created the desired context in which the classic socialism of Marx might now be subject to adaptation and reinterpretation.

Toward a Socialist Commodity Economy

A fundamental rethinking of the "planned" part of the planned commodity economy in 1987–89 was necessitated by the renewed thrust of reform following the Thirteenth Congress. Earlier reforms, such as more autonomy for enterprises, creation of capital markets, and the leasing of small state enterprises, were resumed. Yet these reforms pertained mainly to a reform of enterprises. If the problems raised by critics of the enterprise law in 1986 suggested that enterprise reform was still untenable under an unfair pricing system, deeper price reforms now seemed to be of central importance in the new round of reform.

Price reforms thus far had mainly decontrolled the prices of above-plan goods and granted enterprises more autonomy in the pricing and sale of above-plan goods. The state still retained control over within-plan goods, especially for key inputs and goods. This practice led to a "double-track" price system, one within and one outside state control. The price difference between the two tracks was at least twofold. The coexistence of two official orders of price created obvious loopholes for exploiting price differences and manipulating regulated items, leading to multiple channels of corruption and a resultant multiple price system.[102]

As reform theorists increasingly realized, the integration of the plan and the market such as attempted in the double-track price system had inherent contradictions. The market track remained heavily influenced by the plan track, because the exchange of power for money tainted a truly free market. Since the urban reform of the mid-1980s, it had become increasingly epidemic that various levels of officials involved in the administering, allocating, distributing, and manufacturing of regulated goods utilized their privileged access to profit from the double-track system. Common practices included setting up companies to speculate in regulated goods or exchanging them for graft. Consequently, the market continued to operate through the planned track rather than replacing it.[103] The result was manipulated speculation and shortage, inflation, income gaps, chaos in commodity circulation, and a widespread public discontent at cadre corruption.

Seeing that partial reforms only brought out the worst of both the plan and the market without resolving the irrationalities of the plan, some reform theorists called for additional price reforms to immediately or eventually phase out the price controls under the double-track system.[104] Beginning in the spring of 1988, reform leaders came to accept this line of analysis, with Deng as the primary pusher to accelerate price reform. At his urging in May, Zhao called an extended meeting of the Politburo to study the design and implementation of more price reforms. In May and June newspapers and other opinion forums began to organize discussion of the theoretical basis of a comprehensive market. The justification for the market now shifted from the need to "make up for" the commodity stage of social development to the inadequacy of planning at the primary stage of socialism. The planned commodity economy of 1984 was to be substituted by a "socialist commodity economy." The "planned" part of the economy, once the embodiment of Marx's "product economy" and a key line of demarcation from the market economy, was now regarded as incompatible with the current stage of China's development.

Significantly, the new reformulation on the commodity economy was no longer as controversial as before. Empirical experience with an increasingly multifaceted economy and the fallout of gradual reassessment had made the ideological nature of the issue more blurry. Even leading conservative theorists such as Wu Shuqing and He Jianzhang—the latter a member of the State Planning Commission—had by now conceded the inevitable role of the commodity economy.[105] More relevant to the reform discussions was the practical difficulty of implementing a wholesome socialist commodity economy.

The effort to dismantle planned control and pricing soon ran into a series of difficulties that called the socialist commodity economy into question. One problem stemmed from the staunch opposition from within the top leadership, beginning with the summer meetings at Beidaihe when preparatory studies of price reform were discussed. At a policy consultation conference on July 20, 1988, Zhao introduced the conclusions of these studies, which proposed decontrolling prices, gradual elimination of the dual price system, enterprise reform, and a "New Order of the Socialist Commodity Economy" (under which five cities were to begin to be transformed into complete market economies). Premier Li Peng and Vice Premier Yao Yilin disagreed with the pace and intensity of these measures and assaulted the economic problems caused by Zhao's policies. Yao made a sharp criticism of Zhao's neglect of overall planning, and this was followed by other conservative reformers in the fall and winter of 1988. The price reform measure was left unresolved at the policy consultation conference.[106]

The announcement of continued commitment to price reform set off an inflationary surge and financial panic of unprecedented severity in the summer of 1988.[107] These were largely due to nationwide panic buying and hoarding in anticipation of price decontrol. But they also resulted from the general thrust toward a commodity economy after the Thirteenth Congress, and from increased cadre corruption amid the panic stockpiling of mid-1988. The combined effects of unprecedented inflation and corruption nurtured a disintegration of social order and threatened an imminent outburst of social unrest not unlike the situation on the eve of the 1949 Revolution. The most salient issue for the general public was the glaring social inequality resulting from cadre corruption, or *guandao*.[108] By fall, Zhao's actual and proposed reforms had generated a widely felt economic and social crisis.

The crisis allowed conservative reformers to launch an overall attack on Zhao's policy and leadership and to rally for his resignation. Before and after the Third Plenum of the Thirteenth Congress in September, senior leaders Bo Yibo and Chen Yun talked with Zhao about the involvement of high-ranking cadres' children (including Zhao's own) in corruption and the loss of macro planning. At the central work conference in mid-September and the Third Plenum of the Thirteenth Congress in late September, which were devoted to discussing price reform, Zhao came under criticism on the problems of the economic crisis and rampant corruption. Only thanks to Deng was Zhao saved from being purged.[109] The meetings were followed by measures to retighten central control and crack down on corruption beginning in the fall of 1988. Chen Yun's complaint to Zhao in November vividly reflected the state of the socialist commodity economy at the time and the grave concern of conservative reformers: "I made an investigation at the Central Party School asking them 'what is socialism?' They could not answer. Socialism means putting the economy on a planned and proportionate base. How many ingredients of socialism are still left in our country now?"[110]

Apparently, conservative reformers saw the erosion of the plan, not the irrationality of the mixed economy, as the root of the economic crisis. Strengthened macro control, rather than additional decontrolling of prices, was the necessary remedy. But this line of analysis and its implicit refutation of the socialist commodity economy served only to radicalize a segment of reform theorists and turn the reassessment of socialist economy in yet another direction, especially on the question of ownership.

The Frontal Attack on Public Ownership

Ownership remained controversial as an ideological issue because public ownership was still widely regarded, even by Zhao Ziyang, as a fundamental—and sometimes the only important—feature of socialist economy. As such, discussions on rethinking public ownership generated not only impassioned and extensive debates, but also a new group of reform theorists who stood even farther away from classic socialism than did radical reformers. Because of their proliberty and independent stance in both the economic and political spheres, they may be called liberal reformers.

Among reform theorists whose discourse remained largely supportive or reflective of the reform leadership, pro-ownership reformers such as Li Yining and Jiang Yiwei renewed the rethinking of public ownership in late 1987 along with the aforementioned efforts at price reforms. While mindful of the earlier criticism that the economic environment was not ripe for enterprise reform, this group still favored ownership reform before price decontrol. In their view, it was difficult to change the economic environment at once. Moreover, without full control over the mobility of factors of production, enterprises could not react rationally to market signals. As price reform ran into difficulties after the summer of 1988, the proposal of this group came to receive more attention from Zhao Ziyang and led to renewed interest in enterprise reform.

The approach taken by this group remained within the 1984 frame of the separation of state ownership and enterprise management. Since their emphasis in 1984 was on how to guarantee the autonomy of enterprises, the focus now was shifted to how to ensure the interests of the state. This prompted them to return to the joint-stock scheme deemed amenable to bridging the interests of ownership and management.[111] This approach differed from that of conservative reformers, who did not wish to go beyond the contract responsibility system for state enterprises. It also differed from the views of the emergent liberal reformers, who began to advocate "individual ownership" in early 1988. The joint-share system was approved by the Third Plenum in September 1988 for trial implementation.

The wave of critique of public ownership by the liberal reformers followed the conservative comeback and besieging of Zhao Ziyang after Zhao's failed attempt at price reform in mid-1988, and especially after the Third Plenum in September. Younger and more assertive, some members of the group—such as Chen Yizi, Yan Jiaqi, and Wang Xiaoqiang—worked in Zhao's think tanks under the State Council. Their views flooded reformist journals in the last few months of 1988 and the first few months of 1989, not as articulations of Zhao's inclinations but as independent criticisms of their own. The crux of their critique was that public ownership, being incompatible with a commodity economy, was the root cause of the chaotic market and rampant cadre corruption. In a conversation with *Shijie jingi daobao* in November 1988, Yan Jiaqi asserted that public ownership legitimated central control of the economy and vested power in the hands of cadres, creating a "power-based economy" that destroyed the fair play of the market. Private ownership was the only solution to these problems. In a conversation with Wen Yuankai, a chemistry professor and an influential figure among college students, Yan repeated the charges and questioned "why the ownership issue cannot be thoroughly discussed." He blamed the taboo on "conceptual constraints on fundamental issues" and on the lack of a "political guarantee for freedom of exploration." Chen Yizi and Wang Xiaoqiang also called for "reconstructing" public ownership and "transcending" traditional conceptual confines in looking at private ownership.[112] Chen went so far as to suggest that of the 600 billion yuan invested for capital construction in the state economy from 1958 to 1978, only a third reached the designed productive capacity.[113]

Encouraged by these leading figures, other like-minded liberals began to criticize public ownership as the root cause of economic failures not only at present but also in the past. For a while in late 1988 and early 1989, articles advocating private ownership permeated reformist papers like *Jingji ribao* (Economic daily) and *Jingjixue zhoukan* (Economics weekly), the latter edited by Wang Juntao and Chen Ziming. This climate culminated in the declaration of a "Manifesto of Private Ownership" shortly after the outbreak of the student protests in April 1989, in a big-character poster on the campus of Beijing Aeronautic University. Calling private ownership the "hope of China," it listed "ten crimes" of public ownership, among them the obstruction of the growth of production forces, waste of public coffers, neglect of workers' interests, and lack of real owners and accountability.[114]

Liberal reformers saw public ownership as the root cause of the chaotic market for several reasons. First, ownership reforms based on the separation of ownership and management (for example, contracting output, leasing factories) were insufficient and conducive to a runaway economy. This separation, though serving to reduce state intervention, intensified other problems of public ownership. As the state weakened its control without giving property rights to enterprises, enterprises became more likely to scramble for resources and investments from the state while paying little attention to their efficient use. Enterprises were also more likely to pursue short-term benefits (for example, wage and welfare increases, predatory use of state property, profitable projects rather than long-term investment), since production contracts between the state and enterprises were on a short-term basis and enterprises were responsible for gains but not losses. Furthermore, decentralization allowed local governments to act on behalf of state ownership without any control over them by the state. They were thus able to abuse state ownership for the sake of short-term local interests.[115]

Guandao was blamed on public ownership for similar reasons. Because public ownership meant that no one really owned the enterprise, cadres' lack of concern for the well-being of the enterprise or the state led them to use their control over regulated goods for personal gains. At the same time, it was public ownership that gave cadres administrative powers in the first place: to serve as agents of the state's property rights. With the introduction of the market, the administrator was given the opportunity to become a bureaucratic merchant.[116] The result resembled John Fairbank's observation of the pre-1949 era: "Now the administrator and capitalist combined into one. The result is an unparalleled plundering of the public coffers."[117] Public ownership and the market were thus incompatible for two reasons. First, the absence of proper owners led to the formation of economically irrational interests, that is, the type of enterprise and local interests discussed earlier. Second, administrative functions entailed by public ownership served to distort the market because of cadre intervention.

In this context, liberal reformers saw the only possible way out as either to repudiate public ownership or to backtrack on economic reform. They naturally favored the former course since they traced the root problem of the economy to the "genes" of public ownership. Thus, they opposed not only conservatives' preservation of state ownership, but also radical reformers' partial reform through the joint stock system. Instead, they proposed the distribution of stock shares of state enterprises to all citizens to bring about a system of "individual ownership," a euphemistic term for private enterprise.[118]

Throughout late 1988 and early 1989, liberal reformers made extensive efforts to propagate this proposal. By then, radical reformers actually became their chief opponents in public discussions, since the reformer-dominated media almost excluded conservative voices during the period. Though the call for "individual ownership" did not attain official status, its appearance in public forums suggested tolerance by reform leaders. Some of Zhao's close associates, such as Chen Yizi and Wan Runnan, were known to espouse toleration for cadre corruption, on the ground that it was conducive to the accumulation of private wealth and thus to the emergence of private ownership.

The Dilemma of Socialist Distribution

The expansion in policy and in media discussion of a commodity economy, joint and private ownership, and mobility of the factors of production also created new problems for social distribution during 1987 to mid-1989. Distribution according to labor could no longer apply to many emerging forms of income derived from nonlabor sources, for example, bonds, dividends, stocks, talent, and ownership. At the Thirteenth Congress, Zhao made room for those new sources of income by stating that in the primary stage of socialism, distribution should be based on "multiple forms," with distribution according to labor as the dominant form. However, the introduction of even a limited capital market and cosharing of public ownership would lead to distribution according to capital and ownership. So public discussion in this period sought to find a new principle of distribution.

Parallel to this need for a new distribution ethic was a growing public concern about glaring social disparities associated with two groups of "nouveaux riches." One was the so-called bureaucratic merchants and the other urban private entrepreneurs. The problem now differed from that in earlier periods. Whereas earlier disparities could be attributed largely to differences in ability and effort, now they were widely perceived to have resulted from unfair and shady play.[119] For "bureaucratic merchants" had secured millions by abusing the double-track price system, while urban private entrepreneurs evaded taxes, bribed officials, counterfeited goods, and randomly hiked their prices.[120] These two groups were resented also because their corrupt practices exacerbated other key problems of reform, such as inflation and price disorder. Cadre racketeering of regulated goods, for example, added multiple price increases to major industrial and agricultural inputs, sometimes paralyzing industries and farmers.[121] The problem of unfair inequality was so acute that both reformers and conservatives would later agree that a major impetus of the mass demonstrations of 1989 was the widespread public resentment over corruption and social inequality.

Reform theorists in late 1988 and early 1989 did not avoid this problem of inequity. But radical and liberal reformers diverged in their approach. While the former saw a continued need to emphasize distribution according to labor, at least until a new distribution principle could be devised, the latter found it necessary to embrace fully the distributional principle of the market. For them, official and other types of corruption were caused not by market reforms but by the incompleteness of those reforms: Just as public ownership plagued the functioning of the market, so did central allocation intervene in a fair distribution on the market.[122] Thus, despite the growing inequalities of the late 1980s, liberals favored a new principle compatible with a market economy.

Why did the liberal reformers go so far in this direction when Zhao had all but lost his position and conservatives were making strong efforts to reassert control over the economy? This suggested both the growing independence of reform theorists and the openness of the political climate after the Thirteenth Congress, which lasted until the Tiananmen crackdown of mid-1989. Needless to say, the direction of the liberal discourse became a key target of conservative criticism in the wake of the conservative comeback after mid-1989. A comprehensive criticism of liberal analyses of the market, ownership, and distribution was launched and many policies of radical reformers were contracted to strengthen central control and public ownership, to curtail prices and inflation, and to restore macro-economic balance.

Deng Xiaoping's Spring Offensive of 1992

The political tide began to turn in early 1992, when Deng Xiaoping made a series of speeches to put reform back on the agenda during his inspection tours of several southern coastal cities. Three years of economic consolidation was obviously enough for this senior leader with a young man's impatience with regard to China's development. As before in every important juncture of reform policy-making, Deng started with a redefinition of the ideological context: He declared that the Left tendencies were as harmful to the party and socialism as those of the Right, thus putting a brake on the conservative resurgence since mid-1989. Specifically, the most important aspect of his talks concerned the relationship between the plan and the market. Here, he explicitly deprived both of any ideological nature. "The fundamental difference between socialism and capitalism," he remarked, "does not lie in the degree of planning or the market present in a economy."[123] The point was aimed at restoring the agenda of building a new "socialist commodity economic order," an agenda that had failed Zhao and partly brought his downfall.

Deng's talks became the guidelines for drafting the political report of the Fourteenth Congress, to be held in October. To incorporate Deng's ideas into political and policy lines, the Standing Committee of the Central Committee held frequent meetings, and General Secretary Jiang Zemin delivered several internal and public speeches. Opinions on the draft report were solicited from thousands of officials, representatives, and scholars in and outside the party. Somewhat ironically, the process never generated the kind of passion and heat that had been present in previous national discussions. Partly this may be due to Deng's instruction after the Tiananmen crackdown that ideological debates be put aside to avoid disunity. But partly it was due to the removal of major reform leaders and the exile or eclipse of leading reform theorists and intellectuals, which seemed to have made ideological debates unnecessary. Among those that did occur, three propositions were made about the new economic order on the basis of Deng's southern talks: "A socialist economic order that integrates the plan and the market," "a socialist planned market economic order," and simply "a socialist market economic order." Jiang Zemin leaned toward the last, or the most liberal, version.[124] This version was formally written into the Fourteenth Congress report and adopted as the congress's theme. Though not fundamentally different from Zhao's "socialist commodity economy," the new formulation was significant because a direct reference to "a market economy" became officially acceptable for the first time in post-Mao China.

CONCLUSION

This review of the evolution of the post-Mao reassessment of the Chinese economy from 1978 to 1992 shows clear and persistent contention over the nature of the problems of the economy and the remedies for them. In the late 1970s and early 1980s three political groups—conservers, adjusters, and reformers—battled over how to deal with the excesses of the twin components of China's economy, namely, the sectoral arrangements and the production relations. In the mid-1980s conservative and radical reformers clashed over how to reevaluate the core ingredients of the economic system, especially central planning and state ownership. In the late 1980s three distinct political voices—conservative, radical, and liberal—fought over how to reappraise Marxist theory on socialist economy. The interaction between the political and intellectual levels of discourse also evolved along with the changing issues and battles.

In essence, the disputes among the three groups in the first phase were over three different "projects" of socialism.[125] To the defenders of the Maoist legacy, volunteerism and politics in command in pursuing heavy industrialization and the command economy were noble endeavors at building socialism. To adjusters and reformers, these were subjective pursuits unwarranted by China's objective conditions. Adjusters pruned the heavy industrial model to its Stalinist core, dismissing it as Soviet rather than as socialist. But they did so from the perspective of central planners. Reformers concurred with adjusters on the need to rectify the sectoral model but differed on using the plan as the key to remedying leftist excesses. For both groups, nonetheless, the radical path of development had carried both Stalinism and Marxism to mutant forms. Throughout this initial period, political leadership played a major role in initiating and charting reassessment. Intellectual discussions, though not always dictated by politics, fitted largely into dominant official analyses.

In the second period, the clash between conservative and radical reformers concerned the nature of the Soviet economic model. The former's attribution of leftist excesses to mistaken ideology led them to insist on the basic integrity of established economic institutions. To the latter group, both leftist excesses and past failures to correct them were due precisely to the centralizing tendencies of the command economy. They dismissed the command economy as a Soviet model and saw remedies for economic irrationalities in overhauling, rather than relying on, this model. During the period, political leaders on both sides still set the agenda and tone of public discourse in that they encouraged the range of issues to be explored and elicited intellectual articulation for their respective policy positions. But intellectuals and reform theorists began to be more assertive and independent in that they increasingly made proposals, rather than just justifications, for policymakers.

In the final period under discussion, different views of Marx's original theory of socialist economy accounted for the competing analyses of the three groups. Both radical and liberal reformers held Marx's ideas of product economy and public ownership directly or indirectly responsible for continued economic problems. But radical reformers saw a new economic order possible within the framework of the primary stage of socialism. Liberal reformers, on the other hand, pushed this line of argument to its limit and negated all core components of socialist economy. Conservative reformers reached just the opposite conclusion by blaming the problems in economic reforms on the deviation from socialism. Although the radicalization of liberal reformers was in part a reaction to the conservative surge in the late 1980s, it testified to the increasing independence of intellectual discourse.

The progressive stages of reformulation suggest that the advocacy of diverse paths of economic development was more than rhetoric or post facto justification of policy changes. Instead, it reflected the changing orientations of the leadership and reform theorists. Each reformulation of socialism was substantiated with meticulous elaboration and deepened alongside the challenges of empirical reform, but with consistency in perspective for each group. In different stages of the economic reassessment, conservative reformers had consistently approached economic reform from the perspective of central planners. Along the same line, they had been coherent in placing reform within the basic institutions of traditional socialism. The "Chinese road to modernization" captured the essence of their within-system approach to sectoral and structural change. Reformers and adjusters moved from allies to competitors to opponents on economic reform. But from the very beginning, reformers approached reform from the angle of remedying the systemic features and methods of the economy, be they Maoist, Stalinist, or Marxist. "Socialism with Chinese characteristics" was an evolving concept that came to embody radical reformers' new model of socialist development. The radicalization of some radical reformers into liberal reformers in this context was part of the evolving recognition of the inherent problems of socialist economic institutions.

CHAPTER FOUR

The Reassessment of the Socialist Economic System

DESPITE the seemingly facile progress toward the end of the 1980s, the reassessment of the socialist economy was tortuous throughout the phases that have been discussed. Orthodox socialism provided the opponents of radical reform—first the conservers and later the conservative reformers—with a consistent vehicle to question the direction of reform policies. On each key area of reform—economic organization, ownership, and distribution—they were able to dispute its doctrinal legitimacy and to press for policy adjustments that would keep reform within the bounds of orthodox socialism. These bounds remained equally important issues for the reform leadership, not least because they had to respond to the misgivings of their opponents in order to disarm the latter and secure legitimation for their policy position. Consequently, the reassessment of the socialist economy was not only a political expediency but also an ideological necessity.

Reformulation has not been reduced simply to what can be rendered compatible in one way or another with the views of the founding fathers of socialism, as some may claim.[1] That is, it has not been limited to the argument that past mistakes resulted from deviation from theory. Rather, the crucial difference between the moderate reassessment of conservative reformers and the deeper reassessment of radical and liberal reformers lay in a disagreement over whether the reappraisal should extend to the fundamentals of scientific socialism. Herein lies a central theme of the post-Mao reassessment of the Chinese economy: Were its problems due to errors in practice and in understanding of theory, or to limits inherent in theory? In the efforts to find answers to these questions, important issues were raised concerning the inadequacies of original theory that in turn formed the basis for repudiating past policies.

This chapter examines the content of the three phases of economic reassessment from 1978 to 1992, centering on the core components of organization, ownership, and distribution in the economy. It first reviews the views of founding fathers of scientific socialism and then turns to the Chinese discussions.

Views of Founding Fathers

Traditional doctrine of scientific socialism as upheld by the CCP consists of brief discussions by Marx and Engels and further expositions by Lenin, Stalin, and sometimes Mao. In the original conceptions of Marx and Engels, the principal features of socialism follow antithetically from their criticism of capitalism. From his analysis of the economic operation under capitalism, Marx discovered what Stalin termed the "basic law" of capitalism, that is, the appropriation of surplus value by capitalists. This appropriation is made possible, according to Marx, by three essential elements of the capitalist economy: private ownership of the means of production, which allows for the extraction of surplus value; exchange of commodities at the market, which allows for the realization of surplus value; and commercialization of labor, which allows for the creation of surplus value. Distribution under capitalism, in turn, is determined by the possession of the means of production or the lack thereof. For those not possessing the means of production, labor becomes a commodity in exchange for their share of distribution. Exploitation and alienation result from the deprivation of laborers' right to dispose and distribute their own products because of the lack of ownership of the means of production.

The structural features of the communist society outlined by Marx aim to eliminate those systemic causes of exploitation and alienation. In a society with a common ownership of the means of production, the exchange of commodities and the use of labor as a commodity and a source of surplus value cease to exist. There would be a product economy geared toward the total needs of the community, in contrast to the commodity economy oriented toward profits.

> Let us now picture to ourselves, . . . a community of free individuals, carrying their work with the means of production in common, in which the labor-power of all the different individuals is consciously applied as the combined labor of the community. All the characteristics of Robinson's labor are repeated here, but with this difference, that they are social, instead of individual. Everything produced by him was exclusively the result of his own personal labor, and therefore simply an object of use for him. The total product of our community is a social product.[2]

In his *Critique of the Gotha Programme*, which entails Marx's most extensive discussion of socialist society, Marx wrote:

> Within the cooperative society based on common ownership of the means of production, the producers do not exchange their products; just as little does the labor employed here *as the value* of these products, . . . since now, in contrast to capitalist society, individual labor no longer exists in an inherent fashion but directly as a component of the total labor.[3]

Engels reiterated in *Anti-Dühring* that once society took control of the means of production, the commodity economy would be eliminated, and along with it the control of producers by the products of their labor.

Social distribution, accordingly, would be free from the privileges of private ownership of the means of production. But in the first phase of communist society, Marx noted, distribution would still be based on the "duration or intensity" of one's labor, rather than on one's needs. By this, Marx recognized "unequal individual endowment and thus productive capacity as natural privileges." This recognition was necessary because in a society "stamped with birthmarks" of the capitalist society from which it had just emerged, "right can never be higher than the economic structure of society and its cultural development conditioned thereby."[4]

Lenin followed these stipulations of socialist economy before the October Revolution. In a treatise written in 1894, he wrote that the goal of socialism was to "eliminate the commodity economy and replace it with the communist organization of the commune," where the economy would no longer be regulated by the market but by the producer himself and the means of production would be possessed by the whole society rather than by private individuals.[5] Shortly after the October Revolution, Lenin still envisioned a new Soviet Republic without commodities or money. In 1919 he instructed that the party's current task was to enforce "product distribution" to replace trade.[6] In 1920 he urged the "transition to the exchange of products" to replace the exchange of commodities.[7] In line with these ideas, the party adopted a policy of surplus appropriation and product distribution during the period of "war communism." Surplus grains were appropriated from the countryside to supply the city and the army, while industrial products were distributed to farmers. This policy proved difficult to follow after the war, when patriotic support no longer constituted a rationale for farmers to endure financial sacrifices.

The experience of war communism led Lenin to realize that "in the preliminary period of transition from capitalism to socialism, immediate elimination of the currency is not possible." Particularly in a country of small, dispersed farmers, the transition could only be brought about through "commodity production" and trade.[8] The New Economic Policy replaced surplus appropriation with a grain tax and product exchange through purchase and sale. While summing up the lessons of war communism in 1921, Lenin conceded that to abolish commodity exchange between the town and country was premature and simplistic. In a country of small agricultural producers like Russia, it was mistaken to assume that communist production and distribution would be achieved once the state distributed to factories the grains surrendered by farmers. Rather than relying solely on producers' enthusiasm, Lenin admitted, the state should rely on individuals' economic interest and on economic value to build a solid bridge from capitalism to socialism.[9] Thus, during his lifetime, Lenin came to recognize the necessity of commodity production in the transition to socialism. He did not discuss, however, whether this practice would continue after the transition was completed. For a long time afterward, Soviet orthodoxy closed the possibility of commodity production after the proletariat seizure of power and the establishment of public ownership.

This changed in 1952 when Stalin published his treatise on socialist economy, under the title *Economic Problems of Socialism in the USSR*. Here Stalin recognized the existence of commodity production under socialist economy, that is, the exchange of products based on purchase and sale. He also admitted that the law of value still worked in such commodity production. Rather than legitimating this phenomenon on its own merits, however, Stalin justified it in terms of the presence of two forms of public ownership in the Soviet Union: the state and the collective. Because the collective sector constituted a separate form of public ownership, he argued, those two forms of ownership necessitated commodity exchange. In the state sector, the state had the right to dispose of the products of enterprises. But in the collective sector, farms would dispose of their products only in exchange for desired products through trade. Hence the necessity of commodity exchange between the two sectors.[10]

Although some ideologues saw Stalin's theory as a retreat from pure socialism, most Chinese economists have called it "major progress" in the development of Marxist theory. But Stalin's line of argument, premised on the presence of two different forms of ownership, entails certain limitations on the scope of commodity exchange. For example:

1. Commodity production and exchange will not be necessary once the two forms of ownership are eliminated.
2. Since the means of production in both the state and the collective sectors is socialized, the means of production itself is not a commodity that can be purchased or sold.
3. The law of value applies only to the exchange of personal consumption goods, not to the organization and management of production.[11]

Thus, for Stalin, the existence of commodity exchange was necessary but temporary, and the law of value was applicable but supplementary.

Mao pursued a tortuous path on the question of commodity exchange. During the Great Leap Forward, he attempted to abolish commodity exchange and enforce product distribution. After the devastating failure of the Leap movement, he began to recognize the role of commodity exchange. In a discussion of Stalin's treatise, Mao agreed that commodity production was still necessary, but he differed with Stalin by arguing that the role of commodity production under socialism was determined by the level of production forces. He even gave commodity exchange a larger role than Stalin did by extending it to the sphere of production goods (e.g., machinery).[12] Like Stalin, however, Mao saw commodity exchange as expedient and temporary. Toward the end of his life, Mao not only retreated from these earlier views but went to the extreme of ruling out commodity production altogether, treating them as practices conducive to the restoration of capitalism. Mao even went further than Marx to repudiate the idea of distribution according to labor, equating it with the "bourgeois right" that Marx was willing to permit in the socialist stage. These doctrinal preoccupations of Mao led him to preclude the use of any economic levers or incentives in the economy after the start of the Cultural Revolution.[13]

MODERATE REASSESSMENT

The first period of economic reassessment, between 1978 and 1982, was moderate in nature. It largely involved the rejection of errors made in the past evolution of theory and practice, particularly those in the Maoist and Soviet formulations.

Organization and Management

Initial reassessment of organizational and managerial principles under socialist production refuted Stalin and Mao's theories of commodity production on similar grounds. That is, the market must still play a role in all facets of socialist economy in the sense that the exchange and production of goods should be based on the calculation of economic values. The major reformulation involved abandoning three credos, outlined by Stalin and accepted in the CCP orthodoxy, about the scope and nature of commodity production and exchange under socialism. The new orthodoxy emerged as follows:

1. The exchange of products based on the law of value exists not just between the state and collective sectors, but also within the state sector.
2. Both consumption goods and production goods are commodities that can be sold and purchased.
3. The law of value operates not only in the exchange of consumption goods but also in the process of production involving costs, inputs, and demands.[14]

Reform theorists, whether the more conservative You Lin or the more reformist Xue Muqiao, agreed that the primary basis for abandoning Stalin's teachings was that neither China nor the Soviet Union was endowed with the kind of material and social conditions under which Marx foresaw the construction of a product economy. These included a high level of production forces that determined the level of socialized production (that is, social division of labor and specialization), which in turn determined the level of social planning that could be achieved. Marx and Engels envisioned only one form of public ownership, for they could not have foreseen socialism in underdeveloped societies like China or Russia, which experienced marginal development of capitalism.[15]

For Xue Muqiao, Marx's prerequisites made it structurally untenable for China to have a uniform ownership or, on the basis of this, to exert central planning throughout society. Neither would it suffice for China to adopt only two forms of ownership, namely, state ownership for the city and collective ownership for the countryside. Stalin's notion of two modes of ownership was mistaken in the first place, because he failed to appreciate the vastly uneven levels of development in his largely underdeveloped country. In the case of prerevolutionary China, there was an even lower level of economic development and greater regional disparities. In Xue's words, "several centuries" separated the advanced regions of Shanghai, Tianjin, and Guangzhou from the more backward Xinjiang, Qinhai, and Xizhang, making it impossible to organize production under two modes of ownership and one system of central planning. China's previous efforts to do that had underscored the futility of those attempts. In light of the structural limitations of an underdeveloped society, agreed Xue and the conservative economist He Wei from People's University, it was necessary to water down uniform ownership. In the city there might be collective and individual ownership in accordance with social needs. In the countryside there may be group-based and household-based production according to local conditions. These multiple forms necessitated for them a wider range of commodity exchange than that permitted by Stalin, since a greater variety of economic parties would now be involved in the exchange of products.[16]

A related rationale for broadening the role of commodity production developed in this period concerned the nature of socialized production in China. Du Runsheng, director of the CCP's Research Center for Agricultural Policy, argued that socialized production in the rural sector often amounted to no more than a combination of dispersed small producers, which was quite different from the kind of cooperative ownership outlined by Marx.[17] Xue Muqiao saw this kind of socialization as an "immature socialism built on a seminatural economy," not genuine large-scale socialized production with economic and social links across the economy. He saw the latter as achievable only through extensive commodity exchange, which, if absent, would make it impossible to build the economic base for the type of socialism envisioned by Marx.[18]

While the reform coalition agreed on these reassessments in broad terms, serious differences between conservative and radical reformers remained over the range and nature of commodity exchange. These differences characterized the leadership and policy disputes in 1981–82 over the role of the plan versus the market. Conservative reformers envisioned a supplementary role for the market covering small articles and the above-plan portion of output. Radical reformers objected to the subordination of the market to the plan and proposed instead the incorporation of the market into the plan under centrally guided planning, while leaving details of production and management to enterprises. The dispute was rooted in several conflicting views of central planning.

First, while radical reformers emphasized the limited applicability of planning in China's social context, conservative reformers believed in its basic soundness in both theory and practice. As argued by Chen Yun, in theory Marx derived the idea of planning from his analysis of the anarchic nature of capitalism and the contradictions between production relations and production forces inherent to it. In practice, the planned economies of China and the Soviet Union conformed to Marx's prescriptions. Chen acknowledged the failure of socialist countries to "expand on" Marx's theory on the basis of empirical experience. In particular, he cited the rigidity arising from the sole existence of planning and the absence of the law of value. In this context, Chen praised Yugoslavia for improving the plan by adding the role of the market. But what differentiated him from radical reformers was that for him, the market was only a useful supplement.[19]

Second, radical reformers designated planning as a composite, not an essential aspect of socialism, basing their argument on the recent recognition of the law of value in the realms of production and circulation.[20] Conservatives, however, insisted that planning was an inherent requirement of public ownership. In the latter view, for public will to be expressed in the production process, the public must have control over the means of production, the organization of the labor force, and the management of production, which in turn could be achieved only through central planning. Conversely, such control was just as crucial under capitalism, for it determined the production and extraction of surplus value. If the socialist state was to give up its control over production through mandatory planning, then ownership by the people would not find expression in the production process. So for Xue Xin and Ma Piao, "commodity production" and "commodity exchange" were appropriate terms to describe the role of the market in China, not the term "commodity economy," which designated a more profuse market.[21]

Third, conservatives feared that an emphasis on the limited applicability of Marx's product economy in the Chinese context might legitimize those who questioned whether it was possible or desirable at all to adopt central planning in China. As much as they conceded the underdevelopment of

China's socialized economy, prominent conservative economists such as Wang Jiye, He Wei, and He Rongfei insisted that central planning was both possible and tenable: Central planning did require highly socialized production, but not that it be comprehensive; it only required that major aspects of the national economy be highly socialized. In the Chinese case, they pointed out, these requirements were satisfied by the highly socialized network of large and medium size industries connected through state ownership. On a deeper level, they realized that the real question was whether the Chinese state was capable of exerting optimal planning in the light of so many failures in the past. Nonetheless, they insisted that past failures were often exaggerated and achievements downplayed. More important, they held, past failures such as those committed under ultra-leftism were due precisely to deviation from planning, rather than to planning itself.[22]

Finally, there was also an important disagreement about the nature of planning, with reformers giving a much broader and loose definition to planning. Reformers called for integrating the plan and the market, criticizing Chen Yun's approach as "board and plant integration" (*bankuai jiehe*), or an integration that was piecemeal and incoherent. They also called for including guidance planning as planning. Some also called for associating planning with macroeconomics.[23]

Ownership

The principal judgment on the issue of ownership during the phase of moderate reassessment was that it had been excessively uniform. As argued by Yu Guangyuan and Xue Muqiao, one and the same whole people's ownership existed in the urban sector, and one and the same collective ownership existed in the rural sector, with little variation within each. The result was the lack of conformity with regional disparities or diverse levels of production forces.[24]

This misapplication of public ownership was attributed to dogmatism and the neglect of the nature of China's social transition. On the one hand, past practices were criticized for using "fixed principles," rather than empirical results, as the criterion of policy-making. For a long time the criterion was that the "larger" and the more "public" the scale of an ownership form, the better and more desirable it was. In Yu Guangyuan's words, both policy makers and the public seemed to have an "ordinal table" in mind about the optimal form of ownership: Within public ownership, state ownership was unquestionably superior to collective ownership; and within collective ownership, the commune was absolutely superior to the brigade and the brigade to the team. For Duan Shixian, another prominent reform theorist, such a criterion committed two basic blunders in applying socialism. First, it equated the potential of socialism for greater growth with the existing capacity of socialism. Second, it equated the superiority of public ownership with the level of communal ownership. For Du Runsheng and Gao Hongfan, the collectivization drive of the 1950s, which put small household producers together, did not add up to a superior form of ownership with greater productivity. On the contrary, it could not even preserve the productivity of independent small producers.[25]

As an alternative approach, Duan proposed that the level of production forces in the host society must be the "starting point" in choosing a particular ownership form.[26] The low and uneven level of production forces in China, even Wu Shuqing concurred, was a logical reason to diversify ownership forms and to embrace the notion that "what best promotes production forces in given times and localities constitutes the most superior form of ownership relations." Under the new approach, China's "ordinal table" of ownership forms became multilayered: state, collective, and individual ones in the city, and collective, team, household, and individual ones in the countryside.[27]

But conservative and radical reformers diverged over the degree of adjustment to be made on state ownership. The question of whether state ownership was the best way to represent the "whole people's ownership" was controversial for two reasons: State ownership had a direct bearing on central planning and the extent of enterprise autonomy. For Dong Fureng, state ownership was the root problem of the Chinese economy because it contributed to many of its structural flaws: (1) a highly centralized regulation of the economy by the often arbitrary commands of state agencies, resulting in rigidity and a disparity between plan and demand; (2) the power of the state to appoint managers, rendering cadres accountable to orders from the above rather than to the interests of enterprises and workers; and (3) the incapability of linking the means of production to its real owners (i.e., workers) or of linking workers' interests to enterprise performance, thus stifling local initiative and innovation.[28] Along with Jiang Yiwei, Dong proposed "enterprise ownership" to give enterprises the powers of an independent producer, a proposal that sounded quite bold in the early 1980s.[29] Other reformers, such Wang Mingsheng and Yun Xiliang, would only endorse "enterprise autonomy" at this early post-Mao phase.[30]

For their part, conservative reformers such as Jiang Xuemo, Li Yunfu, You Lin, and Fang Weizhong insisted that state ownership was an essential feature of socialist economy that could not be diluted. It was essential because state ownership provided the mechanism to link divergent enterprises together, just as the market mechanism served to link different enterprises together under capitalism. As such, they saw the state as a guarantee of society's collective interests. State ownership also provided a guarantee against the pursuit of self-interests by enterprises, which conservatives saw as the leading cause of the negative consequences of economic reform. Most of all, state ownership provided the basis for central planning. If it was to disintegrate, the very foundation of socialist economy would be shaken.[31]

Distribution

Early post-Mao rethinking on the theory and practice of socialist distribution sought to restore what reformers took to be the principles of Marx. The key effort involved a critique of Mao's misunderstanding of the idea of distribution according to labor: While Marx allowed the exchange of equal labor embodied in the concept of "bourgeois right," Mao regarded distribution according to labor itself as a bastion of "bourgeois right."

Essentially Mao was criticized for failing to see the difference in social distribution under capitalism and socialism: The former was based on appropriation through *ownership*, but the latter was based on equal exchange of *labor* under a common ownership. As a result, Mao attributed all social and human differences in society to the existence of "bourgeois right," which he set out to eliminate with leveled income. Herein lay the root cause of his policy of absolute egalitarianism, which violated the legitimate interests of the people, stifling their initiative and impeding economic development.[32] One initial rectification of the policy was Deng's new orthodoxy, "Let some get rich first," proposed at the Third Plenum. It encouraged sectoral, regional, interenterprise, and individual disparities through the use of economic incentives.

While the restoration of distribution according to labor was the most doctrinally sound among the reappraisals made thus far, controversy still emerged in and outside the party. This was best reflected in the debate over the socialist nature of double *bao*. For both conservative and radical reformers, distribution according to labor sufficiently legitimated those practices. It adeptly bypassed the real issue raised by the conservers in the debate, that is, the issue not so much of rewards but of incentives under socialism. Although both groups agreed on repudiating ultra-leftist egalitarianism, Fang Weizhong expressed the increasing concern of conservative reformers when he complained about recent abuse of the new distribution ethic.[33]

Overall, in this moderate phase of reassessment between 1979 and 1982, the conservative view dominated in public discussions. The difficulty for reformers stemmed from the inherent contradictions in challenging old practices from within the established doctrinal framework. On a number of key issues they were unable to claim the high ground of adjusters or conservative reformers. The reformist analysis itself, too, did not yet question Marxism, but only underscored its limited applicability to China.

RADICAL REASSESSMENT

The second phase of reassessment, between 1983 and 1986, was heavily marked by the unsettling controversies between conservative and radical reformers. The reformulation of the earlier phase was insufficient to counter the conservative view that commodity exchange could only be supplementary or that state ownership must not disintegrate. For the argument that commodity exchange was necessitated by diverse ownership forms precluded the use of the market within the state sector. The argument that public ownership necessarily required central planning foreclosed the possibility of changing state ownership. Pressured by the need of urban reform in the mid-1980s, radical reformers began to find ways to question the premises of central planning and state ownership. In addition, further rethinking of socialist distribution began to emerge in a manner that threatened to go beyond traditional confines. These efforts marked the radical phase of economic reassessment.

Organization and Management

The principal conclusion reached on this question during this phase was that commodity exchange was necessary not just because China was in need of diverse ownership forms and of exchange among these entities. Rather, there were inherent fallacies in Stalin's theory of socialist economy, including (1) the assumption that the whole people's ownership precluded the existence of individual economic entities with independent interests, and (2) the idea that the absence of such entities rendered commodity exchange unnecessary.[34]

In Marx's conception, the realization of surplus value was possible because of commodity exchange among different owners of the means of production. Cooperative ownership presumably rendered such exchange unnecessary, though this was not spelled out by Marx. Stalin's permission for commodity exchange between the state and collective sectors follows the logic that the need for such exchange arises from different ownership of products. Within the same ownership, so goes the logic, commodity exchange is not necessary. Further, the products of state enterprises belong to the state and so enterprises cannot trade them among one another through the market.[35]

In challenging this line of logic, radical reformers found that the means of production itself actually did not constitute the essence of an economy. More important was the manner in which the means of production interacted with laborers, although the means of production was crucial in determining the manner of this interaction. Under cooperative ownership, laborers were at once owners and laborers, in contrast to the hired labor under private ownership. Accordingly, products created under state or collective ownership were not the results of ownership per se, but the work of a community of laborers. Moreover, since Stalin's so-called two forms of public ownership actually both belonged to the state, it was infeasible to demonstrate the inevitable existence or absence of commodity exchange by ownership forms. Rather, whether or not commodity exchange must occur would depend on social division of labor and ownership of products. The latter was determined by how the means of production and laborers interacted in the production process, not by the ownership of the means of production alone.[36]

Fundamentally, reform theorists argued, it was the interaction of labor and ownership under socialist economy that necessitated commodity production and exchange. Through this interaction, public enterprises became economic entities with their own independent interests. As summarized by reform theorists at the Central Party School, the argument was fourfold. First, even under the whole people's ownership, the economy still comprised numerous individual enterprises, which in turn consisted of a community of laborers associated with a certain amount of state property. Second, because a particular community of workers and an individual worker within it should receive compensation as both laborers and owners, enterprises assumed independent economic interests on behalf of their workers both as a community of laborers and as individual laborers. Third, since the quality and quantity of labor differed, there resulted a diversity of economic interests among enterprises. Further, because individual workers still offered their labor through enterprises rather than through the national economy as a whole, the quality and quantity of labor were manifested only through the products of each enterprise. So finally, to compensate workers according to their labor, each enterprise must see to it that the rewards it received for its products were commensurate with efforts expended. In short, as producers of different products, individual enterprises under socialism attained the status of independent economic entities equipped for commodity exchange.[37]

Independent economic interests of enterprises were also found to exist in the realm of "expanded" reproduction, that is, capital investment for enterprise expansion. To improve the quality and quantity of production, enterprises needed not only to maximize the capacity of existing capital and the means of production but, more importantly, to expand material and human investment. Though investment may be allocated by the state, the lack of linkage between state investment and enterprise performance had led to poor economic results in the past. Enterprises, therefore, should have control over capital investment, which would give them a stake in their further growth and help shape their economic interests as independent entities. In addition, competition among enterprises would help shape independent economic interests of enterprises.[38]

The crux of these arguments was that independent economic interests of production units did exist, and that the realization of these interests must be brought about through the exchange of products as commodities among enterprises. This line of argument refuted the notion that commodity exchange could not be an inherent part of socialism or that the whole people's ownership rendered commodity exchange unnecessary.

Conservative reformers disagreed with this rationalization of an expanded market. For Wu Shuqing, Fang Weizhong, and He Jianzhang, enterprises' economic interests did necessitate commodity production and exchange. But this did not mean that enterprises would gear production toward satisfying the needs of society, as required by socialist economy, without the state to impose common interests and purposes. While recognizing the economic interests of enterprises, they did not see these as the sufficient basis of a dominant commodity economy. For them, public ownership determined the basic unity of interests among different enterprises. What brought these enterprises together to interact with one another was not just their individual interests, but also the common interests of a unified owner, the state. In this context, commodity production and exchange should not be based merely on the conflicting interests of different producers, nor entirely on the unified interests of different producers under one ownership. Instead, they should be based on the fundamentally unified interests of producers who also had their own special interests.[39]

Further, Wu Shuqing argued, the pursuit of self-interest by enterprises should not be the sole motive force of commodity production and exchange under socialism, though it remained important. Under public ownership, the motive force should be to satisfy the needs of all laborers as common owners of the means of production. This motive force, he contended, could not derive from a pure commodity economy.[40]

Finally, Wu argued, because of the unity of fundamental interests among enterprises and the collectivist motive force, labor had a social nature under socialist commodity production. For producers did not work only for their own economic interests but also for those of the larger society. Here it was no long necessary to bring about economic interaction among different producers solely through the market. Rather, that may be done by society through prior central planning. Mandatory planning, then, was a major mechanism on which central planning could continue to rely.[41]

For Wu Shuqing and Fang Weizhong, these points signified that social-ist commodity production was en route to a transition to a product econ-omy, thus possessing features of both the commodity and product econo-mies. In interactions among state enterprises, where the overlap of fundamental interests was significant, the transitional nature was more prominent. In interactions between state and collective enterprises, the commodity nature was stronger. In interactions among collective enter-prises, the commodity nature was still stronger. In their final analysis, the role of the market under socialism was still necessitated by the existence of diverse sectors and owners.[42]

Ownership

In conjunction with the new contention that state enterprises were inde-pendent entities and that state ownership did not need to entail central planning, reformers proposed during 1983–86 that "ownership rights" could be separated from "management rights." The former were defined in terms of the right to possess, benefit from, use, and dispose of the means of production, whereas the latter were defined in terms of the right to manage the means of production, set production plans, improve technology and products, expand production, partially control the dis-posal of the means of production (e.g., leasing), and decide on personnel matters.[43]

The distinction meant that if state ownership could not be changed to enterprise ownership as some had proposed, the state need not have direct administrative control over enterprises either. Diverse forms of manage-ment at the enterprise level could be devised in accordance with degrees of separation of state ownership and enterprise management. There may be (1) complete integration of ownership and management, as under cen-tral planning; (2) partial separation of ownership and management, where enterprises and the state would each retain some rights over production; or (3) complete separation between the two, where the state would exact taxes or rents from enterprises but leave all economic decisions to enterprises.[44]

Proponents of separation of ownership and management advanced three key arguments to justify it theoretically and empirically. As summa-rized by Su Shaozhi, Zhang Xiangyang, and others, the separation of ownership and management as an economic practice historically origi-nated from the emergence of large-scale socialized production, regardless of the nature of ownership. Under small-scale production where produc-tion was barely socialized, the owner of the means of production could and must be involved directly in the management of the enterprise. For example, a small agricultural producer may own and till the land and control its products; or a small landowner or industrial capitalist may hire labor but manages the production process. But separation of ownership and management had to occur where the scale of production became larger, when social polarization in the process of capitalist development forced some to rent property or capital to pursue production. This process produced a stratum of "owner capitalists" and "loan capitalists," on the one hand, and a class of rural tenants and industrial managers, on the other. In addition, the gradual sophistication of management in modern times demanded multifaceted knowledge and skills, so that it became difficult for a single owner or a body of owners to manage directly their own enterprises. Under modern capitalism, this development facilitated the genesis of stock sharing. In this analysis, the gradual separation of ownership and management resulted from social division of labor and commodity exchange, with the function of facilitating economic development. The separation was therefore a "symbol of social progress" and a "general law" of large-scale socialized production, not an inherent feature of capitalism.[45]

A second rationale for separating ownership and management was simply that it was impossible for the state to run directly all of the public means of production in the country. This was due to (1) the size of the public means of production; (2) the limited knowledge of the state over diverse consumer demands, which was necessary for making rational production decisions; and (3) the incapacity of the state to run numerous enterprise with different conditions in a unified way.[46] In the Chinese case, where tens of thousands of state enterprises existed, it was especially impossible for the state to engage directly in managing an enterprise. Hence, the proposed separation of ownership and management would not affect the socialist nature of enterprises because the state's retention of ownership could ensure its goals and interests through state regulation.[47]

A third rationale for separating ownership and management was that enterprises, as economic entities with independent interests, needed certain autonomous decision-making powers. After all, the enterprise had its own interests upon which to calculate its decisions.[48] More importantly, only by recognizing the complete operating "right" (*quan*) and interests (*li*) of enterprises would the state motivate them to take responsibility for efficiency and profitability.[49]

Several forms of separation between ownership and management were proposed in the course of 1983–86. Three of these were most prominent: (1) the contract responsibility system, (2) leased management, and (3) the joint-stock system. In the first form, the output of a production unit would be contracted to competing enterprises, thereby ensuring the interests of both the state and the production unit. The degree of the separation of rights would be worked out between the two parties involved in the contract, thus reducing the arbitrariness of central control yet obligating enterprises to state plans. Here state ownership would be preserved, but capital investment by both parties could lead to mixed ownership in the future.[50] In the second form, the leasing of the means of production to enterprises or individuals totally separated the state and management. Lessees would not be bound by state plans, but need only pay rents and taxes to the state. Capital investment may be shared by the state and the lessees, leading to potential combined ownership.[51] In the third form, the state and enterprises would be separated by having the interests of the owners represented in the form of the stock shares they held. A board of directors, formed by representatives of the shareholders (the state, enterprises, workers, the public), would share decision-making power over management, with the state as the largest holder having the most power. Enterprises, being owned by different shareholders, would become independent legal entities no longer subordinate to any specific state agency. The degree of separation between the state and management would depend on the size of state shares.[52] Similar conceptions of central ownership and external management characterized other proposed forms of separation, such as the asset management system, the vote-sharing system, and the interest-sharing system.[53] But the contract system was the prevailing form of industrial reform between 1984 and 1986.[54]

Conservative reformers objected to the idea that ownership and management may be separated under socialism. They argued that because state ownership is cooperative in character, no social group or individual should benefit from the discrepancies in the type of the means of production they happened to work with. Separation of the state and management would tempt groups or individuals to use the public means of production they happened to occupy to pursue excessively their own self-interests (for example, to choose product types that maximize profits rather than satisfy social needs). Another worry was that the state would not be able to express its interests in production under many forms of separation, rendering it likely to lose macroeconomic control. The leading role of socialist economy, conservatives contended, should consist not just of state ownership or the state's extraction of taxes based on that ownership. It also consisted of actual economic power afforded by the state's control over products and economic infrastructure. If enterprises were given complete user control over state property and products while the state would only collect taxes, then the people's ownership would "exist in name" only. Similarly, if enterprises were to have full decision-making power over capital investment, the state would lose its control over capital construction, comprehensive balance, and rational arrangement of the macro economy. In line with Chen Yun's "supplementary role of the market," conservatives argued that only in cases of small enterprises involving small articles and services could separation of the state and management be granted.[55]

Conservative reformers were particularly opposed to the joint-stock system as a form of separation of ownership and management. The clearest opposition appeared in Wu Shuqing's article in *Renmin ribao* during the 1987 antiliberal campaign.[56] Following Marx's analysis of the emergence of stocks as a result of capitalist development, they disagreed that the practice was an "inevitable result" of socialized large-scale production without a class character. Fan Maofa and others argued in an article in *Jingji yanjiu*:

> Following the development of capitalist production, conventional capitalist private enterprises with their source of capital limited to the personal capital accumulation of the entrepreneurs had difficulty meeting the growing needs of an economy of scale. At the same time, the system of hereditary operators seriously restricted the extensive recruitment of managerial personnel, which was not conducive to raising the level of enterprise management. The joint-stock system, which separates ownership from management, thus emerged as the times require. Through the joint-stock system, capital owned by a greater number of people can be pooled within a short time for developing an economy of scale. With the extensive recruitment of managerial personnel from outside the circle of investors, highly efficient and specialized management can be attained. The emergence of the joint-stock system not only preserved the capitalist system of private ownership but satisfied to some extent the needs of socialized large-scale production.[57]

By the same logic, socialist economy was above the necessity of joint-stock ownership. As argued in the same article,

> China's socialist public ownership system itself represents the complete abolition of the capitalist mode of production. Its capability in pooling funds far exceeds that which is possible under capitalism, and is capable of selecting the most outstanding entrepreneurs for management. Thus, the joint-stock system, which serves the purpose of pooling funds and realizing highly efficient management, does not have much practical significance for Chinese enterprises owned by the whole people.[58]

In addition, Jiang Xuemo, Yang Qixian, Zou Mu, and others were worried that breaking down state enterprises into shares would eventually cause state property to become collective property, and collective property to become private property. Since workers and ordinary citizens could not afford to buy up the bulk of shares, they questioned, would the state's status as the major holder lead to any genuine separation of the state and enterprises anyway? For this reason, they refuted the reformers' argument that the "stockfication" (*gu feng hua*) of state enterprises could curb enterprises' short-term behavior or raise workers' sense of responsibility for state property. On the contrary, the stock system may intensify enterprises' short-term orientation. Finally, the limited shares owned by individual workers would not serve as a more effective incentive than an adequate distribution policy and moral education. Worse still, distribution based on capital shares, entailed by the shareholding concept, was synonymous with capitalism and would even give rise to a parasitic social stratum living off dividends and bonuses.[59]

It should be noted, however, that some of these conservative views were shared by reformers who advocated the priority of market reform and objected to the one-sided emphasis on ownership reform. Short of a good market mechanism that could rationally allocate resources and coordinate economic relations, Wu Jinglian argued, "granting enterprise rights and interests" and promoting "state-enterprise separation" would only lead to irresponsible use of state property without contributing to the overall national economy.[60]

Distribution

In principle, discussions of socialist distribution in 1984–85 still appealed to the idea of distribution according to labor. The new orthodoxy—"common prosperity but not concurrent prosperity"—while conveying commitment to equality, affirmed the need for income differentiation. What distinguished the discussions of this phase from those of the earlier period was a heightened emphasis on what equality and inequality meant under socialism, and whether the consequences of recent reforms violated the socialist notion of equality. Simply put, Chinese reformers came to feel that those who complained about recent inequalities advocated "equality of results," or leveled distribution regardless of labor. Reform policies, by contrast, encouraged "equality of opportunity," or different results from the same "starting point." The former was said to amount to "absolute egalitarianism," while the latter was "genuine equality" under socialism.[61]

Reformers defended recent inequalities by arguing that equality, as advocated by Marx, consisted of political and class equality. Under private ownership, the working class could not enjoy real equality because the propertied class determined social distribution through its control over the means of production. But socialism eliminated political and economic sources of inequality and created the conditions for genuine equality, that is, equal opportunity and labor rights under a common ownership. Since recent income inequalities did not stem from control over ownership and its associated exploitation of labor, they did not constitute inequality in Marx's sense.[62] Rather, those inequalities were attributed to factors unrelated to political and class inequality: (1) differences across enterprises, sectors, and regions in the quality and quantity of their material and human resources; (2) human differences in intellectual and physical ability and in utilization and management of resources; and (3) household differences in the number of working members and dependents.[63] It was ironic, though, that the first group of differences were not considered hindrances to equality. Further, though the "nouveaux riches" were recognized to have violated distribution according to labor, they were seen as a small minority that did not discredit the overall policy of material incentives. As for the fact that enterprises preferred to produce profitable goods rather than small articles of daily necessity, it was explained as an inevitable result of the commodity economy, not a consequence of an erroneous distribution policy.[64]

Since the introduction of urban reform in late 1984 and especially with the blooming of reform discussion in 1986, the concepts of "equality of results" and "equality of opportunity" received more searching analysis. Parallel to the recognition that "a commodity economy" was inherent to socialism, reformers now argued that Chinese socialism should also accept the notions of equality and distribution of the commodity economy. Specifically, equality must be measured by "equality of opportunity" and efficiency, the consummate values of the market economy. In other words, reformers came to see equality as achievable only when there was equality of opportunity and desirable only when it was linked to efficiency.[65]

The perceived linkage between "equality of opportunity" and efficiency led reformers to see inequity in past egalitarian policies that emphasized "equality of results." For Du Runsheng, those policies were inequitable because they were enforced by administrative measures and by "restraining the rich to level with the poor." Further, they "negated the objective law of regulating distribution through the market, resorted to noneconomic means of forceful intervention, severed the link between equality and efficiency, and hindered the mutual promotion of equality and efficiency."[66] An investigative report on the practice of guaranteed employment, prepared by the Research Institute of Chinese Structural Economic Reform under the State Council, concluded that equality achieved at the expense of efficiency resulted in a different type of inequality: Guaranteed employment created feather-bedding, unemployment at the job, and the "iron rice bowl" regardless of job performance. These problems meant inequality for hard-working individuals and cost-conscious enterprises.[67] *Shijie jingji daobao* quoted a Hungarian scholar to the effect that this type of equality actually created exploitation under socialism—of those who worked hard by those who did not. Worse still, as the enforcer of central planning and egalitarian distribution, the socialist state "effectively organized this type of exploitation."[68] The consequence of separating efficiency and equality, reformers concluded, was not "common prosperity," but "common poverty," a type of equality that stifled social creativity and hindered economic development.[69]

Although officials like Du stressed a balance between efficiency and equality, others proposed replacing "equality of results" aimed at egalitarianism with "equality of opportunity" aimed at efficiency. They called for adoption of the latter notion as the new ethical standard in social relations and income distribution. The role of the state would be limited to creating the external conditions of fair competition and putting every social member at the same starting point of the race.[70] Hu Ping, who later became the head of a New York-based dissident organization, pushed the argument for "equality of opportunity" furthest at this time when he wrote that egalitarianism, being imposed by the state, could not constitute a genuine moral standard because it violated individuals' freedom of choice. Further, he alleged that egalitarianism was able to persist in Chinese society because it served to "satisfy the most destructive social psychology of jealousy" and "bring about a special type of social stability."[71] That these views were openly endorsed in *Renmin ribao* by a noted reformist writer in 1986 suggested that Hu's analysis was shared by others.

While conservative reformers supported distribution according to labor, they diverged from the individualistic orientation encouraged under "equality of opportunity" and disagreed with the deemphasis of moral incentives implicit in the exaltation of efficiency. What they really complained about was the one-sidedness of reformers' promotion of the distribution ethic of the market. The dispute over *Shehui bao*'s article on selfishness best illustrated the conservative objection. As reflected in *Renmin ribao*'s editorial renouncing that article, conservatives held that there must always be a balance between individual interests and restraints on selfishness, and that in a socialist society collectivism must remain the ethical norm.[72] In the final analysis, conservative reformers exalted ideological education and moral incentives along with distribution according to labor, not the replacement of traditional ethics by the market ethics of self-interest, competition, and efficiency.

Despite the conservative resurgence at the end of 1986, radical reformers dominated in this second phase of economic rethinking. They overcame the constraints they faced in the first phase and reformulated the orthodoxies that held them back in the earlier period. Nevertheless, the new reformulations did not question the sanctity of the product economy, public ownership, or distribution according to labor per se, but only challenged old ways of applying them. But the claims to new forms of socialist economy did weaken the vigor and coherence of conservative arguments and helped reformers to secure ideological legitimation for putting urban reform into practice.

COMPREHENSIVE REASSESSMENT

Further reexamination of China's economic system in the late 1980s moved to confront original theories of socialist economy. Going beyond the issues of past mistakes and incompatibilities between theory and the host society, the discussions of 1987–89 fundamentally questioned Marx's theory. Concurrent with the efforts to "reconceptualize" socialism and capitalism, which will be the topic of chapter 7, this phase of economic reappraisal de-emphasized systemic features of socialism and stressed common features of modern economic development under socialism and capitalism.

Organization and Management

For both policymakers and reform theorists, the central question that emerged with Zhao's efforts to introduce a "New Order of the Socialist Commodity Economy," beginning in late 1987, was how to conceive of a comprehensive role of the market in a self-proclaimed predominantly socialist economy. Up to then, commodity or market exchange had been justified in one way or another. But could the entire national economy become a "commodity economy," minus the word "planned," thus allowing commodity relations to govern all horizontal and vertical economic interactions? And if so, would this alter the nature of the Chinese economy?[73]

In the course of discussions during the period, radical reformers and even leading conservative theorists such as He Jianzhang and Wu Shuqing came to recognize an inevitable role for the commodity economy, that is, a market throughout the economy, not just limited commodity exchange across sectors and enterprises. The new rationale was that as a form of economic operation, the commodity economy was not intrinsically capitalistic but an "insurmountable stage" of development for any society.[74] Within this broad agreement, though, differences remained between reformist and conservative theorists on the nature and scope of the commodity economy.

The historical stage of commodity economy is "insurmountable" for China, it was now argued, because it was a necessary historical development to replace the "natural economy" antecedent to it. Under the so-called natural economy, commodity exchange was scarce due to the lack of social division of labor and self-sufficiency of producers. Thus during primitive, slave, and feudal societies, all characterized by a natural economy, economic development was slow and evolutionary. But when commodity exchange became the dominate economic mode, specialization and competition greatly enhanced productivity, technology, and efficiency, leading to revolutionary developments in the economy. The replacement of the natural economy by the commodity economy, therefore, was a "great leap" in social development to a superior mode of production.[75]

This purportedly evolutionary process in turn led to an emphasis on the objective conditions (as opposed to the class conditions) that necessitated the emergence of the market. These include (1) a social division of labor and (2) different possessors of the means of production and/or of products, with concomitant different economic interests among them. Since these conditions also existed in the earlier stages of history, albeit in residual forms, the market was thus not an intrinsic feature of capitalist society. Rather, the commodity economy was both a requirement and a product of large-scale socialized production.[76]

This new conception of the origin and function of the market led Chinese reformers to see a basic problem in Marx's concept of product economy. A product economy must be based on a highly developed socialized production capable of societal planning. Yet this product economy was premised on the existence of a large-scale socialized production without the market. In other words, Marx's product economy was built on the premise that the complicated economic activities and social demands of society could in fact be coordinated by means other than the market, specifically, by central planning under cooperative ownership. This seemed theoretically defensible, Xue Muqiao noted, but practice had proven it untenable. In his contention, "large-scale socialized production of the modern day is so complicated that a central planning apparatus cannot possibly manage it."

> The planning for the important segments of the economy has to be divided among many central departments. The planning for the less important segments has to be done by regional agencies. The execution of plans in turn has to be administered by central departments or regional agencies. Both departmental and regional plans exclude horizontal interactions among enterprises. These plans operate along the departmental or regional lines so that within each confine, economic production—large or small—must encompass everything. This practice is not conducive to specialized economic cooperation among enterprises and hinders the development of large-scale socialized production.[77]

To Xue and others, the difficulty that Marx's theory entailed for China was especially great because prior to the Chinese Revolution, China was endowed with neither large-scale socialized production nor a national market. It was thus hardly possible to develop large-scale socialized production by means of a product economy after the revolution. As a result, China's planned economy was built on and patterned after the largely self-sufficient "natural economy" of prerevolutionary days, burdened by a traditional apprehension toward the market that was reinforced by the postrevolutionary ideology. Since the two major conditions for the market still existed in China, that is, social division of labor and divergent interests of owners and producers, the market must continue to regulate its economy. "The commodity economy will be inevitable," concluded Su Shaozhi and colleagues, so long as those conditions persisted, so long as society's products were not ample enough to "flood like spring water," and so long as a unified national system of accounting and distribution could not materialize.[78] Some leading reformers, such as Gao Shangquan and Jiang Yiwei (the former a deputy director of the State Council's Commission on the Reform of the Economic System), went on to characterize a "convergence" of methods between socialist and capitalist economy. Since large-scale socialized production required capitalist economies to adopt some planning and socialist economies to adopt some market functions, they argued, planned and market regulation were "common trends of contemporary economies." Because of this commonality, they no longer saw any need to question "socialist" or "capitalist" when considering economic methods.[79]

Radical reformers nonetheless underscored the essential differences between the socialist and the capitalist market. The most important was that in the ownership of the means of production, the socialist market reflected the interests of different communities of workers under the same ownership. As such it would not lead to the exploitation of workers, as would the capitalist market that reflected the interests of private owners of the means of production. Second, the scope of the market under socialism differed from that under capitalism. Infrastructure such as railways and banks, and important resources such as land and mines, all vital to the macro economy, were not marketable commodities. While allowing most factors of production—capital, technology, labor—to enter the market, radical reformers ruled out labor as a commodity, though there was a discussion of labor as a commodity in 1986. They distinguished between the mobility of labor (change of jobs) and the fluctuation of labor's value according to the market (change in the price of labor). Viewing the former as permissible and the latter as unacceptable under socialism, they insisted that labor could not be used as a commodity to extract surplus value.[80]

Radical reformers were vague about the future of the market under socialism. Xue Muqiao ruled out any eventual elimination of the commodity economy, not because China would be never ripe for transition to a product economy, but because he did not foresee any need to eliminate small owners of the means of production. For him, only key components of the means of production should remain under public ownership. In this context, he faulted Marx for "being methodologically abstract and empirically limited" in ruling out small private producers under socialism. As long as different owners of the means of production existed, he argued, the market would persist.[81]

While conservative theorists largely agreed with these conceptions of the market by the late 1980s, they differed more sharply than radical reformers did with liberal reformers on the nature of the commodity economy. This divergence was to become a focal point of contention before and after the political crisis of 1989. First, liberal reformers either ruled out planning as a systemic feature of socialism altogether or insisted on the market as the basis of planning. They saw the market as an inherent requirement of any modern economy with similar features under socialism or capitalism. The failure of the double-track price system, they claimed, demonstrated the futility of a "socialist commodity economy" and pointed to the need for a complete market.[82] Except for the realms of education, health services, basic research, and the government, they would allow the market to operate in all facets of Chinese life.[83]

Liberal and conservative reformers also disagreed sharply on the scope of the market. For conservatives, the sources of the capital market should be people's income from labor or from dividends based on this income. These should not be the income of speculators who live off manipulating the capital market, which would encourage the emergence of a "parasite class."[84] Liberals, by contrast, did not mind the emergence of social groups who lived on capital gains alone. One even proposed letting superfluous cadres live off stocks so that they would withdraw from politics.[85] Further, conservatives would not allow the labor market to become a means to preserve a labor reservoir and drive down wages.[86] Yet liberals argued that labor could be a commodity under socialism. They saw the commercialization of labor as a means to enhance laborers' sense of self-interest, productivity, and equality of opportunity.[87] In other words, once labor was commercialized, both producers and production would be better off in absolute terms. Along similar lines, a few liberals even favored the exploitation of hired labor at the present stage so that China could develop more quickly to embark on a higher stage when it could eliminate exploitation.[88]

Most of all, conservatives and liberals differed on the requirement of private ownership as a necessary component of the market. While the former did not find it necessary, the latter saw public ownership in any form as incompatible with the market. This point of contention characterized discussions of ownership in the same period.

Ownership

The reassessment of socialist ownership that emerged after the Thirteenth Congress in late 1987, especially after the onset of the economic crisis in mid-1988, focused on the so-called short-term behavior of enterprises and their lack of responsibility for the use or appreciation of state property. Both problems had been highlighted by the "separation" approach to ownership reform. While all three groups of reformers agreed on the need for further reform of state ownership, they differed on the fundamental theoretical and empirical soundness of state ownership.

Radical reformers, such as Xue Muqiao, Yu Guanyuan, and Li Yining, paid primary attention to what they saw as the lack of clearly defined property relationships under existing state ownership. In their view, different central, intermediate, and local state agencies had direct or indirect jurisdiction over different state enterprises, but not a single institution was responsible for the whole of public ownership. That is, there was no "personified representation" of public property. Recent decentralization only made the problem more acute, as state agencies loosened control over enterprises. This lack of "clarification" of property relations in turn led to the lack of clarity in the definition of interests, responsibility, and rights of each party. In this view, while state ownership was still the most realistic form to represent the common will and interest of the public, it needed to be fundamentally refashioned.[89] This assessment largely reflected Zhao Ziyang's approach.

Yu Guanyuan found the basis of this refashioning in the two origins of state ownership. One was Marx's conception of cooperative ownership by the whole society. Another was the immediate postrevolutionary circumstances, when the new state (in China and the Soviet Union) alone was powerful enough to undertake the transformation of former ownership relations. The first origin entailed that state ownership would continue to exist in China since it offered the most feasible way to represent Marx's concept of cooperative ownership. This did not mean, however, that the specific forms of state ownership could not be changed. This was particularly so, Yu stressed, considering the second origin of state ownership, that is, the postrevolutionary circumstances. Thus, both state ownership and the type of state ownership that existed could be legitimately changed.[90]

Proposed reforms on the basis of these views emphasized a new form of public ownership that could provide better links between the people as owners of the means of production and their economic interests. Three such forms were offered: (1) a direct link between the people as owners and their use of the means of production; (2) an indirect link between the two, namely, the means of production would be controlled by parties other than the owners, who could enjoy economic benefits associated with their nominal ownership (e.g., the prereform system); and (3) a "transferred realization" of the people's ownership rights, namely, to entrust these rights to a particular authority, such as a joint stock agency of the state, through which owners could attain economic benefits as shareholders.[91]

Radical reformers agreed that the third form provided the best way at present to resolve the problem of unclearly defined property relations, by institutionalizing public ownership in specific state agencies. The measure was called the "personification of state property," since these "property managing" agencies would assume the status and motivation of legal persons, acting as the responsible representatives of state property. Under this arrangement, state property would be defined in stock shares. State property agencies would hold the shares of the original and later investments made by the state. They would also jointly hold the shares of investment made by enterprises and workers. Importantly, these stock shares—even those held by enterprises—could not be given freely to collectives or individual workers. Under this system, public property would still belong to the state. The "property managing" agencies, staffed by selected professionals, would be expected to act above the interests of individuals and groups, to seek the appreciation of state property in the general interest of public ownership, to discern and implement socially desirable goals, and to oblige the state to be responsible to the interests of the public. Enterprises and individuals might serve in public property managing agencies. But as the leading shareholder, the state would maintain its dominant control.[92] This system was compatible with socialism, reformers assured their conservative critics, because even Marx regarded the shareholding system as a transitional form from the capitalist mode of production.[93]

These assessments largely reflected and endorsed the approach of Zhao Ziyang. Experiments with some form of this shareholding system in Shanghai, Shengyang, Wuhan, and Guangzhou since 1986 had gradually convinced Zhao and other reform leaders that this system offered a new alternative to reform of state ownership. Wu Jinglian disclosed in April 1989 that as early as 1986, when the contract system began to bog down, a strong consensus had emerged among reform leaders that the shareholding system would be the next step of state ownership reform.[94] Though it was not put into effect immediately, thanks in part to conservative resistance, Zhao Ziyang affirmed his determination to promote the reform at the Thirteenth Party Congress in October 1987 and in his talk with Milton Friedman in September 1988.[95]

In contrast to such efforts to improve state ownership, liberal reformers called state ownership a "system of ownerless property." This system, they asserted, was the root cause of all irresponsible behavior toward state property. Unlike radical reformers, they did not see property relations under state ownership as definable. Rather, they found an "inherent contradiction" between that system of ownerless property and a commodity economy, because the latter presupposed free and independent property rights of individual producers. Rather than trying to salvage public ownership by improving its forms, liberals proposed that state ownership be negated totally and individual ownership be introduced.[96]

Like radical reformers, liberals traced the basis of rethinking state ownership to its theoretical and empirical origins, but they arrived at different conclusions. In terms of its theoretical origin, one liberal claimed, state ownership was devised out of normative consideration, namely, the conviction that state ownership could ensure equal property ownership. In terms of its empirical origin, state ownership was adopted on the assumption that it could ensure rational organization of production and resources on a societywide scale.[97] But state ownership had failed on both accounts in the liberal view. On the normative side, equality was achieved at the expense of individual drive. On the empirical side, the state's organization of production and resources proved to have been irrational and inefficient. Moreover, this state role had deprived workers of the rights to organize and allocate their own property. These consequences of state ownership were termed "the genetic deficiencies" of public ownership that had contributed to the problems before and after reform: the lack of incentive for caring for public property and the ineffective use of public property.[98]

To rectify these "genetic deficiencies," some liberals proposed using the production criterion in place of the normative criterion in choosing forms of ownership. For them, private ownership offered the optimal choice because of its demonstrated capability of motivating social members and its demonstrated efficiency. It should therefore be among those advanced and "rational" (*heli*) areas that China ought to absorb from capitalism.[99] Other liberals, following Western "property rights economics," emphasized the idea of "property rights," an idea not just about who owned the means of production but also about resource allocation and the flow of innovation.[100] Borrowing the concept of the "exclusivity of ownership" (the owner's right over economic decisions), Wu Jiaxiang, a member of Zhao's reform "think tank," argued that a major defect of state ownership was the obscurity of property rights stemming from the lack of "exclusivity."[101] By this logic, a partial reform of state ownership was not tenable.

Still other liberals found it more convenient to use a newly emphasized idea attributed to Marx to advocate the elimination of state ownership. This new idea was the "reconstruction of individual ownership" as distinct from Marx's objection to certain features of private ownership. In this reading of Marx, Marx was not opposed to private ownership per se, but only to the use of private property by some to exploit others who did not enjoy property ownership. That is, what Marx and Engels really criticized in their works was "partial private ownership," or ownership by a minority of people. This is a case in which laborers did not own the means of production, while owners of the means of production did not labor, thus contributing to the exploitation of the nonpropertied, hired labor by propertied owners.[102] Yet Marx was not found to oppose a "complete private ownership," that is, ownership of the means of production by all members of society. On the contrary, liberals alleged, Marx advocated a "reconstruction of individual ownership" on the basis of "common ownership of land and the means of production created by labor itself."[103] Based on this reading of Marx, liberals called for a redefinition of public ownership in terms of "social individual ownership," that is, all members of society would enjoy private ownership.[104]

This concept of "social individual ownership" led liberals to propose the disintegration, rather than the clarification, of state property. In contrast to the joint ownership scheme of radical reformers, liberals called for a free and equal distribution of existing state property to all individual citizens. This new form of ownership, they claimed, not only would overcome the deficiencies of state ownership but was markedly different from the system of private ownership criticized by Marx. It would constitute a new concept and form of public ownership with numerous advantages. First, the new form would remedy the problem of "everyone owns public property in name but nothing in reality" and make possible independent property rights and freedom of property transfer. Second, the new form would differ from capitalist private ownership by allowing free association of equal owners and eliminating free possession of labor of the nonpropertied by the propertied.[105] Third, individual ownership offered a way to dispose of cadres who would be rendered useless by the dismantling of central planning and state ownership. If temporarily unemployed, they could become profit-oriented stockholders.[106] Instead of state officials, managers selected by enterprises would be responsible for the interests of their enterprises and accountable to their employees. Finally, individual ownership would legitimate free association of private funds to form stock companies.[107] In short, only by severing public ownership from the state and the political office could its previous problems be fundamentally remedied and its operation made compatible with a market economy.

In contrast to both radical and liberal reformers, conservative reformers saw public ownership neither in need of "clarifying" nor "ownerless." Although admitting its widely acknowledged deficiencies, they saw minor adjustments as necessary and sufficient. As a matter of principle, conservatives objected to the transfer of any portion of state property to collectives or individuals.[108]

The theory and practice of public ownership did not entail ownership by no one but ownership by all, argued Li Guangyuan and Su Xing (the latter a senior economist and vice president of the Central Party School and a conspicuous conservative voice after the Tiananmen crackdown). In theory, this ownership by all denoted several things. First, the state economy served the end of enhancing the material and cultural life of every laborer in society. Second, the products and profits of the state economy belonged to all social members and were shared by them. Third, every social member had the right to use the public means of production through cooperative labor, to receive distribution according to labor, to enjoy social services, and to participate directly or indirectly in production management. Finally, state property was derived from the accumulation of all social members. Importantly, the socialist owner here was not a property owner in a conventional sense but an unprecedented owner of common property. The socialist owner would not privately possess, utilize, or dispose of any portion of common property nor derive income by means of ownership of any portion of common property. Rather, the socialist owner received income through participation in cooperative labor.[109]

For those conservative theorists, state ownership did not relegate workers to be mere employees of the state but embodied ownership of the means of production by the whole people. For state ownership reflected the public's "entrusting" of ownership rights to the state. This relationship of "entrusting" was to be understood in two ways. First, the scale of socialized production and the nature of public ownership rendered it difficult for individual workers to assume all the responsibilities of an owner. If public property were distributed to every social member as liberals proposed, the system of public ownership would collapse and socialized production would be destroyed. Second, public property could be directly or indirectly entrusted to different central and local agencies of the state. The different levels and manners of entrusting did not render the whole people's ownership meaningless, because they entailed not the carving up of public ownership to various parties but only the division of entrusted rights and responsibilities.[110] In short, the system of state ownership, at whatever level of management, did not deprive the whole people's ownership of its significance.

In practice, conservative reformers saw China's choice of state ownership after the revolution as realistic and rational. The establishment of state ownership, Su Xing argued, was facilitated by the seizure of pre-1949 bureaucratic property, in particular the concentrated wealth of the four big families (Jiang, Song, Kong, and Chen) and two-thirds of the nation's banking and industrial apparatus controlled by such groups. The transformation of the bulk of the private sector progressed not arbitrarily but realistically in response to postwar economic and financial conditions, which favored the role of the state to stabilize and unify national finance, prices, and economy. Even at the height of socialist transformation in the mid-1950s, when only a small part of the economy was left to be transformed, the rather hasty process had its logic: Private enterprises simply became overwhelmed by the growing public sector and lost out in the competition. Although Su acknowledged mistakes and lapses during the socialist transformation drive, he emphasized the historical inevitability of the process.[111]

In line with their affirmation of state ownership, conservatives saw the contract responsibility system as an adequate and sufficient solution to the problems of public ownership.

While Zhao and supporters were looking into the shareholding system to deepen ownership reforms, Gao Di, who was governor of Jilin and was to head *Renmin ribao* after the Tiananmen crackdown, countered with an article in *Renmin ribao* under the title "The Contract Responsibility System Is the Road to Deepening Reforms" in June 1988. Along with other conservatives, he argued that the major mistake of the past was that the relations of "entrusting" between the state and the public were taken to mean the state's total authority over public property. In this way, enterprises and workers were deprived of their rights, responsibilities, and interests. The task of reform was therefore to sort out which of these elements should be entrusted to the state and which ones should be left with enterprises. The contract system was to fulfill this task in several ways. By turning the superior-subordinate relationship between the state and enterprises into one of contractual parties, it would change the nature of the relationship between them. By improving the rationality, symmetry, clarity, and stability of the powers between the two parties, it would overcome the excessive and erratic role of the state under previous relations. By linking the interests of the state, enterprises, and individual workers, it promised a realistic form of combining distribution according to labor and the commodity economy, while allowing the state to play a role in balancing the excesses of the commodity economy.[112]

Distribution

Discussions on distribution in the late 1980s centered on two problems. One was the emergence of income from property, stocks, dividends, bonds, and interest, which could no longer be justified by the idea of distribution according to labor. The other was huge profit-making from corrupt activities, now the most visible source of "getting rich first," which was not explicable in terms of equality of opportunity, competition, or efficiency. The key issues here concerned the appropriate forms of distribution under a socialist commodity economy and the sources of unfair avenues of distribution:[113] Was distribution according to labor still compatible with a commodity economy? And was unfair distribution linked to the market?

For radical reformers, distribution according to labor in the classic sense, that is, using a unified standard to compensate labor contributed by all members of society, was a principle of a product economy and thus problematic for a commodity economy. In contrast to the former case, the measure of labor would change and nonlabor sources would enter into the calculation of distribution in the latter case. Changes in the measure of labor would occur for several reasons. First, with the growth of nonstate enterprises, the use of a unified standard to measure labor and compensation would no longer be possible. Second, within state enterprises, the recognition of independent economic interests of production units entailed that economic exchange among them must be based on equality of value, rather than equality of labor. Here, contribution of labor by different enterprises was differentiated from socially necessarily labor, the latter being reflected as "equality of value." Third, reduced mandatory planning and expanded market regulation had eroded the economic conditions for distribution according to labor. Finally, when distribution was still made through the vehicle of currency, social distribution would be affected by such factors as price and interest rates, particularly now that these factors were determined by the market.[114]

In other words, under a socialist commodity economy, the idea of distribution according to labor becomes commercialized distribution according to labor: Labor as a determinant of distribution is replaced by production profits; the state as the central distributor is replaced by the production unit; exchange of equal labor is replaced by exchange of equal value; income disparity based on individual differences is replaced by differences in both enterprise profits and individual labor; and the unitary form of distribution is replaced by diverse forms. For radical reformers, these changes signified a new way of defining "labor," not an abandonment of distribution according to labor.

Distribution according to nonlabor sources could be accommodated within socialism, according to radical reformers. They did recognize the parallels with capitalism, since most of those sources (that is, dividends, bonds, interest, stocks, rent, deposits, loans, assets, leasing) amounted to distribution according to capital, the principle of distribution under capitalism. Under both systems, for example, distribution according to capital was based on the recognition of private capital and on the contribution of capital to the production process (hence a certain degree of exploitation of labor). Under both systems, the expansion of capital depended on "recapitalization," or the reinvestment of interests from the original capital.[115]

However, radical reformers emphasized differences in distribution based on capital under the two systems. For example, the source of capital from which distribution derived was different—mainly from surplus value under capitalism and from the accumulated labor of laborers under socialism. The importance of distribution from capital in overall social distribution was also different—the major source of distribution for capital owners under capitalism and a supplementary source under socialism. The scope of capital flow was different—guided by profit prospects under capitalism but constrained by the overall socialist economy under socialism. Participants in the distribution from capital were different—the largest recipients were "parasites" who lived off interests under capitalism but primary holders were laborers under socialism. Finally, consequences of distribution from capital were different—enhancing the control of hired labor by capital under capitalism but promoting the overall economy under socialism.[116] In short, socialism has the propensity and capacity to contain large-scale accumulation and concentration of capital in the hands of a few.

Radical reformers found other recent sources of distribution justifiable either because they were requirements of the commodity economy or because they benefited the growth of production forces—for example, income derived from managerial and technical skills, mental labor, talent, and risk-taking; or income from a combination labor and capital in household enterprises, rural responsibility systems, private enterprises, Sino-foreign joint ventures, and cooperative enterprises where different parties may contribute technology, labor, and capital.[117] As long as these forms did not impede the primacy of distribution according to labor, Liu Guoguang argued, they should be allowed to exist. After all, he asserted, "Marxists do not simply attend to social justice" in judging a form of distribution. They must also consider whether this form would contribute to the increase of production forces.[118]

For radical reformers, recent inequalities—particularly those associated with cadre corruption—did not result from new distribution mechanisms of the market. Rather, it was the lingering central control over the economy that allowed cadres to manipulate the coexistence of the plan and the market and to profit from price differentials created by it. The result was "the exchange of power for money," as the public called it, or the combination of the administrator and the capitalist that Fairbank noted before 1949. In this analysis, the cause of the most pronounced forms of recent income inequality was not the market principle of "equality of opportunity," but the inequality of opportunity resulting from the monopolistic nature of the planned economy, that is, officials' access to controlled goods. Under this unequal access, the "invisible hand" of the market was trampled by the "invisible foot" of officials, by "official departmentalism" (*guanbenwei zhi*), and by "power-based economy" (*quanli jingji*).[119] The conclusion for radical reformers was the need for a more complete commodity economy and an end to the double-track system.[120]

While agreeing with radical reformers on the legitimacy of distribution according to nonlabor sources, liberal reformers emphasized individual ownership of the means of production as a source of social distribution. On the basis of their idea of "social individual ownership," they sought to revise Marx's thesis that ownership should not be a means of extracting income.[121] They also justified ownership as a source of distribution by asserting the legitimacy of self-interests. The emphasis on collective interests in the past, they claimed, divorced individual interests from social ones. In the end it impeded the realization of social interests as well by hindering the growth of production forces. Adequate concern for individual interests, by contrast, contributed to social progress since the post-Mao reforms.[122] If exploitation of labor was one reason why Marx sought to eliminate private ownership, it was not a concern for some liberals.[123] For them, the new concept of social equality must take efficiency as its value orientation, equality of opportunity as its principle, and the market as its measure of fairness.[124] In line with their emphasis on the role of private ownership in distribution, liberal reformers blamed public ownership as the root cause of cadre corruption. Unlike the radical reformers, they found it insufficient to perfect the market: Public ownership must go because it was the "cradle of feudal privileges and political inequalities."[125]

Conservative reformers disagreed with radical reformers on the scope of distribution according to nonlabor sources and with liberal reformers on the value orientation of social distribution. For them, distribution according to labor must remain the dominant principle, with "labor" still defined by the amount of physical input. Although the principle of equal exchange of value was helpful in determining the amount of labor, they argued, it was likely to encourage money-oriented tendencies and hence should be balanced by the valuation of social interests. The goal of reform, they insisted, was to overcome leveled distribution, not distribution according to labor itself. It was also to encourage hard work, not distribution according to capital and income disparities based on it.[126]

Conservative reformers also objected to an unqualified emphasis on production forces as the criterion of social good. They complained that while many reform writers were enthusiastic in discussing social progress brought about by the commodity economy and defended anything that promoted production forces, they were unwilling to admit the negative consequences, that is, the erosion of social equality, justice, and stability. While production forces may be the motive force of social progress in a broad sense, they contended, the production criterion showed a lack of concern for social values or for the distinction between the capitalist and the socialist.[127] Finally, conservatives objected to the use of individual ownership as a source of social distribution. As a basic principle of socialism, laborers could not privately own or dispose of any portion of cooperative property or derive any income from such possession. They could only participate in distribution by virtue of their labor contribution.[128]

In line with their critique of distribution according to nonlabor sources, conservative reformers blamed corruption and the glaring income disparities caused by it on the value orientation encouraged by liberal reformers. They complained that liberals were shielded by Zhao Ziyang and that they had dominated the media in recent years. In particular, they singled out for attack the advocacy of self-interests and money worship that had allegedly become the "theoretical rationale" for corrupt activities. That is, by encouraging income gaps and private accumulation of wealth, liberal reformers helped to foster illegitimate "nouveaux riches" by moral and administrative indulgence.[129] Social inequalities resulting from such indulgence, conservatives charged in the wake of the 1989 protests, became the social sources of mass discontent; whereas the self-interested individualism championed by liberals became the ideological sources of youth agitation.[130] For conservatives, public discontent over corruption and inequality shown during the protests of 1989 demonstrated precisely the people's dissatisfaction with recent deviation from distribution according to labor. This principle, therefore, proved to have both an ideological and a social base to continue in China.[131]

Until the Third Plenum of October 1988, radical reformers appeared to hold the upper hand in policy and ideology, while liberals dominated many reform journals and opinion forums and conservative reformers remained on the defensive. With the decline of the reform leadership after mid-1989, the radical reform view was eclipsed. Its policies were held responsible for the loss of macro control and planned development in the late 1980s. Liberal reformers became the major targets of conservative attack. Their advocacy of a "complete and free market economy," "individual ownership," and an alternative distribution principle was criticized as a well-mediated rationale for altering the direction of China's reform course.[132] The liberal reappraisal of the economy became the evidence of their alleged efforts to overthrow socialism and establish capitalism in the counterrevolutionary "riot" of June 1989.

The Fourteenth Congress report of October 1992 by and large re-affirmed the platform of radical reformers on all three key elements of the economy. The legitimation of a "market economy" marked the most pronounced breakthrough. There was also progress on the question of ownership. Compared with Zhao's Thirteenth Congress report, Jiang Zemin's new report gave a greater affirmation to nonstate ownership by encouraging (1) "long-term, concurrent development of diverse economic elements"; (2) "diverse forms of joint management by diverse economic elements on a voluntary basis"; and (3) "equal competition among state, collective, and other enterprises in the market place, through which to display the leading role of state enterprises."[133] The significance of these statements, as one *Liaowang* report commented, was to remove the "sword of Damocles" that had long hung over private and foreign enterprises.[134] On distribution, Jiang's report retreated slightly from Zhao's report. While Zhao placed "efficiency" as the "precondition of achieving social equity," Jiang emphasized "balancing efficiency and equity." Nonetheless, the retreat was surprisingly moderate given the intensity of popular discontent with recent social disparities, as best demonstrated during the mass protests of 1989, and given conservative receptiveness to the issue. Even a reformist book on reform theories, written and published by the Central Party School in 1991, devoted a rather critical section to recent disparities in social distribution, a stance rarely taken by radical reformers before.[135]

It is further worth noting that Jiang's above statements also moved beyond the overtly conservative tone of his report a year earlier on the seventieth anniversary of the Chinese Communist party. The post-1992 economic order, then, basically returned to Zhao Ziyang's framework of the primary stage of socialism.

CONCLUSION

The post-Mao reassessment of China's economic system has focused on the theory and practice of three distinguishing features of socialist economy: product economy, public ownership, and distribution according to labor. The central question in the endeavor had been whether past and current problems of the economy were due to inadequacies in the application of socialism or in socialism itself. Divergent answers to the question divided different phases of reassessment as well as different groups of reformers.

The early phase of the rethinking was mainly concerned with errors in past application of models from the Soviet Union and theories from Marx. Both conservative and radical reformers renounced the implementation of a uniform pattern of planning, ownership, and distribution under Mao and Hua. Their mistakes were assessed to be a disregard for reality, for the prematurity of Chinese society, and for the uniqueness of the Chinese context versus that of its Soviet exemplar. These reappraisals legitimated "a supplementary role" for the market and nonpublic ownership, and the restoration of distribution according to labor.

The initial reassessment proved insufficient in the next phase, when the reform of central planning and state ownership required questioning the foundation of the Soviet-type economic system. Three basic assumptions of the model came to be rejected: Stalin's notion of limited commodity exchange under socialism; the unity of state and enterprise interests under state ownership; and the lack of linkage between distribution and human motivation. These efforts established theoretical justifications for a planned commodity economy, a separation of state ownership and management rights, and efficiency and competition in social distribution. Together, the reappraisals of the second phase moved beyond a mere censure of past practices.

The third phase of reassessment touched on the inadequacies and fallacies in the classic principles of socialist economy. Although they disagreed on their implications, radical and liberal reformers shared many conclusions on these issues. On product economy, both came to recognize that it was utopian for the state to organize and manage a highly complex and specialized economy. On cooperative ownership, both came to feel that it was infeasible to maintain state ownership for both technical and human reasons. On distribution, both came to see that it was unrealistic to enforce uniformly determined distribution according to labor. The implications of these conclusions for each group were different but nonetheless profound: While radical reformers qualified original theories, liberal reformers renounced them almost completely.

The problems and deficiencies of the theory and practice of the Chinese economy, as analyzed by radical and liberal reformers, were such only by measure of the so-called criterion of production forces. As the third of group of reformers, the conservatives, repeatedly pointed out, radical and liberal reformers proceeded from the assumption of the failures and demerits of socialist economy, not its achievements and merits. Those failures and demerits, moreover, were gauged against the alleged efficacy of its antitheses. Proceeding from different assumptions and normative criteria, conservative reformers persistently affirmed the basic soundness of the original theory and recognized the need for change mainly in practice.

CHAPTER FIVE

The Noncompeting Nature of the Socialist Political System

As in the economic domain, the rethinking of the socialist system in the political domain first came onto the Chinese political agenda amid efforts to repudiate the policies and ideology of the Mao era and evolved with empirical reforms. Unlike the economic realm, however, the rethinking of the political sphere involved sensitive issues of CCP rule. Here the conflict between the two groups of reform leaders no longer was defined just by their different visions of socialism but was also tempered by their reactions to any reappraisals that appeared to threaten the party's rule. As a result, both groups had consistently been concerned with the preservation of the core of the political system. This foreordained a course of reassessment different from that in the economic arena.

The basic tenets of the Chinese political system are well represented in three of the Four Fundamental Principles, namely, the leadership of the Communist party, Marxism–Leninism–Mao Zedong Thought, and the democratic dictatorship of the people. In clear and simple terms, these principles spell out who leads the country, what kind of political thought guides the country, and how the country is governed. These are by no means empty formulas. Each principle legitimates a fundamental practice of the system: the placing of the party above the state, the hegemony of the party's political doctrine, and the exclusion of segments of society from the political system. Although it is unclear whether they faithfully reflect the visions of the original founders of socialism, those principles seem to have characterized other variants of the socialist political system as well. As such, they have been the focus in the Chinese rethinking and the related political contention.

This chapter chronologically reviews the three major phases of the post-Mao reexamination of the political system: (1) from the beginning of the post-Mao era to early 1986, during which a moderate reassessment occurred; (2) from mid-1986 to the end of 1986, when more radical discussions flourished; and (3) from late 1987 to the end of 1992, a period that witnessed the most dramatic ups and downs in post-Mao reassessment.

THE SEARCH FOR THE SOURCES OF PAST ABUSE

Chen Yun was again the first leader to bring the issue of political change to national attention in the post-Mao era. In his speech at the CCP work conference of November–December 1978, Chen differed with Deng's priority of economic change by proposing the priority of political rehabilitation. Only by reversing the wrong verdicts of the past, he argued, would the major issues of right and wrong be clarified, the nation be united, and the party focus on the Four Modernizations. The verdicts to which he referred involved political leaders and groups who were persecuted before and during the Cultural Revolution, including victims of the Tiananmen incident of 1976.[1]

In a speech at a conference of the Central Discipline Inspection Committee (CDIC) on January 4, 1979, Chen again raised the issue of political change, and this time he linked it to the larger question of the CCP's political fate and socialist cause. Observing that a major deficiency in the past few decades of Chinese and Soviet socialism was the lack of basic intraparty democracy, he criticized Stalin's destruction of routine democracy under Lenin (1917–23) and his establishment of personal rule. Stalin's record as a revolutionary leader, in Chen's view, was primarily stained by his failure in this respect. He made a similar judgment about Mao's record as a leader, which he regarded as pivotal to the success of the Chinese Revolution but instrumental to the "abnormal state" of political life after the revolution, especially during the Cultural Revolution. At worst, Chen noted, even a party vice chairman like Ye Jianying or Hua Guofeng had no opportunity personally to see the late chairman. In underscoring the destruction of intraparty democracy as the root of political wrongs done under Mao, Chen called for reforms to ensure that similar injustices would not recur. For him, such reforms were vital to the survival not only of the CCP as a ruling party but of the international communist movement in general. The CCP's good example would have a positive impact on international communism.[2]

In the hindsight of the collapse of Eastern Europe in 1989 and of the Soviet Union in 1991, Chen's remarks were certainly farsighted. However, while perceptive on how the political system had hurt public confidence in the party and the system, Chen approached political change from the viewpoint of a true revolutionary. His premise was to rid the system of its abnormalities and to restore what he considered to be the fine tradition of Lenin and the Chinese Communist party.[3] The destruction of democracy under Stalin and Mao was seen not as inherent to the system but rather as deviant from it. The misconduct of individual leaders, rather than political institutions, was emphasized.

Although Chen helped to heighten the agenda of reversing wrong verdicts and improving the party's work style, Deng Xiaoping declined to give it immediate attention. In his closing speech at the November work conference, Deng placed political democracy second to economic modernization. The purpose of dealing with past wrongs, he stated, was to "look forward" and smoothly shift the party's work to economic modernization.[4] This line was reiterated at the Third Plenum. Thereafter the media began to affirm the Tiananmen incident of 1976 and the importance of intraparty democracy but did not encourage serious political analyses.[5] Nevertheless, the ending of massive class struggle did constitute a major political change itself. Following the plenum, hundreds of thousands of wrong verdicts were reversed under Hu Yaobang's auspices.[6]

Individual versus Systemic Sources of Abuse

Reversing the wrongs of the past alone did not resolve the question of why they occurred and how to prevent them in the future. At the CCP theory conference in early 1979, many prominent intellectuals were drawn to these questions. Although invited to the conference for the official agenda of addressing the core tenets of the Cultural Revolution, they pushed beyond this agenda to reflect on the deeper sources of the party's arbitrary rule and personality cult during the Cultural Revolution period. Invariably, they traced the Cultural Revolution and the "fascist dictatorship" of the Gang of Four to the lack of democracy in the political system. The raising of many fundamental issues at the conference led some participants to view it as more significant than the Third Plenum.[7] Su Shaozhi, also a participant, even sees the conference as the "most open" in the history of the CCP.[8] For the same reason, it also marked the first major attempt at independent thinking by post-Mao intellectuals.

Li Honglin, for example, pinpointed the reversal of the relationship between the leader and the masses as the major problem of the political system. The personality cult of Mao, he argued, had relegated this relationship to one of the masses' dependence on the leader, not equality between them. The leader was always correct and above criticism while the masses were unconditionally subjected to his absolute authority. It was this lack of popular control over the leader, hence, that must be examined and discarded. Wang Ruoshui, deputy editor-in-chief of *Renmin ribao*, blamed the personality cult on the "traditional forces of small-scale production, the ideology of the feudal emperor, and despotic rule," attributing the ability of a few elites to engineer the chaos of the Cultural Revolution to the masses' fear of speaking out against those in power. The key lesson for him was thus a need to oppose despotic forces and to promote the freedom to "speak out." Yan Jiaqi placed the key blame on the system of political authority. In his view, the destruction of democracy and law during the Cultural Revolution and during Stalin's counterrevolutionary drive of the 1930s had both stemmed from the concentration of highest political power in one person for life. Therefore he found it imperative to place institutional checks on personal power and tenure. Zhang Xianyang condemned the tyranny of Mao's anti-Right bias and his proscription of any objection to Left excesses.[9] Guo Luoji, professor at Beijing University, who would eventually be demoted to Nanjing University for his outspokenness, attacked the personality cult of Mao as "a God-creating movement" and blamed the enslavement of the masses on the distortion of the relationship between leaders and the masses.[10]

Another vocal force in exploring the deeper sources of the Cultural Revolution was the Democracy Wall movement. This movement, which emerged at the time of the November–December work conference in 1978, arose as a result of Deng's ideological offensive to emancipate the mind. During its heyday from November 1978 to February 1979, the movement saw a proliferation of wall posters and self-published journals in the center of Beijing by young activists from the Cultural Revolution period and the 1976 Tiananmen incident. After early 1979 the movement also inspired demonstrations in Beijing and elsewhere by victims of the Cultural Revolution. Three broad categories of issues were raised by the participants of the movement: (1) criticism of Mao and other leaders of ultra-leftist bent and of the Cultural Revolution; (2) demands for redress for the wrongs and injustices inflicted on individuals during the Cultural Revolution; (3) and calls for democracy, rule of law, and human rights. The last was proposed as the diagnosis on the causes of the first two problems and as the key to their remedies.

Different groups within the movement differed significantly on the assessment of the political system. The "socialist democrats" (of whom the Li Yizhe group was a forerunner[11]) favored democratic reforms within the existing system and did not question the fundamentals of the system. The "abolitionists" (of whom Wei Jingsheng is the best known) rejected the possibility of democratic reforms within socialism and advocated systemic change. In socialist practice, they detected the emergence of a bureaucratic ruling class that had come to dominate the masses. In socialist theory, they perceived inherent barriers to democracy in the concept of the proletarian dictatorship that buttressed one-party rule and a unified ideology. To resolve these problems fundamentally, they called for a multiparty system. Some of them saw the United States as the banner of democracy.[12]

The analysis of intellectuals and the Democracy Wall activists proved problematic to the reform leadership. Deng acquiesced to the Democracy Wall in late 1978, when the movement was in its social democratic phase and when he needed popular support in the struggle with the whatever group. But the "abolitionist" forces became predominant in early 1979, coinciding with the convocation of the CCP theory conference. Some participants in the conference, such as Yan Jiaqi, not only sympathized with the movement but had their papers published in the wall journals.[13] The convergence of these two forums represented a powerful intellectual trend. A key concern for Deng was that the efforts to probe into the sources of past injustices and abuses called into question his priority of economic reform.[14] What the Democracy Wall activists advocated was, in essence, the immediate priority of political change, or in Wei Jingsheng's famous words, the "fifth modernization," whereas the theoretical workers placed priority on the "clarification of the major issues of right and wrong" of the recent past, referring not to Mao's misoriented ideology and policy but to their deeper sources. That is, why was his misorientation allowed to occur and persist for so long?

Furthermore, although Deng had secured his initial victory over the whateverists by early 1979, he remained vulnerable before the formal removal of the "little Gang of Four" in early 1980. Toleration of rightist political critiques would certainly arm his leftist opponents and lend himself and his policies vulnerable to their attacks. In fact, Hu Qiaomu would later cite this as a major reason for the party's battle against the Right.[15] In this context Deng spelled out the Four Fundamental Principles at the theory conference on March 30, 1979, days after a crackdown on the "abolitionists" and the arrest of Wei Jingsheng. He spoke of the essence of the radical democratic groups as an endorsement of bourgeois democracy and opposition to the socialist system. He criticized the support for the Democracy Wall movement from the party's theoretical workers and warned them against wavering on the fundamental principles. Theoretical work, he remarked, was to focus on resolving new problems of economic modernization.[16] For a moment, the media turned from its anti-Left emphasis to an anti-Right attack on the Democracy Wall activists. Theoretical workers were called on to "look forward" toward the task of economic modernization.

The immediate result of Deng's anti-Right offensive, as discussed in chapter 3, was a "relapse into ultra-leftism," which in turn led to the resumption of the debate on the criterion of truth in the summer and fall of 1979. Thereafter, the media emphasis shifted back to the worse danger of the Left. The socialist democrats who survived the March crackdown revived in the meantime. By November 1979, however, continued objection from the whatever camp forced Deng to crack down on the socialist democrats, who had by now been radicalized by the arrest and trial of Wei Jingsheng. In justification of this move, Deng remarked in January 1980 that one must not be naive about the "overall inclination and real motives" of the socialist democrats, who too were fundamentally opposed to the party's leadership and socialism.[17] This was immediately followed by two articles in *Hongqi* criticizing their view of democracy.[18] Like the abolitionists, the socialist democrats were now accused of embracing bourgeois concepts of democracy and human rights.

The Socialist System and Its Concrete Mistakes

The resumption of the truth debate in the latter half of 1979, however, generated more rightward impulses than the brief revival of socialist democrats. As the whatever group resurrected the slogans of class struggle and proletarian dictatorship during the "spring relapse," the revived truth debate had to involve "major issues of right and wrong" that were earlier proposed by theorists and intellectuals. After all, these issues were central to the whatever group's claim to legitimacy: Mao's merits and demerits, and the mistakes and lessons of the Cultural Revolution and of the entire Chinese experience since the revolution. In the wake of the Democracy Wall movement, the party was also forced to recognize a "crisis of confidence" among youth and the need to address the issue of political reform.[19] This realization, along with veteran leaders' desire to ensure that events like the Cultural Revolution would never recur, stimulated discussions of political reform. In addition, the beginning of the drafting of the resolution on the CCP history in early 1980 refocused public attention on the place of Mao and Mao Zedong Thought in Chinese history. These developments contributed to a high tide of liberalization from late 1979 to mid-1981. Not only did public discussions flourish in legitimate forums, but underground publications of surviving dissidents persisted throughout the period.

The new twist in this round of rethinking was given by Deng himself. In the same January speech in which he rebuked the antisocialist nature of the socialist democrats, Deng defended the CCP against the criticism that capitalism had proved superior to socialism by drawing a distinction between socialism as a system and the concrete practices of a given socialist country. This bifurcation was not exactly new, being rooted in Mao's distinction between the "state system" (*guoti*, the class nature of the state) and the "political system" (*zhengti*, the structures of the state).[20] But it provided a convenient basis at this juncture for defending the Chinese political system from the rightist assault while allowing rectification of its "concrete practices." Nonetheless, Deng stressed that such improvement was only to serve the four modernizations, political stability, and the party's leadership.[21]

Partly yielding to external pressure and partly to provide party guidance on political reform, Deng formally placed the reform of the party and the state on the political agenda at an enlarged meeting of the Politburo in August 1980. In a thorough speech on "The Reform of the Leadership System of the Party and the State," he used the distinction between the state and the political system to analyze the deficiencies of the Chinese system, which only a short while ago he himself had prohibited. He delineated the main problem of the political system as the overconcentration of power and its major consequences—bureaucratism, inefficiency, and the lack of popular initiative in economic modernization. Quite sharply, he pinpointed three key sources of the overconcentration of power: a high degree of centralization entailed by the command economy, the monistic leadership of the party (*tang de yiyuanhua lingdao*), and patriarchal and feudal traditions. Describing them as problems in the party's system of organization and operation, he admitted that they were responsible for the mistakes of Mao and the Cultural Revolution and were crucial to the legitimacy and future of the party.[22]

Deng's emphasis here was obviously on those "concrete structures" of the political system that were defective; problems emphasized by the wall activists and intellectuals, such as the nature of one-party rule and ideological monopoly, were not mentioned. Deng's emphasis was reflected in the political reforms carried out between 1980 and 1982: abolition of life tenure of party and state leaders, restoration of the constitution and the presidency, strengthening of the legislature and the legal system, and expansion of elections and local power.[23] In large measure, those reforms aimed to restore the 1954 constitutional order of socialist democracy and legality patterned after the Soviet Union, as Richard Baum has pointed out.[24] It is not surprising that conservative reformers such as Peng Zhen were the leading forces in these early political reforms.

The paradigm of a "state" versus "political" system also provided reform theorists and intellectuals with a framework in which democracy could be used as a reference point to discuss the problems of the past and the prescriptions for the future. The idea of a "political system" legitimated the concept of "democracy" as a form of government, while the idea of a "state system" qualified it as "socialist." The resulting discussion between 1980 and 1982 marked major progress in rethinking the Chinese political order. If in the past the party's mistakes could be only attributed to individual leaders, be they the Gang of Four, Hua Guofeng, or Mao, the recognition of a deficient political system now permitted the discussion of the mistakes in the party's exercise of power.

Although this framework by and large guided public and intellectual discussions, some again went beyond the official boundaries. Li Honglin not only characterized the periods of the Cultural Revolution and the Great Leap Forward as "feudal fascism" but extended this criticism to the entire seventeen years before 1966.[25] Zhang Xianyang also traced the "fascist dictatorship" of the Cultural Revolution to political practices since the early 1950s.[26] Wang Ruoshui proposed a wholesome negation of Mao and Mao Zedong Thought during the discussion of the draft resolution on the CCP history.[27] The extension of their critique to the entire CCP rule since 1949 suggested that these critics saw the problems of the system as more serious than mere deficiencies in "concrete practices."

Two other groups touched on similar themes in their exploration of the "major issues of right and wrong" and the deficiencies of the political order. In the well-known "wound literature," which flourished during the recent tide of liberalization, writers and artists produced a flood of bitter accounts about the fate of individuals in the hands of the party's darker policies. Bai Hua's "Unrequited Love," a short story about a patriotic intellectual who returned from overseas but was persecuted to death in his homeland, was emblematic of this recent genre. Other literary works touched on the thorny subject of the existence of a privileged bureaucratic class. One major hit was Ye Wenfu's play, "General, What Is the Matter with You?" Another was a play called "If I Were Real." The latter told the story of a city youth sent to the countryside who posed as the son of a high-ranking cadre in order to return to the city, and who would have succeeded had he truly been an official's son. Before being banned in early 1980, the play was very popular during its brief appearance on stage, indicating that resentment of bureaucratic privileges had a popular base.

Still another group, the surviving dissidents, especially the former socialist democrats, carried the thesis of "bureaucratic class" to its logical conclusion. By now they came to share the "abolitionist" view that a "bureaucratic class" had arisen within the party and that this class was an inevitable result of the political and economic system. China's problems could only be resolved by overthrowing this class, they argued, because the contradiction between this class and the masses constituted the "leading contradiction" of society.[28] Commenting on the party's recent initiative of socialist democracy, Wang Xizhe and Xu Wenli, the two most prominent of the surviving dissidents, questioned the party's program of implementing democracy from top down. Such a program was bound to meet with bureaucratic resistance, they argued, because democracy ran counter to the interests of the bureaucratic class. As an alternative, they proposed democratic reforms from "bottom up" in the tradition of the mass movement of the Tiananmen incident of 1976.[29] The implication of this analysis was that because of the existence of a bureaucratic class, the party itself was the obstacle to democracy.

Together, these theoretical workers, writers, artists, and dissidents posed troubling questions about the prospect of genuine socialist democracy, which even Deng could no longer tolerate. The swing back began with a Politburo meeting in November 1980, at which Hua Guofeng's mistakes were criticized and his resignation accepted. As part of their objection to this move, leftist officials attacked the negative effects of Deng's emancipating the mind, such as those just discussed. To disarm his critics from the Left, Deng called for a tightening of political control in the following month. Two central documents were issued in early 1981 to ban underground publications and forbid deviation from the Four Fundamental Principles in official publications. In the next few months, Wang Xizhe and other publishers of underground journals were arrested. The special commentators of leading papers began to reverse their liberal tone by emphasizing the people's dictatorship and the Four Principles in early 1981.[30]

It was in this political climate that *Jiefangjun bao* published a special commentator's article on April 20, 1981, criticizing Bai Hua's "Unrequited Love." Bai was singled out as the start of the army's intended public attack on recent liberalizing tendencies. The army was most upset about the proposed negation of the late Chairman Mao in the discussion of the draft resolution on the party's history. Just ten days earlier General Huang Kecheng had published an article in the army daily and *Renmin ribao* on the appropriate evaluation of Mao.[31]

Jiefangjun bao's public attack on Bai Hua may be seen as a maneuver of the military to preempt the Sixth Plenum, at which the draft resolution was to be passed and Hua to be further demoted.[32] But the general ideological retreat since early 1981 suggested that the dismay with excessively liberal writings was shared by the reformist leadership. Deng did give prior approval for the public censure of Bai's work. Hu Yaobang had also made a summary criticism of the recent exposé literature at a meeting of artists in early 1980.[33] Deng particularly sympathized with the army's discontent for efforts to repudiate Mao and Mao Zedong Thought. This dismay became a key impetus behind the ensuing campaign against bourgeois liberal tendencies.[34] Insofar as the army took the initiative in criticizing the Right, the significance was that the attack was aimed at a wider scale than the reform leadership had hitherto attempted. Deng's response to the Right, after all, had so far focused on underground dissidents. *Jiefangjun bao*, on the other hand, called attention to ideological deviance in the legitimate literary and theoretical forums. And it did have a point: rightist tendencies were further demonstrated by the refusal of *Renmin ribao* to reprint the *Jiefangjun bao* article attacking Bai Hua. Hu Jiwei and Wang Ruoshui were respectively director and deputy editor-in-chief of the paper at the time.

After scoring a victory over the Left at the Sixth Plenum in July, Deng moved to deal with the Right in August. With his endorsement, the lukewarm criticism of "Unrequited Love" thus far extended to a centrally directed, nationwide criticism of "bourgeois liberalization tendencies," even though he and other reform leaders may not have intended it to become another political campaign. In Deng's talk to key propaganda officials on July 17, in Hu Yaobang's speech at the CDP's symposium on problems on the ideological front on August 3, and in Hu Qiaomu's remarks at the same symposium on August 8, all three leaders voiced concerns over the "Unrequited Love" phenomenon in the recent period. In essence, these concerns centered on how to view the "dark side" of the CCP's thirty years of rule and of the current society: to look upon them as intrinsic problems of socialism or as isolated policy and leadership failures. "Unrequited Love" was seen to fall into the former approach and represented a "general ideological trend" in recent theoretical, literary, and journalistic circles. Insofar as the reappraisal of the political system was concerned, this trend was said to have pitted the party's leadership against democracy and posed the former as incompatible with the latter. Like the abolitionists and socialist democrats, those circles were criticized for blindly extolling the bourgeois concept of democracy.[35]

The distinction between the socialist system and its concrete practices, then, failed to resolve the problem of critiquing the concrete mistakes of the system without questioning its basis. From the viewpoint of the leadership at least, any probing into the deeper causes of the dark side of society called into question the socialist system and the party's leadership.

The Socialist System and the Repression of Humans

Between the antiliberal campaign of 1981 and the reinitiation of political reform in mid-1986, discussion of political reform, at least that initiated by the leadership, experienced a relative hiatus. One reason was that the adjusters' platform prevailed in 1981–82, and reform was to be subordinated to it. Another reason was that measures to establish a manager-responsibility system in urban reforms had created a controversy among radical and conservative reform leaders over the role of the party secretary at enterprises. Because the new system would transfer major production responsibilities to the professional manager, conservative leaders worried about the erosion of the party's leadership at enterprises. But the most important reason for the shelving of political reform at the top was a lingering apprehension over possible resurgence of rightist tendencies. Deng, in particular, did not want political controversies or campaigns adversely to affect his economic priority.[36]

Yet amid official inattention, intellectuals again ventured to look into China's "state system" on their own initiative from a new perspective. This time, they raised the questions of humanism and alienation in socialist society. The inquiry into the treatment of human beings under socialism grew out of intellectuals' post-Mao reflection over the sources of the arbitrary persecution and inhuman treatment of "class enemies" during the Cultural Revolution. Initial discussions occurred mainly in academic circles and received little attention from the party.[37] But as the scope of interest and discussion increased, the topic even became one of two themes of officially commemorative symposiums on Marx's centenary in March 1983.

The discussion of humanism (*rendaozhuyi*) beginning in 1980 focused on the search for a justification within the Marxist framework for valuing the individual as a human being, not just a class-based social being. Intellectuals traced the place of humans in Marxism, from which the class conception of humans was derived in the first place. The battle line in the discussion was most sharply drawn with reference to the question "Is the person the starting point for Marxism?" which appeared in the title of a number of articles and at least one book.[38] Among the first to raise the question and argue for the person as the starting point of Marxism was Wang Ruoshui and Ru Xin, the latter the head of the Institute of Philosophy at CASS.[39] The debate pitted those who argued that the person per se was the starting point of Marxism against those who insisted that the socially defined person was his primary concern.

The first group, represented by Wang Ruoshui, argued on the ground that Marx never denied that "the person is the highest being for humans," but only that he opposed approaching the being of human "abstractly" without regard for the social context. For this group, humans possess an inherently common nature that entitles each person to the being of human.[40] The second group disagreed on the ground that while Marx was concerned with the abstract human being, it was the "actual" person as a totality of social relationships that constituted the essence and the starting point of his analysis.[41] The emphasis of the first group was on the intrinsic value of the human and his or her self-realization, whereas that of the second was on the socially defined value of the human and his or her development in the social context. The crux of the revisionist view of the first group was that if the human per se was the original goal of Marxism, then humans should be the end, not the means, of socialism.

The revisionist view has a profound implication. Under the socialist system, social institutions and practices were oriented to maximize the realization of the goals of revolution and communism. Human beings, Wang suggested, were sacrificed to achieve the elusive higher goals.[42] Further, in the name of the class-based conception of the person and social goals, the Gang of Four were able to exaggerate "class struggle" and ruthlessly persecute whomever they considered to be class enemies.[43] In this way, the class-based goals of socialism deprived the individual of the basis for defending himself or herself as a human being. The ultimate contention of the revisionists was that if the human was the starting point for

Marx, it was necessary to restore humanism as the highest value and goal of socialism. Accordingly, Marxism should be subsumed under humanism: the Marxist goal of common well-being among humans should contribute to, rather than supersede, the humanistic goal of individual well-being. Thereby the class nature of the socialist "state system" was deemphasized.

Reflections on alienation (*yihua*) followed from this assertion on the value of the person as human being. For those who regarded humans as the highest goal, alienation of humans became the gravest failure of the Chinese system. In his original article that started the debate on humanism, Wang Ruoshui already argued that alienation existed in the ideological, political, and economic spheres of China. Others found that alienation constituted the "concentrated manifestation of all maladies of socialism." Some even claimed that the theory of alienation provided the "most scientific explanation" of all prevalent problems of Chinese society.[44] Although few ventured to link alienation directly to socialism, the concept as originally delineated by Marx implies the self-estranging nature of a subject's activities. As Zhou Yang wrote in 1982, "What is referred to as alienation is that, in the course of its development, a *subject* creates its own antithesis through its own activities and that, as an external and alien force, this antithesis in turn opposes or dominates the subject."[45] Although Zhou denied that alienation in Chinese society was caused by socialism, the underlying reference to the systemic causes was inescapable. As leading conservative literary critic Lin Mohan would later contend, the "subject" in the Chinese context could only refer to the socialist system and its members.[46] Wang Ruoshui, in arguing that the translation of the CCP from a party in opposition to a ruling party created alienation, also placed an implicit blame on socialism.[47] This deeper meaning of alienation made it a highly sensitive topic. Until 1982 Zhou and other moderates refrained from endorsing it as an explanatory concept under socialism.

It was in this context that Zhou Yang gave a key presentation at the CCP symposium on the centenary of Marx. As an event led by Hu Yaobang, now the party general secretary, Zhou and other participants apparently had ample freedom to express their own views. Drafted with the help of Wang Ruoshui, Zhou's speech dwelled in length on humanism and alienation under socialism. On humanism, Zhou suggested a compromise by placing the concept under Marxism rather than the other way around. On alienation, his key message was identical to Wang Ruoshui's ideas since 1980:

> The socialist system is superior to capitalism but this does not mean alienation no longer exists in socialist society. In economic development, we failed to recognize the laws of socialist construction and in the end reaped the bitter fruit we sowed. This is alienation in the economic domain. Because democracy

and the legal system were inadequate, public servants of the people were able at times to abuse the power entrusted to them by the people. This is alienation in the political domain. As for ideological alienation, the best manifestation is personality cult, which is somewhat similar to the religious alienation criticized by Feuerbach. . . . We can overcome alienation through the socialist system, for the roots of alienation do not lie in socialism but in the (specific) structures and other aspects. The Emancipation of the Mind put forth at the Third Plenum is designed to overcome ideological alienation. The reform of economic and political structure . . . are intended to overcome economic and political alienation. . . . Understanding Marx's concept of alienation has great significance for promoting and guiding our current reform.[48]

Although Zhou was careful enough to say that alienation was not due to socialism, the very use of the concept appeared politically pernicious to conservative leaders. After some digging, Yu Qiuli revealed, they discovered a proliferation of writing on humanism and alienation in recent years and a few instances where alienation was directly attributed to socialism.[49] The political implications of this linkage gave the conservatives an edge in the ensuing leadership disputes over whether or not to launch a campaign against recent intellectual deviance. This factor, arguably, more than any other contributed to the success of the conservative lobbying. The power explanation that highlighted Deng Liqun's conflict with Hu Yaobang could not convincingly demonstrate why Deng Liqun, an ideological official at the lower rank of the party stratum than the general secretary, Hu Yaobang, could actually win over the latter. Nor could it completely explain why Deng Xiaoping would endorse an antiliberal campaign simply to acquiesce to Deng Liqun and other conservatives.[50] As the campaign against "spiritual pollution" unfolded after Deng's speech at the Second Plenum of the Twelfth Congress in October 1983, conservatives launched an overall assault on the general moral and ideological degeneration in recent times.[51] Revisionist discussions of humanism and alienation came under a focal attack. Wang Ruoshui, as a leading proponent of alienation who defied central orders to publish Zhou Yang's article in *Renmin ribao*, was dismissed from his deputy chief editorship. Hu Jiwei, head of *Renmin ribao*, lost his post as well.

In an authoritative article summing up the debate over humanism and alienation, Hu Qiaomu pinpointed the political significance of the recent intellectual interest in the two concepts. Fundamentally, he saw the assertion of the value of the person as advocacy for individual authority against the authority of society as represented by the state. The emphasis on intrinsic human value was counterposed to the socialist emphasis on class will, he noted. In linking alienation to socialism, he further argued, proponents of humanism and alienation were seeking to blame the injustices done to individuals and other problems of Chinese society on the repression of the individual will by the societal will. In this sense, the concepts of humanism and alienation challenged the ideological, economic, and political authority of the socialist state. Further, the idea of the "abstract person" (as opposed to the socially defined "actual person") espoused the bourgeois concept of the individual and, inevitably, the bourgeois form of democracy based on it.[52]

If Hu Qiaomu's analysis of the proponents' intentions was correct, then we may see the intellectual discussion of the concept of humans as an attempt to question China's "state system," that is, the class nature of the Chinese state. In the intellectual analysis, China's "political system" exhibited despotic and arbitrary tendencies because its state system justified the imposition of a "societal will"—one often determined by political leaders—on individuals. Hereby the deficiencies of the state system and the political system were linked: The nature of the state system had contributed to the problems of the political system. This analysis marked a step forward from the distinction earlier between the socialist system and socialist methods. But precisely because of this, it failed to gain official acceptance.

REFORM OF THE NONCOMMODITY MODEL OF THE POLITICAL SYSTEM

It was not until mid-1986 that political reform would again be placed on the political agenda and provoke a new round of political reassessment. Three major factors led to the resurrection of political reform at this juncture. First, Zhao Ziyang discovered in 1985 on an inspection tour in Wuhan that after urban reform was introduced in late 1984, the devolution of powers to enterprises had not really been achieved. Rather, the state and party apparatus at various levels sought to retain or reassert those powers. Further, the ambiguity between the authority of the manager and that of the party secretary in enterprises hampered the development of the autonomy of the manager encouraged by reform.[53]

Second, with the widening of economic reform since 1984, the reform leadership increasingly realized that economic reform could not be carried out alone. Urban reform was more complicated and all-encompassing than rural reform, affecting not only established institutions but social attitudes, interests, and the entire social fabric. In Zhao's words, urban reform was "a gigantic project involving the entire social system of extreme difficulty and complexity."[54]

Finally, increased economic corruption since urban reform had caused controversies at the top as to its causes and remedies. The reform leadership linked both to the political system. The conservative leadership, emphasizing the negative influences of the commodity economy and the opening to the outside, prescribed remedies with the traditional control mechanisms of ideological and disciplinary tightening. By initiating political reform, the reform leadership hoped to divert the blame from economic reform and to find long-term solutions.

Beginning in January 1986, Hu Yaobang began to prepare the ideological context for political reform by calling for the development of Marxism and the discarding of outdated concepts and theories. From June Deng Xiaoping also called repeatedly for the preparation of political reform. Other reform leaders made a series of speeches to mobilize public opinion. In July Wang Zhaoguo outlined the principles and direction of political reform. In August Wan Li discussed some contents of the envisioned political reform. It was clear from their statements that the immediate objectives were to overcome political obstacles to economic reform, improve efficiency in policy making and implementation, and raise people's initiative through a more open political process.[55] Although Hu Yaobang was known to have a genuine belief in promoting democracy and played a key role in putting political reform back on the agenda, the overall orientation of the official platform in 1986 was still to treat political reform more as a means than an end. This was especially so because a CCP Commission on Political Reform, established at Deng's recommendation, was staffed with more people who leaned toward Zhao's policy positions than those who leaned toward Hu Yaobang: Hu Qili, Tian Jiyun, and Peng Chong headed the commission while Bao Tong, Yan Jiaqi, Zhou Jie, and He Guanghui were its members.[56] Tian and the four members were close to Zhao.

The difference between Zhao and Hu Yaobang was one between a pragmatist and idealist within the same reform camp.[57] As the prime minister and the person who was responsible for the economy, Zhao emphasized the separation of party and state organs as the focus of political reform to help economic reforms. As the party's general secretary, however, Hu was concerned about the weakening of party organs by such a separation and emphasized a general democratization as the focus of political reform. Personal experience also contributed to their divergent approach. As a longtime grass-roots administrator, Zhao was concerned about concrete issues of economic well-being that were basic to the masses. As a longtime party official, Hu Yaobang was interested in issues of party ideology and organizational principles.[58] Hu's resistance to the separation of the party and the state, interestingly, put him in the conservative camp on this matter and also led to a little-known animosity between Zhao and Hu.

Whatever the leadership orientation and emphasis, they did not deter academic and media circles from seizing the occasion to address serious issues of political reform, or from going beyond the official framework. In particular, three developments in 1986 contributed to an unprecedented blooming of public discussion on the political system. The celebration of the thirtieth anniversary of the Hundred Flowers movement led the media and reform officials to encourage a climate of what Zhu Houze, the new CDP head, called "generosity, relaxation, and tolerance."[59] Then, on August 30, *Renmin ribao* publicized Wan Li's remark that "political questions can be discussed," thus removing the taboo on discussion of political issues.[60] Finally, the context of "developing Marxism" in 1986 helped to ease the fear of ideological stigmatizing. The result was a flood of symposiums, forums, and articles on political reform in the second half of 1986, constituting, as Harding observed, a design of political and ideological pluralism previously unseen in the history of the PRC.[61] Three groups of intellectuals led the public discussion: (1) those who worked in the Commission on Political Reform, such as Yan Jiaqi, whom some may link to Zhao as his intellectual supporter; (2) those who had been prominent intellectual articulators of reform, such as Su Shaozhi and Li Honglin at CASS, whom some may link to Hu Yaobang as his intellectual supporters; (3) and those who contributed to the discussion as social scientists, such as Wang Huning of Fudan University and Li Shengping of the Institute of Marxism-Leninism at CASS, both around thirty years old then. Whether or not these groups had any ties to the central leadership, they contributed to the discussion largely from their own perspectives rather than as supporters of particular leaders.[62]

Although the focus of 1986 was no longer the sources of past abuse but the political barriers to economic reform, public and intellectual discussions still probed into fundamental aspects of the political system. Because emphasis was now on the interaction between the economic and political system, rather than on the deficiency of the political system, intellectuals and reform theorists were able to transcend the constraints of the bifurcation between the state and the political system. Specifically, public discussions developed in three directions in 1986.

First, the question of political reform was approached from the point of why the political system had become a barrier to economic reform. Three major problems in economic reform prompted the inquiry. One was the "reassertion of economic powers" by state administrative organs after their supervising powers were supposedly devolved to the enterprise. Instead of streamlining, such state organs usually established trading companies through which to reassert lost powers. These new "administrative companies" sought to retain economic powers over the supply of inputs and rations and the distribution and sale of products. In this way, administrative organs continued to dominate enterprises under the now legitimate cover of trading companies. Through these, moreover, state functionaries could profit from the double-track price system by trading rationed inputs and scarce products. The practice subjected enterprises to continued administrative meddling and became a leading source of economic corruption.[63]

A second problem arose in the course of enterprise reforms over the role of factory managers versus that of party secretaries and/or party committees. Whereas formerly party organs exercised dominant control in the name of the "unified leadership" of the party, the new "factory manager responsibility system" was to delegate economic powers to the manager. In the course of the previous two years, serious conflicts had grown between managers and party organs over the appointment and dismissal of intermediate-level cadres at plants. While these powers belonged to managers under the reformed system, the party secretary was still responsible for "guaranteeing and supervising" these matters. While enterprises were to become relatively autonomous entities, they remained under the "leadership" of affiliated ministerial organs and local governments. These ambiguities created confusion about who had the final say in horizontal disputes (within enterprises) and vertical disputes (between enterprises and supervising authorities). For conservative officials, the transfer of power to managers threatened to erode the party's leadership. For many reformers, continued party participation in the economy amounted to interference in state affairs.[64]

A third problem concerned the role of local party organs versus local state organs in managing local economic affairs. Although party organs had been encouraged to stay away from economic and other affairs of the state apparatus, local party organs continued to perform administrative functions on behalf of local state organs under the pretext that the focus of the party's work was now economic construction. As a result, the problem of overconcentration of power persisted, while local state organs continued to have difficulty formulating their own differentiated and effective system of administration.[65]

The above three problems became the basis for questioning the political system. In the ensuing discussions, the first problem was attributed to the combination of political and economic functions in the state, while the other two to the lack of differentiation between the functions of the state and the party. Since reformers' attention in 1986 was on the linkage between political and economic structures, they saw the overconcentration of power as at least partly related to the planned economy. Central planning required not only strong political functions but also direct management of the economy through a highly centralized and multilayered administrative system. For Wang Huning, the central question was therefore one of changing the functions of the political system, the separation of the political and economic, and of the party and the state, in accordance with the replacement of the command economy by the commodity economy.[66]

In the administrative-command orientation entailed in the planned economy, reformist writers also saw the roots of some general problems of the political system, such as excessive bureaucracy and administrative inefficiency, dictatorial and arbitrary style of officials, and, above all, the lack of democracy and popular input in the policy process. In other words, a command economy had justified a strong central role in all spheres of society. Interestingly, this emphasis on the economic source of bureaucratism in the political system resembled Deng's observation in his 1980 speech on political reform, although this point was not pursued by Chinese theorists back then because of their different priorities at the time. In the discussion of 1986, however, the command economy as a source of bureaucratism and despotism became a major reference point around which reformers explored the deficiencies of the political system and the basis for reforming them. In the words of Su Shaozhi and Wang Yizhou, attention to the political consequences of the command economy pinned down a core "Stalinist" root of China's political system.[67]

Another angle from which the issue of political reform was approached in 1986 was the relation between economic modernization and political modernization. One-sided economic modernization was insufficient, many found, because many of the problems arising out of economic reform also stemmed from the lack of corresponding modernization of other spheres of society, especially traditional culture and the political system embedded in it. China's "premodern" cultural legacy was now summarily referred to as the "feudal legacy," "feudalistic influences," or "feudal ideology."[68] Su Shaozhi, a leading critic of the "feudal" aspects of Chinese politics, linked the surge of economic corruption since reform primarily to "feudal influences." Such phenomena as cadres' children going into business with favorable access, obtaining licenses and ration privileges through official ties, smuggling regulated goods with immunity, and speculating in scarce goods and foreign currencies all resulted from the "feudal" vestiges of official privilege, nepotism and cronyism. Economic corruption should not be blamed on the "enterprising spirit" of capitalism, he suggested, because those corrupt business activities exhibited not the commodity relations of capitalism but the patriarchal relations of "feudalism."[69]

Su and others also extended this criticism to some larger problems of the political system. At the heart of official abuse of power, they claimed, was the lack of popular and institutional control over powerholders. Official privilege was but one manifestation of a strong "feudal legacy" intimately related to the overconcentration of power and the lack of democracy. In this regard, they found that many aspects of the Chinese political system were "feudalistic" in nature: the unequal status between leaders and subordinates, rule by a few sagacious emperors, "uniformity of thinking" (*da yi tong*), hierarchy in social relations, lack of checks against absolute power, and the lack of citizen rights and rule of law. Common practices and work styles among officials were also seen to be heavily tainted with "feudal influences," for example, autocratic and patriarchal leadership style, subordination of law to power, paternalism, factionalism, clan mentality, neglect of science and talent, and nepotism in official appointments. At the level of the masses, lingering feudalistic orientations included the belief in "holy emperor," a dependent psychology, a tolerance of "god's misdeeds," tolerance of political despotism but not social disparity, conservatism and conventionality, backwardness and ignorance, and fear of change and competition.[70]

These analyses again coincided with Deng's analysis in 1980 that "feudal" remnants were among the important causes of the problems of the political system. But reform theorists moved further in 1986 by pondering the basis of lingering "feudalism." From the interaction between economic and political structures, they found that the persistence of the "feudal" ideology and superstructure was due to the persistence of the feudal economic base. This meant that the traditional small-scale, self-sufficient peasant economy continued to have its hold on society after the establishment of socialist economy. The conclusion drawn from the discussion of the political system from the modernization perspective was clear: To uproot the economic base of the "feudal" legacy, China must develop the commodity economy and its associated values that would facilitate political modernization.[71]

Still another angle from which the political system was reassessed in 1986 was the "development of Marxism," a favorite platform of Hu Yaobang aimed at a more flexible approach to Marxist and non-Marxist theories. One distinct theme in this discussion was the need to absorb the "cultural achievements" of other civilizations, especially those outside the Marxist system of thought. In the words of Zhu Houze, recently promoted from among Hu's political base, Marx's theories were originally formulated on the basis of non-Marxist materials, and so the development of Marxism should not be limited in a self-enclosed framework of Marxist theories. The positive ideas of even the bourgeoisie may be adopted and used for socialist society.[72] In the context of 1986, special attention was given to political concepts from the world outside Marxism. One reform leader singled out the ideas of freedom, democracy, human rights, and humanism. If these ideas were dismissed as unacceptable because of their bourgeois origins, he asked, "What's there left for socialism?" Would socialism only talk about "dictatorship, punishment, and struggle"? How would the "superiority of socialism" be exhibited then?[73]

Several factors led Chinese reformers to see these concepts as not exclusively bourgeois in 1986. First, many of those concepts, Su Shaozhi argued, were put forth during the French Revolution by both the bourgeoisie and the working class. Second, they were developed in the struggle of the rising bourgeoisie against feudalism, a task that precisely faced China at present. Finally, political democracy was a concomitant result of the market economy.[74] The implication was that if democracy was a common aspiration of rising social groups against feudalism and a requirement of the market economy, the class nature of democracy had been overemphasized in the past. Nonetheless, there was only open endorsement of the electoral system, the system of checks and balances, and rule of law, not the more sensitive multiparty system.

In short, the dominant themes of the reassessment of the socialist political system in 1986 centered on the newly found link between the market economy and political democracy. Since small-scale peasant production, the planned economy, and the indiscriminate exclusion of bourgeois concepts had contributed to the failure to develop democracy, many reformers believed, it was the central task of political reform to overcome these problems.

This direction of reassessment was insufficient for some more radical intellectuals. Emboldened by the political atmosphere of 1986, a few of them ventured to push the discourse further. Though they were not the sole proponents in 1986, Fang Lizhi and Wang Ruowang—the former the head of the Chinese University of Science and Technology in Anhui and the latter a writer in Shanghai—were the most vocal spokespersons of a negative political reappraisal. In the course of 1986 each made a series of speeches on university campuses and in other public forums that later earned them the label "instigators" of bourgeois liberalization. Unlike mainstream reform theorists, Fang and Wang directly referred to the political system as "modern feudalism." Fang saw the preeminent feature of Chinese "feudalism" as the combination of political power and moral authority in the state, which, he asserted, continued to exist under CCP rule. For him the socialist system was basically the old "autocracy and despotism" under a new nationalistic cover. Wang also saw in the PRC a basically "feudal regime painted with a socialist face." He complained that the discussion of political reform thus far had failed to touch on the essence of the matter, namely, the party's leadership. Both Fang and Wang called for the importation of the Western political system and particularly American-style democracy, including the multiparty system and the general capitalist system.[75]

At the other end, the growing obliteration of the distinction between socialist and bourgeois democracy was exactly what worried the conservative leadership. During the drafting of a central document on "socialist spiritual civilization," which went on from January through the fall and was to provide guidelines for political and ideological reforms, a heated controversy arose between conservative and reformist officials over the insertion of a refutation of bourgeois liberalization. The phrase referred to the "negation of the socialist system and the advocacy of the capitalist system" that could apply narrowly to outspoken liberals like Fang and Wang but more broadly to reform theorists as well. Reform leaders headed by Hu Yaobang opposed the insertion as insistently as veteran leaders objected to its exclusion. Unlike his stance on such controversies over economic matters, Deng eventually endorsed the position of conservative reformers, thus resolving the issue in favor of the latter group.

On other key issues of political reform as well, the resolution that emerged from the political negotiations and was adopted in September contained compromises endorsing political change, on the one hand, and defining its boundaries, on the other. The document affirmed the concepts of democracy, liberty, and equality but emphasized the need to "critically inherit" these bourgeois ideas. Marxist versions of these concepts, the resolution stated, were different from the bourgeois ones "in principle." The document endorsed the promotion of democracy as the goal of political reform but placed it under the "party's leadership" and the "people's democratic dictatorship." It endorsed the general direction of political reform but offered no specific program as desired by radical reformers.[76]

The high expectation for change generated by the discussions of the summer and the ensuing disappointment with the resolution soon set off a wave of student demonstrations across the country at the end of 1986. The demonstrations started in the city of Wuhan over poor food and shelter on campus but quickly spread in Anhui and Shanghai, where Fang and Wang had made most of their recent speeches. Eventually students' calls converged over demands for a faster implementation of political reform and for freedom and democracy, sometimes of the Western type. These protests confirmed conservative leaders' misgivings about continued dangers of bourgeois liberalization.[77] Again with the backing of Deng, these leaders launched a crackdown on the demonstrations and a political campaign against recent bourgeois liberalization. Not only were the more outspoken Fang Lizhi, Wang Ruowang, and journalist Liu Binyan expelled from the party, but some of the most prominent reform theorists since 1978, such as Su Shaozhi, Li Honglin, Zhang Xiangyang, Yu Haocheng, Wang Ruoshui, and Sun Changjiang, were either demoted or expelled from the party. Hu Yaobang was dismissed as the general secretary of the CCP for his tolerance of bourgeois liberalization and, in particular, for his objection to a repudiation of bourgeois liberalization in the resolution on spiritual civilization.[78] But Zhao Ziyang may also have played a role in Hu's downfall, because of Hu's opposition to separation of the party and the state. At the very least, Zhao did not try to help Hu.[79]

In the ensuing campaign against bourgeois liberalization in early 1987, conservative critics disparaged recent discussions of both reform theorists and "abolitionists" like Fang and Wang. They complained that discussions of democracy and liberty had been "abstract," that is, making no distinction between the nature and form of democracy, so that bourgeois democracy was one-sidedly propagated as "democratic" whereas its real "monetary" nature was deliberately ignored. In a series of commentaries on the student demonstrations, Deng concurred with the distinction between two kinds of democracy and reiterated that the kind promoted by the party was not the Western bourgeois type. Conservative critics also dismissed the analysis of the "feudal despotic" feature of the political system as indiscriminate and political, as it groundlessly equated the basis of socialism to feudalism.[80] Furthermore, because political reform was ostensibly necessitated by economic reform, some conservative officials and critics extended their attacks to the economic realm. Arguing that the "deeper roots" of bourgeois liberalization lay in economic liberalization, they complained that only those who talked about bourgeois liberalization were being opposed (namely, Hu Yaobang), while those who practiced it were not (namely, Zhao Ziyang). Opposition to liberalization on the political front, in short, must be accompanied by similar efforts on the economic front.[81]

In sum, radical reformers' political reassessment and their argumentation for political reform from the economic perspective failed to secure them a solid framework of political discourse and action. Conservative reformers still refused to see any link between China's economic base and its political system. As for Deng, though he seemed to recognize the linkage, he apparently saw political reform in instrumental terms: it was desirable as long as it promoted economic development but not so if it threatened the stable environment for such development.

The Frontal Attack on the "Totalist" State

The need for continuing economic reform put political reform back on the agenda a hundred days after the start of the antiliberal campaign. Twice in April 1987 Deng signified his support for resuming economic reform by talking to visiting foreign delegations about "poverty is not socialism." In June he directly urged accelerating economic reform and resuming political reform, a month after Zhao Ziyang's May 13 speech at a meeting of officials from ideology and media circles, made with Deng's endorsement.

In the speech, Zhao responded to the recent attacks by conservative officials and critics. On political reform, Zhao criticized those who took the anti–bourgeois liberal campaign to mean that political reform would no longer be carried out; those who equated the separation of the party and the state with the negation of the party's leadership; and those who regarded the advocacy of democracy as bourgeois liberalization. In response, he placed "reform and opening" (known as the "two basic points") on a par with the Four Fundamental Principles. He also announced that political reform was to be an important agenda item of the Thirteenth Congress.[82] In the following month, *Renmin ribao* carried two editorials to publicize the content of Zhao's speech. The change of tone at the top soon put conservative critics on the defensive and reform theorists back on the offensive. As conservative officials would later complain, the proliferation of bourgeois liberal trends in the late 1980s began with Zhao's "suppression" of the 1987 antiliberal campaign.

The objective of political reform nonetheless remained unchanged for Deng and Zhao: to create a political environment conducive to the commodity economy. In Deng's words, political reform was to help strengthen the "party's leadership" and the development of "production forces." Democracy was not part of the objective but an "important means" of reform.[83] In a speech outlining his political reform program shortly before the Thirteenth Congress, Zhao stressed some of the same issues that led to the political reform discussion in 1986—the separation of the party and the state, the change of their functions, and the implementation of the manager responsibility system.[84] The agenda of Hu Yaobang and Zhu Houze in 1986 was visibly absent. In his political report to the Thirteenth Congress, Zhao continued to speak of political reform in terms of replacing a wartime legacy unsuited for peacetime modernization efforts and a socialist commodity economy. Socialist democracy was a long-term goal to be achieved through a gradually evolving process. The report adopted the program proposed by the Commission on Political Reform, created in 1986. It emphasized the separation of the party and the state, an agenda originally opposed by Hu Yaobang.[85]

Still, the favorable climate surrounding the Thirteenth Congress sparked a renewal of public discussion of political reform. With the consolidation of Zhao's leadership at the Thirteenth Congress and an ideological context of "reconceptualizing socialism," the tone and content of public discussions soon returned to the levels of 1986. With the onset of the economic and corruption crisis in mid-1988, moreover, these discussions took a drastic turn that was to develop into a comprehensive reassessment of the political system by intellectuals and reform theorists on their own initiative.

The impetus for the new round of reassessment was the need to diagnose the causes of the economic crisis and to refute conservative leaders' assault of the market and of Zhao's leadership. Attention was again turned to the political system because, in the view of some reform theorists, none of the immediate causes of the economic crisis and corruption was inherent to the market, that is, the monopoly of market channels by officials, unfair and ruleless competition fueled by access to office, and the combination of the official and the capitalist. For these theorists, the economic crisis was due to the failed emergence of a genuine market rather than the existence of one. Although some of the same factors fueled the examination of the political system in 1986, intellectuals and reform theorists went further this time.

For some, such as Sun Liping, Li Ming, and others who were not members of Zhao's "brain trust," the reform designs and priorities of the center were part of the problem. That is, the order and nature of the reform program was at the root of the economic crisis and cadre corruption. Premised on the primacy of economic reform, this program avoided the political aspects of the old economic system. Because the problems of the planned economy did not reside in the economic system alone, however, market mechanisms introduced after reform still could not function as expected. This was belatedly recognized by reform leaders, but their political reform agenda remained ill premised by stressing the separation of the party and the state and their adaptation to the market. The underlying assumption was that if party and state functions were adapted, a genuine market would inevitably develop, and this market would in turn lead to political democracy. Yet for the critics of this reform program, including the famous Hu Jiwei, the sequence should be reversed: In a political context where the agents of the old apparatus refused to renounce old functions, political democracy must be a precondition rather than a result of the commodity economy. If there were no prior democratic reforms, party and state functions could not change.[86]

The lack of a democratic political system was held responsible for the economic crisis and corruption in another sense. The design of the faulty reform program was blamed on the very lack of democratic input in the policy-making process. On the one hand, reform policy-making was limited to a small circle of Zhao's brain trust, whose main concern was the transition to a commodity economy. Even after the economic crisis of 1988, their favored program continued to be enterprise and price reforms. The major criticism against such a program was that the previous ownership and price system were embodied in multilayered state agencies, and that they could not be truly transformed without prior reduction of the agencies representing them.[87] At the same time, Hu Jiwei cited the lack of media openness—another major deficiency of the political system—about policy-making errors, including those of Zhao, as contributing to the failure to contain economic chaos and cadre corruption.[88]

Reform theorists on Zhao's brain trust team, such as Yan Jiaqi and Cao Siyuan, did place the blame on the political system, but not on the reform leadership or the sequence of reform. For them, the problem was not just the persistence of the old administrative strata but the absence of built-in limitations against the absolute political power. In a departure from Zhao, they argued that reform was a matter not just of adapting old party and state functions but also of checking the behavior of officials under a system of undefined and unlimited powers. Along this line, they criticized the conservative insistence on traditional methods of control, namely, ideological education, administrative command, and mass campaigns, which had lost efficacy in the wake of the Cultural Revolution and now served to delay the development of institutional and legal mechanisms of control.[89]

Despite the variation in emphasis, reform theorists within and outside Zhao's circle concurred on the determining role of the political realm in the Chinese context. The emphasis of both groups was no longer the interaction between the economic and political spheres, or the contributing role of economic reform to political reform. Rather, the consensus was that because the state combined most functions of society in itself, it controlled the economic and other spheres of society. Many leading intellectuals, such as Yan Jiaqi, Su Shaozhi, Wang Yizhou, and younger ones Li Ming and Han Kang, used Tang Tsou's term "totalism" to describe the phenomenon.[90] In this analysis, political reform must take precedence over other reforms.

Another aspect of the public discussions of political reform from 1988 to mid-1989 centered on the analysis of what to do with the ongoing economic crisis and cadre corruption, which, like the diagnosis of the crisis itself, reflected the analysts' basic assessment of the political system. Overall, the public discussions disagreed with the central leadership's response to the crisis. The center's response was twofold. The conservative approach called for Zhao's resignation as the general secretary, a retreat from economic reforms, and a crackdown on corruption. The last two measures were carried out in the fall and winter of 1988. The reformist approach was to defend Zhao's leadership and policy with a new legitimating theory summed up under the idea of "neo-authoritarianism," proposed by some of Zhao's advisers and allies, among whom Wu Jiaxiang, a junior member of the Office of the CCP Central Committee, was a chief proponent.

Neo-authoritarianism defended Zhao by arguing that economic transition must precede political democratization and that the separation of the economic and political spheres must remain the immediate goal of political reform. To achieve both, the leadership must have sufficient "authoritative power" to eliminate structural and human barriers. The period of transition to the market was therefore to be marked by strong central power in politics but its renunciation in the economy. The resultant economic development and interest pluralization, so the theory argued, would eventually lead to political democratization.[91] This new authoritarianism was partly aimed at strengthening Zhao's leadership so as to press through with the unpopular price reform and to withstand the conservative assault. Wu Jiaxiang overtly objected to the immediate implementation of democracy because elected representatives of special interests might seek to damage or avoid the creation of a healthy market. Chen Yizi, Wang Xiaojiang, and a few other members of Zhao's brain trust advocated "elite democracy," referring to the replacement of senior policymakers with young, knowledgeable, modern-minded elites like themselves.[92]

For intellectuals and reform theorists, both the immediate remedy for the economic crisis and the long-term solution to China's political order was political democratization. Outside Zhao's circle, Li Ming (of the CASS Institute of Philosophy) and Hu Jiwei called for an immediate slowing down of economic reform and the "running ahead" (*chao qian*) of political reform.[93] Among those more closely associated with the reform leadership, Yan Jiaqi favored concurrent "political democratization," "ideological pluralization," and "economic privatization."[94] But "political democratization" was still the top priority even for the latter group, directed pointedly at conservative leaders who were trying to deal with the economic crisis by a coup against Zhao and by old command measures. From these conservative maneuvers, Yan and Su, along with prominent theorists Cao Siyuan and Wang Yizhou, saw the deeper patterns of Chinese politics that not only threatened current reforms but were also responsible for the major mistakes and tragedies in the history of the People's Republic. These patterns were summarily referred to as "nonprocedural politics," that is, the absence of institutionalized procedures for policy-making, for the transfer of leadership, and for the resolution of conflicts among political actors. They were seen as the major deficiencies of the political system that only genuine democracy could eradicate.[95]

If these analyses were still largely prompted by the problems of economic reform, a series of developments in late 1988 finally turned intellectuals and reform theorists to view the issue of democracy as an inherent need of political life, not just a necessary condition for economic development or for redressing past wrongs. The trend began with reaction against the veteran leader Wang Zhen's criticism of the television series "River Elegy" at the Third Plenum of the Thirteenth Congress in September.[96]

Scripted by the writer Su Xiaokang, "River Elegy" was a documentary of contemporary Chinese introspection on the flaws of Chinese culture that had served to hold the country back in modern history, especially vis-à-vis the advent of the West. Su Xiaokang used Marx's theory of the Asiatic mode of production as a central theme of the piece, placing implicit blame on political "despotism" and the weakness of capitalism for China's lagging behind. Although Wang's remarks came too late to ban Su's work from the public, they caused an uproar among writers and artists who feared ideological tightening.

Indeed, Wang's criticism signified the beginning of a conservative offensive to reassert control over leading academic and cultural realms. At the symposium in memory of the decennial of the Third Plenum, organized by the now conservative-staffed CDP in mid-December, a number of leading reform theorists, such as Yu Guangyuan, Wang Ruoshui, Tong Dalin, and Su Shaozhi—some of whom were closely associated with Zhao—were invited not as regular attendees but as "special invitees" who had "erred before." Others were simply excluded from the meeting. Although most of them refused to attend, organizers of the symposium still controlled its content and exchange among participants. But Su Shaozhi, the only "special invitee" who showed up, gave a speech in which he attacked the 1987 campaign against bourgeois liberalization, the self-styled Marxist-Leninists who suppressed freedom of expression, and the treatment of Marxism-Leninism as a taboo subject. The CDP, infuriated by Su's speech and its subsequent publication by *Shijie jingji daobao* despite CDP warnings, threatened to take action against him.

In late December Yu Guangyuan, Wang Ruoshui, Su Shaozhi, Yu Haocheng, Yan Jiaqi, and other leading theorists gathered at a cultural symposium to complain about the "cultural squeeze" being enforced by the conservative leadership. Under the editorship of Hu Jiwei, they commemorated the Third Plenum and the truth debate of 1978 with a collection of essays, *Mengxin de shike* (The moment of sudden awakening), with the theme of opposing ideological monopoly. Meanwhile Hu Jiwei also began to edit two book series on the theory and practice of democracy. A magazine called *Xin qimeng* (New enlightenment) made its debut in October, having evaded the censor system for periodicals by registering as a book series. Contributors during its brief existence included well-known theorists Bao Zunxin, Jin Guantao, Li Honglin, Yu Haocheng, and the maverick and would-be activist in the 1989 Tiananmen protests Liu Xiaobo. Early 1989 saw the decennial of the Democracy Wall movement, at which Fang Lizhi led a series of petition movements to ask for the release of Wei Jinsheng and other dissidents.

The direction of these developments placed the question of the treatment of the individual under socialism back at the center of political reappraisal. For reform theorists and intellectuals, at the heart of the intellectual insurgence against the recent conservative tightening was the issue of citizens' rights versus the authority of the party. Following this theme, public discussions developed along three major lines. First, the value of democracy was explored for its own sake, which, many now found, was the guarantee of the intrinsic value of individual human beings and their full development and expression. Second, in the efforts to reopen the discussion of humanism and alienation under socialism, Hu Qiaomu's authority in arbitrating the debate in his 1984 article was challenged. Finally, from the discussion of the rights of individuals and the diversity of human beings, the thesis of a "diversity of truth" began to emerge as a rationale for pluralistic democracy.

The intellectual insurgence subjected Zhao Ziyang to additional conservative attacks. Throughout late 1988 and early 1989, veteran leaders criticized Zhao for his ideological laxity and his weakness in fighting corruption. For example, Zhao refused to watch any movies for the purpose of censorship, and he gave indirect protection to "River Elegy" by offering a copy to a visiting foreign prime minister. He also indulged corruption by arguing that it was an inevitable part of the transition to the market. Conservatives were most resentful of his tolerance of restive intellectuals, many of whom were under his umbrella. Thus Bo Yibo complained about Zhao's tolerance for "vicious" attacks on the party by "rightist intellectuals." Wang Zhen saw Zhao's ideological and political lines as "basically a little to the right." Chen Yun faulted Zhao for the failure to handle "public opinion, ideological and theoretical work" properly and suggested that "the proletarian ideological position has now been almost completely lost to and occupied by various bourgeois factions." Hu Qiaomu's complaints in February 1989 best reflected the conservative mood: "The political differences between ourselves and Comrade Zhao Ziyang came to light in May 1987. Whether or not we should oppose bourgeois liberalization and whether or not a tendency toward bourgeois liberalization exists within the party are major matters of political principle. If we acted strictly in accordance with Comrade Deng Xiaoping's instructions two years ago, the situation within the party and in the country, I think, would not have become so chaotic."[97] To placate conservatives, Zhao made a series of efforts at the end of 1988 and the beginning of 1989 to strengthen "party building." To sustain Deng's patronage, he took a cautious stand toward intellectuals' call for political reform to deal with economic problems and corruption.[98]

The Tiananmen protests of mid-1989 broke out against this backdrop of a general crisis of reform and an intellectual challenge to the political system. The two phases of the protest movement reflected the themes of the political reform discussion of late 1988 and early 1989. In the first phase, that is, before *Renmin ribao*'s editorial of April 26, students demanded a repudiation of the party's last antiliberal campaign and the rehabilitation of its victims. After the editorial, which warned against a minority of people instigating "turmoil" and violating the Four Fundamental Principles, students shifted their focus to cadre corruption. The new emphasis did not go beyond the party's leadership or socialism. Politically legitimate and outreaching, it was instrumental in rallying mass involvement in Beijing and widespread support elsewhere, leading to the second or popular phase of the movement. Many themes in recent discussions of political reform were echoed in both phases of the movement, for example, the party's authority to launch antiliberal campaigns, "procedural" politics through dialogue and the People's Congress, unlimited power of officials, sources of China's backwardness, and, most of all, media openness and democratic controls to redress official corruption and problems in economic reform. Still, in both phases of the protests, participants as a whole refrained from advancing any calls that violated the Four Fundamental Principles, though antiparty and antisocialist slogans were occasionally seen or heard.

Nonetheless, the post–June 4 leadership blamed the outbreak of the movement on the surge of bourgeois liberalization since September 1988. In the words of Wang Renzhi and Wu Shuqing, the protests represented the culmination of ideological confusion among the youth created by a handful of "instigators," who consisted of the leading reform theorists, radical intellectuals, and other active participants in reform discussions in recent years.[99] This confusion had allegedly been manifested in these aspects. First, those discussions linked recent corruption to the political system, obscuring the distinction between a majority of good cadres and the misdeeds of a few. As a result, some protesters sought to overthrow the entire system on the pretext of eradicating corruption. Second, the discussions obscured the class nature of democracy and the distinction between socialist and bourgeois democracy. This created a climate in which class consciousness was abandoned, a situation conservatives found perilous after the "counterrevolutionary riot" of early June. In short, the intellectual advocacy of unqualified democracy was faulted as the inspiration for the student movement of 1989.[100]

Not surprisingly, many of the intellectual activists of 1988–89 who were discussed earlier, whether or not they played any direct role in Tiananmen, were either arrested, forced into exile, or criticized after June 4. *Shijie jingji daobao* and *Jingjixue zhoukan*, which published many radical views in 1988–89, were closed down. The two editors of the latter paper, Chen Ziming and Wang Juntao, received the longest sentences among those arrested after the crackdown. Conservative theorists, who complained about the earlier monopoly of the media by reformers, now embraced the opportunity to criticize systematically the reform theorists and to engineer a return to the class view of democracy. Some of Deng Liqun's allies and supporters, such as Wang Renzhi, Xu Weicheng, and He Jingzhi, were promoted to head the CDP. Wu Shuqing became the new president of Beijing University, the hotbed of student unrest. Gao Di became the head of *Renmin ribao*.

Political reform obviously became a touchy issue after the Tiananmen episode. Rather than political reform, Deng Liqun began to talk about "class contradictions" and "class struggle," terms that had almost disappeared from public discourse only a short while before.[101] Jiang Zemin did not even mention "political reform" in his report on the seventieth anniversary of the CCP in July 1991. Instead he spoke of "dictatorship of the proletariat," another term rarely seen in recent years.[102] His emphasis as well as that of the party in general was now on improving the party's relationship with the masses and on "party construction" (*tang de jianshe*), both important issues after Tiananmen.[103] But all these did not mean that discussion of political reform was prohibited. In fact, the Central Party School published a book in 1991, *The Political Program of Chinese Socialist Democracy*, whose arguments corresponded closely to the reformist discussions in 1986.[104] In his southern talks in the spring of 1992, Deng Xiaoping too avoided touching on political reform. "Political reform" did finally reappear in Jiang's report to the Fourteenth Congress in October 1992, but obviously not as part of a prior agenda. The congress stimulated little public discussion of political reform or related reform measures.

CONCLUSION

The post-Mao reassessment of the political system evolved in a direction similar to that of the economic system, but in a markedly different manner. As in the economic domain, the political reappraisal generated much controversy among leading groups over the nature of the problems and the type of appropriate remedies. It evolved from critical analyses of mistaken Chinese practices in the late 1970s to that of fundamental errors in the political system in the late 1980s. But unlike in the economic domain, the course of political appraisal had been much more tortuous and contentious. Much more often than in the economic sphere, reform theorists, intellectuals, and social critics formed a distinct voice independent of the political leadership that encouraged political discussions from time to time.

In the economic sphere, reform theorists and intellectuals usually enjoyed the support of reform leaders, who not only elicited but also utilized intellectual contributions in policy-making or in policy battles. They enjoyed leadership support even in periods of intense controversy and contention, for reform leaders had both the consensus and the determination to rectify the sources of past failures, to overcome the limits in the basic confines of socialism, and to prevail over the conservative leadership. As a result, intellectual discourse largely fitted into the orientation and framework of the reform leadership, except for that of the liberal reformers in the late 1980s. It formed part and parcel of the mainstream analyses acceptable to the reform leadership who dominated the policy arena in most periods throughout the post-Mao era.

In the political realm, however, the reform leadership's political support for intellectual efforts and its endorsement of intellectual views were not matched nearly as well. Serious discussions of past theory and practice were still invited, but constrained each time it had gone too far. Radical reform leaders either had to compromise under pressure from conservative forces, as in the campaigns of 1979, 1981, and 1983, or risked political reprisals, as in the crackdowns of 1987 and 1989. Despite a common definition of "bourgeois liberalization" and a set of compromises on political and intellectual discourse made between conservative and reformist leaders in the resolution of 1986, the distinction between within-system reappraisal and dissidence became increasingly blurred: While the campaign of 1979 was delivered at dissidents, later campaigns were aimed at intellectuals both within and outside the system. Hence in the political domain, three distinct groups—rather than the two dominant ones in the economic domain—battled over how to reevaluate the Chinese political system throughout the post-Mao period: the conservatives, the official reformers, and the intellectual/social critics.

Why did the reassessment of the political system evolve differently? Why did political leaders respond differently to intellectual discussions on the political system? One factor was the policy priority of the reform leadership. Although Hu Yaobang was genuinely concerned with political change to avoid the recurrence of the Cultural Revolution and other abuses, Deng and Zhao were preoccupied with economic modernization. From the beginning Deng recognized that the deficiencies in the political system were conducive to bureaucratism and the overconcentration of power. In the course of economic reform, Zhao and Deng also came to see incompatibilities between the political system and the desired economic order. But they still subordinated political reform to the goals of raising systemic and economic efficiency.

The evolution of the political reassessment also showed that the group of leaders who sponsored economic reappraisal were ideologically immobilized in the political realm. In the former domain, they were willing to confront systemic problems because this did not threaten the legitimacy of the regime as a whole. Buttressed by dialectical and historical materialism, even Marx's original theories could be modified to suit "Chinese characteristics." In the political domain, however, to face the systemic problems would threaten the foundations of the regime's legitimacy. The critics of 1979–81 called into question such milestones of the Chinese socialist movement as the Cultural Revolution, the Great Leap Forward, and Mao's leadership and Mao Zedong Thought: all important parts of the party's legacy. The critics of 1986 and 1988–89 called into question such basic characteristics of the political system as the all-embracing functions of the state and the absolute power of officeholders. What is important about these inquiries is not that those issues were raised, but that they were linked to the socialist system.

The political contention within the leadership also had an important impact on the course of the political reassessment. The whatever group had good reasons for urging the suppression of the Democracy Wall activists and other critics in 1979 and 1981, because the probing into the systemic sources of Mao's personality cult and arbitrary rule threatened their rise to power in the last stage of the Mao era. This group could also use the emergence of ideological deviance against the practice group, whose reversal of the Mao line spurred that deviance in the first place. Conservative reformers were mainly concerned with the return to genuine socialism and the correction of its distortions. Their vision of socialism consisted largely of the Soviet model that they cherished before the Cultural Revolution. This vision, in Baum's characterization, was but the post-Stalinist tradition of socialist democracy and legality.[105] But unlike in the economic realm, this group was ideologically mobilized in the political domain because of the Four Fundamental Principles and because of the party's concern with its monopoly on power and with political stability. As a result, they were able to use these concerns to circumvent the direction of public discussions, as they did in 1983, 1987, and 1989. By demonstrating the danger of political liberalization, they could at least temporarily impose their political agenda.

In the final analysis, conservative and radical reformers shared a view of the noncompeting nature of the political system. For the former group, this was symbolized in the "class nature" of the socialist state and democracy. For the latter group, this class nature was increasingly irrelevant, but a pluralistic political order was no acceptable substitute because of its perceived individualistic and anarchic orientations. In this context, neither the assertion of individual human value, nor the requirements of a commodity economy, nor the necessity of checks on political power was sufficient to secure a rationale for a fundamental rethinking of the socialist political system.

CHAPTER SIX

The Reassessment of the Socialist Political System

THE POST-MAO reassessment of the political system took a more difficult route than that of the economic system. It has also not been translated as much into practice. Nonetheless, in the evolving search for the sources of and solutions to past abuses and failures, many important issues were raised concerning the problems of the socialist political order. This chapter discusses these substantive issues. It draws mainly on the discourse of mainstream reform theorists and intellectuals, who carried out the bulk of the discussions. Although their discourse has not been always endorsed by the reform leadership and has often been rejected by the conservative leadership, the reassessment itself has been encouraged and often tolerated by the reform leadership. In this sense, it reflects the major directions of the post-Mao political reassessment. The chapter also draws from the statements of political leaders and other officials on political reform.

VIEWS FROM THE FOUNDING FATHERS

The founding fathers of scientific socialism had said very little about the two aspects of the socialist political system that interested Chinese reformers, that is, the nature and forms of the proletarian state. Both Marx and Engels did elaborate generally on the theory of the state, which, along with their theory of revolution, became the basis of Communist doctrine on this matter. One Marxist conception views the state as part of a superstructure that is determined by the economic base of a given society. The essence of the state, in this view, is its role as an instrument of class rule.[1] The nature of the bourgeois state is thus a dictatorship of the bourgeoisie against the proletariat. Parallel to this conception is Marx's treatment of the state as a symptom of alienation, a condition enabling class exploitation, with its sources in the material conflicts of the bourgeois society.[2] After the overthrow of bourgeois rule, the proletariat must establish its own dictatorship, at least in the transitional period, to bring about the "revolutionary transformation" of capitalist society into a communist one.[3] The new state would be proletarian in nature in terms of its relationship to social class. It may be inferred here that the new state ceases to be a form of alienated life.

Marx's conception of the state is more complex than its simple designation as class dictatorship, however. In his earlier works, he exhibited uncertainty about the relationship of the state to social class. Of several "possible relations" between the state and the dominant economic class he studied, the state could be relatively autonomous of class and society.[4] In one early work, Marx noted the tendency of any state to arrogate to itself powers beyond those originally delegated to it by the society that created it. In another work, he observed the extraordinary preponderance of the state over society under Oriental despotism.[5] These insights have two implications for the new proletarian state. First, this state can also become autonomous of the society that created it. That is, it is capable of imposing its will on society, including the proletariat. Second, this state can perform services other than those for a single dominant class. That is, even a proletarian state, because of its autonomy inherent in the very nature of the state, is capable of serving the interest of society as a whole. Unfortunately, these insights received little attention in the CCP doctrine. Its narrow conception of the state as class dictatorship was influenced by the manner and timing in which Marxism was introduced to China—through Bolshevik Russia—and by the lack of access to Marx's earlier works.[6]

As for the specific forms of the proletarian state, Marx and Engels had said even less. But one thing seems clear from Marx's analysis of the bourgeois state: He found the form of the political state less significant than its class nature. For him even a "democratic republican state" cannot really liberate the individual and eliminate alienation, because class and other material differences remained beneath the institutional structures of the state. "*Political* emancipation" represents a great progress for Marx, but it was not "the final form of human emancipation," for it was only emancipation within "the prevailing social order." True freedom would be achieved only when the social order that produced alienation had been eliminated.[7] It follows, therefore, that if the new state can transcend private property and class differences, the proletarian nature of this state is more crucial than how its power is exercised. This emphasis does not prove Marx's neglect of the form of proletarian rule, but it certainly lends support to greater attention to the class nature of the new state.

Empirical conditions led Lenin to address the questions of both the nature and the form of the new state, although his contributions were conditioned by objective circumstances. In *State and Revolution*, written in response to the sudden prospect of a successful Bolshevik revolution, Lenin elaborated on the postrevolutionary state. Here he followed the narrow conception of the state as an instrument of class rule, extracted from the texts of mature Marxism. From the oppressive nature of the bourgeois state in Russia, he stressed the need to destroy the old state apparatus and to replace it with proletarian rule.[8]

Elsewhere, Lenin considered the structures of the new proletarian rule.

Before the October Revolution, he envisioned a form of government called the soviet, with an armed force of workers and peasants closely tied to and easily supervised by the people, a body of officials duly selected by popular election, and a close relation with different trades and professions. Although his idea of the vanguard party, developed earlier as an instrument of revolution, showed disregard for ordinary workers, Lenin ascribed to it benign functions in the new state. The vanguard party would mobilize, educate, and lead the people so as to integrate them into political life and to combine the parliamentary system with direct democracy. That is, the people's representatives would perform both legislative and executive functions. Despite the element of the party, Lenin embraced the idea of workers' self-government, as reflected in the well-known slogan "all power to the Soviet."[9]

Objective constraints led Lenin to alter his theory in practice. Once the party seized power and established the soviet, he discovered that governing various spheres of society was more complicated than he had thought and that direct self-government by workers was neither possible nor practical. This realization was enhanced in the civil war of 1918, when domestic and foreign pressures led him to modify his vision of the soviet rule and to stress centralization in several areas. Government by the whole people was changed to that by the vanguard party. The power of the Central Party Committee was expanded, and the soviet structures were subordinated to party structures. Democratic centralism became the new governing principle. A vertical appointment system replaced the electoral system. Political centralization during the civil war corresponded with war communism in the economic domain.[10]

In the course of the war Lenin came to see many problems with political centralization. As the postwar Tenth Congress of the Communists Party of the Soviet Union admitted, the highly centralized institutions created excessive bureaucracy, detachment from the masses, official privilege, distortion and repression, and cadre abuse.[11] Amid his retreat from war communism through the New Economic Policy, he proposed a series of political reforms, including separation of the functions of the party and the soviet to overcome the replacement of the latter by the former, establishment of agencies to supervise party and state organs, reform of state institutions, improvement of the legal system, and reform of the cadre selection process.[12] These reforms, however, took little effect in the first few years of the new regime. Lenin remained dissatisfied with the operation of its political institutions. While he commended the establishment of a new state under workers and peasants, he continued to urge the reform of institutions.[13] Unfortunately, these last words were unheeded by his successor, Stalin. Instead, Lenin's creation of the vanguard party and democratic centralism were utilized to extremes and remained the core features of the socialist political order not only in his own land but elsewhere.

Mao at first paid attention to both the nature and form of the new proletarian state. Before the revolution, he articulated a theory of "people's democratic dictatorship" for the new state, which spelled out the class nature of the new state (dictatorship against landed and bureaucratic bourgeois classes) and the form it was to take (democracy for the people).[14] Not long after the revolution, Mao indicated that with the establishment of proletarian rule, the form of political life became central. In 1956 and 1957 he developed the thesis of "the correct handling of the contradiction among the people," emphasizing that after the completion of socialist transformation, the handling of the nonantagonistic contradiction became the focus of national political life.[15] Even after the Antirightist movement of 1957, he still observed in 1958 that after establishing the people's own government, the relationship of this government to the people was basically one of an internal relationship among the people, that is, no longer an antagonistic relationship of one class against another.[16]

Beginning with the Antirightist movement, however, and especially after the intraparty and interparty disputes of the late 1950s and early 1960s, Mao began to put more emphasis on the class nature of the new state, both in theory and in practice. In 1962 he reaffirmed his delineation, made during the Antirightist drive of 1957, of a principal contradiction between the proletarian and bourgeois classes in socialist society. Moreover, he extended this contradiction to the entire historical phase of socialism, making "class struggle as the key link" the central focus of Chinese political life. This view led him to be preoccupied with ensuring the proletarian nature of the state, launching incessant political campaigns in the subsequent years aimed at dictatorship against the class enemy. The form of the proletarian state, or democracy for the people, was ignored and substituted by mass campaigns. It was against this legacy of Mao as well as that of international communism that the post-Mao reassessment was placed.

Moderate Reassessment

During the first phase of political reappraisal, from the late 1970s to the early 1980s, the imperative of the reform leadership was to advocate political reform without undermining public confidence in the system as a whole or succumbing to the analysis of the Democracy Wall activists. The resultant emphasis on a distinction between the "state system" (which class rules) and the "political system" (how to rule) opened the way for reform theorists to discuss legitimately the sources of the wrongs and injustices of the Cultural Revolution without threatening to negate the fundamental system. This bifurcation became a useful framework for examining the political maladies of the Mao era.

A key point raised in this phase of discussion was that during the Cultural Revolution and much of the past three decades, the state system had been overemphasized to the neglect of the political system. Both Li Honglin and the more conservatively inclined Lu Zhichao traced this one-sided emphasis to an assumption that once the issue of "which class rules" was resolved, the question of "how to rule" was concomitantly ensured. Under this assumption, much attention was paid to defending the class nature of the state and eliminating its enemy, but rarely to improving the form of government. Thus constant efforts were made to pursue the "key link of class struggle," the "dictatorship of the proletariat in all fronts," and "continuing the revolution." But there were few specific measures by which citizens could exercise their political rights. As a result, the political system had many deficiencies: the weakening of the People's Congress since 1958; the destruction of all people's representative organs from 1966–75; the absence of laws and courts; arbitrary search of residences, arrest, and the use of torture in that period; suppression of public opinion; life tenure of officials; official immunity from law; personality cult; and one-person rule.[17] In Yan Jiaqi's words, despite the founding of the People's Republic, the question of "what kind of People's Republic" had not been seriously addressed. Consequently, the political system, namely, the form and manner of government, had failed to reflect the state system, namely, the rule of the people.[18]

In theory, the one-sided emphasis on the state system was attributed to a distorted understanding of Marx's concept of the dictatorship of the proletariat, rather than the concept itself or its Leninist origins. Rather, Feng Wenbin, an official and researcher at the CCP's Party History Research Office, stressed two misunderstandings. First, while Marx ascribed it to the transitional period from the proletarian seizure of power to the establishment of its own rule, the CCP extended it to the postrevolutionary period. Second, while the objective of the proletarian dictatorship after the revolution was the rule of the people, not the struggle against the bourgeoisie, the CCP exclusively emphasized the latter and ignored the former. As a result, the forces of the bourgeoisie were overestimated well after the revolution, and issues falling within the realm of "nonantagonist contradiction" among the people were extended to the realm of "antagonistic contradictions" and handled by dictatorship. The most telling manifestations were the notion of "class struggle as the key link" and the idea of "continuing the revolution under the dictatorship of the proletariat." These tenets were now seen as ideologically absurd from Marx's original point.[19]

Both official and intellectual analyses assigned serious consequences to the one-sided emphasis on the state system. One was the extension of class struggle to people arbitrarily labeled as class enemies. The resolution on CCP history cited a series of major events after the revolution: the Anti-rightist movement of 1957, the persecution of Peng Dehuai in 1959, the call to wage "class struggle throughout the entire socialist stage" in 1962, the assault on "capitalist roaders within the party" in the Four Clean-ups campaign of 1965, the Cultural Revolution, and the campaign against "bourgeois rights" in the mid-1970s.[20] More broadly, Feng Wenbin and Yan Jiaqi saw the excessive emphasis on the class nature of the new state and its rightful dictatorship as responsible for Stalin's drive to eliminate counterrevolutionaries in the 1930s. In this view, the exclusion of segments of society predicated in the concept of class rule provided the rationale for exaggerating the presence of class enemies. The overestimation of class enemy, in turn, called for ever greater dictatorship of the proletariat. Further, because of the neglect of the form of government, class struggles were often determined by a few leaders, who, in the name of proletarian dictatorship, not only carried out excessive struggles but in the process concentrated absolute power in their own hands. As a result, the truly proletarian nature of the state became destroyed or void.[21]

Another major consequence of the one-sided emphasis was the pretext it provided for Lin Biao and the Gang of Four. These people were accused of utilizing the class emphasis to serve their own political purposes, through instigation of "down with everything" and an "all-round civil war," smashing of political institutions, persecution of veteran leaders and other political enemies, arbitrary arrest, and destruction of the freedom and lives of many innocent individuals. More importantly, they were able to exploit the dictatorship of the proletariat because the "political system" was deficient and incapable of protecting the people from becoming the targets of proletarian dictatorship.[22] As one report noted,

> The reason why the "Gang of Four" could wantonly condemn [the people] as "counterrevolutionary" was . . . because the people were not in a position to safeguard their right to free speech, and . . . there were no clear laws providing scientific, clear-cut stipulations as to what constitutes counterrevolutionary crime. . . . As the people could not safeguard their right of a free press, the "Gang of Four" were at will to . . . make all means of mass communication toe their line. And because the people could not safeguard their freedom of assembly, the "Gang of Four" could wantonly proscribe all meetings, parades, and demonstrations against them on the charge that these were "counterrevolutionary." As the people could not safeguard their freedom of conviction, the "Gang of Four" were given a free hand to imprison those who thought for themselves. . . . As the people could not safeguard their freedom of person, the "Gang of Four" set up kangaroo courts and slaughtered innocent people at will.

The result was that "socialist democracy gave way to feudal despotism married to twentieth-century fascism."[23]

The key theoretical consequence of the confusion over the state and the political systems was said to be the confusion it created with regard to the concept of democracy. This confusion was twofold. First, since the class nature of the state was taken to be of decisive importance, democracy was relegated to the realm of the political system, as something secondary and dispensable. Second, democracy as a concept was often equated with bourgeois democracy that had no place under socialism. In the post-Mao judgment, such a view of democracy was misconstrued for two reasons. First, the exclusion of democracy was detrimental to the proletarian nature of the Chinese state by ignoring the content of democracy. The content of democracy referred to the status of different classes under different types of democracy. Thus the content of socialist democracy should reflect the leading status of the people and should be an inherent part of the Chinese state system. The dismissal of democracy as "bourgeois democracy," in this view, had served to hurt the leading status of the people. Second, the equation of democracy with many forms of bourgeois democracy, such as elections, parliament, and a multiparty system, prevented the socialist system from adopting some of them, even though they were not exclusively bourgeois. Without a democratic political system to guarantee the interests of the people, Wu Jialin of the People's University concluded, the proletarian nature of the Chinese state was actually undermined.[24]

While the inclusion of democracy in both the state and the political systems marked a major change from previous treatment of the concept, reform theorists were careful to distinguish socialist democracy from bourgeois democracy at this time. Here they differed from the "abolitionists" of the Democracy Wall movement. Especially after the crackdown of spring 1979, they generally joined the reform leadership in rejecting the rightist conception of democracy, which was characterized by a denial of any distinction between socialist and bourgeois democracy and by a belief that "the form [of democracy] is everything." The designation of democracy to both the state and the political systems allowed a reformist response to this view. As the state system, Zhang Xianyang, Wang Guixiu, Wu Jialin, and others argued, socialist democracy differed from bourgeois democracy on the key question of who ruled: the working class or the bourgeois class. It was this class nature, rather than the forms alone, that determined the superiority of a particular type of democracy.[25] However, this class view of the state was precisely found by "abolitionist" groups to be the root problem. For example, the Thawing Society faulted proletarian dictatorship for "splitting mankind," while the Democracy Forum called it the "source of all evils."[26] In essence, these groups attributed the wrongs of the Mao era to the differential treatment of individuals legitimated by proletarian dictatorship.

By contrast, the primary concern of reform theorists at this time was the form of government, not the class nature of the state. Because they emphasized that the content of democracy may differ, Li Honglin and Wu Jialin were able to argue that socialist democracy could share structural features with bourgeois democracy at the level of forms, thanks both to "historical continuities" and the superiority of bourgeois democracy to the "feudal fascism" of the Cultural Revolution.[27] To justify these arguments, some found from the scattered observations of Marx and Engels an outline of the form of the proletariat state, consisting mainly of their observations on the French Revolution of 1848 and the Paris Commune of 1871. In this claim, classic masters saw in the Paris Commune a new type of government based on the bourgeois republic, a transformed "social republic" that was to be a ready form of proletarian rule.[28] The specific forms of bourgeois democracy now viewed as palatable for socialist democracy included freedom of speech, press, and assembly, equality before law, multicandidate direct election by secret ballot, and direct contact between the electorate and elected representatives. The parliament and multiparty systems were ruled out because of their "inherent" class nature.[29]

Several symptoms were ascribed to the lack of democracy under the Chinese political system. In his 1980 speech on the reform of the party and state system, Deng cited three: (1) a highly centralized system of administrative control over the economy, politics, culture, and society; (2) overconcentration of power in the hands of party committees; and (3) feudalistic leadership style.[30] But only the second was the focus of official and public interest at this time because it seemed to be the most pressing problem. In particular, much attention was on the question why the form of the state had contributed to this problem. Three major sources were identified.

The first was the concentration of power in the hands of the party in the name of upholding the party's leadership. This was a bold argument in 1980, as testified by the fact that several articles making this point were published in the name of special commentators.[31] The exclusive emphasis on the party was blamed on the one-sided view of proletarian dictatorship, because the party was taken to embody proletarian rule. The party's leadership, in turn, became a direct administration of all spheres of life and all details of affairs, with decision-making powers in all policies and with the attribution of ultimate authority to the party in all matters. An assumption had then developed that if party organs were not involved or consulted in the affairs of the state and society, there would be disrespect for or deviation from the party. This manner of the party's leadership was criticized for assuming all functions of the state through control of the executive, legislative, judicial, and economic organs, and all spheres of society through control of social and mass organizations. Nonparty entities were stripped of independent operational functions, or they would be considered as weakening the party's leadership. Finally, in the name of the "party's unified leadership," the party placed itself above law.[32]

Such overconcentration of power, moreover, resulted in the concentration of power in the hands of a few party committee secretaries, and often in the hands of the first secretary. This was then legitimated as the "unified leadership" of the party and the "command of the first secretary." During the Cultural Revolution, almost every first party secretary of a province was concurrently the governor and army commander in that province. Such arrangements practically eliminated political division of labor, deprived other organizations and departments of any room to exercise their functions, and reduced local branches to a dependent status of asking for party approval on everything. In the end, all these contributed to blind leadership and bureaucratism of party committees. This style of party leadership also enhanced the personal power of the first secretaries, whose personal inclinations were often equated with the party's leadership. These individuals became above criticism because the party was above criticism. They could impose their will as the party's will. Their opinions and decisions could not be disputed because the party's unified leadership must be upheld. Together, these problems were identified as the major sources of one-person rule, patriarchal leadership, and personal dictatorship that had characterized much of Chinese politics since the Great Leap.[33]

A second reason why the political system resulted in the overconcentration of power was said to be the lack of institutions to express the proper relationship between the party and the masses. Under the assumption that the party represented the interests of the people, party policies were neither made with the input of the masses nor carried out under their supervision. The concentration of power in party committees shrank the influence of mass organizations and the rights of citizens. Few mechanisms existed to solicit the people's opinion. Popular elections became ceremonies because "leaders prepare the candidate lists while the masses simply circle their approval." Under the pretext of the "party's leadership," officials could also overturn elected candidates at their personal whim. Equally frequently, officials deprived popularly elected institutions of any actual power. As a result of its divorce from the masses, two *Hongqi* articles conceded, many of the party's past policies not only failed to represent the people's interests but ran counter to them, the foremost examples being the Great Leap Forward and the Cultural Revolution. Ultimately, they cited the party's inattention to mass opinions and interests as the most important cause of the policy errors in the history of the CCP.[34]

The lack of sound institutions to guarantee the proper relationship between the party and the masses turned the party's status of leadership into one of "rulership," according to Xiong Fu. Xiong, deputy editor of *Hongqi* who was forced to make a self-criticism at the 1979 theory conference for his journal's stance in the truth debate, had now tuned himself to the tone of Deng's 1980 speech on political reform. The emphasis on the party's leadership and the "command of the first secretary," he now admitted, encouraged a situation in which some cadres took the party's leadership to mean setting themselves above the masses, issuing orders, intervening in all matters, and making arbitrary decisions. Even ordinary party members sometimes placed themselves above the masses, giving themselves more say in public affairs and the liberty to command others. Some cadres were even in danger of turning the relationship between the party and the masses into one of class oppression. "Some people went so far as to take our party's leadership status into capital for personal power," he wrote. "They regard the masses in their districts or departments as 'subjects' under their rulership. They wave the banner of 'leadership over everything,' . . . acting like arrogant overlords and suppressing democracy. Some even abuse public office for private benefits. . . . They have turned their leadership position into the position of rulers."[35] The result, another *Hongqi* article argued, was the reversal of the relationship between the party and the masses: The servants of the people became their masters while the masters of the state became its subordinates.[36]

A third reason why the political system contributed to the overconcentration of power was the emphasis on centralism in implementing Lenin's principle of "democratic centralism," according to several articles in *Hongqi* and *Renmin ribao*. Centralism should be based on democracy, namely, full expression by the masses and the formulation of policies on the basis of their elected representatives. But democracy was played down in the early history of both the Soviet and Chinese party because of the special circumstances of war and revolution. Unfortunately, after the Revolution, that transient practice was carried on by both parties. In the CCP's thirty years of postwar history, therefore, excessive battles had been waged against those accused of "disobeying the leadership," "establishing independent fiefdoms," or "making rival claims with the party" because they insisted on the autonomous power of their organizations. But excessive centralism was never criticized. The assertion of centralism grew even more intense after 1958, when the party attacked the adventurist tendencies of local cadres, on the one hand, and the rightist tendencies of Peng Dehuai, on the other.[37] Moreover, the "democracy" part of democratic centralism was too often sacrificed because it was treated as a means to centralism, so that its meaning was subjected to the needs of centralism. A prime example of emphasizing democracy was the staging of "mass democracy" during the Cultural Revolution to aid intraparty struggle. A prime example of ruling out democracy was the advocacy of "complete dictatorship" by Lin Biao and the Gang of Four.[38]

The ultimate effect of the overconcentration of power was said to be the "alienation of power" (*quanli yihua*). As both Xiong Fu and a *Hongqi* special commentator conceded, centralized power deriving from the party's leadership and democratic centralism had, in the course of its operation, created its own antithesis: It became contrary to the party's leadership and the principles of democratic centralism. Thus the power of the party became that of individuals, the use of power for the interests of the party became its abuse to damage those interests or to dominate the party, the submission of individuals to the organization became the submission of the organization to a few individuals, and the submission of the minority opinion to the majority opinion became the submission of all opinions to those of the leader himself. These problems, in turn, contributed to the characteristic maladies of the political system: the suppression of critical voices, the monopoly of power by officials with life tenure, the cultivation of factionalism by political speculators, and the deification of individual leaders to whom all achievements of the country were attributed.[39]

Despite the open admission of these problems, official accounts rejected Li Yizhe's designation of a "bureaucratic class" within the party. According to the Li group, a principal contradiction between this class and the masses was inherent in the Chinese system, and it could not be resolved by the party's top-down reforms. The implication was that the political power of party officials, buttressed by the notion of proletarian dictatorship, had become the basis of a class domination over society and that only by dissolving this political power would the dominant class be eliminated. The Li group thus defined the basis of a dominant class in terms of political power, contrary to Marx's economic definition.[40]

In response to these claims, mainstream analyses were careful to balance its critique of the past with affirmation of the integration of "democracy and dictatorship" and "democracy and centralism."[41] The advocacy of democratic reform from "bottom up" was criticized for its "worship of mass spontaneity," its alleged anarchic tendencies, and its attempt to renounce the party's leadership.[42] Xiong Fu also defended the party's continued leadership by arguing that because the party took the maximum interests of the entire society as its goal, it was able to stand higher and see further than the masses, to transcend immediate and local interests, and not to cater to short-sighted sectarian interests.[43] Refuting Li Yizhe's noneconomic definition of social class, another *Hongqi* article insisted that a "bureaucratic class" could not exist in China because it did not have any economic base under public ownership of the means of production.[44] In the final analysis, the thesis of a "bureaucratic class" and the proposal of "bottom-up" reforms were rebuked as attempts to counterpose the party against democracy and deny the party's leadership.

In short, in this early round of political reassessment, past misunderstanding of the nature of the proletarian state and its relation to the form of the state was a focal point of discussion. As in the economic arena, the emphasis at this time was on the Maoist excesses in implementing socialism. Neither the Marxist concept of proletarian dictatorship nor the Soviet model of democratic centralism itself was questioned.

RADICAL REASSESSMENT

During the second phase of political reassessment, from June to December 1986, the imperatives of economic reform drew reform theorists away from questions involving the roots of past political wrongs and injustices. The focus shifted to the structural basis of a political system unconducive to a commodity economy and political democracy, with attention to two major issues: (1) the sources of the administrative-command nature of the Chinese political system, as opposed to (2) the origins of the coordinating-procedural nature of a democratic political system. The relationship between a commodity economy and political democracy provided the key framework for analyzing these issues, just as the bifurcation between the state and the political systems served as the analytical scheme in earlier discussions.

Although the initial interest in probing the linkage between a market economy and democracy was prompted by the needs of economic reform, the theoretical exploration of 1986 was premised on Marx's view of the determining effect of the economic base on the superstructure. In this context, several aspects of a commodity economy were said to be conducive to the evolution of a democratic political system.

The first was the exchange of products among producers on the basis of economic values. This exchange allegedly contributed to a social division of labor and socialization of production, gradually replacing scattered, small-scale production with widely integrated and specialized large-scale production. Socialization of production, in turn, led to changes in the mode of social interaction. Thus under the premarket traditional "natural economy," economic exchange flowed mainly along *vertical* lines, for example, between tenant peasants and landlords, and between landlords and the government. Socially, this vertical exchange produced networks of social relations of personal dependence, upon which the feudal superstructure rested. Under a commodity economy, however, social interaction developed along *horizontal* lines, that is, free exchange of products among equal producers, a division of labor based not on personal dependent relations but on the value of commodities, and free movement of labor. These features contributed to the dissolution of the feudal bonds of personal dependence.[45]

Another aspect of a commodity economy conducive to developing democracy was said to be the special economic interests of commodity producers. As relatively independent economic entities, these producers were responsible for their own profits and losses, thus forming independent economic interests. As parties to free market exchange, they no longer dispensed their products according to the feudal relations of landlord and tenant but rather had the freedom to dispose of their products as they wished. These two conditions—commercial interests and the free will of producers—contributed to the formation of a new social class with a common political platform advocating economic and political liberty. This rising bourgeois class, in turn, became the social basis for overthrowing the feudal political order.[46]

The exchange of equal value entailed by a commodity economy, it was further argued, presumed the equality of the individuals involved in commodity exchange. As the commodity economy developed, the principles of equal exchange and fair play extended to other spheres of social interaction. In the political domain, the idea of equality became the ideological basis of political democracy. Importantly, the idea of equality born out of the commodity economy differed from the notion of egalitarianism born under the traditional "natural economy." In the latter, the relatively undifferentiated livelihood among small, self-sufficient producers was based not on freedom and competition but on a conservative and insular pattern of production. There egalitarianism sought the equality of *result*, or relatively equal distribution among small producers. Under the commodity economy, individual producers sought the equality of *opportunity*, that is, equal starting points and equal subjection to the rules of the game of free competition and economic pursuit. Only out of this type of equality, it was concluded, could there arise the necessary outlook to abolish sacred rulers and develop participatory democracy.[47]

Because a commodity economy generated a diversity of economic interests, it was further argued, it also created conflicts among different social groups, which in turn necessitated changes in the form of the state. To mediate those conflicts, new political procedures evolved to replace the arbitrary rule of feudalism. To accommodate different economic interests, there emerged political parties and a system of checks and balances. To guarantee the freedom and equality of commodity exchange and to regulate increasingly complex commodity relations, the supremacy of political power came to be challenged and the subordination of power to law was affirmed. Thereby the rule of law replaced rule of man.[48]

Finally, a commodity economy was found to operate according to the rules of competition, the selection of the superior and the elimination of the inferior. As reflected on the superstructure, economic interests prompted different social groups to elect their own political representatives. The result was the replacement of the feudal hereditary system and life tenure by periodic popular election.[49]

From these connections between a commodity economy and political democracy, reform theorists concluded that because China's traditional and socialist modes of production both excluded a commodity economy, they had impeded the development of political democracy. If the peasant economy of the precapitalist era sustained a "feudal" superstructure, the command economy of the postrevolutionary era helped to create a highly centralized bureaucratic superstructure. The command economy, moreover, was said to have failed to break the hold of the peasant economy, thus compounding the socialist superstructure with a "feudal" one.

In tracing the sources of a persistent "feudal" legacy under socialism, reform theorists followed Deng Xiaoping's analysis of 1980 in pinpointing the incompleteness of the Chinese Revolution.[50] In the analysis of Su Shaozhi, Wang Yizhou, and others, traditional China was a dominant peasant society with a long-lived small peasant economy and ideology. Yet the Chinese Revolution, characterized by the "encirclement of the city by the countryside," was undertaken largely by those who were directly or indirectly from the peasant class, including the majority of party cadres, army ranks, and intellectual supporters. To Su and Wang, where the peasant contribution lent a unique strength to the Chinese Revolution, it also gave rise to its special weakness, namely, the heavy influence of small peasant producers. After the revolution, the party tackled the "feudal" legacy only in the areas of marriage and land reforms. It never made systematic efforts to repudiate "feudalism" politically, economically, and ideologically. This neglect became more serious after the Antirightist movement of 1957, when the party turned its attention to the struggle against capitalism.[51] These analyses echoed Wang Xiaoqiang's discussion of "agrarian socialism" in 1980, which was then suppressed by Hu Qiaomu.[52]

Several features of the small-scale peasant economy had allegedly laid the economic base of a "feudal" superstructure. Self-contained and self-sufficient, small producers produced primarily for family consumption rather than for the market. Without commodity exchange and a social division of labor, they were limited to repetitive simple reproduction, dated technology, and conservative production patterns. Tied to the land and less mobile than commodity producers, they were ill informed and likely to resist change. Economically weak and psychologically vulnerable, they were unwilling to endure the uncertainties of the market and likely to resist it. Fearing competition and desiring stability, they sought the assurance of egalitarian distribution even if it meant common deprivation for all. This psychology was best reflected in the phrase "Worry not about scantiness but about unequal distribution," a traditional slogan of Chinese peasant rebellions and a widely shared value of the Chinese populace. Thus in traditional China a set of values had evolved to rationalize the status quo: Agriculture was esteemed as the highest trade while commerce was demeaned as the lowest; "righteousness" (*yi*) was valued while "profits" (*li*) were slighted; and the merchant was placed at the bottom of the social strata. To ensure stability and governance, the traditional state sanctioned these values and institutionalized them in the form of an official Confucian ideology.[53]

This socioeconomic base entailed a series of consequences for China's traditional superstructure, argued reform theorists. Unable to defend themselves against the uncertainties of nature or to protect their economic interests as part of a social group, small producers were anxious to have some higher "saviors" decide their fate and bestow them favors. So they cherished "holy emperors," "sagacious ministers," and "upright magistrates." Once they accepted rulers as deified figures, they willingly held them in absolute supremacy and allowed themselves to be at the mercy of "gods." The result was the rule of man as the ethos of the peasant society, with concomitant life tenure and hereditary officeholding for officials, personality cult, loyalty to the "emperor," arbitrary rule, worship of power, obedience of the masses, lack of restrictions on officials, and proliferation of abuses such as the use of office for private benefits, bribe taking, and the circumvention of laws.[54]

At the same time, because the small producer was tied to the land and lacked physical mobility, the patriarchal clan system evolved to dominate the peasant society. Human relations were determined by blood relations rather than economic or other interests. The head of the family or clan became the authoritative ruler. The patriarchal system extended from the family to the society, and from social relations to the political organization of the state. The alleged impact on politics included the patriarchal and autocratic traits of officials, the granting of titles to family members, political hierarchy, nepotism and favoritism, emphasis on seniority, patronage seeking, factionalism and sectarianism, the turning of superior-subordinate relations into personal dependent relations, the treating of one's domain of jurisdiction as a personal fiefdom, and the circumvention of law for family and friends.[55] The rule of man and patriarchy were summarily said to form the "despotic" (*zhuanzizhuyi*) character of China's "feudal" political system.

The Chinese Revolution failed to destroy the economic base of "feudalism" and thus the "feudal" superstructure, reform theorists suggested, because the planned economy perpetuated the noncommodity and bureaucratic nature of the traditional society. In the countryside, the revolution carried out only one of the two tasks essential to the transformation of small peasant production into large-scale socialized production, that is, the socialization of agriculture. The other task—the commercialization of agriculture—was not carried out. Worse still, the socialization of agriculture was achieved without the required material base of commercialization and was thus built upon a "sandy beach" of dispersed small producers.[56] Although extensive marketing networks in traditional China have been documented by William Skinner, Chinese reformers emphasized the dominant mode of production for a dominant segment of the peasant population.[57]

Further, reform theorists agreed with Deng's analysis that the socialist transformation of ownership in the mid-1950s occurred much too quickly so that the scale of collectivization became unrealistically high.[58] As ever higher levels of collectivization were hastily pushed, so the argument went, commercialization seemed less and less necessary to leaders. As a result, collective agriculture developed along the traditional patterns of self-sufficiency, while horizontal relations among producers failed to emerge, and vertical ties between peasant producers and the state persisted. That is, small peasant producers continued to exist under the facade of larger production units, where they became connected with other producers through bureaucratic administration, rather than through social division of labor or commercial relations. They were still self-sufficient producers who interacted mainly with the state: After retaining the bulk of products for self-consumption, rural collectives handed over to the state whatever they were assigned to produce. In 1980, 60 percent of all agricultural output was still consumed by peasants, while 15 percent was commercially exchanged. In this way, the small peasant economy and the planned economy were neatly integrated, serving to inhibit the development of a commodity economy.[59]

In the industrial sector, reform theorists found, large-scale socialized production on the basis of commodity exchange also failed to take shape despite the emergence of a sizable national industry. Here, the organization of production was seen as the problem: The various sectors and enterprises were not organized along the horizontal lines of commodity exchange relations but rather were vertically organized into departmental and regional enclaves. The "feudal" economic mode was not dissolved but reproduced here: Production units interacted not with one another but with the state. Worse than in the "feudal" mode, every detail of the production process—from investment to management to marketing—was administratively determined by state planning agencies. The criteria used in decision making were not the supply and demand of the market but often the political needs and subjective will of politicians. Production units were left with little autonomy to dispose of products at market value.[60] In short, the planned economy inhibited the development of commodity economy in the urban sector as well.

A welter of adverse effects on the political system were attributed to the integration of the traditional and the planned economy. One was the combination of political and economic functions in the state. Because the state assumed direct organization and management of production, allocation, and distribution, it had to establish a complex hierarchy of administrative organs. As a result, a large number of state organs—two-thirds of the entire state apparatus—performed economic functions. Although the rest of the state apparatus was not directly involved in economic management, they often had control over personnel matters. As a result, all decisions over production or personnel matters of the enterprise had to go through different levels of the state apparatus. Under the precept of the party's leadership, moreover, the power of state organs was centralized in the party committees, whose authority in turn resided in the hands of a few party secretaries. The combination of political and economic functions in the state led to a number of problems: excessive powers of politicians, a huge bureaucracy, impromptu and monopolized decision making, mutual obstruction between party and state organs, and suppression of grass-roots initiative and creativity.[61] These characterizations are consistent with Kenneth Lieberthal and Michel Oksenberg's findings on the policy-making structure in China.[62] Although their analysis emphasizes the bureaucratic impasse that often frustrates central initiatives, it reinforces the Chinese view that the political apparatus as a whole overwhelms grass-roots units.

The state management of the economy further resulted in highly centralized control over other aspects of the society, from political to cultural, a practice similar to the "feudal" tradition of "all-embracing uniform rule" (*da yi tong*).[63] That is, the planned economy created a system of rule that entailed the use of administrative-command methods by the state. These methods, in turn, became institutionalized as the routine ways of governing society, affecting not only academia and the arts, but even areas of personal life and thinking.[64]

The planned economy was further faulted for stifling the people's sense of individual interests necessary for the development of democracy. Because the planned economy presumed the uniformity of interests among the state, the collective, and the individual, it could not reflect the actual interests of different production units and producers whose contributions differed. For reform theorists, this obscured the existence of conflicting interests among divergent groups and therefore inhibited fostering a sense of equal exchange and fair competition. These in turn affected the development of democracy in two ways. First, the denial of differences and conflicts among the people nullified the necessity of developing a mechanism to coordinate and protect diverse interests. Second, the absence of perceived economic self-interests prevented the people from desiring elections, since their personal stakes were not involved. Such an underdeveloped sense of political equality led them to accept political authoritarianism and economic egalitarianism.[65]

These tendencies, moreover, were reinforced by constant official efforts to resist bourgeois influences. Although these efforts were made in the name of defending socialism, now they were alleged to have proceeded from a "feudal" perspective: The bourgeois concept of equality was opposed on the basis of "feudal" hierarchical values (for example, cadre privileges were legitimized); the idea of the autonomous individual was opposed on the basis of "feudal" relations of personal dependence (for example, the superior-subordinate relationship between cadres and the masses was permitted); the bourgeois concept of rule of law was opposed from the point of the "feudal" rule of man (for example, officials were above the law); and finally, the bourgeois ideas of diversity and risk-taking were opposed on the basis of a "feudal" psychology of conservatism and conformity.[66] In short, as Su Shaozhi and Wang Yizhou declared, the marriage of the small peasant and the planned economy resulted in a political order that combined "feudal despotism" with Stalinism.[67]

From the linkage between a noncommodity economy and the problems of the concomitant superstructure, some reform theorists found it necessary to rethink the nature of the socialist state. The Marxist theory of the state and the proletarian dictatorship, Liao Gailong and Wang Zhenyao argued among others, placed exclusive emphasis on the state as an instrument of class oppression, as opposed to a coordinating organ of general social functions, such as the management of public affairs. After the transition to socialism, in particular, the proletarian state should lose a significant part of its class nature and become a state of all citizens on an equal political basis. This meant that no segment of the citizenry should be regarded as politically more advanced or backward, in the manner that the concept of proletarian dictatorship presumed the political superiority of the proletarian class. This presumption was deemed impractical because the industrial working class made up only a small part of the Chinese population. It was also judged to be theoretically harmful, because it justified the immunity of the state from law, on the pretext that the state must act above law in the struggle against class enemies.[68]

This line of rethinking was also extended to the bourgeois state. In their view, past conceptions of the bourgeois state overemphasized its class nature and neglected its general social functions. Since the economic base determined the superstructure, an article in *Minzhu yu fazhi* argued, many functions of the bourgeois state were necessitated by the commodity economy rather than by class rule. Further, because the commodity economy was now permissible under socialism, the socialist state could share some features with the bourgeois state.[69] Specifically, the socialist state could inherit those aspects of the bourgeois state that had developed from the rising bourgeoisie's struggle with the "feudal" order: the separation of powers, the system of checks and balances, rule of law, competitive elections, the coordination of conflicting economic groups and interests through procedural and pluralistic politics, and, most of all, the concepts of democracy, freedom, and equality.[70]

The administrative-command state, formed on the basis of a noncommodity and planned economy, should therefore be transformed to a state based on institutional and legal rule compatible with a commodity economy. However, Chinese reformers by no means advocated a *regulatory* state of the classic capitalist type that would not take on *developmental* functions typical of other East Asian states.[71] Rather, they proposed (1) limiting the scope of party and state power and (2) changing the manner of exercising this power. In Yan Jiaqi's words, the first involved a redistribution of power between the party and the state, among state organs, and between state and nonstate organizations. The second involved a redistribution of power between superior and subordinate organs.[72] The crux of the matter, Yan, Li Honglin, and many others agreed, was to place limits on the power of the party and the state at all levels.[73]

The second reform was to transform direct, command governance into indirect, procedural governance. As several members of the Central Party School suggested, the party should change its role from physically running the country to providing "overall leadership" (through general policy lines, communication with the public, and supervision of the state). The party should also change its method of leadership from direct to indirect involvement (recommending instead of appointing officeholders, having branches within state and social organs instead of dominating them, publicizing party lines instead of imposing them). Finally, the party would play its vanguard role through the exemplar role of its members.[74]

The state, on the other hand, was to be solely responsible for the aspects of running of the country that involved the constitution and laws, the economy, education and culture. This meant that the party's programs would not become policies unless enacted as such by the state, and the party's ideological work would not supersede education and culture.[75] In essence, these proposals aimed to strip the party of any actual policy role and to transfer policy-making to the state.

While this guiding role of the party was compatible with the traditional Chinese conception of the state as moral authority, one difference was crucial: Whereas in imperial China both political and moral functions were combined in the state, the idea of the party's "overall leadership" proposed to separate the two by assigning moral functions to the party and political functions to the state. This was perhaps the most signifi-cant aspect of the political discussions in 1986: it advocated a separation of the party and state, on the one hand, and of the state and society, on the other.

Reform theorists were vague, however, on how to implement those proposals. Because of orthodox Marxism's emphasis on the economic base, their underlying assumption was often that a rational separation of power would automatically follow the growth of the market. The fallacy of this assumption was to become the focus of examination in the next phase of reassessment.

COMPREHENSIVE REASSESSMENT

With the resumption and intensification of economic reform after late 1987, the continued inability of party and state organs to relegate power became more apparent. As optimism on the positive impact of the market on political reform declined, reform theorists again turned their attention to the political sphere. In analyzing the sources of the economic crisis and cadre corruption in 1988 and early 1989, they now emphasized the polit-ical basis of the economic system and its problems. The concept of "total-ism" (*quannengzhuyi*) provided the key analytical framework of discus-sion in the late 1980s.

The radical discourse entailed by this concept was adopted not only by many younger intellectuals but by such leading reform theorists as Yan Jiaqi, Su Shaozhi, and Wang Yizhou as a standard reference, in an increas-ing departure from the reform leadership behind which they had rallied. The idea of totalism was used to denote the "monistic, pyramid style" of the political power structure, under which all aspects of society—political, economic, and other institutions—were organizationally subordinated to the party apparatus. Characterized by the "use of political power to ad-minister everything," totalism allegedly caused a "combination of the party-state-economy" on the one hand and a "combination of power-ideology-culture" on the other,[76] that is, the total control of the party over society.

Totalism entailed that the reform of any aspect of Chinese society was a political question because it would involve the undoing of aspects of totalism. As Li Ming, Han Kang, and some other younger reformers pointed out, price reform would touch the powers of state agencies re-sponsible for price setting. Ownership reform threatened the powers of state agencies in charge of industries. Political and economic reform, then, could not be accomplished simply by having some agencies transfer or renounce their old functions according to market requirements, but must involve giving up the whole concept and practice of totalism. This was at the root of why economic organs had been unable to give up their administrative functions, state organs unable to devolve their powers, and party organs unable to separate themselves from government and public sectors.[77] The question for the political reform discourse was, then, where did totalism originate and why did it still persist?

A moderate view emphasized its historical sources. As noted by the concept's original author Tang Tsou, totalism was rooted in the special conditions of the Chinese Revolution, as the result of the "total" response to the "total" crisis faced by China in the early twentieth century.[78] In his Thirteenth Congress report, Zhao Ziyang also spoke of the "excessively centralized political system" as one "born out of the revolutionary war era, shaped during the period of socialist transformation, and developed in the course of large-scale mass movements and the constant intensification of command planning." Some found historical circumstances to have given rise to the all-powerful state in two ways. Wang Yizhou stressed that the interwar and early postwar periods called for a set of command structures, leadership skills, and mobilization methods best equipped to deal with the threats from opponents of the revolution and with domestic chaos.[79] Sun Liping conceded that the postwar modernization drive, belatedly made possible by the revolution and the unification of the country, required a strong central government to enforce speedy and effective change.[80] In addition, the special position of the party upon the revolution sanctioned its leadership over the state and society, giving rise to a "double government" that reached into all corners of society.[81]

Some, such as Su Shaozhi, blamed the guiding ideology of the CCP partly for creating totalism. For him, the highly centralized political system was not determined by historical circumstances alone. CCP credos that advocated the leadership of the party, the dictatorship of the proletariat, class struggle, transformation of production relations, transition to communism, and suppression of bourgeois ideas also helped to shape the Chinese political system. Because of this ideological basis of the political system, Su argued, any substantive reform would not be possible without change in the party's ideology. For without an appropriate ideological base, radical reform ideas or programs would always be resisted as heretic by those who seek to defend orthodoxy.[82] Yan Jiaqi shared Su's implicit point here that the strength of the conservative counterattack in late 1988 rested partly upon their charge of Zhao Ziyang's ideological deviation. Because ideological correctness served as the basis of political legitimacy, Yan noted, ideological deviation was a serious matter for a leader since it entailed the loss of legitimacy. As examples of victimization by ideology, he cited Mao's demotion of Peng Dehuai for his "rightist opportunism," of Liu Shaoqi for his "capitalist road," and of Chen Boda for his "pseudo-Marxism."[83] Zhao Ziyang, too, argued Yan, was under attack because of his political opponents' exploitation of ideology.[84]

Yan Jiaqi and Li Ming also emphasized that persisting totalism was intimately tied to the unwillingness of officials to relinquish control, since the all-powerful functions of the political system were embodied in the personal power of individual officials at all levels.[85] Li Ming attributed unwillingness at the top to conservatism and habitual forces, but he blamed the resistance at the middle and lower levels on vested interests. In his analysis, the huge ranks of party and state functionaries had formed a stratum of "bureaucratic privileges" and "special interests" that resisted change.[86] Because the totalist structures of the party and state remained in place, so Li's analysis went, those functionaries could pursue new interests under economic reform through the old power structures. Rather than reducing or adjusting their functions, they integrated their old powers with new market opportunities, for example, obtaining state-rationed goods through official access and selling them for market prices. This integration of the cadre and the capitalist became the ultimate cause of the unprecedented severity of official corruption in the late 1980s. In this view, the relative success of rural reform was due to the elimination of the administrative apparatus at all levels of the commune, leaving decision making directly to the peasant household. Political reform, then, was a question of how to eliminate old political functions and what to do with old functionaries. This was a problem, Li recognized, too sensitive for the reform leadership to touch. In this regard, he championed Japan's Meiji leaders for adeptly and resolutely abolishing the samurai class.[87]

On a broader level, the all-embracing functions of the political system had contributed to a pattern of "nonprocedural politics," according to Yan Jiaqi, Su Shaozhi, Sun Liping, and others.[88] This was manifested in several areas: The political system lacked a legal-institutional basis of political authority, a representative legislature (the National People's Congress being such an institution largely in name), an independent judiciary system, institutionalized procedures governing the exercise and limitation of power and the relationship between the party and nonparty organs, and institutionalized channels for public participation and expression.[89] In short, because of the lack of procedural politics, the "form" of socialist democracy did not exhibit the "content" of socialist democracy.

The absence of procedural politics had contributed to the use of numerous nonprocedural means in Chinese politics, Yan Jiaqi, Sun Liping, and others also argued. One was the constant use of political campaigns to deal with political problems or economic tasks, such as the Great Leap Forward and more recent campaigns to enhance spiritual civilization.[90] Intense, massive, and sometimes violent, these erratic movements quickly fell into rituals without ever touching the roots of the problems they intended to address. The recurrence of old problems after each campaign necessitated a return to new campaigns, further reinforcing the neglect of institutional mechanisms.[91] The most recent example, Luo Haiguang and others cited, was the use of campaigns to deal with cadre corruption, a matter falling under the realm of law enforcement. Because of inattention to procedural politics, even law enforcement was ineffective and plagued by the official position of many corruptors who could act above law. Other procedural means of control, such as the media, were restricted out of concern for the party's image and social stability. As a result, there had been a routine neglect of cadre abuse. But when disputes among the leadership arose over the effects of reform, campaigns were launched to counter corruption. Such efforts often generated sympathy for corrupt officials, who seemed to be victimized by opponents of reform. When the reform momentum resumed in the wake of a political campaign, corruption would resurge to new levels. This situation culminated in the economic and social crisis of late 1988 and early 1989.[92]

Another highly destructive aspect of nonprocedural politics was said to be the lack of procedures and rules in the transfer and succession of power. This absence meant that changes in leadership could occur only amid intraparty struggles or following the death of leaders, so that leaders' mistakes could rarely be rectified unless a transfer of leadership occurred. The lack of mechanisms to regulate intraparty conflicts also meant that opposition within leadership was not tolerated and had to be eliminated by "unprocedural" means. The fates of Peng Dehuai, Liu Shaoqi, Lin Biao, the Gang of Four, and Hua Guofeng all illustrated these features of nonprocedural politics. This political style was also found to be true of the international communist movement, such as Stalin's persecution of Bukharin and other political opponents, the rise and downfall of Nikita Khrushchev, and Gorbachev's "palace coup" against conservatives in his party. By criticizing these nonprocedural maneuvers, Yan Jiaqi, Cao Siyuan, and others intended to show the illegitimacy of conservatives' efforts to oust Zhao Ziyang. Once again, Yan warned, there was a danger of an intraparty struggle in the Cultural Revolution style and a "nonprocedural transfer" of power. He also saw in this incident the systemic cause of the Cultural Revolution, namely, the lack of institutional control over arbitrary exercise of power. Quite boldly, he suggested that this root problem persisted despite senior leaders' staunch efforts to repudiate that tragic event.[93]

Still another aspect of nonprocedural politics was found in the closed and personal nature of the decision-making process at the highest levels. Because final decision powers were concentrated in the "supragovernment" of the Politburo or in the hands of a single leader, any change in the individual will of a leader or in leadership could result in major changes in power structures and even massive social turmoil.[94] The extreme example was Mao's decision to launch the Cultural Revolution, made in the small temple of a remote village.[95] The result, Sun Liping noted, was unpredictability and inconsistency in policy over the past few decades:

> When nonprocedural methods like political campaigns are used to solve problems, [policies] inevitably tend to be indiscriminate and extreme. When indiscrimination and extremeness reached their limits, [leaders] have to turn back and then go to the other extreme. Between the two extremes have been incessant adjustments and rectification. Over the past thirty years, we can say that at least half of our time has been spent on adjusting and rectifying policies. However, these adjustments and rectification were themselves carried out by political campaigns. This only created the condition for going to the other extreme in the next circle.[96]

One folk saying thus summarized the popular perception of policy inconsistencies: "The party is like the moon—it's different on the first and fifteenth of the month."[97]

Those who saw the root problem of the political system in its "unprocedural" and "totalist" power opposed the advocacy of "New Authoritarianism." These included not just those who complained about the exclusive nature of Zhao's policy circles, such as Li Ming, but also some who were inside his circle, such as Yan Jiaqi and Cao Siyuan. They objected in principle to giving any new authority to any individuals, leaders, groups (that is, an "intelligentsia elite"), or ideology (that is, neo-authoritarianism), for whatever seemingly justifiable purpose. The disasters of recent decades, Yan Jiaqi insisted, had stemmed from precisely the same rationale. If any new authority should be established, it must be the authority of the constitution and law, which were the only guarantees of procedural politics.[98] In practice, some argued, to forcefully push economic reform from above, as New Authoritarianism advocated, would not resolve the crisis of reform, since it would not reduce the public's unwillingness to bear increasingly difficult economic burdens. The most dangerous aspect of the current situation, they suggested, was not a lack of authority, but the massive abuses and social costs passed onto citizens who were not involved in the political process. If democratic controls were not immediately instituted to channel public discontent and enhance public identification with the system, some warned with foresight, the masses may have to resort to nonprocedural means to express their discontent.[99]

As these discussions raised the character of the political system to the first importance, some no longer treated democracy as a mere precondition for economic modernization but as something of intrinsic value. Totalism was now criticized not only for its hindrance to economic development but also on normative grounds. Conversely, democracy was now held desirable not only because of its empirical effectiveness but its moral superiority. The intrinsic value was the realization of a person's worth as a human being. Democracy was said to guarantee this realization on several grounds.

First, democracy, with its premise of the people as their own rulers and as the main body of society, was the political expression of respect for the dignity and individuality of human beings.[100] Because democracy guaranteed freedom of thinking, individuality, and autonomy, individuals need not succumb to a higher will or goals. In this context, some intellectuals found the discussion of humanism and alienation of 1983 still pertinent. During the Mao era, they observed, the major problem was indeed the lack of respect for the rights and freedom of members of society, as the humanists of 1983 argued. Insofar as any individual will and development incompatible with the goal of socialism were subject to criticism and the "micro self" was subordinated to the "macro collective," members of society were turned from the end of the socialist revolution to its means. As the humanists of 1983 argued, individuals were sacrificed to maximize the realization of politically defined social and class goals. The lack of awareness of and respect for one's human value further created the cultural condition for political despotism. In the end, the "free development of the full potential of all people" as Marx promised failed to materialize, and the lack of opportunities for such development reduced socialism to an "empty slogan."[101]

Second, democracy was seen to be capable of guaranteeing political rights to *all* members of society, not just certain segments of it.[102] This rather idealistic argument was made on the ground that the concept of democracy did not preclude any particular group from participating in the political process, as did the concept of the dictatorship of the proletariat. Although the latter may be necessary during the transition to socialism, Yu Guangyuan contended, a socialist society should adopt a form of political rule in which all members enjoy equal political rights. As he wrote in memory of the May Fourth movement in April 1989, proletarian democracy should no longer be qualified by "class dictatorship," because any residual class struggle "no longer requires a political system that must exclude one or more classes from the socialist community with democratic rights."[103] Apart from the changes in historical and social conditions, Wang Yizhou observed, the determination of which segments of society to exclude from political rights under socialism could be difficult and arbitrary. For the concept of proletarian dictatorship was often abused to justify the persecution of anyone in the past. Finally, proletarian dictatorship was criticized as exclusive because its class view of political rights required everyone to think and act as a member of the proletarian class, thus depriving all the right to independent thinking. The result, Wang concluded, was the "dehumanization" of citizens by the denial of their individuality.[104]

Not only the scope of rights but also the kind of rights differed under democracy and proletarian dictatorship. Yan Jiaqi distinguished between the advocacy of political rights to achieve social justice and the advocacy of social equity to achieve social justice. Marx did not ignore the importance of the political sphere, Yan claimed, for he regarded the resolution of the political issue as a fundamental solution to the social issue.[105] Here, Yan seemed to argue that Marx viewed the proletarian seizure of power as the precondition to social equity, which was to be based on socialist production, ownership, and distribution. Yet socialism had only achieved a facade of social equity, added Su Shaozhi and Wang Yizhou, because leveled distribution did not provide opportunities or reward for the more able and the ambitious. Further, egalitarian distribution must be enforced through command of a higher authority. The result was that "political despotism becomes a twin brother of social egalitarianism." That is, despotism was a political condition of egalitarianism.[106] Without dismissing social equity as a political goal, Yan Jiaqi went on to argue, real social justice could only be achieved through political democracy, because it was easier for people to tolerate disparities resulting from human differences than to tolerate inequalities caused by an unfair political system in which the people could not influence the selection of their government or its policy output.[107] For Yan and other supporters of individual ownership, private property did not conflict with social equity. Rather, it was part of those individual rights that enhanced citizens' sense of democracy.

Finally, democracy was capable of contributing to the full development of human beings by guaranteeing a "diversity of truth." A dictatorship of the proletariat was seen as less equipped to do so because of its class world view and its doctrine of the total truth of the objective laws of history. Democracy was held to allow the "diversity of truth" by recognizing (1) the right to independent thinking and (2) the equality of diverse schools of thinking. Writing on Chinese intellectuals' feeling of loss since the 1949 Revolution, the noted literary critic Liu Zaifu argued that intellectuals may have a less staunch class stand than workers and peasants, but their views were not necessarily wrong or less valuable. On the contrary, intellectuals' questioning mind was more valuable from the point of "modern cultural norms" symbolized in the early part of the May Fourth movement.[108] In an essay on the upholding of Marxism, Li Honglin questioned the constitutional stipulation of "adherence to the Four Fundamental Principles." These principles should only apply to party members, he argued, because ordinary citizens should have the right to choose their own beliefs.[109] Others proposed that the spirit of equality and plurality should apply to Marxism itself. That is, there could be pluralistic thinking toward

Marxism on the basis of contention among equals.[110] Still others, notably the renowned literary critic Xia Yan and journalist Hu Jiwei, questioned the authority of the party and Hu Qiaomu to arbitrate the debate on humanism and alienation in 1983. They were particularly indignant about the treatment of Zhou Yang, whose essay on the debate triggered the 1983 antiliberal campaign. As a citizen, they insisted, Zhou Yang did not violate any law by speaking on those issues. As an individual, Zhou should be entitled to freedom of expression, even though what he espoused may be wrong. For both Xia and Hu, the injustice of the episode spoke strongly for the correctness of Zhou Yang's advocacy of humanism, because the pressure of the 1983–84 campaign had struck him ill and confined him to bed since then.[111]

In this connection one writer openly called for "a reorientation of the Marxist normative standard" in *Renmin ribao*. The Marxist world view was no longer adequate, he suggested, because it gauged right and wrong only with regard to the interests of the proletariat. In the contemporary world, the central value of Marxism should be redefined as the full development of the human being and the harmonious development of the entire society and the entire humankind.[112] This new normative standard summed up the arguments that reformers made to justify the replacement of the proletarian dictatorship with democracy.

While emphasizing democracy as a fundamental value, reform theorists were not oblivious to the question of the relation between democracy and social progress. This has been a primary concern of Chinese intellectuals since China's confrontation with Western civilization. As China's national priority became the strengthening of the country to catch up with the West, many among earlier generations saw democracy as a means to bring out human potential for the progress of the nation.[113] Essentially, the post-Mao reform leadership shared this pragmatic, instrumental interest in democracy. For Deng, the objectives of political reform were to overcome bureaucratism, raise administrative efficiency, enhance popular initiative, and, above all, promote the development of production forces.[114] Reform theorists' elevation of the individual as the end of democracy was partly in response to the Dengist elevation of the production forces as the criterion of all progress. In their view, Deng's criterion did place less emphasis on the class goal of society and thus allowed the individual and society more room for development, but it did not alter the teleological nature of Chinese society and the neglect of the individual.[115]

Deng was also faulted for deliberately turning the people's attention away from noneconomic needs and rights. In a mirror reversal of conservative criticisms of Deng's reforms, reformist critics questioned his underlying assumption that economic development would lead to the development of other spheres. They pointed out that the moral breakdown of the

Chinese individual and the corrosion of the state apparatus, as witnessed in the recent frenzy of corruption, had shown the futility of economic determinism. Without downplaying the importance of production forces for social progress, these critics argued that the human factor should be the most essential component of production forces and that social progress would be the concomitant, rather than the end, of democracy.[116] In other words, democracy should have priority over efficiency and be viewed as its precondition. This marked the essential difference between the "idealistic approach" of reform theorists and the "instrumental approach" of the reform leadership on the question of democracy.[117]

"Democratization" was upheld in the Fourteenth Congress report as a goal of the party's political reform. But more than in the Thirteenth Congress report, Jiang emphasized building "socialist democratic politics with Chinese characteristics" and "absolutely not a Western-type multiparty and parliamentary system." There was no longer any mention of "separation of the party and the state" or "decentralization of power," which would involve changing relationships among major political actors. Rather, the proposed reforms were mainly technical in nature: improving the People's Congress, the decision-making process, the legal system, and the administrative system. Thus, the report returned the official discourse on political reform to the early post-Mao framework of reforming the "forms" of the system. Unofficially, a society now consumed by *xia hai* (going into the sea, or business) seemed at least temporarily to have damped any real enthusiasm for discussing political change.

CONCLUSION

The post-Mao reassessment of the Chinese political system consistently centered on the sources of past and present problems and their appropriate remedies. As in the economic sphere, the line of inquiry moved from analysis of past mistakes in theory and practice to inherent problems in original theory. It began with the Maoist application of the Marxist theory of the proletarian dictatorship and the Leninist principle of democratic centralism, then moved on to the economic roots of the administrative-command superstructure, and finally confronted the Marxist origin of the class nature of the socialist state. Two central themes emerge from the three phases of reassessment. One is the relationship between the nature and the form of the socialist state; the other, the relationship between socialism and democracy.

During the first phase, from the late 1970s to the early 1980s, emphasis was on Chinese misunderstanding of the nature of the socialist state that had led to serious errors in the "form" of government. Although the 1979 theory conference went far in critiquing the political system, the mainstream analysis (especially after Deng's Four Fundamental Principles) did not challenge the defining principle of the Chinese state (the proletarian dictatorship) nor its organizing principle (democratic centralism). Rather, only the overemphasis on proletarian leadership and centralism was diagnosed as the cause of a deficient form of government that had contributed to the abuses and injustices as well as the misconception and dismissal of democracy during the Mao era. The nature of the proletarian state was not linked to its deficient form.

During the second phase of reassessment, in the mid-1980s, the nature and the form of the Chinese state were linked through the analysis of the impact of the economic base on the superstructure. Here the emphasis was on the errors in the Soviet model of overcentralization and in Marx's theory of proletarian dictatorship. From the linkage between a noncommodity economy and the deficiencies in the Chinese state, between a commodity economy and the democratic features of a bourgeois state, there emerged a recognition that the Soviet-type planned economy had contributed to a socioeconomic base conducive to a defective form of government. Moreover, there was the realization that the Marxist theory of proletarian dictatorship overemphasized the class nature of the state to the neglect of the nonclass functions of the state. Because of this neglect, the nature of the socialist state also had a relation to its deficient form.

Finally, during the final phase of reassessment, in the late 1980s, the nature of the Chinese political system became the focus of reexamination. The central problem came to be identified in its group-based and teleological character,[118] that is, a political order geared at the realization of certain group interests and future goals. It is based on Marx's concept of proletarian dictatorship and expressed in Lenin's leadership of the vanguard party, Mao's class doctrine, and Deng's Four Fundamental Principles and economic ideology. The group-based and teleological nature of the Chinese state was criticized on structural and normative grounds. Structurally, it was faulted for contributing to the unchallengeable authority of the party that resulted in totalism. Normatively, it was blamed for contributing to a disregard for the intrinsic values and rights of individual members of society. In the final analysis, the nature of the socialist state had a direct relation to its flawed form.

Apparently, the central concern of post-Mao reform theorists, intellectuals, and social critics was the deficiencies of the Chinese political system, and this perspective guided their reassessments. As major victims of political campaigns under both Mao and Deng, they emphasized the negative aspects of the political order. As a segment of society prone to independent thinking, they focused on questioning the authority of the party to define the value orientation of society. As a politically competent group whose expression had often been constrained, they were willing to go further than the reform leadership to challenge the sanctity of the system. Because their rethinking was conditioned in the context of Chinese politics, these critics tended to accept the positive ideals of democracy without questioning its limitations in theory and practice.

Herein lies the fundamental difference between the reassessment of social groups (reform theorists, intellectuals, dissidents) and the ruling clique (both conservative and reform leaders): For the former, the basic problem of the Chinese political order was that the state had too much power; for the latter, it was how this power was used.

CHAPTER SEVEN

The Reconceptualization of Socialism

THE STRENUOUS efforts to reassess and rectify the practice and theory of the socialist economic and political system have raised serious questions about socialism itself as a principle for organizing and guiding Chinese society. If socialism requires such extensive adjustments, why should China continue to be concerned with it? After all, the issues raised in the economic and political reappraisals have pointed to many deep problems in China's adoption of socialism. Does socialism fit China's national conditions? What does Marxism entail for China now that many of its assumptions are no longer unquestionable? What do changing conditions at home and abroad mean for China's socialist path? What do the contradictions between reality and Marxist doctrine signify for socialism as a theory and historical problematic? These questions, in turn, raise the fundamental issue of the fate of socialism in China. What should be the place of socialism in reform and in China generally? These questions are among the most important confronting both the leadership and the public. They also constitute the most fundamental aspects of reassessment that have been undertaken.

Rather than breaking entirely with the socialist framework, the Chinese Communist party has opted for the accommodation of Marxism to the contemporary world, an effort summed up in the Thirteenth Congress report as the "reconceptualization of socialism" (*dui shehuizhuyi de zairenshi*). The host of questions raised above, nonetheless, are more than what politically expedient adaptations can resolve. Thus, although the efforts to deal with those questions were connected to the needs of policymakers, they were not simply manipulations to justify whatever was required of them. Nor were those efforts mere political weapons to wield against political opponents, although they were used in political battles. At the intellectual level, the "reconceptualization" of socialism has been a gradual process of recognition of the characteristics of China's national development. At the political level, it has been a response to those on the Left who abhorred deviation from the socialist path of development and those on the Right who derided the feasibility of this path. The two levels of discourse were not always distinguishable, and they interacted to influence each other.

This chapter first reviews the evolution of the Chinese rethinking of socialism as a generic theory and mode of social development from 1978 to 1992 and then examines the content of that process.

THE EVOLUTION OF THE RECONCEPTUALIZATION

The first inquiry into the feasibility of socialism in the post-Mao period was sparked off by the thesis of "undeveloped socialism," proposed at the time of the 1979 theory conference by Su Shaozhi, then a member of the theoretical group at *Renmin ribao*. The ideological thrust of the conference and the political climate at the time was to reexamine Mao's "class struggle as the key link." Much of this effort was focused on analyzing the historical stage of Chinese society to redefine its nature and its basic contradictions. In the process Mao's designation of the principal contradiction came to be renounced. In an article published in the May issue of *Jingji yanjiu*, however, Su Shaozhi, with coauthor Feng Lanrui, went beyond a mere repudiation of Mao's theory to call into question the nature of Chinese socialism.[1] Their thesis aroused a controversy and a considerable amount of trouble for Su, but it was to have an important impact on the Chinese rethinking of socialism.[2]

The Debate over the Socialist Nature of Chinese Society

Their central argument was that Chinese society could not be termed "completely socialist" because it did not achieve the level of socioeconomic formation originally envisioned in scientific socialism. This may not sound too novel, given the plethora of discussions on China's "backward production forces" at the time and mentions of the "lower stage" (*diji jieduan*) or "early stage" (*chuji jieduan*) of Chinese socialism by such figures as Xue Muqiao.[3] But while these references were made in the context of discussing economic reform, Su and Feng's article was a systematic discussion of the larger question of the nature of Chinese socialism. Following Marx's distinction between a lower and higher stage of communism, Su and Feng differentiated in the lower stage between (1) a transitional stage from capitalism to socialism, subdivided into (a) a transitional period (from the proletariat's seizure of power to the basic completion of social transformation) and (b) undeveloped socialism; and (2) developed socialism (socialism as envisioned by Marx). China fell under "undeveloped socialism" because it still possessed many qualities that were not fully socialist:

> The characteristics of undeveloped socialism are the two forms of public ownership, commodity production and commodity exchange. Capitalists have been basically eliminated as a class but there are still capitalist and bourgeois remnants, even feudal remnants. There also exist quite a few small producers, class differences among workers and peasants . . . and the force of habit of

small-scale producers. The production forces are still not highly developed. And there is not an abundance of products. . . . Therefore, the transition toward socialism has not yet been completed.[4]

The immediate implication of the relocation of China to a "presocialist" stage of development was a Marxist rationale for policies such as those recently introduced in the countryside. But the significance did not end here. The logic of the thesis also suggested that with the persistence of presocialist elements in Chinese society, the country lacked the material base to embark on a transition to socialism. Su made the point more explicit in another article by refuting the formulation, established at the Eighth Party Congress in 1956 and restored by the post-Mao leadership, that the principal contradiction of Chinese society was that between "an advanced social system" and "backward production forces." Though the official reinstatement was intended to underscore the importance of production forces, Su found it problematic. For this formulation meant that a society could in fact have a political/economic system more advanced than its level of production forces. This was doctrinally unsound, to say the least, because it conveyed the idea that production relations could be created regardless of the objective state of production forces. Instead Su asserted that China did not yet possess the material basis for a full transition to socialism.

> The socialist system consists mainly of production relations. Whether a production relation is advanced or not is determined by just one criterion, namely, whether or not it can meet the demands of production forces and facilitate their development. Although some production relations, such as commune ownership, may be superior to ownership by the production team in terms of the stage of development, in rural China today, where manual labor remains predominant, only ownership by the production team, rather than by the commune, would be the type of production relations capable of measuring up to the level of production forces and facilitating their development. If . . . commune ownership is adopted, it would damage the development of production forces.[5]

The notion of "undeveloped socialism" posed a serious challenge to the legitimacy of Chinese socialism. On the one hand, it shed light on a lingering "feudal" legacy that was increasingly blamed for the "autocracy" of the Mao era. On the other hand, the "undeveloped" nature of Chinese society made a logical argument for retreat from socialism. Not surprisingly, the notion received mixed responses. Some, who appeared to be writing independently, disagreed with the analysis.[6] Others concurred that since China was still in a transition to socialism, it should return to the policies of New Democracy, or the period prior to the socialist transformation of 1956.[7]

The sensitivity of this line of analysis, of which Su was a conspicuous articulator, became evident in the ensuing official reactions. Deng Lijun, CASS vice president and party official, organized a meeting to criticize Su Shaozhi, now a member of the CASS Institute of Marxism-Leninism. This resulted in Zhu Shuxian's rebuttal of Su in *Jingji yanjiu*.[8] Deng's hostility toward Su was partly due to the latter's close association with Yu Guangyuan, CASS president, but the root cause was still their incompatibility of mind: Su was close to Yu because they shared outlooks and views.[9] Su's thesis also came to be implicitly censured in many subsequent public forums. In his National Day speech in 1979, Ye Jianying devoted a paragraph to declaring that China had indeed entered the socialist stage, albeit in its "infantile phase" (*youzhi jieduan*). The theory was also targeted during the crackdown on socialist democrats in mid-1981.[10] During the campaign against bourgeois liberal tendencies in late 1981, it was again singled out as an antisocialist current. In his keynote speech at the CDP symposium to lay out the themes of the campaign, Hu Qiaomu devoted a long paragraph to criticizing the major arguments of underdeveloped socialism.[11] In his October 1983 speech on spiritual pollution, Deng Xiaoping also criticized those who questioned the socialist nature of China.[12] As admitted by other officials, Su's thesis was identified as part of the "rightist trend" begun with the Democracy Wall movement and a major instance of "deviation from socialism" targeted by Deng's declaration of the Four Basic Principles.[13]

The official rebuttal offered by Hu Qiaomu, Feng Wenbin, and others contended that the notion of "undeveloped socialism" overemphasized the undeveloped nature of Chinese society and conversely underestimated its socialist nature. These two fallacies, moreover, were related: The former was to show that China was not ready to be a socialist society, while the latter was to suggest that China was indeed not fully socialist. The theory was a matter of concern because, Hu Qiaomu noted, it lent a theoretical rationale to opponents of socialism and contributed to a growing crisis of faith among the youth with respect to the superiority of socialism.[14]

Su Shaozhi was singled out perhaps because his analysis of the stage of China's development did represent a dangerous trend in recent intellectual discussions. Writing in a local college journal even before Su's articles appeared, one scholar located China in the transitional period, which was even earlier than the stage pinpointed by Su Shaozhi.[15] The young researcher Wang Xiaoqiang, who was later picked up by Chen Yizi to become part of Zhao's economic team, dismissed Chinese socialism as "agrarian socialism" built upon a "feudal" legacy and a peasant economy.[16] A related discussion that occurred around this time renewed debates about Marx's theory of the Asiatic mode of production.[17] Although limited to historical circles, it raised many similar questions. From the fact that Chinese intellectuals had never been able to reach consensus about that theory nor to find Marx's five modes of production totally fitting, historians now questioned Stalin's dismissal of the former to impose the latter. In particular, they probed into the nonconformity of either theory with Chinese history to uncover the deeper problems of Marx's unilinear view of evolution. The questions raised by the historians were relevant to understanding both Chinese history and Chinese socialism: for example, the generality and particularity of human progress, multilinear versus unilinear paths of evolution, and the weak development of capitalism in China.[18] Some aspects of the Asiatic mode theory, such as communal ownership and the despotic state, were not linked to the analysis of the present in the historians' discussions. On the contrary, efforts were made to rebuke Karl Wittfogel's linkage of the socialist state to Asiatic despotism.[19] At this juncture, historians were interested in the special features of Chinese development and their import for Marx's theory of five modes of production. This emphasis echoed Su Shaozhi's point about the questionable nature of Chinese socialism. Not surprisingly, these analyses suffered a fate similar to that of Su's. At Hu Qiaomu's instruction, discussion was closed on "agrarian socialism" thereafter.[20] The discussion of the Asiatic mode of production also came to be discouraged during the 1983 campaign against spiritual pollution.

The seriousness with which the regime reacted to these intellectual discussions suggested also the relevance of the issues Su and others raised about the applicability of socialism in China. This was in itself a contribution to Chinese rethinking. In an indirect wrap-up of the controversy over the stage of Chinese development, the resolution on CCP history (June 1981) concluded that although Chinese socialism was in its "early phase of development" (*chuji de jieduan*), China had indeed entered the stage of socialist society.[21] The emphasis here was that China was already a socialist society. Nonetheless, the very use of the phrase legitimated the concept of a preliminary stage in which Chinese socialism remained.

The Centenary of Marx: Developing Marxism under Contemporary Conditions

The centenary of Marx in March 1983 is often remembered for Zhou Yang's paper that touched off the campaign against spiritual pollution. From the point of view of this study, equally important was the theme of "developing Marxism under contemporary conditions" marking the various forums and papers devoted to the occasion, which ushered in a second wave of discussion on socialism. The circumstances of this discussion had changed considerably from those of the earlier period, when discarding Mao's legacy was of central concern. By early 1983 the conflict between conservatives and reformers within the reform coalition had moved to center stage. The question was no longer how to defend ideological discontinuity, but how to find proper paths of national development. The centenary offered an occasion to discuss the application of Marxism in China, which was the original premise of Su's thesis.

Hu Yaobang again played a leading role in moving forward party ideology. In his commemorative address, he proposed treating Marxism as a "developing science" and warned against isolating it from "other cultural achievements of mankind." This meant that Marxism should be integrated both with "other human knowledge" and with "indigenous conditions." The latter, he warned, could not be bypassed as dogmatists wished. In encouraging greater attention to "Chinese characteristics," he called for the use of Marxist epistemology to handle properly the relation between the "general" and the "particular" and to avoid obscuring the latter with the former.[22] Indeed, the distinction between socialism as a general theory and China as a host society was central to the discussions at the centenary. At the CDP's commemorative symposium on March 8–11, Yu Guangyuan, Su Shaozhi, Zhou Yang, Song Zhenting, the economist Ma Hong, and the recanted former supporter of the two whatevers and now CASS vice president Hu Sheng all elaborated on the special problems of applying Marxism.

Su Shaozhi was again a leading voice in the discussion. He moved beyond his earlier thesis that it was premature to adopt socialism in China. Rather than saying that practice did not fit theory, he now stressed that theory did not fit reality, that is, Marxism had a limited applicability to Chinese reality. Importantly, he was still developing his critique from within a Marxist perspective. Following the dialectical materialist line, he proposed an "epistemological study" of socialism to pin down its theoretical "origins" and its "added features" from later practice. Within the original theory, he made a distinction between those principles fundamental to any socialist society and those specific only to a given society, a distinction he found applicable to the works of Lenin, Stalin, Mao, and Marx himself. In his view, China's mistakes in the past were twofold: (1) a dogmatic adherence to Marx's universal laws of socialism regardless of "Chinese characteristics," and (2) an equation of the birthplace of the first socialist country with the sole correct application of Marx.[23] These analyses found ready agreement among Yu Guangyuan, Fan Ruoyu (vice president at the Central Party School), and others.[24]

A central issue for Su and the others was the discrepancy between Chinese society and the type of society in which Marx envisioned socialism to germinate. This was but another way of posing the question raised by Su's notion of "undeveloped socialism," that is, the feasibility of applying socialism in China's current stage of development. The first problem of "Chinese characteristics," Hu Sheng and Song Zhenting agreed with Su, was a generic one: the difficulty of applying socialism in an underdeveloped country. This was so because Marx predicted the triumph of socialism in developed capitalist countries where a high level of commodity economy and large-scale socialized production existed. Upon the proletariat's seizure of power in such a social context, society would be able to exert a unitary public ownership and eliminate commodity economy.[25] But Su no longer sought to question the feasibility of adopting socialism in an underdeveloped country. Rather, he conceded that the triumph of socialism in such countries had become a recent "historical trend," as almost all postwar socialist revolutions occurred in underdeveloped countries. He admitted that this reality "enriched" Marxism rather than "discredited" it.[26] Nonetheless, the problems posed by the emergence of socialism in societies that Marx did not foresee were numerous and complex. Song, Hu, and Su noted the following:

1. A lower stage of development than that envisaged by Marx and Engels, with feudal, semifeudal, semicolonial elements, and even remnants of serfdom and the clan system still present.
2. The lack of the material prerequisites of socialism, such as a large-scale socialized production essential to public ownership and a product economy, or a highly educated population and technical personnel.
3. The lag of production forces behind production relations and superstructure, with the concomitant surviving influence of precapitalist social relations, psychology, and ideology.
4. Subjugation to the encirclement, even the intervention, of capitalist countries. As most underdeveloped countries had suffered from imperialism, there was a need to balance the absorption of the positive achievements of capitalist countries with the preservation of national independence and dignity.[27]

These generic difficulties in turn posed a second problem for those Chinese Marxists: the special difficulties of each underdeveloped country in adopting socialism. In the Chinese case, these included a large and predominantly rural population, limited financial and technological resources, a weak industrial base, and the lack of a capitalist legacy to run a commodity economy.

These difficulties and problems, however, led not to the conclusion that China should not adopt socialism, but only to the determination that it should adopt "socialism with Chinese characteristics." The founding fathers, Song Zhenting noted, never stated that underdeveloped countries could not make up for a commodity economy and large-scale social-ized production *after* the triumph of the socialist revolution. Thus, for him, the "special" features of China's socialist road lay in the prior seizure of political power and then the use of this power to build a socialist society and learn what other societies had acquired under capitalism. For Hu Sheng, "Chinese characteristics" meant that China should not be "ob-sessed" with a "pure and perfect" socialism based on the "general laws" prescribed by Marx. Similarly, for Su Shaozhi there should be no stan-dardized or immutable model in building socialism. They agreed that if the general laws of founding fathers were applied arbitrarily and the growth of production forces was impaired, socialist development would be "impeded" rather than enhanced.[28]

It is not clear how far this line of developing Marxism would have gone without the interruption of the campaign against spiritual pollution later that year. Although these discussions did not come under direct attack during the campaign, Su Shaozhi's "undeveloped socialism" was again criticized, this time by Deng himself at the Second Plenum of the Twelfth Congress that formally launched the campaign. Su's thesis had to be criti-cized along with those of humanism and alienation because they were all seen as part of a general intellectual trend to negate socialism.[29] Su was further subject to an internal self-criticism during the campaign.

The bifurcation of socialism and its Chinese application, though not new, became more prominent in public consciousness with the recent dis-cussions. By June 1983 Zhao Ziyang was talking about the reform of an "outdated" model of socialism.[30] In public debates over urban reform in late 1983 and 1984, the idea of a Chinese model provided a key rationale to jettison the Soviet model. The concept was also incorporated into the 1984 resolution on urban reform. The recognition that socialism did not entirely fit Chinese reality marked a step forward from the party's earlier denial of the arguments of "undeveloped socialism."

The Blooming of Hundred Schools in 1986

After the campaign of 1983, the reassessment of socialism as a general theory experienced a brief hiatus from late 1983 to early 1986. Several reasons underlay its eventual revival in early 1986. First, at the Party Con-gress in September 1985, conservative leaders consolidated their eco-nomic retrenchment and the anticorruption drive of 1985, both aimed to rectify the negative consequences of urban reform, by placing the study of Marxism and the building of spiritual civilization on the party's political agenda. For the reform leadership to resume the momentum of reform, therefore, it was necessary first to redefine the ideological context. Sec-ond, the expansion of a commodity economy and opening to the outside since urban reform posed many challenges to both the traditional and socialist ethos of a noncommodity economy. The emergent value crisis called for a value reorientation of society. Finally, in the public discussion on cultural modernization since 1985, questions had been raised about the place of Marxism in Chinese political culture. To accommodate these developments, reform leaders, particularly Hu Yaobang, saw the need for Marxism itself to be modernized.

Reform leaders thus sought to redirect the "study Marxism" campaign into a "develop Marxism" campaign. At a meeting of the CCP Secretariat in January 1986, Hu Yaobang proposed that the party shift its ideological work to this task in the new year. In the same month at the Central Party School, Hu Qili introduced Hu Yaobang's call for "developing Marxism" as one of the Secretariat's agendas for 1986.[31] Then in a front-page article in *Guangming ribao*, Yan Jiaqi enunciated this task as a major shift of the focus of the country's theoretical work since the debate on the truth criterion. Whereas the debate of 1978 was to resolve the question of how to handle correctly Mao's teachings, Yan wrote, the current shift was aimed at "how to handle Marxism scientifically."[32] In the May issue of *Hongqi*, CASS President Hu Sheng urged that the development of Marxism be the key theme in current academic discussions. In his May Day speech, Hu Qili suggested that Chinese ideology should accommodate the new values and concepts that had arisen out of reform. In a July speech at the Central Party School, Wang Zhaoguo again stressed the centrality of ideological development in the new period by summing up the key lesson from the party's major blunders in the past as the "errors of dogmatism."[33]

Reform officials also spelled out the direction and manner of the theoretical shift in 1986. First, the "development" of Marxism should be taken as a precondition to "upholding" of Marxism. Second, the focus of development was to break away with those conclusions that had proven "outdated" or "not entirely correct" by practice. Finally, development should include incorporating "other cultural achievements of mankind," as Hu Yaobang had called for in 1983. Zhu Houze specifically suggested that development should not be limited to the traditional framework of Marxism.[34] As for the manner of "developing," Yan Jiaqi warned against treating Marxism as "sacred classics" and called for "equality before the truth" in public debates. Hu Sheng stressed that Chinese acceptance of Marxism before 1949 was based on its truth, not coercion, and that Marxism should not "compel people to believe in it."[35]

Reform theorists, ideological workers, and scholars responded enthusiastically to these calls with a flux of discussions in newspapers, magazines, and symposiums. Following the party's call to remove obsolete and incorrect credos, they eagerly explored various problems in both the content and the methodology of Marxism. Regarding the content of Marxism (that is, the theories of scientific socialism, political economy of capitalism, and philosophy), discussants sought to locate deficiencies in Marxism arising from "methodological limitations," "lack of empirical tests," and "changes in time and circumstances."[36] In Su Shaozhi's words, the main objective was to meet the challenges to Marxism posed by "new problems in the contemporary development of socialism," "new characteristics in the contemporary development of capitalism," and "new methodologies advanced by modern science and technology."[37]

On the challenges posed by contemporary socialism, many cited the diversity of models across socialist countries and the tortuous development within one country, the location of Chinese socialism in a primary stage, the failure of some predictions of scientific socialism to materialize and the appearance of other, unanticipated elements, and the widespread recognition of the necessity of reform across socialist societies. In response to these challenges, Su Shaozhi, Wang Yizhou, Yu Guangyuan, and others proposed a "reconceptualization" of socialist theory that would correct its outdated aspects. On the challenges posed by contemporary capitalism, they saw problems in Marx's predictions about the slowing down of production growth under capitalism, the absolute impoverishment of the proletariat, the sharpening of class struggle, the decay of monopoly capitalism, the inevitability of imperialist war, and the prospect of social revolution in capitalist countries.[38]

Regarding the methodology of Marxism, the essential problem was identified in the epistemological and methodological basis of dialectical and historical materialism. Here Marx was criticized, though somewhat inaccurately, for placing an exclusive emphasis on the independence of the objective world from the subjective one and on the deterministic role of material forces in the historical process.[39] The implication was that Marx neglected the role of human actors in the cognitive process and, consequently, in historical evolution.

The diagnosis of the methodological fallacies of Marxism generated the most interest among theoretical circles and was to have a major impact on Chinese rethinking on socialism. In May 1986 philosophers held the PRC's first symposium on the relationship between cognition and subjective norms. In October they convened the first conference on new achievements in philosophy, during which the topic "humans and their subjectivity" was the favorite among participants. Interestingly, their assertion of the subjective will was not in the direction of Mao's politics in command but just the opposite: Their emphasis was to underscore the role of subjective choice, human intelligence, normative preferences, technology, and pluralistic thinking in human evolution.[40] Su Shaozhi drove the point home when he observed that Marxism lacked attention to the psychological aspects of the motive force of social evolution. This helped to explain, he added, why the record of socialist economies failed to support Marx's assumption that once the proletariat seized power, production forces would develop rapidly. Only by questioning this assumption, he argued, would one understand why productivity under socialism had long been inferior to that under capitalism.[41] This new emphasis on human factors was to provide an intellectual foundation for the critique of public ownership and the assertion of political rights in 1988–89.

A few radical intellectuals, however, went further to suggest the futility of developing Marxism. In his campus talks delivered in the course of 1986, Fang Lizhi asserted that Marxism had already proven to be a failure in theory from Marx to Mao and a failure in practice from China's experience over the past three decades. Similarly, Wang Ruowang attacked Chinese socialism as "utopian and fictional designs" that took "fantasies for correct goals." The result was what he called "over three decades of historical abnormalities." For them, Marxism was not worth developing. In Fang's words, "Marxism as a science has completed its historical mission. Now we need to search for new truth." This search, moreover, would consist of a "free competition" between the Four Fundamental Principles and a "wholesale opening" (*quanfangwei*) to the West. The perceived failure of Chinese socialism also suggested to them the futility of the socialist road. Because of its lingering feudal legacy, Fang claimed, capitalism rather than socialism was the proper remedy for China. Wang also saw most things under Chinese socialism as "feudal practices" painted with a Marxist face. Deriding China's skipping of capitalism, he called for "making up for" the capitalist stage of social development.[42]

At the level of political elites, the development of Marxism was a highly contentious issue between reformists and conservatives. Central to the conflict was a disagreement over the priority of developing versus upholding Marxism and the relative danger of dogmatism versus deviation. Whereas reformers insisted on the priority of development and the greater danger of dogmatism, conservatives argued the opposite. Shortly after Hu Yaobang's call for developing Marxism in January 1986, Peng Zhen took advantage of a speaking opportunity at Zhejiang University to emphasize the study of Marxism. Defending all major components of Marxism, he refuted those who saw the proponents of studying Marxism as "conservative" and "antireformist." Instead, he attacked bourgeois theories as "undeveloping" and "ossified" for their defense of capitalism.[43] In April, at a conference on the ideological work of state enterprises, Deng Liqun addressed the priority of upholding Marxism and complained about recent deviations in public discussions. As a statement from the party's leading ideological official, Deng's passage is worth quoting in some length here.

There are lot of comments nowadays about the upholding and development of Marxism. We think that the two are unified and inseparable. In August 1980, Comrade Deng Xiaoping made a speech on the reform of the leadership system of the party and the state. . . . When the section in which he addressed the party's leadership was being edited, the word "improvement" (of the party's leadership) was at first placed before the word "upholding" (of the party's leadership). But he said no, "upholding" should come first: Only by "upholding" can we improve and "improve" is to help "uphold." The same holds true for Marxism. It is not appropriate to only talk about development and not upholding. Recently, some articles separate the two. They talk about studying newly developed Marxism, but do not mention or ignore the study of basic principles of Marxism.[44]

During the drafting of the resolution on spiritual civilization, the controversy over "develop" versus "uphold" Marxism became a key area of contention between conservative and reform leaders. The relative importance of "develop" versus "uphold" determined the nature of ideological reformulation: If "develop" was secondary to "uphold" Marxism, reformulation would be partial. The ordering of the terms also determined the place of socialist ethics in "spiritual civilization": Whereas the precedence of "develop" would allow a greater scope of values that were consistent with the market, the precedence of "uphold" would preserve a greater use of moral incentives. In the final version of the resolution, "uphold" maintained priority over "develop." But in a political compromise, the resolution disparaged both those who held Marxism as rigid dogmas and those who "negate the basic principles of Marxism, regard Marxism as outdated, and blindly worship some bourgeois philosophies and social theories."[45]

In the wake of the student protests at the end of 1986, recent discussions of developing Marxism were blamed for causing a value confusion among youth and for encouraging bourgeois liberalization. Many were criticized for counterposing "develop" to "uphold" and opposing Marxism in the name of developing it. Fang Lizhi and Wang Ruowang were accused of utilizing the controversy to repudiate Marxism.[46] Su Shaozhi lost his directorship of the CASS Institute of Marxism-Leninism and a research project on developing Marxism that had received government funding earlier that year.

The Formulation of the Primary Stage of Socialism

In managing the aftermath of the student protests in early 1987, Zhao Ziyang recognized that political opposition from both the Left and the Right was linked to socialism. As he noted in his May 13 speech, the crux of recent conservative attacks was that ideological deviation on the economic front had contributed to the spread of bourgeois liberalization on the political front. The conservative argument had a legitimate point: Orthodox Marxist theory does offer a coherent view of life, in which change in one aspect affects the whole. As for the opposition from the Right, the influence of liberal individuals among students did demonstrate the crisis of socialism. The advocacy of making up for the capitalist stage in China also had a point from the Marxist perspective. To safeguard economic reform while allowing himself to maintain a stand against both the Left and the Right, Zhao saw the need to make socialist theory more coherent with his reforms.[47]

Ironically Su Shaozhi's notion of "undeveloped socialism" now provided the basis for a new socialist theory. Shortly after the student protests, Zhao's chief adviser Bao Tong called on students to study the "primary stage" of Chinese socialism. As a "young horse," he said, Chinese socialism should not be compared to the "old horse" of developed capitalism. Just as Mao wrote the theory of "New Democracy," he urged, so the nation now needed a theory of the "primary stage of socialism."[48] Such a theory was also to be aimed at the Left opposition. In his speech at the Spring Festival celebration on January 29, Zhao called on "all who care about China" to study the country's stage of development and be realistic about the necessity of reform. The notion of the primary stage of socialism offered a ready starting point not only because of its intellectual appeal but because of its gradual acceptance by the party. After all, the recent resolution on spiritual civilization did use the phrase "our country is still at the primary stage of socialism" (*chuji jieduan*). In a letter to Deng Xiaoping on the drafting of the Thirteenth Congress report, Zhao formally proposed using the primary stage of socialism as the theoretical basis of the report. Since this concept was not to emphasize China's "unsocialist" nature or the unfeasibility of socialism, as did Su's original thesis, but to highlight China's weak material base, Deng did not find it objectionable. In fact, he endorsed a more materialistic conception of socialism. "What we want," he remarked in April, "is a socialism superior to capitalism" but not a "socialism of poverty." In his May 13 speech Zhao rebuked "those who judge socialism only by production relations in disregard for production forces." In the same month a group under Zhao's leadership began to draft the Thirteenth Congress report based on the theory of the primary stage of socialism.[49]

In the following months, the drafting became a national effort to rethink socialism. Seven major drafts were produced, often under Zhao's direct chairmanship, with the participation of over five thousand national and local officials, social scientists, and members of non-Communist parties. Many discussion sessions among leading theorists were also held. Heated discussions were also conducted in papers and magazines, and many individuals sent their suggestions to the central party.[50]

These discussions centered on the question of how to work out the arguments of the theory of the primary stage of socialism. Many dilemmas were inherent in such a theory. If the level of production forces was to be the basis for determining this primary stage, might this suggest the inadequacy of socialism for China because it did not attain the level of capitalist production forces? If the principal contradiction of this stage lay in that between production forces and production relations, might this suggest the need to remove socialist production relations? And finally, if retreat from socialism needed to be defended from dogmatism, might this encourage bourgeois liberalism?[51] The resolving of these questions laid the foundation for the full development of the theory of the primary stage of socialism and its adoption at the Thirteenth Congress in November 1987. The congress report also endorsed the reconceptualization of socialism on a full scale and took the initiative by summarizing twelve points of reconception that had been made in the post-Mao period. Many books and articles appeared subsequently to elaborate on these points, among which three were most prominent and had a semiofficial status. One was the book project on the "Development of Marxism in China since the Third Plenum" by the CASS Institute of Marxism under the editorship of Su Shaozhi and Zhang Xiangyang. Stopped during the 1986 antiliberal campaign, it was restored after the Thirteenth Congress as one of the major research projects in the government's seventh five-year plan. The other two collections were undertaken by the Central Party School. One provided theoretical interpretations and the other integrated theoretical interpretations with policy developments.[52]

With the conservative resurgence and the radicalization of reform theorists since the fall of 1988, the reconceptualization of socialism took on a new dimension. In the same way that public ownership was being repudiated and the value of the human being reasserted in this period, the reassessment of socialism in late 1988 and early 1989 involved a questioning, and sometimes an outright negation, of Marxism. While within-system reformers such as Su Shaozhi and Wang Ruoshui still proclaimed their faith in Marxism and their objection only to orthodox Marxism, the more liberal minded were hardly patient to make the distinction, much as were the conservatives. The radicalization of the reconception of socialism coincided with three landmarks in the Chinese experience with Marxism: the seventieth anniversary of the May Fourth movement and of the October Revolution; the fortieth anniversary of the Chinese Revolution; and the decennial of the debate on the truth criterion. As they reflected on the evolution of Marxism in modern China amid its current crisis, even leading students of Marxism such as Zhang Xianyang, Ruan Ming, and Wang Yizhou came to question Marxism as a guiding principle of the nation. Viewing the political and economic system as the root cause of the ongoing crisis of reform, some blamed official ideology as the "fundamental barrier" to reform.

The advent of this "negative" discussion, conservatives would later complain during the campaign against bourgeois liberalization after mid-1989, created the intellectual climate for the outbreak of the "antiparty," "antisocialist," and "counterrevolutionary" turmoil in the spring and summer of 1989.[53] Jiang Zemin emphatically spoke against "ideological pluralization" and the weakening of Marxism and socialism in his speech observing the party's seventieth anniversary. But by late 1992 the tone was drastically moderated in his Fourteenth Congress report. Still, mindful of the pitfalls of the primary stage theory and partly to make a departure from Zhao Ziyang, the drafting committee for the Fourteenth Congress adopted "socialism with Chinese characteristics" as the theme and the theoretical basis of the congress's report. This term slightly mitigated the emphasis on China's backwardness and unfitness for socialism, as entailed in the primary stage theory that underlay Zhao's Thirteenth Congress report.

THE CONTENT OF THE RECONCEPTION OF SOCIALISM

A major breakthrough in the Chinese reconception of socialism was marked by the adoption of the notion of the primary stage of socialism at the Thirteenth Congress. Heretofore, the reconception had touched on the incompatibilities of the Soviet and Marxist models of socialism with Chinese reality and on deficiencies in Marxism. But the notion of the primary stage went far beyond these efforts to re-create a theory of socialism for China. Paradoxically, the framework of discourse set by this theory encouraged both a negative reconception of socialism in the late 1980s and a return to a more orthodox conception after mid-1989.

The Development of Marxism

The conclusion on developing Marxism that emerged after the Thirteenth Congress was that this development should not be subject to an "elusive balancing of words" between "develop" and "uphold" or to the influence of individual idiosyncrasies. Rather, any development should be gauged by scientific and operative methodologies.[54] These methodologies found their clearest elaboration in the CASS project edited by Su Shaozhi and Zhang Xiangyang.

The first was based on the bifurcation of fundamental and specific principles developed in the truth debate of 1978. To be more precise, Su and Zhang now differentiated between three levels of Marxism: (1) the world view and methodology, including dialectic and historical materialism; (2)

theories on issue areas, for example, Marx's notion of socialist society and the theory of social revolution; (3) discussions of a specific society or historical period, for example, the slave society. As the methodological and epistemological guide to lower levels of principles, the higher levels of principles had greater universal applicability and stability. And of these highest principles, dialectical materialism constituted the most fundamental. Su and Zhang concurred with Deng in ascribing "seeking truth from facts" as the "philosophical basis" and the "highest methodology" of Marxism.[55] In this light, the development of Marxism meant the "regeneration" of lower principles under the guidance of higher ones.

The second methodological imperative concerned whether or not any development should be made or had been made correctly. The criterion proposed here was none other than the test of practice. Applied to China's reality, the practice criterion was now equated with the criterion of production forces. This equation was given not just in Su and Zhang's book but also by such prominent theorists as Yu Guangyuan, Wu Jiang, Gong Yuzhi, and Sun Changjiang.[56] The argument was that because production forces were the ultimate determinant of production relations and superstructure in a society, they must form the empirical parameters of the practice criterion. In other words, the production criterion made concrete the practice criterion by defining "what kind of practice." In developing Marxism, therefore, whether new ideas contributed to the promotion of production forces was to gauge whether they "developed" or "distorted" Marxism. An example was Mao's theory of "continuing the revolution." Though once praised as the "third milestone" in the development of Marxism, it proved to have run counter to Marxism because it pushed the national economy to the verge of collapse.[57] But in an ironic reversal of Mao, the criterion of production forces went to the other extreme.

Another methodological consideration in developing Marxism concerned the significance of new ideas specific to the Chinese context. This point was made in response to conservatives who doubted that such ideas could be genuine developments of Marxism because of their limited universal significance. Su and Zhang's book replied that because Chinese additions helped to expand the applicability of original theory, they were indeed one way of developing Marxism. This could even be a more important way of developing because the application of socialism in an underdeveloped country of the East enriched the meaning of classic socialism by relating to similar social contexts in other countries. Examples were Lenin's theory of revolution in isolated, underdeveloped countries and the Chinese theory of the primary stage of socialism.[58]

The final approach to the development of Marxism was that incompatibility between the original and the added must be viewed in terms of the contrast between the fundamental and specific levels. The incompatibility may stem from empirical changes, or the original theory may be incorrect in the first place, as, for example, Marx's notion of a product economy. Since the Chinese experience had proved that the absence of a market was not conducive to the growth of production forces, a "negation" (*fouding*) of Marx's theory on this matter amounted to a development of Marxism compatible with historical materialism. This process of differentiation and negation, Su and Zhang argued, provided students of Marxism with the "methodological freedom" to develop Marxism.[59]

The empirical emphasis in ideological development, explicit in the official approach, has in effect deemphasized the normative stand of Marxism. The elevation of "practice" and "production forces" to the first priority obscures the human actors involved. As Su and Zhang conceded, some people may wonder, "does not any [social] class proceed from reality, including the bourgeoisie"? Their response resembled Xing Fensi's reply to similar concerns raised during the 1978 truth debate. That is, owing to differences in social class, class stand, viewpoint, and values, observation and interpretation of reality differed among divergent social groups. Thus the bourgeoisie was likely to refuse to recognize those aspects of reality that ran counter to their class interests.[60] This attention to normative bias, however, falls short of answering the challenge from the Right, that is, the role of subjective choice in ideological thinking: *Who* determines *what* practice should test the correctness of ideology? Does being part of the working class entail a uniform allegiance to Marxism or to the party's production criterion?

These questions obviously went beyond the official frame of analysis. They attracted special interest in the late 1980s, when the upholding of Marxism as the sole source of truth came to be questioned, often by the same reform theorists who played an active part in developing Marxism. In an article observing the decennial of the truth debate of 1978, Yu Guangyuan proposed extending the scope of that debate to the question of whether any truth should be "concrete" and not "abstract."[61] In other words, any truth, including the Marxist fundamental principles, should not be absolute and immune to evidence of empirical change. In their articles on the subject, Su Shaozhi and Wang Yizhou complained about the ethic of *da yi tong* that suppressed "pluralistic thinking."[62] Two writers argued in *Guangming ribao* that "truth does not mean that it is absolutely correct, or that it is held by one school only."[63] A third writer complained that Marxism had been deified as if it embraced all human truth and no other schools of thought were needed.[64]

Still others saw the diversity of truth in terms of a need to replace the fundamental principles of Marxism. Zhang Xiangyang, coeditor of Su's project on developing Marxism, attacked the fundamental fallacy of Marxism in a Hong Kong–based paper in early 1989. Historical materialism was "mechanistic," he wrote, because of its "extreme rationalism." This made Marx's analyses of human society and capitalist society simplistic. For example, Marx mechanistically emphasized the deterministic role of private ownership and failed to foresee possible changes in later periods. Zhang also disputed Marx's world view by suggesting that private ownership and its concomitant class struggle were no longer central to contemporary capitalism.[65] Others advocated abandoning the starting point of Marxist philosophy, the counterposing of materialism against idealism. Instead, Chinese political thought should shift to the study of the person as the first question of philosophy.[66]

The assertion of the human role and pluralistic thinking ultimately led many to the conclusion that because of the inherent limitations of the materialist epistemology and methodology, the fundamental principles of Marxism could not be absolute truths, and that, further, the development of Marxism would not suffice to transcend those limitations.[67]

The Reconception of Socialism

The central contention in the reconception of socialism was that China must break away from its unrealistic approach to socialism in the past. That approach was unrealistic because it emphasized the normative requirements of socialism, not its material prerequisites.[68] Specifically, three misconceptions of socialism over the previous decades were identified concerning (1) the stage of China's social development; (2) the model of socialist development; and (3) the relationship between efficiency and equality.

Regarding China's stage of development, consensus emerged on the incongruence between the actual state of Chinese socialism and the ideal state of Marx's socialism, in analyses ranging from those in *Hongqi* and *Renmin ribao* to those in *Jingji ribao*. China was previously judged to have completely entered the socialist stage, many analysts now acknowledged, because attention was paid only to the general features of socialism, not the special characteristics of China. A proper reappraisal of the developmental stage was highly important, because an overestimation in the past had contributed to the lack of objectivity in policy making: Based on the judgment that China had entered the socialist stage, past leaders did not allow production relations of earlier social stages. Conversely, institutions that exceeded China's stage of development were pursued simply because they were socialist.[69]

The purpose of redefining the stage of Chinese socialism was not just to recognize its peculiarity but also to conceptualize it from the point of view of its unique historical position. The notion of the primary stage was designed to serve both purposes because it differentiated Chinese socialism from Marx's ideal type, on the one hand, and from socialism of other countries, on the other. In other words, the notion referred to a special stage that an economically and culturally underdeveloped country like China must experience in adopting socialism.[70]

Su and Zhang attributed past misconceptions on the question of stage above all to "subjective factors," that is, a dogmatic understanding of the general principles of Marx and a lack of recognition of the peculiarity of China's conditions. These errors led to a failure to appreciate China's "structural untenability" to enter fully the socialist stage at once: the incompatibility between Marx's socialism born out of developed capitalism and Chinese socialism born out of semifeudalism and semicolonialism. This failure was a mistake of divorcing theory from reality. But this mistake was seen to differ from the cognitive errors of the ultra-leftists, because objective factors were also responsible for the CCP's impetuosity on the issue of developmental stage. Su and Zhang discussed two such factors rooted in the revolutionary experience of socialist countries: the military style of leadership and the neglect of individual interests.

Owing to the wartime environment in which most socialist states were born, they argued, socialist leaders were forced to adopt a developmental strategy aimed at rapidly catching up with more advanced capitalist countries. In this context, socialist leaders easily applied familiar methods of handling military tasks to the building of new societies, namely, a high-speed, mobilizing strategy that sought to defy objective constraints. This military style had some merits initially, because social change could indeed be engineered immediately and dramatically upon the revolution thanks to the social base of the revolution. Unfortunately, socialist leaders took these temporary victories as the rationale to engineer radical changes well after social circumstances had changed. The more important change, they argued, concerned the interests of social groups. Before the revolution, the major conflict of interests existed among different social classes. Hence the party could successfully mobilize the masses on the basis of their class interests. But after class conflicts were resolved by the revolution, individual and collective interests within the working class became important. Yet leaders exhausted the public's initial enthusiasm and willingness for self-sacrifice to pursue unrealistically higher and higher stages of socialism.[71]

If the retreat into the primary stage allowed some "presocialist" elements to exist, the problem arose as to how to justify the reform of the remaining, socialist portions of society. To deal with the problem, Su and Zhang defined the term primary stage in two ways. First, this was a stage of socialism based on an underdeveloped commodity economy (the presocialist portion). Second, any socialist production relations built on such a base cannot be perfect (the socialist portion). The latter point justified not attempts to march toward ideal socialism but rather constant reforms to accomplish the tasks of the primary stage.[72] Those tasks were, interestingly, quantified in GNP per capita increases according to the party's long-term plans. Thus the GNP per capita was to be doubled every decade beginning in the 1980s and to reach the state of a middle-level developed country by the middle of the next century. The primary stage of socialism, begun in the 1950s, would thus encompass over a hundred years.[73]

Regarding the model of socialist development, the consensus was that China should no longer cherish those institutions that were not necessarily socialist in nature but were formed under special historical conditions. The established economic and political systems were primarily such institutions referred to here. According to Su and Zhang, the political system was partly a legacy of the revolutionary struggles that required a highly centralized, command structure. This system was still effective in the early postrevolutionary period in resisting imperialist blockades, protecting national independence, and reviving the economy. But after the consolidation of power and socialist transformation, the political system should have changed accordingly. However, administrative and command functions were preserved as inherent features of socialism.[74]

Similarly, the adoption of the Soviet command economy was facilitated by postwar circumstances, including the urgent need to unify finance and the economy, transform the private sector, and accelerate industrialization. As the transition was completed and the state-owned economy grew stronger beginning in 1957, Su and Zhang contended, many of the mechanisms to control the economy and the private sector were no longer necessary or adequate. In fact, some drawbacks of the command economy were already apparent during the period of transformation (the 1950s) but were compensated for by the presence of the mixed economy then: The private and collective sector supplied small goods and services unavailable from the state sector. Once socialist transformation was complete, the drawbacks of excessive control became clearer. Rather than changing the command economy, however, leaders sought to push it further, beginning with the Great Leap Forward of 1958. In the next two decades, the overcentralized political and economic system combined to stifle China's development.[75]

Regarding the relationship between efficiency and equality, the key reappraisal was that equality was not linked to efficiency or the criterion of production forces in the past. Because the goal of equality was a major rationale for adopting socialist production relations in the first place, those production relations were kept intact to ensure equality in terms of leveled income, even if they were not conducive to efficiency in terms of raising productivity. As a result, equality was achieved on the basis of a low level of production forces. The resultant "common poverty," even though equal, was now rejected as not genuine socialism. Deng simply redefined the goal of socialism in terms of efficiency.

> Of the many lessons we have to sum up, a very important one is this: we should make clear what is socialism and how to build socialism. . . . The primary task of socialism is to develop production forces and to elevate the standard of the material and cultural life of the people. Our twenty years of experience from 1958 to 1976 have told us: poverty is not socialism, socialism is to eliminate poverty. It is not socialism to not develop production forces and raise the people's living standards.[76]

Elsewhere Deng pronounced that to "uphold socialism" was to develop production forces. In simple paraphrasing, Deng emphasized efficiency on the ground of socialism's promise of a high level of production forces, and he ended up equating efficiency with socialism.[77]

In their book, Su and Zhang acknowledged that a high level of production forces was only a means, not an end. They saw the original intention of Marx as a search for a social system conducive both to the growth of production forces and the development of the person: The former was a means in being a precondition to and guarantee of the latter. But under China's current conditions, they argued, it was materially impossible to attend to both at once. Rather, the appeal of socialism could be expressed only in better standards of living for the people. In their words, "at the primary stage of socialism, the fundamental demand of our people is to shake off poverty and become prosperous." To define socialism in terms of production forces, therefore, "reflects the urgent aspiration of the people" and would "make socialism more scientific and more attractive" to the people. To allow the development of the person in the long run, they added "common prosperity" to the "development of production forces" as the twin goals of Chinese socialism: The latter was to lay the foundation for the former, which, in turn, was to prepare for the full development of the person.[78]

Overall, the emphasis on the material base did help to refute political forces on the Left. After all, it appeared doctrinally sound to justify China's retreat from socialism from the Marxist view of the primacy of production forces and the progressive stages of social development. But the same emphasis also lent support to the assertion of the Right that China's socialist production relations contradicted its level of production forces, and that therefore China should go back in history to "make up for" the capitalist stage of development. Forced to face this dilemma in the wake of the 1986 student protests, the Thirteenth Congress report thus rebuked the "epistemological errors" of the Left and the Right.

The belief that under the specific historical conditions of modern China, the Chinese people could not bypass capitalism and embark on the socialist road, amounts to a mechanism on the question of revolution and development. This is an important epistemological source of rightist errors. The belief that the primary stage of socialism can be bypassed without a major development of production forces and a highly socialized production, commercialization, and modernization is utopianism on the question of revolution and development. This is an important epistemological source of leftist errors.[79]

In other words, to the challenge from the Left, the report replied that a particular social stage could not be arbitrarily bypassed. But to the challenge from the Right, it answered that a particular stage needed not be mechanistically followed.

Although their personal views belonged to the category of the Right castigated here, Su and Zhang attempted to resolve the above dilemma in their semiofficial book. They admitted that the discrepancies between theory and practice in Chinese socialism opened a "new horizon" for understanding the relation between production relations and production forces. One could no longer claim that a particular mode of production of a country was "solely determined by economic factors." This did not mean, however, that historical materialism had totally lost its credibility. For them, historical materialism was a scientific methodology for the analysis of the general trend, not the specific processes of historical development. Attention must be paid to the interaction of different factors, including the role of the superstructure in social transformation. In the Chinese case, superstructure (Marxist ideology and the CCP) played an obvious role in China's historical "leap" from semifeudalism to socialism.[80]

Yet the very analysis of "specific processes" raised two crucial issues that Marx declined to elaborate, at least in those of his writings emphasized in the CCP doctrine. These were (1) the role of human choice in historical development and (2) the possibility of diverse modes of production other than those dictated by historical materialism. As noted by the female researcher Hong Yingsan, the historical positioning of the "primary stage" of socialism was problematic in the framework of Marx's stage theory: It was at once precapitalist and postcapitalist. The peculiarity of this stage implied that history was multilinear rather than unilinear, and that factors other than production forces could determine the mode of production in a given society.[81] The implication of this analysis was more problematic: Unilinearism meant that China should not adopt socialism because it did not go through the capitalist stage, while multilinearism implied that China needed not adopt socialism because socialism was not an inevitable stage of human evolution. Fundamentally, Su and Zhang realized, the real question was "do people have freedom to choose a particular set of production relations?" For them, Marx did not exclude this possibility, as testified by his theory of the Asiatic mode of production—except that Marx placed this choice in the context of given production forces.[82] But others overtly questioned the inevitability of a particular mode of production as outlined by Marx's stage theory. The history of human civilization, they declared, was a matter of human beings' "subjective choice."[83]

Some intellectuals carried this line of analysis to its logical conclusion by late 1988 and early 1989. They raised the fundamental question in all Chinese efforts at rethinking socialism thus far, that is, the desirability of socialism. The question was especially relevant by mid-1988 when reform had gone as far as it could within the system. Both ownership reform and political reform hinged on the larger question of what to do with socialism: An overall negation would open the way for individual ownership and pluralistic politics advocated by liberal reformers. The view of leading reform theorists was ambivalent at best. For Wang Yizhou, the socialist system had passed the test of survivability but not that of superiority in the seventy years of its existence since the October Revolution. He attributed the latter failure to two factors. Structurally, the system's "survivability" depended on its control mechanisms, not its superiority. Historically, the system had been burdened by a heavy "feudal" legacy in nearly all the countries that adopted it. Thus Wang no longer complained just about "feudal elements" as he and others did in 1986. Rather, he drew structural parallels between "feudalism" and socialism: (1) the self-sufficient, noncommercial economy and the planned economy; (2) "feudal despotism" and the all-powerful party-state; and (3) *da yi tong* and the CCP's unified ideology.[84]

Some other prominent figures went further by calling Chinese socialism a complete failure. At a symposium at Beijing University in December 1988 and then again in an article in January 1989, Jin Guantao, editor of the "Toward the Future" book series, spoke of the "trial and failure of socialism" as "one of the two legacies of the twentieth century." Ge Yang, editor of the weekly *Xin guanzha* (New observation), added that "some may regard [Jin's] criticism as too harsh, but I think it's still too light and insufficient." She predicted that a "high tide to criticize socialism" would occur on the seventieth anniversary of the May Fourth movement.[85] In an April issue of *Shijie jingji daobao*, Wen Yuankai declared the "failure" of the Chinese Revolution. "History has painfully made a great and tragic conclusion," he wrote, "that China must carry out a second revolution." The tone of these statements approached that of the more established "bourgeois liberals" such as Fang Lizhi, who continued his attacks despite his demotion in 1987. Writing in a Taiwan-based paper in January 1989, Fang called the fortieth anniversary of the Chinese Revolution and the seventieth anniversary of the May Fourth movement "symbols of China's disappointment and hope." The root cause of that disappointment, he said, lay in socialism.[86]

The conclusion drawn from this line of assessment was that China, as a nation and a civilization, must abandon a mistaken choice of social system and make a new choice. In one statement reflective of the intellectual mood in early 1989, a scholar referred to China's failure in politics, economy, ideology, values, and institutions in the last forty years as a "failure of cultural choice."[87] In his television series "River Elegy," Su Xiaokang blamed China's backwardness on its "yellow civilization" and its Asiatic mode of production, while hailing the "blue civilization" for the modern advancement of the West. In more extreme expressions, some among the younger generation asserted that China would have been better off had England colonized it after the Opium War, or had Japan won World War II.[88] In other words, China would be better off had it not adopted socialism. The reassessment of socialism, then, ultimately led to the negation of its track record and the embrace of its opposite.

The Reconception of Capitalism

The reconception of capitalism was intimately related to the reconception of socialism because of their opposing relationship to each one. Specifically, this reconception came to focus on the sequential and horizontal relationship between the two systems for two reasons. First, the CCP's past emphasis on the presocialist nature of capitalism had served to treat any adoption of capitalist methods as historical retreat and deviation. Second, the CCP's emphasis on the diametrical contrast between socialism and capitalism had served to categorize the relation between the two systems as inherently hostile and incompatible. Within the official framework, the reconception was formally made in the Thirteenth Congress report in November 1987. Outside that framework, Xu Jiatun and Tong Dalin were most prominent. Xu was a former provincial head who became the chief Chinese representative to Hong Kong in the 1980s, and Tong was a deputy director of the State Council's Commission on Economic Structural Reform.

In rethinking the sequential relationship between capitalism and socialism, a new emphasis developed regarding the continuity between capitalism and socialism. One source of this continuity was attributed to the fact that any new mode of production must necessarily be born out of an old mode. Just as Marx's theories of transforming the old world were based on a critical analysis of it, so a new world must bear some marks of the old. Another source of continuity between socialism and capitalism was ascribed to the fact that contemporary capitalism had exhibited a "greater capacity for creating human civilization" than Marx expected. Hence capitalism was now seen as capable of offering more for socialism to absorb than had previously been believed (especially the market, political democracy, rule of law, and civil service). A final source of continuity between the two systems was seen in their parallel coexistence in the contemporary world.[89]

The rethinking of the horizontal relationship between socialism and capitalism centered on Lenin's theory of the "imperialist age" in which international communism was situated. This theory enunciated the general crisis of capitalism, the inevitability of imperial war, the inevitability of revolution spurred by war, and the containment of war by revolution. The CCP had long upheld the theory, at least in doctrine. Although Chinese foreign policy based on these theories was abandoned in the 1970s, Lenin's theory continued to be taught in classrooms, and official revision of the theory was made only in Zhao Ziyang's Thirteenth Congress report in November 1987.

In redefining the nature of the contemporary age, Zhao used a statement that Deng made in 1985: "The major themes of the contemporary world are peace and development."[90] By "peace and development," Deng reversed Lenin's view of the international environment and the task of proletarian countries. In other words, "war and revolution" were no longer the determinants of the relationship between former imperialist and proletarian countries. In elaborating the characteristics of this new age of "peace and development," the collections of the Central Party School and of Su and Zhang pointed out four empirical changes since Lenin. First, the decline of ideological confrontation and the presence of nuclear deterrence had changed the East-West relationship from "war" into "peace"; and the end of colonialism had changed the North-South relationship from "revolution" to "development." Second, progress in science and technology had strengthened the vitality of capitalism and created a new arena of international competition different from the war and revolution of the earlier age. Third, economic interdependence had reduced the likelihood of imperialist war. Finally, reform across socialist countries had brought the socialist world into the world market in greater coexistence with capitalism.[91]

The rethinking of capitalism again generated impulses unintended by official efforts. Exploiting the official emphasis on the changing nature of contemporary capitalism, some analysts tried to make deeper analyses of the vitality of capitalism. Apart from scientific progress, which was a nonideological element, Tong Dalin pointed to changes in the superstructure and production relations—both ideologically charged elements—that had invigorated contemporary capitalism. One was the nature of ownership. Owing to the proliferation of stocks, he asserted on the basis of dubious facts, big companies were no longer the private property of a few financial oligarchs but rather the common property of tens of thousands of shareholders. Another change lay in the nature of the capitalist state. Because the market reflected the free will of individuals, he again idealistically claimed, government regulations could not just serve a few individuals or a social class, but only the entire society.[92] Elsewhere, Tong suggested that changes in production relations under capitalism had rendered Marx's theory of exploitation obsolete and that capitalist society had embraced Marx's emphasis on the human being. By contrast, he contended, the individual person had been abandoned by Communist movements since Lenin and been reduced to the "least valuable thing" in China.[93] Others, including Xu Jiatun, pointed to the emergence of macroeconomic regulation, the welfare state, and the middle class that had ameliorated socioeconomic structures and class relations under capitalism.[94]

For Yu Guangyuan, these structural adjustments suggested that capitalist production relations might allow greater development of production forces than Marxist teachings could ever predict.[95] For Xu Jiatun, the antifeudal ideology and rule of law developed under capitalism were superior to the "feudalistic" ideology and institutions of China.[96] Still others, whose views were openly published in such papers as *Renmin ribao* and *Guangming ribao*, saw a growing "convergence" of socialism and capitalism, for example, the increased use of planning under capitalism and that of the market under socialism, the separation of ownership and management under both systems, and similar patterns of modernization. A few even saw the engulfing of the world by the industrial civilization and its replacement of the agrarian civilization. In this light, the increasing parallels between China and the capitalist world were historically inevitable because China was embarking on a path already traveled by developed countries. On the basis of this "convergence" thesis, these advocates called for ending the practice of asking "socialist" or "capitalist" (*xing "she," xing "zi"*) when new policies were considered.[97]

This "convergence" thesis became the other side of the production criterion, according to which any forms of production relations—no matter which system they came from—could be used so long as they contributed to the growth of production forces. The reconception of capitalism, in this line, served to deideologize both capitalism and socialism.

The Place of Marxism in Chinese Political Culture

The official concern with the place of Marxism in the Chinese value system is best reflected in the efforts to build "socialist spiritual civilization," a party platform since 1981 and written into the Thirteenth Congress report as one of the Chinese "developments" of Marxism. The function of socialist spiritual civilization, as noted by Dirlik, is to check against the danger of ideological retreat in the efforts to reorient society.[98] Indeed, the 1986 resolution on spiritual civilization warned that if the ideological aspect was neglected, "we will be not able to guarantee the socialist direction of our modernization course, and our socialist society will lose its goals and ideals." Paradoxically, the type of material civilization pursued in economic reforms appeared to be incompatible with a spiritual civilization based on Marxism. The place of Marxism in Chinese spiritual civilization, therefore, must be redefined. Essentially, the post-Mao reappraisal here was that Marxism still provided the dominant values, but no longer the only values.

The first redefinition of the place of Marxism concerned the source of social values and ideals. In the early 1980s the place of Marxism was central in the concept of socialist spiritual civilization. "Communist ideals" were prescribed as the "core of socialist spiritual civilization" in both the Sixth Plenum of the Eleventh Congress in 1981 and the Twelfth Party Congress in 1982. By late 1986, however, the term "communist ideals" was dropped from socialist spiritual civilization in the party's resolution on spiritual civilization. In its place, the resolution made a distinction between the "communist ideals" of the party and a "common ideal" of society defined as the building of a modern and democratic country. Because it was unrealistic to demand the masses of commitment to communist ideals at present, the resolution stated, a common ideal of the nation would reflect the aspirations of the people from all walks of life and avoid alienating those committed to national modernization but not to communism. The mandate of communist ideals, on the other hand, applied to members and active followers of the party. Another redefinition of the place of Marxism involved public morality. Again the 1986 resolution divided public morality into "socialist ethics" for the majority of the people and "communist ethics" for party members and cadres. The former endorsed distribution according to work, competition, material incentives, and individual interests. But in a departure from the bourgeois emphasis on the individual, socialist ethics would emphasize the "integration of individual, collective, and state interests," and individual interests should complement rather than contradict collective or state interests. Party members and cadres, on the other hand, were to adopt self-sacrifice and moral incentives as norms of public morality. The resolution summarily blamed the party's failure to make a distinction between socialist and communist ethics, between the masses and party members, and between ethical standards of the present and the future, for past lapses into "absolute egalitarianism."

Third, the place of Marxism was redefined in terms of its relation to other aspects of cultural and intellectual life. Ideology was to be limited to the area of spiritual civilization and to play a guiding rather than an all-encompassing role in the spheres of education, culture, science, and the arts. Su and Zhang, in particular, blamed a lack of a civic culture in Chinese society on the replacement of culture and education by ideology. For them, construction of this culture should form the "foundation" of spiritual civilization, for it would provide the basic avenues of fostering higher ideals, beliefs, and ethics. Without this foundation, ideology would have little upon which to build.[99]

Finally, the place of Marxism in China was redefined in relation to the place of "cultural achievements and civilization" of the non-Marxist world. In the new conception, the dominance of Marxism would no longer mean the exclusion of other schools of thought. In this connection the resolution on spiritual civilization stated that the concepts of democracy, liberty, and equality represented a "major liberation of the human mind" in the struggle of the rising bourgeoisie and the working class against feudal despotism. As such, they were historically progressive and should be inherited by socialism. However, the practice of these principles should differ in the two systems given their class nature and composition.[100]

These redefinitions of the place of Marxism in Chinese political culture in turn inspired an intellectual challenge initiated by some of those who had led the mainstream line of reconception. As conservative officials tightened their "cultural squeeze" in late 1988, these intellectuals began to turn attention to the basis of the official claim to ideological correctness. Was Marxism able to dominate Chinese political culture because of its claim to truth, or was it because of its officially sanctioned position? The latter, they answered.

Su Shaozhi saw the problem in the combination of political and moral authority in the state. This allowed Marxism to have a privileged status vis-à-vis other schools of thought. Even worse, it permitted self-proclaimed advocates of Marxism to use this status to castigate perceived heretics.[101] Li Honglin also pinpointed the problem in the official place of Marxism that excluded the legitimacy of all other philosophies and theories.[102] In a call to end the ideological monopoly of Marxism, two other scholars proposed that there no longer be one "unified, standardized, and authoritative system" in Chinese political thought.[103] A single school of thought was harmful, all concluded, because politicians could insist on "upholding" aspects of it that were politically useful.

The monopolistic position of Marxism was partly attributed to the "cultural distortion" of Marxism in China, particularly a "feudalization of Marxism." "Feudalization" referred to the centralized system of thought in the imperial tradition of "abolishing all schools of thought but Confucianism." In the words of Ruan Ming, a contributor to the book *Mengxing de shike*, "the integration of Marx and Emperor Qin Shihuang could only lead to the domination of Marx by the Emperor and the domination of democracy by despotism." In the same collection, Wang Ruoshui called the struggle against dogmatism and "feudalism" the "dual tasks of the enlightenment movement" in the late 1980s.[104] Wu Dakun, a noted historian who refuted Karl Wittfogel in his articles in the early 1980s, argued in mid-1989 that the legacy of the Asiatic mode of production had an impact on the persisting economic bureaucratism and political despotism of present-day China.[105] Writing on "five distortions in the sinification of Marxism," still another scholar called Chinese Marxism the "neo-Confucianism" of modern China. The Chinese tradition of annotating classics, using moral doctrine as means of political and social control, and conformity to collective thinking and values, he asserted, all contributed to the "feudalization" of Chinese Marxism.[106]

Following these analyses, the most important task in the reconception of socialism was to change the centrally sanctioned position of Marxism so as to create the political conditions for a "diversity of truths." Wang Ruoshui went back to his humanistic emphasis to justify a person's subjective preferences and challenge Marx's theory of cognition.[107] In a book on the "A Philosophy about the Person," Jin Guangtao made similar arguments.[108] One scholar directly used the recent emphasis among philosophers on the role of the subject in cognition to justify a theory of subjective choice: If the human being, not the material world, determined human cognition, then one's subjective preferences had a crucial impact on how each person perceived the world.[109] In the final analysis, the assertion of the subjective role justified the freedom of choice in one's world view, and therefore a rejection of an imposed world view.

The Fourteenth Congress report said relatively little on the issues discussed in this chapter: the development of Marxism, the reconception of socialism and capitalism, and the place of Marxism in Chinese "spiritual civilization." It affirmed the "upholding and development of Marxism" without giving priority to either. It basically affirmed the Thirteenth Congress line on the developmental stage, developmental model, principal contradiction, and motive force of development of Chinese socialism. It endorsed "absorbing and utilizing" the achievements of capitalist countries. On spiritual civilization, the report actually played down Marxism and gave more attention to a more current problem, the erosion of public morality in recent times. Apparently, the post-1992 leadership is determined to focus on the "socialist market economic order" and not to risk other ideological ventures to change major directions of the country.

CONCLUSION

Much as in the political sphere, intellectuals displayed considerable independence from the official framework of analysis throughout the three stages of the post-Mao reconception of socialism, even though it was the reform leadership that encouraged the efforts at each stage. As a result, the intellectual discussions were not always incorporated into the official platform or endorsed by the political leadership. In the initial phase from the late 1970s to the first half of the 1980s, the official view defended socialism as the guiding principle and path of national development. Despite admitting failures in past efforts at building socialism, the party objected to the questioning by some intellectuals about the adoption of socialism, for fear of raising doubts about the legitimacy of Marxism and the CCP itself. Empirical difficulties and problems in building socialism were assessed as rooted not in the unfeasibility of adopting socialism, but in mistaken practices.

By the mid-1980s the pressures of reform compelled reform leaders to confront the issue of the adequacy of socialism as the guiding thought and path of Chinese society. They came to recognize the challenges that the contemporary world had posed to Marxism and the implications for Chinese socialism. Difficulties and problems in Chinese socialism became linked to limits within the original theory that had constrained the choice of political and economic structures. But this recognition did not yet lead to a rejection of socialism, except among a handful of intellectuals, but to attempts to locate the incorrect and outdated aspects of Marxism and to develop correct new ones.

Officially sponsored development of socialist theory materialized finally in the late 1980s with the theory of the primary stage of socialism. As a distinct theory of socialism appropriate to Chinese reality, it was intended to overcome the limits in Marxism and offer guidance to Chinese practice. But the direction of reassessment thereafter created the context and momentum for many intellectuals to confront the fundamental question beneath all post-Mao efforts to reassess socialism, namely, the very position of socialism in China. Some of the very intellectuals who made theoretical articulation for the official reassessment also came to pursue that line of analysis in their more independent writings.

The officially guided reconception and intellectuals' more provocative reconception came up with different answers to the questions posed at the beginning of this chapter. Within the official framework, the rethinking of Marxism, socialism, capitalism, and the place of Marxism came to the conclusion that socialism, in its traditional version, did not fit China's national conditions in many respects. But this did not spell the end of Marxism or socialism for China; it only entailed that they must be adjusted in accordance with national characteristics. Nor did the discrepancy between the original theory and the empirical world mean the end of socialism as a social goal and historical problematic; it only signified that there was a greater complexity in terms of its empirical realization, such as a temporary retreat into an earlier stage of social development.

Beyond the official framework, however, socialism was found to be unfit for China on both philosophical and empirical grounds. Philosophically, the basic methodologies, normative assumptions, and historical and social analyses of Marxism were untenable, incorrect, or outdated. These entailed that Marxism was no longer a desirable source of first principles and that socialism was no longer a feasible path of national development. Empirically, the very discrepancies between Marxist theory and Chinese reality, and the very need for a "retreat" into an earlier stage of development, ruled out unilinearism in human evolution and the inevitability of the Marxist path. The conclusion drawn from this line of reconception was the need to search for alternative truths and forms of national development.

The reconception of socialism had been influenced by political needs as well as subjective assessments of China's national experience. Advocates of both the intrasystem and negative reconception did not question their own methodologies, assumptions, and limitations in their analyses. For the former, the heavily materialist view of the primary stage framework was based on a rather one-sided reading of classic works and tailored to the needs of economic reform. It emphasized the incongruence of socialist economic institutions with the economic base but played down the incompatibilities in the political sphere. But the official analysis was not a totally manipulated political discourse. It evolved incrementally and quite logically, at least from the Marxist perspective. In this sense it did represent a learning process and what some leaders really thought was wrong with Chinese socialism.

The more negative reconception of socialism, increasingly made by formerly intrasystem analysts, reflected even more genuine a process of learning and intellectual soul-searching. These analysts, especially the leading reform theorists, consciously went beyond their expected role as supporters and interpreters of official discourse to question this discourse itself. They were ingenuous in using Marxist analytical tools to discredit Chinese socialism, and in using Chinese socialism to discredit Marxism. But the intellectual analysts of socialism were also political in the sense that they, like the liberal critics of China's economic and political system, held some fundamental normative biases against socialism. These biases and other problems in their critical analyses will be discussed in the next chapter, as part of the response from conservative reformers who assumed a basically affirmative approach to socialism.

CHAPTER EIGHT

The Response to the "Liberal" Reassessment of Socialism

THE POST-MAO reassessment of socialism reviewed thus far suggests a prevailing struggle against dogmatism on the Left, that is, the political forces that refused to adapt to the interpretation and application of socialism to the extent desired by more reformist leaders. At the same time, reformulation in the officially guided line of inquiry was largely within the socialist framework of reference. In keeping with this frame, there had been a consistent struggle against "liberalism" on the Right in the same process, namely, the social and intellectual forces that had been targeted in the five campaigns against bourgeois liberalization, as discussed in chapter 5. The demarcation of "bourgeois liberals" here is not so much to determine whether they were antisystem or intrasystem analysts, but whether officially they were perceived to have stepped out of the permissible bounds of public discourse. From the perspective of this study, those political campaigns had served the purpose of checking the impulses generated by official reassessment and responding to the so-called liberal variant of reappraisal.

The recurrent attacks on rightist deviance can be seen as a function of elite power struggle, or as an instrumental use of ideology to maintain political control amid desired loosening in the economic realm.[1] But the strenuous and periodic efforts to balance between the Left and the Right reveal on a deeper level both the consistency and the seriousness with which the regime as a whole had responded to the "liberal" analyses. The striking parallels in the issues raised and the types of deviance attacked during each campaign testify further to this point. Moreover, despite the different alliances of political forces that initiated the five political campaigns, each campaign was backed by the supreme "engineer of reform," Deng Xiaoping himself. The links among the five campaigns illustrate the seriousness of the ideological conflicts that underlay the different schools of reassessment. They also evidence the boundaries of the official school.

This chapter looks into the official/conservative response to the "liberal" reassessment. It first reviews the key areas of this response that emerged in each anti–bourgeois liberal campaign and then looks at the content of the official critiques as a whole.

EVOLVING THEMES OF THE EFFORTS AGAINST
BOURGEOIS LIBERALIZATION

Each of the five post-Mao campaigns against ideological heterodoxy followed a period of officially encouraged relaxation and reformulation. One central concern of the campaign initiators had been that in each period of relaxation, certain public discussions went beyond the originally intended line of reformulation.

During the Democracy Wall movement of 1978–79 and the theory conference of early 1979, a common array of issues raised by the two forums caused great concern among the party leadership. First, criticisms of the mistakes of the Cultural Revolution and the late Mao era developed into analyses of the undemocratic nature of the Chinese political system, leading to the conclusion that the socialist system was inferior to the capitalist system. Second, criticisms of Mao's mistakes during his late years extended to a negation of his entire life and thought, leading to misgivings about the party's entire history and its capacity to lead. Finally, criticisms of the arbitrary persecutions during the Cultural Revolution extended to calls for freedom, democracy, and human rights, often explicitly of the Western type.[2]

In the campaign of spring 1979 against these trends, the negation of socialism was targeted as the fundamental problem of the recent surge of rightist tendencies. Because they criticized the lack of democracy, freedom, and human rights under socialism, the wall activists were accused of attributing the leftist excesses and injustices of the Cultural Revolution to proletarian dictatorship and the party's leadership. Because they extolled the guarantee of political rights under capitalism, they were also found guilty of championing that system as superior. "What those [democrats] really think," Deng remarked, was that "socialism is inferior to capitalism, and that mainland China is inferior to Taiwan."[3] The special commentators of the leading media organs also emphasized the antisocialist nature of the wall analysts, on the ground that they sought to dismiss this system as inherently incapable of providing their desired political goals.[4] Similarly, intellectuals' support for the wall movement, emphasis on the systemic roots of the Cultural Revolution and Mao's mistakes, and objection to the Four Fundamental Principles were criticized for showing doubt about the party, socialism, and Marxism. Thus, not only conservative officials Hu Qiaomu and Wang Renzhi but also Deng Xiaoping reproached both groups for contributing to an already serious "crisis of confidence" among the public after the Cultural Revolution.[5] In other words, those groups would not have been considered a formidable danger were they not perceived to have questioned China's fundamental system.

In the campaign against bourgeois liberal tendencies in the fall of 1981, major official complaints focused on public discussions of the dark side of society as inherent to socialism. The intellectual trend exemplified by "Unrequited Love" was held, in Hu Qiaomu's words, as a threat to public confidence in the political system and to the "spiritual health and political stability" of the country.[6] In his elaboration of the campaign on behalf of the party, Hu singled out the theoretical front as the most representative of the "Unrequited Love" phenomenon, with spillover effects in arts and literature. He enumerated several issue areas where the phenomenon was particularly prevalent.

In discussing "issues of fundamental importance," Hu complained, some sought to go beyond the framework of Marxist theory and Chinese practice of the past few decades. In discussing the Chinese Revolution and the socialist experience, some questioned China's choice of the socialist path, refused to see the achievements of socialism, and even called for a return to earlier stages of history (a clear reference to proponents of "underdeveloped socialism"). In analyzing Mao's mistakes of his late years, some negated the Mao Zedong Thought entirely, thereby seeking to discredit the whole history of the party, the entire national experience under its leadership, and the application of Marxism in China. In discussing democracy, some refused to accept the party's leading role born out of the revolution and castigated it as incompatible with popular initiative; or they excluded the concepts of dictatorship, law, centralism, and discipline in their consideration of democracy. In examining the mistakes of the party, such as the Antirightist movement, the Cultural Revolution, feudalistic styles of leadership, cadre privileges, and bureaucratism, they linked these to the party's systemic incapacity to lead the country.[7]

All three leaders who made public statements in the 1981 campaign—Deng Xiaoping, Hu Yaobang, and Hu Qiaomu—disparaged this line of criticism for deviating from the correct, intrasystem analysis. When Deng first commented on the army's request to conduct a public criticism of "Unrequited Love" in March 1981, he endorsed it on the ground of a need to contain both leftist and rightist tendencies. By August, after he viewed the movie version of the story and read internal reports about similar works, Deng was alarmed by the scope and intensity of recent "liberal" criticisms. Faulting Bai Hua for conveying solely the impression that the party and the socialist system were bad, Deng compared the impact of such works to that of the Democracy Wall activists.[8] In his campaign speech, Hu Yaobang concurred that Bai Hua's work represented a dangerous trend.[9] This trend was objectionable, Hu Qiaomu remarked, because it deliberately "distorted the history and reality of China's socialist society." In its various manifestations, the Gang of Four and the like were depicted as if they represented the party; traumatic events like the Cultural

Revolution were portrayed as if they were socialism itself; and the sufferings of a few victims were described as if no touch of brightness could be seen in the country.[10] Though Deng and Hu Yaobang were reluctant to launch an all-out political campaign in 1981, they agreed with Hu Qiaomu that such probing into the systemic causes of China's "dark side" must be resolutely opposed.

The campaign of late 1983–early 1984 against spiritual pollution also focused on the antisocialist nature of the discussions of humanism and alienation and other similar intellectual trends at the time. In his speech initiating the campaign, Deng remarked that the theories of humanism and alienation must be criticized because, rather than helping the people to understand past and existing problems of society, they would lead them to doubt and negate socialism, and to not appreciate its superiority.[11] He also rebuked other similar tendencies on the ideological front, including the advocacy of "abstract democracy" to endorse the freedom of speech for counterrevolutionary views; the contention that the media should place its "affinity to the people" above the "affinity to the party" (which was put forth by Hu Jiwei in response to the criticism that he should not have published Zhou Yang's article on humanism in *Renmin ribao*); skepticism about the necessity of the Four Fundamental Principles; the inquiry into whether China should or could adopt socialism and whether the CCP was a genuine proletarian party; and the advocacy of "everything for money" in place of socialist values.[12]

Criticisms of the discussions of humanism and alienation, by their intellectual critics Xing Fensi and Lu Zhichao as well as by Deng Xiaoping and Deng Liqun, again focused on the fundamental implications for Chinese socialism. Because the application of alienation in the Chinese context suggested that alienation did exist under socialism, this analysis was said to undermine socialism's claim to its capacity to eliminate alienation. Because alienation was used to explain the goals of reform, this concept was said to advocate that past failures were indeed caused by the system's neglect of the person. Because the emphasis on intrinsic human nature affirmed the "abstract" conception of the person devoid of class relations, advocates of alienation and humanism were said to champion the capitalist system premised on the individual.[13]

The major themes of the anti–bourgeois liberal campaign of late 1986 to early 1987 reflected similar concerns of the regime over the negation of the socialist system, though the issue areas were expanded. Here the major accusation against those who dominated the opinion forum during the liberalization of mid-1986 was that they had carried the negation of socialism and Marxism to new levels. For example, the party's call to develop Marxism was used to oppose Marxism; its efforts to introduce political reform were utilized to propound Western democracy; its emphasis on political reform to promote the economy was extended to calls for a marketization of both economic and political spheres; and its attention to the basis of the centralized political system was turned into exaggerated criticisms of the feudal basis of Chinese socialism. Most seriously, official encouragement of absorbing "cultural achievements of other civilizations" was exploited to spurn the nation's choice of developmental path born out of the Chinese Revolution. As a *Hongqi* article complained, some went so far as to champion the opening of China by the Opium War, on the claim that the intrusion of capitalism into feudalistic China was a positive thing, and that had it come earlier, China "would be far different from what it is now."[14] Others, like Fang Lizhi, were censured for using the party's liberalization to advocate "wholesale Westernization." Such advocates must be taken seriously, Hongqi warned, because they represented a "social trend" that sought to "negate the socialist system and adopt the capitalist system."[15]

This trend, not surprisingly, was identified in the literature of the campaign as a primary source of inspiration for student protesters and other young skeptics of the party and socialism. Conservative leaders in particular saw the problem of bourgeois liberalization as a calculated negation of socialism and sought a return to orthodoxy as the solution. Reform leaders such as Zhao, on the other hand, saw it as merely symptomatic of an inadequate assessment of Chinese socialism. His campaign efforts, therefore, focused on addressing the question of how the youth and the public should look at the record of socialism in China. As part of the effort *Renmin ribao* published several articles, of which three received Deng's praise. Chen Junsheng, a reform official under Zhao's State Council, wrote on the appropriate methods of comparing the capitalist and socialist systems. Hu Sheng, CASS president, deliberated on the historical context of China's socialist choice. Zhao Fusan, CASS vice president, discussed the appearance and the reality of Western culture and values. Deng Xiaoping concurred that the ideological confusion of youth stemmed from their inadequate assessment of socialism. But for Deng, as for conservative leaders, the intellectual "instigators" of student protests must not be tolerated because the type of bourgeois liberalization they advocated had gone beyond the party's reform platform and amounted to calling for "taking the capitalist road."[16]

Despite the popular base of the mass protests of mid-1989, the antiliberal campaign that followed in late 1989 and 1990 focused on the comprehensive reassessment of socialism among media and intellectual circles in 1988 and early 1989. This reassessment, as criticized by conservatives such as Wang Renzhi and Wu Shuqing, had served as the intellectual preparation for the political rebellion of mid-1989. The radical and liberal reform theorists and intellectuals were indiscriminately attacked together as "bourgeois liberals" for their alleged attack on socialism. For example, their analyses of the economic crisis and cadre corruption in 1988–89 placed the blame on the nature of the socialist system. Their discussion of the "totalist" nature of the state implied that so long as this totalism was not relinquished, reforms would not succeed. Their questioning of the choice of socialism and the place of Marxism in China insinuated the futility of preserving a social order and belief system whose possibilities of renovation had been exhausted. Their call for the privatization of public ownership and the cultivation of a middle class endorsed basic elements of the Western social order. Finally, their praise of European colonialism and Westernization suggested their extreme dissatisfaction with China's choice of political, economic, and value systems.[17]

As summed up by Wang Renzhi, the protest movement of 1989 represented the culmination of a fundamental conflict between the party and a handful of "instigators" over the direction of China's reforms and of the country in general.[18] Accordingly, conservatives who now dominated the media and other opinion forums launched a comprehensive critique of "bourgeois liberal" tendencies in the entire post-Mao period. "Bourgeois liberals" were accused of seeking to repudiate the socialist system and adopt the capitalist system since the late 1970s, from the denigration of certain periods of CCP rule to the negation of its entire revolutionary history, from the analysis of "feudal" influences to depictions of the "feudalization" of Chinese socialism, from the call for "making up for" the capitalist stage to open proposals for abandoning the socialist path, from the advocacy of abstract humanism and democracy to direct attacks on the people's democratic dictatorship, from the assertion of the priority of developing Marxism to the renunciation of its guiding role, and from the criticism of specific historical incidents and leaders to the negation of the entire international Communist movement.[19] The overall "liberal" platform was summarily characterized as "political pluralization, economic privatization, and ideological liberalization" in the direction of the capitalist system.[20] In the final conservative judgment, the sharp challenge presented to the ethos of the regime by the radical and liberal intellectuals was responsible for the loss of youth allegiance to the system and the party.

In sum, the five political campaigns from 1979 to 1990 focused on issues involving the proper reassessment of China's socialist experience and the desirability of socialism. The reassessments made by the social forces on the Right were characterized by at least part of the Chinese leadership as "bourgeois liberalization," defined by Hu Qiaomu as "consciously or unconsciously advocating the abandonment of the socialist path in the political, economic, social, and cultural spheres and the adoption of the so-called free capitalist system."[21] Whether or not this had indeed been the intention of the "bourgeois liberals," their reevaluation was "antisocialist" as measured by the official framework of analysis. As such, it had elicited repeated official reaction in the form of political campaigns.

THE RESPONSE TO THE "LIBERAL" REASSESSMENT

The parameters of the official definition of the framework beyond which reassessment becomes bourgeois liberalization were articulated in each campaign by party leaders and theoreticians. The analysis here will consider three key areas of post-Mao reassessment: value reorientation, developmental path, and institutional arrangements. The post-Mao value reorientation, symbolized in the Emancipation of the Mind, had been instrumental to the policy and ideological rectification after 1978. The reexamination of the nation's developmental path, epitomized in the notion of the primary stage of socialism, had made possible the rejection of the Soviet and Marxist models of development. The reevaluation of the institutional arrangements of socialism, embodied in the reform of central planning and state ownership, had justified a "multiform" economy. Yet in each of these areas, lines of demarcation had been drawn to check deviation from official boundaries.

The Exercise of the Emancipation of the Mind

Bourgeois liberal trends flourished in each period in the atmosphere of the Emancipation of the Mind encouraged by the regime. Hence to define the framework of "emancipation" had been a central issue in each of the five political campaigns. Summarily, the official policy of emancipating the mind pertained specifically to the rejection of leftist thinking and to the resolution of "new situations" created by economic reform. In reference to the Democracy Wall movement, Deng noted in early 1980 that emancipation applied to the "removal from the shackles of habitual forces and subjective biases, to the study of new situations and the solution of new problems." It should "never deviate from the Four Fundamental Principles or impair the stable and lively political environment. The entire party must have a consensus on this point."[22] Hu Qiaomu stated during the 1981 campaign:

> The Central Committee holds that the Emancipation of the Mind, primarily and principally, means to liberate our cadres and masses from the shackles of the "Left" mistakes of the Cultural Revolution and the period preceding [the

present regime], from the shackles of the "two whatevers," and to return to the scientific path of Marxism–Leninism–Mao Zedong Thought and the fine tradition of seeking truth from facts."[23]

Deng Liqun in the 1983 campaign and Zhao Ziyang in the 1986–87 campaign drew the line more sharply between the economic sphere and the political/ideological spheres.[24] As public discussions sharpened in the late 1980s, Wang Renzhi and others in the post-Tiananmen campaign differentiated the Emancipation of the Mind from the negation of the socialist system "as a whole."[25]

The alleged mistakes of the "bourgeois liberals" were that they pursued the emancipation of the mind beyond the scope of "leftist errors" and the specified "new situations." Thus regarding the Democracy Wall activists of 1979, Deng accused their "emancipation" of having gone "on the opposite side of the party and the people" and of threatening the "political environment" of the country.[26] Regarding the exposé literature in the early 1980s, Hu Qiaomu complained that "some comrades" extended their criticism of leftist mistakes to major aspects of Chinese revolutionary and socialist experiences.[27] In the campaign of 1983 the theories of alienation and humanism were castigated for questioning the goals and values of socialist society. In the campaigns of 1986 and 1989 liberals' Emancipation of the Mind was attacked for advocating the "importation of bourgeois thought": The party's calls for "opposing dogmatism," "developing Marxism," and "contending and blooming" were all exploited to "peddle Western bourgeois philosophy and political theories" so as to replace Marxism.[28]

The imposition of limits on the Emancipation of the Mind seems in apparent contradiction to the practice criterion promoted by the party to discredit the very practice of ideological monopoly. The party justified this on two grounds. First, it drew the line of permissible truth on the basis of Deng's bifurcation between fundamental and specific principles of Marxism. For Deng, the Emancipation of the Mind campaign was intended to discard the ultra-leftist distortion of Marxism, which made no distinction between fundamental and transitory principles and treated "whatever" as truth. Emancipation was aimed at the transitory, not the fundamental aspects of party ideology. Thus differentiated, the regime's insistence on adherence to socialism became compatible with, rather than contradictory to, the Emancipation of the Mind. The logic of the argument is that it was the fundamental principles of dialectic materialism that dictated the Emancipation of the Mind in the first place. The second justification for placing limits on the Emancipation of the Mind follows from here. As the basic world view and method of social analysis, the fundamental principles of Marxism were supposed to serve as the "cognitive and methodological" tools in the observation and analysis of reality. In particular, a *Hongqi* article stated, the Marxist conception of humans and history must be the guiding values and designs for China in its search for a viable path of development and for appropriate forms of social arrangement.[29] In a word, the Chinese society must rely on Marxism for basic affective and analytical categories in defining its social goals and values.

The regime, however, never found its own policies of economic non-orthodoxy and political orthodoxy contradictory. In the economic realm, reform and opening were justified by the primacy of "practice" and "production forces" derived from the so-called fundamental principles. In the political and ideological arena, "bourgeois practices and values" must be opposed, in Hu Qiaomu's words, so as to safeguard the socialist framework "in principle." Hu first elaborated on these forbidden practices and values in the campaign of 1981:

INSTITUTIONAL:
bourgeois parliamentary system
two-party system
electoral system
bourgeois freedom of speech, publication, assembly, and association

ATTITUDINAL:
bourgeois individualism
materialism and profit orientation
bourgeois way of living and hedonism
moral and artistic standards
concept of "natural rights"
worship of the capitalist system and the capitalist world[30]

Since the instrumental use of ideology in the economic realm cast much doubt on the regime's own faith in its doctrine, bourgeois liberals increasingly tried to challenge these "forbidden zones" in the political and ideological domains. Hence, in the latest two campaigns, the CCP took pains to draw the distinction between its economic reform and the capitalist road. The theory of the primary stage of socialism and the slogan of "one focus, two basic points" were direct products of the effort to mediate economic nonorthodoxy and political orthodoxy. In the words of Gong Yuzhi, deputy director of the CDP in the late 1980s, the practice criterion of 1978 was to legitimize "emancipation" from ultra-leftism in order to build socialism with Chinese characteristics, whereas the production criterion of the late 1980s was designed to justify the primary stage of socialism.[31]

Two major factors were held responsible for bourgeois liberals' periodic violation of the limits on the Emancipation of the Mind. First, these liberals were said to pit the policy of emancipation against the Four Fundamental Principles. That is, they deprived this policy of its Marxist premise. As Deng complained in 1979, liberals equated the party's emancipation policy with the "absolute freedom" to say whatever they liked.[32] Hu Qiaomu made a similar criticism in 1981 when observing that some comrades took the policy of "Let a Hundred Flowers Bloom" to be the party's *sole* policy in the ideological realm. Heuristically he distinguished that this policy was meant to define the *manner* of intellectual and literary exploration, not the *content* of such discourse. The latter must be guided by the party's policy of upholding the "leading role of Marxism in all political and ideological spheres of society."[33]

Another source of unrestricted emancipation was blamed on the tendency of "skewing toward the Right" in post-Mao political and ideological policy. The charge was first made by the "whatever" group during the 1979 and 1981 campaigns and by conservative reformers during the subsequent campaigns. The essence of this alleged skewing was a failure among leading ideological circles to draw a clear line between dogmatism and the Four Fundamental Principles. This failure, conservatives charged, resulted from a "predisposed fear of leftism" in post-Mao China: Because of the tremendous harms done by ultra-leftism during much of China's socialist experience, the party sometimes went to the other extreme of exclusively stressing opposition to the Left. The result was the proliferation of bourgeois liberalization throughout the decade and its inevitable explosion in 1989.[34]

This problem of "skewing to the right" for fear of leftism reflects a perennial dilemma of the post-Mao dual direction course, that is, the need to combat dogmatism in economics and liberalism in politics. The logic of official orthodoxy, however, defies such an incoherent orientation. Because of the coherent nature of Marxism, conservative forces could extend an anti–bourgeois liberal campaign in the political front to the economic front, which often served their actual political objectives. Faced with rising leftism in the midst of each campaign, Deng Xiaoping had to reverse the political tide to check leftism. Thus the surge of leftist forces in each of the post-Mao campaigns compelled him to circumscribe the offensive against the Right. In 1979, when the whatever group took the opportunity of political tightening to attack economic liberalization, Deng quickly shifted to reemphasize the greater danger of leftism. Deng and Hu Yaobang agreed to modify the scope of the 1981 campaign after Zhao Ziyang warned them of repercussions on economic reform.[35] When the campaign of 1983 got out of control and extended to social and economic spheres, reform leaders again pointed to the negative impact on economic reform and moderated the campaign within twenty-eight days of its commencement. In the campaign of 1986–87, when conservative leaders linked the rise of bourgeois liberalization in the political realm to the liberalization policies in the economic realm, Zhao quickly enacted measures to exempt economic reform from attack and in time put an end to the campaign itself.[36] The campaign of mid-1989–90 survived the longest because of the severity of the Tiananmen "riot" and because of the demise of Zhao's leadership. But in his spring talks of 1992, Deng Xiaoping once again turned the tide and faulted the Left for posing a greater danger. Such cyclical responses testify to the persistent need for, as well as the difficulty of, maintaining a dual-direction ideological course.

Various manifestations of bourgeois liberalization had been attributed to deviations from the Marxist world view and methodology in the exercise of the emancipation of the mind. In evaluating past and current practices of the regime, official critics charged, bourgeois liberals proceeded not from an acceptance but from a rejection of the fundamental soundness of the socialist system. This normative stand was linked to their attitude toward Marxism, that is, their denial of the "scientific truth and basic assumptions" of Marxist analytical criteria.[37] In other words, the fundamental problem here was that a significant portion of intellectuals, whose allegiance was crucial to the regime's maintenance of monopoly of truth, no longer pledged allegiance to the official brand of truth. In response, conservatives rejected the bourgeois liberal claim that Marxism was outdated, that it did not conform to China's realities, and that it was only one school among a "diversity of truth."[38] Conservatives dismissed such arguments as exaggerating the historical and analytical limitations of Marxism and using the "diversity of truth" as a pretext to peddle their cherished brand of truth, that is, Western values.[39] He Xin, a CASS researcher in his early forties who became a leading academic defender of socialism after mid-1989, argued that Marxism had a lasting significance for China by having offered four crucial elements: an ideological weapon against colonialism and imperialism, a useful economic theory for an underdeveloped country to gather capital rapidly for industrialization through state ownership, a pro–working class stance that helped to spare the Chinese people the misery of the early industrialization process, and a unifying force for China's political unification and economic modernization.[40] In short, Marxism had been and remained fundamentally relevant to China's national development.

On a deeper level, the CCP and conservatives in particular recognized that intellectuals' disillusionment with Marxism stemmed from the track record of socialism in postrevolutionary China. The question of an appropriate appraisal of this record had thus been another central issue in the official response to the "liberal" reassessment of socialism.

The Assessment of the Socialist Road

The key question raised in the "liberal" reappraisal of the Chinese socialist experience involved the fundamental soundness of the adoption of the socialist path in light of its inadequate performance. In authoritative responses by Chen Junsheng, Hu Sheng, Hu Qiaomu, Liu Danian, and others, the "liberal" view was summarily criticized for its alleged underlying assumption that had China not taken the socialist road, it would have developed better. This assumption was found to be "synchronically" mistaken, as it denied the historical necessity of China's choice of socialism. It was also found to be "diachronically" mistaken, as it juxtaposed the achievements of Chinese socialism to those of developed countries without regard for historical and social contexts. In addition, the "liberal" view was seen as normatively biased, because it passed specific imperfections of socialism for systemic deficiencies.

The major argument raised against the "synchronic" negation of socialism was that this perspective failed to appreciate the fact that generations of Chinese had already tried the capitalist road but all failed. This Chinese endeavor was traced back to the Westernizing movement of the 1860s, the Restoration movement of 1890s, the warlord period, and the Guomindang era. These efforts all failed, both conservative and reformist critics argued, mainly because of the West's subjudication of China under semicolonialism. For Hu Sheng, the presence of Western colonial powers was the most important factor in preventing China from developing a strong capitalist economy. The "imperialist invaders," he argued, introduced some new modes of production in the colonies according to their own needs and interests while retaining other indigenous social and economic relations for the same purposes. Thus the feudal landed class, which formed the basis of indigenous rulers in China, was not only preserved but turned into a compradore capitalist class dependent on imperialist powers. Lacking real control over national sovereignty and autonomy, the Chinese were never able to develop capitalism freely, or to utilize foreign trade and capital in accordance with indigenous needs and interests. To Hu Sheng, the only historical period in which capitalist development was able to flourish in China was between 1914 and 1918, when major imperialist powers were preoccupied with the war in Europe.[41]

Another reason for China's previous failure to develop capitalism was attributed to the tremendous economic and human costs incurred by colonial invasions, extortion of war indemnities, and civil wars backed by Western and Japanese colonial powers. The reformist official Chen Junsheng stressed that China had genuinely wanted to pursue the capitalist road, but its constant humiliation at the hands of the West eventually turned, as Mao had put it, the "earnest pupil" to search for alternative ways of national development. The result of China's failure to develop capitalism was the lack of an indigenous bourgeois class strong enough to put an end to semicolonialism and semifeudalism and to lead the nation on a modernization path. This role had to be assumed by the CCP along with the support of the peasant and working class.[42]

The emphasis of the "liberal" argument, however, is on the futility of half-measure reform efforts in the past as well as in the present. The post-Mao economic reform, so the argument goes, is similar to the policy of "Chinese learning as essence and Western learning as practice," which had contributed to China's previous failures to modernize and develop capitalism. In response, official critics contended that generations of Chinese intellectuals had indeed admired and pursued Western democracy before eventually abandoning it. This historical fact was particularly emphasized in the campaign of 1989–90, because of the overtly pro-Western orientation of student protesters. Authoritative critics repeatedly cited the futile quests of Kang Youwei, Liang Qichao, Sun Yat-sen, the May Fourth youths, and founders of the Communist party such as Chen Duxiu, Li Dazhao, and Mao Zedong to highlight the inevitability of China's choice of socialism.

Hu Qiaomu and others made a special point of citing Li Dazhao's transition from a passionate democrat to the first Chinese Marxist in the early twentieth century. Pointedly, they noted that the process of Li's transition distinguished him from other progressive intellectuals at the time who were equally in despair about China's plight but unable to find an effective remedy. While other intellectuals opposed colonialism and feudalism on the basis of the Western concept of *individual* freedom, Li came to realize that he must do so on the basis of *society*'s happiness and emancipation. The individualism of the former group eventually lapsed into anarchism. But Li turned to question seriously Western values and the relevance of the newly founded Chinese Republic to the welfare of the masses. The outbreak of World War I led Li to recognize further the social destructiveness of Western values. Li was quoted observing that "the war has cast much doubt on the authority of European civilization" and that "Europeans themselves now have to reevaluate the real value of their civilization."

Following this disillusionment, Li was said to have doubts about Western conceptions of social development and human evolution, particularly social Darwinism and Malthusianism. If these theories were originally viewed as justifications for European colonialism, now Li came to realize that the "development of capitalism" and the desire of capitalist countries to build huge "economic empires" were at the root of the colonial conquests and the military rivalry among European countries. Social Darwinism and Malthusianism did not explain human development but served only as the pretext for imperialism and war. This understanding contributed crucially to Li's shift to the Marxist view of history and of capitalism, and eventually to the socialist mode of development.[43] In citing Li's gradual change of faith, the CCP sought to show that the persistent Chinese rejection of Western ideas was not accidental.

Indeed, sometimes Chinese sufferings in the hands of Western colonial powers were cited as the primary reason for the rejection of the capitalist system on moral grounds. In an article on China's decision in the early 1950s to adopt socialism, Hu Qiaomu revealed that China's colonial experience and its continued isolation by a hostile West after 1949 were decisive factors in this choice.[44] The historian Liu Danian blamed "socially pernicious" imperialism for having played a "special role" in affecting China's choice of socialism, because the impact of colonialism on China's class composition made a socialist revolution inevitable, and the revolution made a rejection of capitalism logical.[45] These arguments, emphasized by the regime after mid-1989, were clearly motivated by a desire to counter student protesters' call for American democracy and to dismiss Western responses to the military crackdown. But in previous campaigns, the role of imperialism had consistently been cited in official defense of China's choice of socialism.[46]

By appealing to history, the CCP further refuted the argument for a "free choice" of social order proposed among intellectual and student circles since 1988. As Liu Danian wrote in his post-Tiananmen commentary, China's choice of socialism was not a subjective or unpopular choice, even though the CCP was the leader of this choice. No other independent political force existed in the pre-1949 period that could assume the leadership in the national struggle against colonialism and feudalism. Nor was there any other political force to mobilize the masses of the working class. The CCP's mobilization of the lower classes naturally entailed, both Liu and Hu Sheng stressed, the adoption of socialism in the interest of the lower classes. Had the class composition of the revolutionary forces been different, the choice of the social system might have been different. The argument implicitly criticized the narrow interests of the intellectual strata in opposing the socialist choice.

Diachronically, the CCP rebuked bourgeois liberals for using an "ahistorical methodology" in comparing Chinese socialism to the capitalism of developed countries. This methodology was found to underlie bourgeois liberals' doubts about national progress under socialism and their advocacy of the need to "make up for" the capitalist stage. Not only conservatives but even Hu Yaobang and Deng Xiaoping criticized this line of comparison for imputing China's relative backwardness on socialism and attributing the achievements of developed countries to capitalism.[47] In the late 1980s, when some intellectuals and young students grew more vocal in their admiration for capitalism, the refutation of "ahistorical comparison" became a centerpiece of official response, beginning with Zhao's associates in early 1987 and intensifying after mid-1989.[48]

First, official critiques depicted "diachronic" comparisons as unscientific because they ignored such factors as historical conditions, geography, economic and cultural levels, and international contexts. For example, capitalism had developed for a few hundred years in the West, and its accumulation stage was dependent on "bloody and ruthless" plundering of colonies through "unjust" invasions and wars. Non-European countries, including China, made significant material and human sacrifices for the development of Western and Japanese capitalism. In the Chinese case, war indemnities alone measured up to incalculable amounts. Moreover, as a late developer and prime target of imperial scrambling, China could not have developed into a Western-type advanced country even with the adoption of capitalism. Rather, it would only be reduced to a poor dependency of developed countries by the latter's economic and political power, such as the use of international debts and international division of labor. These arguments were particularly emphasized in the post-Tiananmen critiques, not only by such prominent conservatives as Gao Di, Lu Zhichao, and He Xin, but also by Deng Xiaoping himself.[49]

Second, official critiques contended that the success of East Asian NICs did not prove the failure of socialism in China. Apart from their small size and island economies, Chen Junsheng pointed to the unique historical, international, and financial opportunities that benefited the NICs, and to the lack of such conditions that contributed to less favorable growth in other, more established capitalist countries in Asia.[50] He Xin put special emphasis on the fact that the NICs' favorable opportunities were due precisely to their geographical position vis-à-via mainland China, which was subject to hostile isolation and embargo by the West.[51] Finally, official critics argued that the performance of Chinese socialism did not compare unfavorably with countries on a similar level of development with China. For Chen Junsheng, China was methodologically comparable only to India because of historical and demographic similarities. This comparison, he found, did not suggest the superiority of the Western system. Moreover, of the many countries that adopted the capitalist system, only a handful were actually successful. The conclusion for him was that as a late developer, China needed a strong state and public ownership to allocate macro priorities and ensure national independence. Because socialism fulfilled these needs, it had achieved what China failed to do for over a hundred years before the revolution.[52]

A final official rebuttal was that "liberal" analyses often made no distinction between the specific deficiencies of institutions and practices from the nature of the socialist system. The emphasis in the "liberal" analyses was to find something fundamentally wrong with the system. As Hu Yaobang and Hu Qiaomu complained in 1981, the antisystem treatment of the dark side of Chinese society tended to give one-sided explanations or to depict it as the prevailing trend of society. For Hu Qiaomu, Bai Hua's "Unrequited Love" sought to interpret the Cultural Revolution in terms of a deified leader's arbitrary manipulation of the masses. Such an interpretation mocked the people's blind faith in a party and leadership that allegedly betrayed them. Similarly, the two Hus saw the suggestion of a "bureaucratic class" as an attempt to pinpoint its root in the inherent contradictions of the socialist system.[53] Conversely, bourgeois liberals were criticized for taking minor changes under contemporary capitalism as fundamental ones that had altered the nature of capitalism.[54]

Likewise, the theories of alienation and humanism were criticized for linking the party's mistakes to socialism by depicting those mistakes as the alienation of the individual by the collective. The real objective of the two theories, a *Hongqi* article claimed, was to attribute economic "alienation" to public ownership, political "alienation" to the party's leadership, and ideological "alienation" to the dominance of Marxism.[55] On the issue of feudalism, Xiong Fu criticized bourgeois liberals for exaggerating residual remnants by suggesting structural similarities between feudalism and socialism: the party's leadership and feudal autocracy, the planned economy and the noncommodity agrarian economy, the leading role of Marxism, and *da yi tong*.[56] On the issue of the causes of the economic reform crisis and cadre corruption in the late 1980s, an article in *Beijing qingnian bao* faulted "bourgeois liberals" for laying the blame on the systemic features of socialism, that is, public ownership and the so-called totalist state.[57]

For both conservative and reformist leaders, the problems and failures of Chinese socialism lay in nonsystemic sources. One was the legacy of the prerevolutionary society. Such persisting problems as bureaucratism, cadre privileges, and arbitrary rule, both Hu Yaobang and Hu Qiaomu stressed, were "feudal remnants" rather than systemic features of socialism.[58] Another source was the blunders of individual leaders and policies. The two Hus gave this explanation for the Antirightist movement of 1957; the Cultural Revolution; the ultra-leftism of Lin Biao, the Gang of Four, and Mao's later years; the neglect of economic laws and economic affairs, and the personality cult.[59] Wu Shuqing and others also offered this explanation for problems in the economic reform and the surge in cadre corruption in the late 1980s.[60] Since these problems were products of policy and individual failures, so the logic went, they could be rectified by eliminating those mistakes rather than the entire system. Still another source of the problems of socialism was attributed by Hu Yaobang and

Hu Qiaomu to imperfections in specific structures, for example, imperfections in the specific forms that the party's leadership and socialist democracy should take, and in the specific ways that public ownership could be arranged.[61]

The fundamental departure here, as Xiong Fu well argued, lay in the normative and analytical stand of official and "liberal" analyses. The "liberal" critique of feudalism proceeded from a "bourgeois" perspective by assuming that capitalism was the natural cure for China's "feudalized socialism." In Xiong's perspective, however, "feudal remnants" should not become the basis to equate socialism with feudalism, because class formation and economic relations differed under the two social modes.[62] In the case of "Unrequited Love," Hu Qiaomu pointed out, Bai Hua adopted a "negative" normative stand by linking the Cultural Revolution to the arbitrary nature of the party's rule. The correct stand, Hu suggested, should emphasize the party's miscalculation of class struggle and revisionism.[63]

Similarly, proponents of the theses of alienation and humanism were said to be mistaken because they took the "abstract" person as the goal of human progress and the reference point of social analysis. In his summing up of the debate on the subject, Hu Qiaomu concluded that a divergence over basic norms and analytical methodology contributed to the fundamental conflict between the two sides in the debate. Advocates of humanism, he charged, derived their critical stand from the supposedly "class-free" norms of the bourgeoisie.[64] As for the crises of economic reform and cadre corruption, the two underlying causes of the 1989 mass protests, conservatives blamed them on Zhao's policies of tolerating a private economy, individual interests, and economic corruption at the expense of the public economy. In response to the "liberal" critique on the question, conservatives insisted that it was reformers' unconditional embrace of bourgeois values and practices that contributed to the widespread corruption, social inequity, and economic crisis of the late 1980s.[65] In the final analysis, the "liberal" reassessment of the socialist road was accused of aiming not at the improvement of socialism but at its negation.

The Evaluation of Institutional Arrangements

Another key issue raised in the intellectual reappraisal of China's socialist experience concerned the form of the political system. This question is at the root of the unrelenting criticism of socialism for lacking democracy and the unremitting interest in Western democracy. Here bourgeois liberals were summarily criticized for making no distinction between the essence and form of democracy and idealizing Western democracy. Rather than asking "what kind of democracy," they championed the seemingly democratic form of bourgeois democracy and failed to see its essence. By contrast, the CCP emphasized the essence of democracy, that is, the ownership of the MOP that determined the fundamental questions of who ruled, who was ruled, and whose class interests were served in a political system.[66]

In drawing a distinction between the essence and form of bourgeois democracy, official accounts faulted bourgeois liberals for obscuring the fact that socialist democracy was superior to bourgeois democracy in essence, if not in form. Three superior features were attributed to socialist democracy in this respect. First, democracy was linked to social justice under socialism. But the concept of "natural rights" underlying bourgeois democracy could not lead to social justice under capitalism, short of certain "human-given" rights to ensure equitable social distribution. This is so because under capitalism, private ownership resulted in the inequality of citizens in reality: Property was a decisive factor in determining the amount and weight of political power available to social groups. By establishing public ownership, socialism eliminated this root of the bourgeois essence of Western democracy. Socialism was therefore able to combine democracy and social justice. Second, because public ownership guaranteed the economic interests of the working people, the socialist system entailed democracy for the *majority* of people in essence, notwithstanding its shortcomings in form. By the same token, bourgeois democracy, based on private ownership, amounted to *minority* rule in essence by ensuring the interests of a few. Finally, socialist democracy was "explicit about its class stand" while bourgeois democracy was "hypocritical" in its claim to universal equality, freedom, and democracy. This claim was dismissed as an instrument to obscure the essence of bourgeois democracy.[67]

Several structural forms in Western democracy had been particularly championed by bourgeois liberals to underscore its superiority vis-à-vis socialist democracy: the multiparty system, parliamentary procedure, and the electoral process. In response, official critiques countered that these forms were the most deceptive aspects of bourgeois democracy. The multiparty and parliamentary systems served to only coordinate different interests within the ruling class, whereas the electoral system helped to perpetuate, rather than harm, those interests. In the more sophisticated analysis of mid-1989–1990, the electoral process was criticized as "deceptive" because members of the working class could neither afford to run for office nor manipulate politicians, nor could they really learn about the candidates because of "behind-the-scenes deals" and "professional image manipulation." To explain the ability of the bourgeois electoral apparatus to win over the working people against the latter's interests, conservatives attributed it to the bourgeois class's capacity to manipulate public opinion.[68] Since none of the parties under this system actually represented the interests of the working class, Deng argued in 1980, the bourgeois political institutions could not have real representativeness or legitimacy.[69]

Here, the campaign of 1989–1990 paid particular attention to the role of the media in manipulating public opinion, because the events of mid-1989 alerted the authorities to the media's impact. The postcrackdown critique contended that the bourgeois class, through its control of the media, was able to achieve the "deception, anesthesia, and thought control" of the public. The slogan of "freedom of the press," a major call of the students during the demonstrations, was found to be a most effective means to disguise the bias of the media. For it obscured the fact that freedom of the press was premised on the interests and power of the media's owners and advertisers, and on the restriction of potentially destructive views. One *Beijing ribao* article even argued if China were to permit such freedom of the press by whomever had the money, the control over the direction of public opinion in China would fall into the hands of the United States, which had the financial ability to sponsor this control.[70] Another point that came to be realized in the wake of mid-1989 was the power of advanced communication technology, which "dramatically increases the media's capacity to influence public perceptions and feelings and makes unconscious victims of the masses."[71] Sensationalism and impressionistic journalism in Western reports of the student protests even led some Chinese commentators to see a "rumor-mongering" tendency of the bourgeois press. One commentator observed that such freedom of the press actually amounted to "dictatorship of the press."[72] This criticism of the sensational Western media actually rang quite true from my own months of experience in China during and after the 1989 protest movement.

The class-based conception of democracy that buttressed the party's own ruling status had been frequently challenged by bourgeois liberals. Official critiques dismissed such challenge as normatively biased. In the campaigns of 1979, 1981, and 1983, official criticisms centered on the "individualistic" claim of the liberal vision of democracy. In the Democracy Wall movement, dissidents criticized the differential treatment of social groups epitomized in the "dictatorship of the proletariat," such as those statements that faulted it for "splitting mankind" and for being the "source of all evils." Wei Jingsheng charged that "modern socialist states without exception neither acknowledge nor protect the equal human rights of the individual members of society." These views, in turn, were dismissed by Deng as advocating individual "self-interest" and opposing a social order that put society ahead of the individual.[73] In 1981 Hu Qiaomu criticized intellectual exaltation of the concept of "divine rights" for purporting individual-based democracy. Hu's criticism of the humanism and alienation theses in 1983 also involved the assertion of the individual, which he saw as a rejection of a social order that valued the authority of the community and placed limits on the individual. From the materialist conception of human beings, he rebuked the concept of "divine rights" as a "utopian bias" that legitimated the bourgeois class's vision of social order.[74]

As "liberal" calls for Western democracy grew increasingly more sophisticated and agitated, official critiques also paid attention to the subjective bias of the proponents of Western democracy. Wang Renzhi made this point when pointing out that the discussions of humanism and alienation championed individualism as a "timeless and class-free" ideology of all humankind." This "bourgeois" view was but to serve the depiction of Western democracy as "universal and eternal."[75] In 1989–1990, a similar thesis attributed to Yan Jiaji was singled out for attack, namely, the assertion that "there is no distinction between democracy of the East or the West" and that "democracy will be the consensus of the world."[76] Other variants of the same idea under attack after mid-1989 included Fang Lizhi's call for "wholesale Westernization" and Liu Xiaobo's equation of European colonialism with Westernization and of Westernization with "globalization" (*quanqiuhua*).[77] In other words, Liu saw the mission and impact of European colonialism as having brought universal values and practices to the non-Western world. In essence, these individuals espoused that there was no distinction between the essence and the form of democracy, and that the superior form of Western democracy meant its superiority in essence.

The claim of Western democracy to universality was rejected on the ground that the history of the modern West had itself been shown to be a "history of aggression" against other nations and that therefore Western democracy did not entail genuine democracy, equality, and justice.[78] As several authoritative critics argued in the 1989–90 campaign, Western democracy was a weapon of European colonial powers in the late nineteenth century. Viewing democracy as the highest form of civilization created by Europe, these powers felt they had the "right" to impose their vision of society around the world. In political values as well as in geography, race, culture, and social system, it was these powers that had a "consensus" about Western superiority. But this was a consensus not shared by China then because of its suffering under imperialism and during the two world wars. It was such doubts that led many Chinese to realize the cultural- and class-bound nature of Western democracy, among them the once fervent believer of democracy Li Dazhao. For conservative critics, the function of Western democracy had changed since the collapse of colonialism after World War II. Ideas like "democracy," "freedom," and "human rights" had since then become ideological weapons to undermine the socialist world or to make Eurocentric judgments on third world countries.[79] In short, Yan's "consensus" thesis, in ignoring these facts and biases, was intended to weaken the party's ideological and moral ground against Western democracy and thereby justify the latter's importation.[80]

The postulate of the "diversity of truth" was criticized as another subjective bias underlying the "liberal" opposition to socialist democracy. Proponents of the postulate argued that "only through a multiparty system can truth be grasped all-sidedly, chances of mistaken policies be reduced, and the interests of the majority be guaranteed."[81] In other words, the thesis justified pluralistic democracy on the claim of the diversity of opinions among individuals and groups. Not surprisingly, it became an influential argument for pluralistic democracy during the high tide of liberalization in 1988–89. In response, post-June 4 official critiques appealed to the Marxist orthodoxy that the prevailing ideology of any class society must necessarily be the ideology of the ruling class. Several *Qiushi* articles identified the class nature of bourgeois ideology in its staunch antisocialist stance. One described the ideology of bourgeois society as a set of values centering on the idea of the market.[82] On these grounds, the diversity of opinions under bourgeois democracy was found questionable: If "pluralism" pertained to the fundamental character of a polity, then there was little pluralism in Western democracies because competing groups agreed on the basic framework of capitalism. But if "pluralism" referred to diverse social groups in a society, then it existed "not only in the West but in the East."[83] Following this logic, conservative critics concluded that rather than advocating the "diversity of opinions" among social groups on an equal footing, bourgeois liberals actually propounded the dominance of their own version of social order. Specifically, this order would favor the so-called middle class to the benefit of the political ambitions of leading bourgeois liberals, who would have the leisure and finances (from private ownership and foreign sponsorship) to run for political office.[84]

If, as the conservative critics rightly claimed, subjective criteria were inevitable in choosing political beliefs and institutions, the issue became one of how to determine these criteria and by whose authority. While intellectuals challenged the party's authority to make the choice for society, official critics stressed the historical context in which China's socialist choice was made. But this emphasis also led them to recognize the pertinence of the question raised by students and intellectuals as to whether, under changed international and domestic conditions, the choice of socialism may be reconsidered. Official responses, in turn, combined appeals to convictions from history and ideology. Avoiding the question of the institutional basis for a new choice, Hu Sheng placed the issue in the perspective of the materialist conception of history. Thus viewed, socialist institutions remained optimal for China, because a "return" to capitalism would entail the initial stage of capitalism in an underdeveloped country with all the concomitant social conflicts and class contradictions. Since the Chinese people already rejected the capitalist mode of the accumulative stage of industrialization in the 1949 Revolution, there was little need for the masses to go through the painful stage of beginning capitalism again.[85] For Deng Xiaoping, the social disparity and instability ensuing in a developing capitalist China would be simply too great for a country of China's size.[86] These criticisms hit at the intellectuals' own class bias for a social order that may not serve the interests of the masses.

In short, the specific structures of the Chinese political system should be reformed, but the "class nature" of the polity was not to be changed.[87] Marxism was still to provide the dominant truth, both because China had historically discovered so and because Marxism identified with the interests of the masses.[88] Institutionally and doctrinally, therefore, there would be no legitimacy for alternative political forces that may be on an equal footing with the CCP in the Chinese context.

CONCLUSION

The struggle against bourgeois liberals, as symbolized in the five post-Mao political campaigns, illuminated the dilemmas of the Chinese reassessment. The officially encouraged line of reappraisal could not accommodate those on the Left or the Right, and the regime was constantly forced to confront both. These dilemmas were epitomized in Deng Xiaoping, who had been the central figure behind the efforts to transform socialism as well as behind every campaign to circumvent the impulses generated by this process. Nor did other reformist officials want the socialist framework abandoned, though they had often been victims of those campaigns.

The resultant middle road had been marked by a reformulation of socialism, on the one hand, and a preservation of the socialist orientation of society, on the other. In encouraging the Emancipation of the Mind, the regime insisted on maintaining its basic assumptions about political values as well as the scope of change. In launching a reassessment of socialist practices, the regime did not sanction questioning socialism itself or the socialist path of development. In initiating political reforms, the regime would not permit political forms incompatible with its choice of social order. In other words, the rethinking of the theory and practice of socialism may not lead to repudiation of the socialist foundation of China.

Rather than being a mere function of elite politics, however, the struggle against ideological deviance and intellectual heterodoxy had been a part of the party's efforts to retain the socialist ethos as a conventional means of self-expression, legitimation, and political control. As intellectuals extended ideological reformulation in the economic realm to the political and the ideological, the party found itself facing a formidable threat to the basis of its moral authority and, inevitably, its political authority. Demands for unlimited Emancipation of the Mind threatened the foundation of the monopoly of truth and the party's assumptions about what was right and wrong. The weakening of Marxism by bourgeois liberals had done away with a "common language" between the regime and certain segments of society, leaving a void for "bourgeois" ideas to fill. Doubts over the socialist road raised questions not only about the party's choice of developmental path but also the legitimacy of the party that insisted on the choice. Calls for a "diversity of opinions" threatened the party's claim to being the best representative of the people's interests. Together, these challenges may indeed have provided, in Hu Qiaomu's words, a coherent "ideological basis" for an alternative system of political values and social order that threatened "public confidence in the political system and spiritual health and political stability" of the country."[89] As adeptly noted by Andrew Nathan, Deng Xiaoping was not entirely wrong in attributing the "turmoil" of 1989 to the sharp challenge presented to the ethos of the regime by intellectuals.[90]

No less important than political and ideological concerns, however, were the moral and cultural concerns associated with the endeavor to preserve socialism. From the point of the regime, "liberal" forces not only challenged the fundamentals of socialism but espoused a vision of social order that the older generation fought to reject. This vision was unacceptable for reasons that went beyond the threat to the CCP's authority. Fundamentally, this alternative vision lacked a solid cultural and national basis, at least in the CCP view. The fate of bourgeois liberals' challenge to the regime in post-Mao China stemmed essentially from this difficulty. Thus far, it had failed to discredit coherently the CCP's appeal to China's historical choice and national experience. This may ultimately account for the regime's consistent efforts to fight bourgeois liberalization and for its efforts to readjust socialism, rather than cynically bypass it.

CHAPTER NINE

The Chinese and Soviet Reassessments of Socialism: A Comparison

LIKE CHINESE reform leaders, Mikhail Gorbachev also encouraged the reappraisal of socialism as a means of diagnosing past problems and articulating reforms. These efforts were expressed in such platforms as "new thinking," the "renewal of socialism," and the promotion of "humanistic and democratic socialism." Because the Chinese party eventually blamed these efforts for the erosion of socialism that heralded the collapse of the Soviet Union in late 1991, it is interesting to address the important question raised by the Chinese reactions here. That is, what is the role of ideological reappraisal in the divergent directions that reforms have taken in these two countries and the different fate that socialism has experienced in the two cases?

A comparison of the Chinese and the Soviet cases will help shed important light on this question and will also highlight the peculiar sequence and content of the Chinese reassessment. This chapter makes a comparative examination of the process and content of reassessment in post-Mao China and the Soviet Union under Gorbachev. It focuses on the prevailing view in both cases, that is, the views of reform leaders and their supporters.

THE PROCESS OF REASSESSMENT

In both countries, the rethinking of socialism began with methodological questions, that is, questions of appropriate approaches to the theory and practice of socialism. This focus was necessary to justify change while pledging ideological commitment to the system.

The Initial Phase: Methodological Questions

In the initial phase of the Chinese reassessment, that is, during the controversy over the truth criterion in the late 1970s, the principal target of rethinking was the whatever group's blind adherence to Maoism, which forbade any change from the previous course of policy and ideology. Through the exposure of the fallacy of Hua's dogmatism and of Mao's radical socialist tenets, there developed a new approach to the understanding and construction of socialism that stressed regard for the empirical context of theory and the host society. Thereby the post-Mao reform leadership delegitimated Mao's radical course and began to shift the country away from it.

In the initial phase of the Soviet reassessment, from the late Andropov period (1984) to Gorbachev's first two years in office (1985–86), the key target of rethinking was also dogmatism in the understanding of and approaches to socialism. Beginning in 1984 two established credos began to be reexamined among intellectual and official circles: (1) the theory of "developed socialism" of the Brezhnev era, which denotes that socialism is fully mature in the Soviet Union and established on thoroughly socialist production relations, and (2) the idea of "automatic adaptation" under socialism, which suggests that once socialism is established, its production relations will automatically adapt to production forces and create unlimited scope for the latter's growth.[1] Both tenets endorsed the fundamental soundness of existing production relations and had become absolutized in theory and practice. As Gorbachev would later complain, "such ideas were actually identified with the essential characteristics of socialism, viewed as immutable, and represented as dogmas, leaving no room for objective scientific analysis."[2]

At the heart of the thesis concerning the developmental stage reached by the Soviet Union was the conception of the basic tasks appropriate to that period. Based on unrealistic assessment, two previous Soviet leaders had proclaimed extravagant goals for Soviet society that led to miscalculated economic policies. The Third Party Program of the CPSU, adopted under Nikita Khrushchev in 1961, had designated a transitional period that would culminate in the attainment of communist society by the early 1980s. Accordingly it pronounced the full-scale construction of communism as the practical task of the country. At the Twentieth CPSU Congress in 1971, Leonid Brezhnev toned down Khrushchev's rash promise by interposing a new and lengthy stage of "developed socialism." Although it postponed communism indefinitely, the new concept was still used to convey the great achievements and the fundamental soundness of the existing Soviet order, said to be "moving in just the right direction."[3] With emphasis on the successes rather than real problems of society, the concept again served to disorient practical policy and was as resistant to change as Hua's whateverism.

The Soviet reassessment started precisely with a retreat from "developed socialism." In 1984 Yuri Andropov and Mikhail Gorbachev began to qualify the level of socialism achieved in the Soviet Union by describing the country as "at the beginning" of a lengthy stage of socialist construction. The task of the present also became to "improve developed socialism," which signified imperfections in the system and therefore the need for reform.[4] After the April plenum of 1985, at which Gorbachev assumed the leadership of the CPSU, the question of the place of "developed socialism" received much attention in public discussions of the new party program to be adopted at the Twenty-seventh Party Congress. Some wanted to raise it to even higher levels while some wanted to do away with it altogether. At the Twenty-seventh Congress in February 1986, Gorbachev criticized the concept for justifying complacency while overlooking failures in society. The new party program retained the concept but made minimal references to this deeply entrenched tenet of Soviet ideology. Rather, the program emphasized the "all-around improvement of socialism," not the transition from socialism to communism.[5] Thereafter the term "developed socialism" soon disappeared from Soviet political vocabulary. Months later, Gorbachev spoke only of a "developing socialism."[6]

If the retreat from "developed socialism" acknowledged imperfections in Soviet society, the rejection of the notion of "automatic adaptation" indicated the locus of these imperfections. In his address at an ideological conference in December 1984, Gorbachev first disputed this idea by arguing that "the correspondence between production relations and production forces is not reproduced just itself, but requires constant, purposeful work in the perfecting of the entire economic system of socialism." This was so because some elements in socialist production relations could become obsolete, and their preservation "may bring about a deterioration of the economic and social situation."[7] At the Twenty-seventh Congress, he further refuted the "automatic adaptation" thesis by discussing why old production relations had become obsolete. Placing the blame on the historical conditions of emergency circumstances under which those relations took shape, he sought to distinguish them from socialism itself.

Beginning with the Twenty-seventh Congress, Gorbachev also promoted "new thinking" to overcome bureaucratic and public apathy toward reform. Many of its themes echoed those of Deng's offensive to emancipate the mind. One theme was to reject dogmatic concepts and practices and to grasp new notions of socialist economic forms. Another theme was to adopt a "Leninist" creative and realistic approach to accessing reality and to adjusting policies.[8] A related theme was to promote "dialectic thinking," namely, to "view reality in all of its aspects, in constant movement, with its contradictions, and as the new struggling against the old."[9] As Gorbachev put it, "the new mode of thinking that all must master is dialectic thinking. As Karl Marx notes, dialectics does not revere anything and is critical and revolutionary by its nature."[10] The essence of the new thinking, then, like Deng's dialectic materialist approach, was to overcome dogmatism and inculcate a new value basis for action.

Despite the similar rhetoric, the Soviet leadership was more committed to the existing order at this early stage than were Chinese reform leaders. They sought to "improve" socialism, with emphasis on the "acceleration" of economic development through intensified technical progress, as opposed to the "stagnation" of the Brezhnev era. "Restructuring" of the economic system was a secondary task. Politically, Gorbachev's call for openness and democratization was largely instrumental, aimed at aiding the party's economic agenda.[11] From the beginning, the Soviet effort was not circumscribed by an elaborately articulated set of fundamental principles or suppression of dissent, as in China's campaign of early 1979. Rather, Gorbachev's primary targets were "conservative and ossified forces."[12]

The Second Phase: Growing Divergence

In the next phase, however, Soviet reformers moved further than Chinese reformers in pinning down the sources of the problems of established socialism.

From the CCP work conference of April 1979 to the eve of the urban reform in 1983, the focus of Chinese reexamination shifted to the mistakes and excesses of Chinese socialism beyond those of the Mao's radical project. This effort proceeded largely from a basic affirmation of the existing system. In the economic domain, it emphasized past excesses in applying the Soviet sectoral and economic models, tracing their sources to the lack of recognition of Chinese conditions. In the political domain, the official reexamination emphasized the neglect of the "form" of the proletarian state. Intellectual and literary discussions that questioned the class nature or human costs of this state were suppressed in the campaigns of 1981 and 1983.

During the second phase of the Soviet reassessment, from the January plenum of the CPSU in 1987 and the eve of the Nineteenth All-Union Conference in July 1988, the difficulty of reaching consensus at the top and of implementing reform at the bottom led Gorbachev to urge "a deeper understanding of the critical problems" of the Soviet system. For this purpose the January plenum of 1987, convened after several postponements due to conservative resistance, formally started the reexamination of the Stalinist roots of the Soviet system. In his report at the plenum, Gorbachev explicitly distinguished socialism from its present forms, which he traced to the Stalinist periods of 1930s and 1940s. Importantly, he attributed the identification of those forms with true socialism to "a negative influence" on the theoretical front that helped to make certain forms of social relations into immutable dogmas.[13] No longer seeing them as simply imperfect and in need of improvement, he declared those forms "retardation mechanisms." This assessment in effect called for the replacement, not just the reform, of existing production relations.

These themes soon stimulated a nationwide rethinking of Soviet history, especially the Stalinist period. In various opinion forums, truth and honesty were urged in the writing of Soviet history to expose "incrustation and deformations." Impeding forces in the current restructuring process were traced to the bureaucratic and administrative-command legacy of the Stalin era. The excesses and necessity of the collectivization and other events in the early phase of Soviet socialism were debated. The so-called blank spots in Soviet history that used to be taboo areas were explored. These discussions remained within the socialist framework, since the negative aspects of history were depicted as Stalinist "distortions" and reform was presented as a way to correct them so as to return to Lenin's genuine socialism.[14] But in calling the roots of the Soviet economic system into question, Soviet reformers began to go beyond their Chinese counterparts. Interestingly though, the heavy industrial model of development that took shape in the extraordinary conditions of the 1920s and 1930s did not become a central or even minor part of the historical reexamination. Both official and public attention was on "restructuring" of the economic system, which formally became the party's agenda at the June plenum of 1987, accompanied by pathbreaking reform measures.[15]

In the political arena, the Soviet divergence was still more pronounced. "Openness" and "democratization" were no longer treated as instrumental goals of the party but as fundamental values. Since the January plenum of 1987, Gorbachev depicted democratization as "the essence," "the basis," and "the soul" of restructuring; and "thorough openness" as something that would not only better inform the public but also allow fundamental rethinking of the country's past and present. To ensure genuine democratization and openness, he now advocated "pluralism of opinion within socialism" and opposed a monopoly of ideas under socialism. In line with his emphasis on socialism's capacity to ensure diverse opinions and interests, he offered what would become a potentially destructive concept: humanism. The ultimate goal of restructuring, he declared at the January 1987 plenum, was to display fully the "humanistic nature" of socialism.[16] This goal was specifically juxtaposed to the "alienation" of the people under the old system.

Although both pluralism and humanism were emphatically placed within socialism at this time, no campaign was launched to suppress Gorbachev's liberal opponents (the Left in the Soviet case), who were impatient with the pace of reform and advocated more radical changes. The leading spokesperson of this group in the party, Boris Yeltsin, was dismissed as first secretary of the Party Committee of Moscow in November 1987, after attacking the party's lack of resolve in reform.[17] But the major target of Gorbachev's criticism and organizational reshuffle remained his conservative opponents (the Right in the Soviet case).[18] By October 1987 half of the ten members who were in the Politburo at the time of Gorbachev's inauguration had been replaced. A. N. Yakovlov, a liberal-minded reformer, was promoted to serve as Gorbachev's chief ideological aide. Partly owing to this curbing of conservatives, the CPSU was able to negate the roots of the system and advocate the pluralistic, humanistic direction of socialism forbidden by the Chinese leadership.

The Third Phase: Conceptual Departure

It was only during the third phase of Chinese reassessment, from 1983 to 1986, that the reform leadership finally rejected the basis of the old economic system and paid attention to the interaction between the economic and political reforms. Although empirical reform had gone much further in the Chinese case than in the Soviet case at the comparable stage,[19] the Soviet-type command economy was negated in principle by the CCP only in the 1984 resolution on urban reform, while the basis of the Soviet-type political system came to be questioned only during the 1986 discussion of political reform. As in the Soviet case, political reassessment was called forth by the demands of economic reform and was intended to serve the latter. But unlike in the Soviet case, political reappraisal did not take on a life of its own, nor did it lead to a fundamental reexamination or negation of CCP history. The Chinese leadership never lost sight of the instrumental role of political reform, as reflected in its emphasis on a separation of the party and the state, but not a change of the leading role of the party or its doctrine. Efforts by intellectuals and reform theorists to advocate political democracy on the basis of a market economy were suppressed in another antiliberal campaign in early 1987.

From the Nineteenth All-Union Party Conference of the CPSU in July 1988 to the eve of the CPSU Plenum in February 1990, the Soviet leadership again moved ahead of the Chinese with an entirely new direction of rethinking. Two key events marked the new direction of this period. First, the Nineteenth All-Union Conference altered the focus of Soviet reform by shifting the party's priority from the economic to the political sphere. This shift was made as Gorbachev came to recognize the determining role of politics in a Stalinist system and its all-encompassing control over society.[20] Along with the prioritization of political reform, the Nineteenth Conference made several conceptual breakthroughs in CPSU ideology. Going beyond the espousal of "pluralism of opinions" within socialism, the conference advocated a pluralism in the political system that could facilitate "democratic expression" and the "formation of the interests and will of different classes and social groups." Pluralism was even elevated to the level of "democratization" and "openness," as one of the three "revolutionary proposals" of the CPSU. The conference also stressed the separation of the party and the state, but emphasized the power of state organs by restoring Lenin's slogan of "all power to the Soviet." This only helped to hasten the decline of the leadership of the party. Finally the Congress proposed "humanistic and democratic socialism" to replace the so-called barracks-type socialism.[21] This new concept marked a fundamental change in the goal of Soviet reform from the "improvement" of socialism to the replacement of "deformed socialism."

Gorbachev's article on socialism and reform in the November 26, 1989, issue of *Pravda* was another monumental event in this phase of Soviet reassessment. Here his elaboration on "humanistic and democratic socialism" made many novel departures from the previous CPSU doctrine. Gorbachev no longer described reform as a way to correct distortions of socialism, but as a means to "fundamentally transform the entire social edifice." Moreover, he no longer depicted reform as a return to the "Leninist vision of socialism" but declared that even Lenin did not have a complete program of building socialism. Instead, he portrayed restructuring as a way to correct the main direction of the international Communist movement that had gone astray for over a century. This point in effect negated the history of Soviet socialism and that of the international Communist movement. In this context, Gorbachev affirmed social democratic parties, which were dismissed as genuinely socialist by Lenin after 1914. At the same time Gorbachev equated humanism with the essence of socialism and endorsed "humanistic norms" as the priority of all aspects of social life. This implicitly played down the class basis of political rule and social goals in the classic conception of socialism. Finally, Gorbachev called for ending the ideological confrontation between the socialist and capitalist systems on the basis of a reevaluation of contemporary capitalism. While the official Chinese reconception of capitalism stressed the historical and synchronic links between the two systems, Gorbachev saw the two systems as in an evolutionary process of a similar content and called for their "cooperation" to replace "confrontation."[22]

In short, fundamental changes had occurred in Gorbachev's thinking on Leninism, socialism, capitalism, and international communism in this period that far exceeded the level of official Chinese rethinking at a comparable stage. Although Gorbachev still maintained a balanced opposition to both the Right and the Left in rhetoric, his reaction against conservatives on the Right was far stronger organizationally. At the extraordinary session of the CPSU Central Committee in September 1988, five senior leaders—including the long-term leader Andrei Gromyko—were replaced. Ye. K. Ligachev, the second-ranking leader in the party who was in charge of the Secretariat and the party's ideological work, was demoted to head the party's agricultural work. V. A. Medvedev, a liberal-minded reformer, was promoted to the Politburo to take charge of party ideology. In April 1989, 110 retired members and alternate members of the Central Party Committee and members of the Central Inspection Committee were asked to resign from their remaining posts. In September 1989 the Central Committee discharged all remaining members, except Gorbachev himself, who were serving in the Politburo when Gorbachev first assumed office. These organizational reshuffles helped to weaken political opposition to Gorbachev's platform.

The Fourth Phase: Fundamental Departure

From mid-1987 to mid-1989 a new conception of socialism finally emerged in official Chinese thought, expressed in the idea of a primary stage of socialism. But instead of defining socialism in terms of new goals and features, it reflected a retreat to a supposedly earlier stage of socialism. Based on a selective use of Marxist methodology to justify the centrality of the economic base, the concept neglected those aspects of Marxism that addressed humanistic concerns. Thanks to its material emphasis, the new conception made a major departure from Marxism in the economic sphere, but it contained minimal adjustments in the political sphere. Beyond the official framework, some intellectual discussions during this period did reach the level of the Soviet reappraisal with its critique of the "totalism" of the Chinese state and its assertion of humanism and universally based democracy. But this line of analysis was not incorporated into official thought. Instead, it came to be attacked, in the antiliberal campaign after mid-1989, as a key source of incitation in the student protest movement of spring 1989.

By contrast, the Soviet Union witnessed a complete departure from established socialism from the February plenum of 1990 and culminated in the July plenum of 1991. Two key events marked this historical phase of Soviet political development: the end of the Communist party as the leading force of society and the transformation of this vanguard party into a political force on an equal footing with other political parties. The CPSU plenum in February 1990 made major decisions concerning the leading status of the CPSU, including a constitutional revision to end the legally and politically superior status of the Communist party, creation of a multiparty system to accommodate the emergence of new political forces, and establishment of a presidential system to replace the Politburo.[23] These ideas were enacted in the third extraordinary session of the Supreme Soviet in the following month, among them the abolition of the Article 6 of the Soviet Constitution, which guaranteed the party's leading status.

The Twenty-eighth Party Congress of the CPSU, held in July 1990, was another key event in the development of humane, democratic socialism. The conference was held amid intense battles among liberal, centrist, and conservative forces in the party over the parameters of humane, democratic socialism. Conservatives, headed by Ligachev, opposed the weakening of the party's ideological and organizational functions and its claim to promoting the working class's interests.[24] Liberals, led by Yeltsin, advocated changing the CPSU into a parliamentary party, renouncing democratic centralism, and embracing universal human values.[25] Centrists, represented by Gorbachev, supported universal human values but, unlike liberals, advocated a vanguard CPSU operating through parliament and a partial retention of democratic centralism.[26] Although the congress preserved Gorbachev's basic line, the outcome leaned toward liberals' "Democratic Platform" by formally redefining the goal of socialism and the nature of the party along the so-called universal human norms of individual and pluralistic development. The congress program integrated socialism with universal human values, a vanguard with a parliamentary party, and democratic centralism with political rights to have minority opinions and coalitions. It abandoned references to "planning" or "public ownership" and proposed the market economy as the "only choice" to replace the command economy.[27]

The CPSU plenum of July 1991, devoted to the draft of a new party program under new conditions, saw the CPSU's final effort to reassess and readjust socialism before its disintegration later that year. In his plenum report, Gorbachev went further than he had at the Twenty-eighth Congress in reassessing socialism, communism, and the role of the party. On socialism, he went beyond his past criticism of "incrustation and deformations" to negate its entire theory and practice, calling the Stalin era a "totalitarian legacy" and the post-Stalin era a form of "post-Stalinism." On communism, he justified the abrogation of communism as the goal of the CPSU on the ground of its proven utopian nature. "It must be admitted that our experience, and others' as well, gives us no reason to believe that this goal is realistically attainable in the foreseeable future."[28] On the role of the party, he made the most drastic change by deemphasizing its class nature. The party would no longer see itself as the political vanguard of class revolution and liberation but as a party of "democratic reforms, political and economic freedom, social justice and universal human values," and a party that would fight for "general civil concords" and its electoral victory. He endorsed renaming it the "Social Democratic party," a name that the Bolsheviks had left behind in the 1910s, although he did not approve of actually doing so because many party members had deep attachments to the concept of communism.

These remarks of Gorbachev, as some delegates at the plenum complained, amounted to "abandoning Marxism-Leninism," thereby "weakening the domestic communist movement." This direction of events culminated in the conservative coup attempt in the following month to restore the old order and the rapid disintegration of the Soviet socialist order after the coup's failure.

The processes of the Chinese and Soviet reassessments have shown several contrasting features. First, after the initial phase of reassessment, Soviet reformers were a step ahead of the Chinese at each comparative stage of reappraisal. Second, although both began reassessment with the economic arena, the Chinese leaders consistently focused on this sphere, while the Soviet leaders turned from the economic to the political. Third, the Chinese "liberal" view, which approached the level and tone of the Soviet mainstream analysis was frequently suppressed by the regime. By contrast, despite Gorbachev's consistent efforts to balance between conservatives and liberals, no political campaigns were ever launched in the entire Gorbachev era to suppress liberal views in order to placate conservative pressure. On the contrary, the mainstream discourse under Gorbachev increasingly tilted toward the liberal view.

THE CONTENT OF REASSESSMENT

These divergent processes were intimately related to the content of the Chinese and Soviet reassessments. Here differences in three key areas of rethinking distinguish the character and direction of reassessment in these two countries. These are the reexamination of past socialist experience, the treatment of the person under socialism, and the place of the Communist party in society.

The Evaluation of the Past

Analyses of past socialist experience are indices of the nature of change in reforming socialist countries, because they suggest the problems to be rectified and the remedies to be sought. In this sense the reexamination of the past is a prerequisite for appropriate reforms. From the beginning, the Chinese reform leadership encouraged a one-sided and half-hearted reappraisal of the past. While forthcoming about the economic sphere, Deng discouraged the reexamination of the political mistakes of the past, against the advocacy of the same by conservatives (for example, Chen Yun) on the one hand and social forces on the other. Politically Deng was concerned about the potential divisiveness of these in the face of the need for national unity in the modernization drive. Ideologically he was mainly interested in new ideas to guide and justify economic reform.[29] Partly to avoid division and dissent, the CCP eventually made a formal reappraisal of its past in the resolution on CCP history in 1981. As an official version, it served to justify the official program and direction of reform.

In analyses of mistakes of the past, the CCP had been careful to insulate the fundamental socialist system, political and economic, from questioning. Instead, it sought to place the blame for past tragedies on the blunders of individual leaders, on mistaken approaches to socialism, or on the gap between Marxist theory and Chinese reality. That is, they were aberrations rather than intrinsic consequences of the system. Similarly, although much was made of the indiscriminate adoption of the Soviet model and the premature establishment of socialist production relations, there was no explicit and serious consideration of whether collectivization of agriculture should have been carried out in the first place, whether the heavy industrial model and the planned economy should ever have been copied, or whether socialist production relations should be adopted at all.

In critiquing the mistakes of past leaders, the CCP was also careful not to link them to the fundamental Chinese system or to negate them in total. Mao's blunders were depicted as exceptions in comparison with his positive achievements. The only CCP leaders that could be completely negated were the Gang of Four. But even here, the link between the Gang and Mao was carefully severed so as not to undermine the legitimacy of Mao, the CCP, and the Chinese system as a whole. Despite the CCP's negative view of past tragedies and of the blunders of past leaders, legitimate judgments could be made only within its frame of analysis.

At first Gorbachev also appeared apprehensive about reexamining the past, for the same reasons that concerned Deng. "If we start trying to deal with the past," Gorbachev remarked in the summer of 1986, "we shall dissipate our energy." But at the January plenum of 1987, he admitted that clarification of "some basic issues," especially issues of the historical origins of current forms of socialism, was essential to reaching a consensus about the urgent necessity of reform. One month later he proposed that there should be "no blank pages" in the history of "the years of industrialization and collectivization."[30] Rather than setting parameters on historical reassessment, Gorbachev permitted the opening up of even the most troubling questions about CPSU history, particularly the Stalin era, although he resisted questioning Lenin initially.

Thus, in analyzing the mistakes and failures of the past, Gorbachev and like-minded reformers were willing to link them to the Soviet system and even to make a wholesale negation of it. The use of "deformed socialism" to describe the political and economic system created in the Stalin era clearly conveyed the idea of fundamental deficiency.[31] Although initially utilized to suggest the influence of the Stalinist legacy on the present, the term was later applied to Soviet socialism from Stalin to the present. Such characterization in effect delegitimated the foundation of the Soviet system and called for its total removal. Following the notion of "deformed socialism," the entire history of the CPSU came to be characterized in terms of several models of socialism, none of which was regarded as genuinely socialist: the war communism" of the interwar and revolutionary period, the "authoritarian-utopian socialism" of the 1920s, the "authoritarian mobilization-type socialism" of the 1930s and 1940s, and the "authoritarian-bureaucratic socialism" since the 1950s.[32] By July 1991 the entire "theoretical and practical model of socialism" of past decades was declared "bankrupt" by Gorbachev. The Stalin era was then described even more negatively as a "totalitarian-bureaucratic system," and the whole post-Stalin period became "post-Stalinism" because, while "the mass repressions were ended . . . the basis of power and control remained in the same administrative-command system, based on the absolute supremacy of state ownership."[33] The negation of the entire system and the de-legitimation of a greater part of Soviet experience after the revolution could not but encourage the liberal forces to raise serious questions about the legitimacy of the CPSU itself. Yuri Afanasyev, historian and USSR People's Deputy, for example, accused the CPSU of having "led the country nowhere" for seventy years.[34]

In critiquing major tragic events under CPSU rule or past leadership mistakes, the Gorbachev leadership did not avoid linking them to the Soviet system. At first he accepted Stalin's collectivization drive with reservations about the excessive coercion used, while rejecting Bukharin's position on the matter as failing to appreciate the "time factor." But soon he came to acknowledge the negative consequences of collectivization, especially the destruction of the peasantry.[35] This change of attitude encouraged public inquiries into major milestones of the Soviet experience: collectivization of agriculture, the early phase of industrialization, the purges of the 1930s, and the coercive internal policies of the postwar years—to mention just a few major issues.[36] Even the dissident critiques of previously repudiated figures, such as those of Bukharin, were revived.

The Gorbachev leadership was even more willing to negate past individual leaders in whole or in large part. Stalin was completely repudiated by a depiction of his reign as a "period of personality cult" and a "totalitarian legacy." Khrushchev came to be viewed in a more positive light, but greater emphasis was still placed on the negative effects of his subjectivism and bureaucratism. Brezhnev's reign was labeled "a period of stagnation," suggesting an overall failure.[37] In this way, Lenin was left as the only positive leader in CPSU history who had genuine socialist visions, if not completely correct designs. This kind of official approach encouraged some liberal critics to attribute the deeper roots of Stalinism and the ills of the Soviet system to this founding father himself, and eventually to the original theory of Marx.[38]

The Treatment of the Person under Socialism

What fundamentally distinguishes the Chinese and Soviet reassessment, not only in the reexamination of the past but also in the formulation of present and future goals, is also the treatment of the person under socialism. In the Chinese case, the leadership never used the human factor as the yardstick of past failures and current reforms. In analyzing the root causes of past failures, emphasis was on the misorientation of the party's agenda away from the economy and the adoption of improper production relations and political forms. In analyzing major consequences of past policies, emphasis was on the excesses of class struggle and their impediment to the growth of production forces. The remedies, therefore, lay in the reorientation of the party's agenda and the rectification of those aspects of production relations and superstructure that obstructed economic development. The CCP rejected an alternative analysis of past failures offered by social critics and liberal intellectuals, which viewed the deemphasis of the person and the class orientation of society as the root cause of past problems. Because the latter analysis saw alienation of the person as the principal consequence of past policies and proposed democracy based on a universal conception of the person as the solution, the CCP dismissed it as propagation of bourgeois values with their own class biases.

In the Soviet case, by contrast, Gorbachev adopted the concepts of alienation and humanism as the key frame of reference for reappraising Soviet socialism. The designation "deformation of socialism," above all, was based on the judgment that the annihilation of the "humanistic potential of socialism" had occurred under the old "authoritarian-bureaucratic system."[39] In this analysis, human alienation became a key measure of the CPSU's failures. As Gorbachev noted, socialism should consist in ending "the social alienation of man . . . from power, from the means of production, from results of his labor, from his spiritual values."[40] Yet in reality, many of its practices "suppress the initiative of the people, alienate them in all spheres of vital activity and belittle the dignity of the individual."[41] This alienation was identified by Soviet social scientists in the political, economic, and ideological spheres: the alienation of the working people from political power due to the administrative-command system, from the means of production and results of labor due to state ownership and leveled income distribution, and from spiritual value due to the incongruence between words and deeds.[42] Tayana Zaslavskaya, perhaps the best-known Soviet sociologist and reform theorist, argued that the ruling stratum of party officials has in effect turned into a new "ruling class" through its control of the political and economic system, thus causing the alienation of the people from power.[43] Others concurred that if "commodity fetishism" caused human alienation under capitalism in Marx's analysis, then "fetishism of power" was at the root of social alienation under socialism. That is, "the source of the new alienation is not property in the means of production, but a form of political and ideological control over the means of possessing this property."[44]

Although such alienation was attributed to "deformed socialism" rather than to socialism itself, the collective (class-based) and teleological orientation of socialism was held responsible for the neglect of the person, much as in the analysis of Chinese intellectuals. In the Twenty-eighth Congress program, the CPSU acknowledged the impact of the class orientation of socialism on the neglect of the person. "New forms of man's alienation from property and power," it said, had been engendered by "the statization of all aspects of public life and the dictatorship exercised by the top party and state leadership in the name of the proletariat."[45] Elsewhere Gorbachev admitted the harm that the teleological orientation of the socialist project could do to the people. Speaking on the socialist choice at the February plenum of 1990, he remarked, "we are moving away from a dogmatic understanding of that idea, refusing to sacrifice people's real interests to schematic constructs."[46] The question was even raised as to whether a socialist society of workers' direct government and cooperative labor could indeed eliminate alienation. One social scientist suggested that such a society was not equipped to do so because here "the individual is reduced to a cog in a wheel." In his view the provision of civil rights would offer more genuine prospects of the "emancipation of labor."[47]

Just as human alienation was used as the yardstick for past failures, so was its elimination upheld by the Gorbachev leadership as the goal of restructuring. This humanistic emphasis was summed up in the concept of humane, democratic socialism and was specifically reflected in three reformulations. First, in this new conception, the development of the individual, rather than the realization of schematic social designs, became the highest goal of social development. As early as 1986, in his Twenty-seventh Congress report, Gorbachev already elevated human life and the full development of the person to "the highest value," more important than the implementation of socialism itself. "If progress in one area is accompanied by human loss," he remarked later that year, "not just psychological or political loss but also physical loss, then the system that causes such loss should be doubted."[48] Since then he repeatedly described the purpose of restructuring as to display the "genuine humanism" of socialist mode of life, the "humanistic potential of socialism," "the full development of the person." In the Twenty-eighth Congress in 1990, the CPSU formally declared that "the object of social development is the individual; living and working conditions worthy of present-day civilization are created for him or her; their alienation from political power and from the material and spiritual values is overcome, and their active inclusion in social processes is ensured."

Second, in humane, democratic socialism, universal human values were emphasized over class-based values. Addressing an Italian audience in 1989, Gorbachev spoke of establishing "the priority of universal human values in the world."[49] At the Twenty-eighth Congress, he stated that the new ideology of socialism would "assimilate anew universal human values, not as something that is alien in a class sense but as something that is normal for normal human beings. These values have been worked out over centuries and millennia, after all, and we know what neglecting them has brought us."[50] Accordingly, although the CPSU still pledged allegiance to socialist and communist goals, it no longer emphasized the building of a classless society. Instead, even the communist future came to be defined in the neutral terms of a universal humanism. As the Twenty-eighth Congress program stated, "The party's social ideal incorporates humanistic principles of human culture and the age-old desire for a better life and social justice." Or as Gorbachev remarked at the July plenum of 1991, "the realization of the socialist idea and movement . . . can be achieved successfully only in the course of the general development of civilization."

Moreover, the means of achieving these ideals also changed for the CPSU. It was no longer necessary for the masses to transform an unjust society through violent struggle and revolution, or in Gorbachev's words at the July plenum in 1991, "with a forcible coup, the establishment of the dictatorship of the proletariat, and the class struggle, carried through to eliminate the hostile classes." This was so, he explained, because the masses had no other means in the past, but now changes in economic well-being and social structure and the presence of democracy and trade unions made it "possible and necessary" to achieve socialist goals through reforms.[51] In a socialist society, the means of achieving those ideals also changed from the construction of production relations and superstructure of the proletariat to the use of "everything valuable that exists in other societies, in their economies and social sphere, political life, organization of production and everyday life, science and technology, culture, and spiritual and intellectual creativity."[52]

A third aspect of humane, democratic socialism was that the new socialism posited itself as part of the overall civilization of humankind, rather than as an ideology of an exclusive camp that emphasized opposing groups. The embracing of "universal human values," Gorbachev enunciated at the Twenty-eighth Congress, meant the entrance of socialism into "the stream of worldwide transformation" and its "inclusion in the overall progress of civilization."[53] The recognition of the commonality of human progress also became the basis of ending the demarcation of socialist and capitalist mode of thinking and development. Because of reforms in both systems to correct their respective flaws and because of an increasing array of common issues facing mankind, Gorbachev and Soviet reform theorists saw an increasing "convergence" of socialism and capitalism.[54] Therefore, Gorbachev remarked at the February plenum in 1990, "We must renounce everything that led to the socialist countries' isolation in the mainstream of world civilization, and an understanding of the paths of progress as a constant confrontation with a socially different world."[55] This new thinking, in his words, was aimed at "uniting the world, not splitting the world."[56]

Thus the new ideology of the CPSU no longer emphasized the guidance of Marxism-Leninism in all its activities. Rather, the emphasis was now on commitment to socialism as broadly defined, incorporating both the thought of the classic masters and the revolutionary experience and empirical changes of the twentieth century. As the Twenty-eighth Congress program asserted, "The CPSU favors a creative approach to the theory and practice of socialism and their development along lines of a constructive comprehension of the historical experience of the twentieth century and the legacy of Marx, Engels, and Lenin, free of dogmatic interpretation." This new socialism would embrace "the best achievements of human reason and the world's accumulated experience in effective economic management, the solution of social problems, and the development of democratic institutions." These words suggested little concern for whether those other schools of thought and practice were non-Marxist or even anti-Marxist. Ultimately, the assertion of the universality of human beings and human values in these various ways amounted to the deideologization of socialism.

The Place of the Communist Party

The place of the Communist party in society remained another taboo area in the Chinese reassessment. Three issues were particularly important here, namely, the (class) nature of the party, the source of the party's leading status, and the legitimacy of alternative political interests and views. On each of these issues, the CCP refused to make fundamental reformulations. Although it renounced class struggle as a major phenomenon of Chinese society, the party still retained the class nature of the party (that is, the dictatorship of the proletariat) to justify its rightful vanguard role. Although it reduced the use of ideology as the source of its legitimacy, the party was still reluctant to accept the legal and institutional basis of power and more willing to cling to the historical basis of its dominant status. Although it broadened the framework of political and intellectual discourse, the party still rejected non–class-based rule to allow political opposition. In short, the place of the party could not be questioned to erode its monopoly on power and truth.

The Soviet reform leadership, on the other hand, fundamentally rethought the place of the party in society. First, the renunciation of the class nature of the party practically delegitimated its rightful vanguard role. With the adoption of humane, democratic socialism in the party platform since July 1988, the idea of the individual gradually replaced the concept of the working class as the leading force and the purpose of socialism. The party's new commitment to "universal human values and humanist ideals" also helped to obscure the class orientation of the party.[57] Eventually the party came to be defined as "a voluntary union of like-minded people," not just of the working class, although its policy still professed to express "the interests of the working class, the peasantry and the intelligentsia."[58] The CPSU's abandonment of its class nature, most significantly, made it no longer ideologically tenable to exclude segments of society from political life or target them as enemies of the state.

The renunciation of its class basis in turn enabled the CPSU to affirm popular and institutional bases of political power. The Twenty-eighth Congress program stipulated that political power should derive from "[the] sovereign will of the people as the only source of power"; whereas the state, under the control of society, could not act above the society but only "guarantees the protection of individuals' rights and liberties and their honor and dignity regardless of social status, sex, age, national origin, or religion." Further, political power should derive from electoral contestation and the rule of law, through which "free competition is exercised by all public-political forces operating within the framework of the law."

The recognition of the popular and institutional bases of power also legitimated the equality of expression by diverse and opposing political interests and forces, not just the monistic expression of the party or pluralistic expressions within socialism. The Twenty-eighth Congress program put other political organizations on a par with the CPSU as political forces that "express the political and occupational interests of the working class, the peasantry, the intelligentsia, young people, servicemen, and veterans." In proposing the removal of the constitutional guarantee of the "leading role of the CPSU" and of the party as "the nucleus of the political system," Gorbachev remarked in May 1990 that there should be "equal opportunities for the CPSU and other political and public organizations to take part in legal and democratic forms, naturally—in public and political life and to struggle for the implementation of their programmatic aims."[59] Although the CPSU still "intends to struggle for the position of ruling party," he said on another occasion, "it intends to do this strictly within the framework of the democratic process, renouncing any legal and political advantages."[60] The legitimation of alternative political forces and opinions, in turn, de-legitimated the Party's monopoly on power and truth.

In sum, the content of Chinese and Soviet reassessment diverged in three major areas. First, the CCP encouraged an incomplete reexamination of the past in that it avoided a total discrediting of the established system or a linkage of past mistakes and failures to it. But the CPSU's rethinking of the past acknowledged the fundamental deficiency of the old system and attributed past failures and mistakes to it. Second, the partial approach of the Chinese leadership led to its emphasis on the level of production forces as the key measure of past problems and the basis for current reforms. But the more thorough approach of the Gorbachev leadership led to its emphasis on the treatment of the person as the key measure of past failures and the reconstruction of socialism. Finally, the CCP's incomplete analysis of the past and the treatment of the person in turn failed to lead to a fundamentally rethinking of its role in society. But the restoration of the person as the fundamental goal of socialism led the Gorbachev leadership to renounce the party's dominant place in society vis-à-vis other organized groups.

Conclusion

This comparison of the Chinese and Soviet reassessments of socialism has revealed two major differences in these two cases, both of which reflected as well as had an impact on the divergent directions that reforms took and the fate that socialism experienced in the two countries. First, in terms of the process of reassessment, the Soviet reappraisal did not experience a zigzag course as in the Chinese case. In the Soviet case, there was not a deliberate lag in the political sphere nor periodic campaigns to check the impulse of officially sponsored reassessment. Rather, this impulse was allowed to develop in directions that may not have been intended or expected by the leadership. Second, in terms of the content of reassessment, the Soviet reappraisal went beyond the major taboo areas of the Chinese case. It uprooted the foundation of the established system, political and economic, by pruning it down to its Stalinist core; it exposed the normative deficiency of this system by establishing the person as the goal of political life and social development; and it delegitimized the political vanguard of that system by recognizing the legitimacy of competing political opinions and interests.

Why did the Chinese and Soviet reassessment evolve differently? Why did the Soviet leadership go further than the Chinese leadership in the content of its reassessment? One explanation, somewhat ironically, lies in the soundness of China's initial economic reappraisal and economic reforms. Both the Chinese and Soviet leadership started with changes in the economic arena. After renouncing the Maoist model, the Chinese leadership began to critique and scale down the Soviet model of sectoral arrangements, that is, the strategy of heavy industrial and quantitative growth, as well as the Soviet model of command economy. The former effort was aimed at shifting investment and growth to agriculture and light industry, while the latter sought to introduce a "supplementary role" of the market and nonpublic ownership. These twin processes of readjustment and reform proved successful, which in turn encouraged the Chinese leadership to continue focusing on the economic sphere. The empirical success of economic reform also encouraged a belief in the possibility of a separation of the economic and the political spheres, permitting a lag in the latter.

In the Soviet case, it was the lack of success in the early periods of economic reform that forced the leadership to turn to the political sphere. From the Chinese perspective, three major factors contributed to the initial failure of Soviet economic reform. First, the Soviet leadership failed to reassess and readjust the heavy industrial model at the outset of reform. Thus, investment and growth patterns remained distorted in that they still focused on the heavy industrial sector, including the defense industry. Second, microeconomic reforms at the enterprise level were not accompanied by proper macroeconomic ones at the national level, leading to chaos in the economy. Whereas Chinese reforms preserved the necessary macroeconomic control while encouraging competition among production units, Soviet reforms were centered on increasing autonomy of enterprises and dismantling state plans, without effective pricing, financial, and tax policies to retain macroeconomic control and ensure microlevel competition. Third, economic reforms were implemented half-heartedly and ineffectively in the Soviet case. The Soviet leadership did pay attention to this third problem, viewing it as the result of cadre resistance and public inertia. This perception led to the shift to political reform in order to overcome bureaucratic foot-dragging. However, once political reform became the focus of national attention, the political sphere grew overheated and eventually out of control, shelving economic reform and further delaying it.[61]

The balance of political forces in each case also accounts for the divergent processes and outcomes of ideological reassessment in the two countries. Although Chinese veteran leaders had mostly been retired by the mid-1980, they continued to play an active and often decisive role in national politics through informal influence. Their strength contributed to the readjustment policy and a balancing of old and new economic measures, helping to ease the pace of transition and offset the excesses of reform. Conservative leaders were also a leading force in defining the limits of reassessment, cracking down on dissent, and upholding the Four Fundamental Principles.

In the Soviet case, Gorbachev's frequent and adept organizational maneuvers helped to weaken increasingly the political and ideological strength of conservative forces. Important junctures of reform were always accompanied by a discharge of veteran leaders and officials. Ideological work was put into the hands of liberal-minded reformers, whose control of national discourse helped to influence the discussion and formation of policy agenda. The weakness of conservative input was at least partly responsible for the more radical nature of the Soviet reassessment and the one-sidedness of the Soviet reforms. Apart from the generational factor, a greater adherence to democratic centralism within the Soviet party may be a major reason for the successful organizational reshuffles of Gorbachev and the quiet departures of conservative officials. That is, Gorbachev could always get his organizational reshuffles and reform measures adopted in the party because party officials and Central Committee members observed the principles of democratic centralism, even while they may personally disagree with his proposals. In the Chinese case, arbitrary disruption of normal political procedure by senior leaders and Deng's unwillingness to alienate them contributed to the persisting influence of conservative forces. By contrast, Chinese intellectuals were much weaker both in number and in social strength compared with their Soviet counterparts.

Leadership also made a difference. At the outset of reform, the two countries shared a legacy of economic failures and human tragedies. The latter legacy, symbolized in China's Cultural Revolution and the USSR's Stalinist terror, was perhaps the most devastating and disturbing postrevolutionary experience for both nations. Why did similar experiences lead to such divergent directions and outcomes in the rethinking of two essentially similar systems? The orientation and determination of Chinese and Soviet leadership clearly made a difference here. The Chinese reform leadership, of both conservative and reformist leanings, was reluctant to negate the past totally, especially the period before the Cultural Revolution, because a part of their own past and therefore legitimacy was at stake. They consistently treated economic reform as their top priority because of China's more apparent need for economic development, the paralysis of the economy since the Cultural Revolution, and an exhaustion with the political sphere after years of politics in command. Thus, constantly alluding to the chaos of the Cultural Revolution, Deng repeatedly emphasized political stability as the precondition of economic development and even the highest political good. Gorbachev, by contrast, was willing to negate the past thoroughly, partly because he was not personally tied to it. He placed humanistic goals above economic ones and accepted the priority of political reform, because he seemed to believe genuinely that these measures could salvage socialism and give it a new life. He did not place limits on his "new thinking" with any fundamental principles, because, like Hu Yaobang, he was an idealistic Marxist who genuinely cherished popular rule. Compared with Deng, Gorbachev seemed almost naive in believing that reformed socialism would remain the dominant national choice without an economic base or a vanguard party.

Finally, differences in national histories and cultures also help to account for the divergent outcomes of the reassessments in the two cases. The legacy of semicolonialism and imperial invasions certainly made the Chinese leadership more reluctant to embrace completely those values and practices that were perceived as belonging to the "other system." The memory of the warlord period and the Cultural Revolution also made them particularly concerned with the instability of political change. The greater distance between the Chinese and Western civilizations also made it harder for them to accept, in Gorbachev's words, "joining the mainstream of the world civilization," because this would immediately cause qualms about Westernization. The absence of these factors in the Soviet case, by contrast, made it relatively easy for Gorbachev to talk about the reconciliation of the two social systems, and the returning of the Soviet Union to the "mainstream of the human civilization."

CHAPTER TEN

The Post-Mao Reassessment of Socialism and the Chinese Socialist Experience

SHORTLY after Deng Xiaoping's southern tour of spring 1992 to resurrect reform from the retreat of previous two years, reform theorists and intellectuals who had been active before mid-1989 reemerged to rally for the renewal of reform. At their first few symposiums after Deng's new offensive, two central topics were the "reconception of capitalism" and the "reconception of socialism." Aimed at the conservative officials and theorists who had become dominant after mid-1989, the thrust of these discussions was to defend the need for socialism to learn from contemporary capitalism and to oppose a new whateverism that questioned "socialist" or "capitalist" in "whatever" matters.[1]

The four phases of the Chinese reassessment of socialism from 1976 to 1992 discussed in this study have illuminated the evolution and function of this controversy in the post-Mao era. Though the vigorous resumption of economic reforms since 1992 has not been accompanied by significant theoretical discussions and conceptual innovations, ideological issues have not become irrelevant. Apart from Deng's instruction that ideological debates be put aside, the absence of debates can be attributed to the fact that the basic ideas underlying the new drive to expand the market economy and to reform state enterprises were well developed before the mid-1989 retrenchment. In fact, post-1992 reforms have reflected many ideas previously embraced by the radical reform leaders and intellectuals, except now they are being put into practice rather than just being talked about and debated. In this context, the declining importance of ideology and ideological discussions ironically signifies the important roles that post-Mao reassessment has already played and completed.

The Chinese rethinking of socialist theory and practice, as the collateral result of the post-Mao search for the sources of the problems of Chinese society and the solutions to their remedies, has been an integral part of the overall reform course and of the Chinese socialist experience in general. This final chapter considers the important characteristics of the post-Mao Chinese rethinking. It also contemplates the ultimate effects of the Chinese reassessment for the fate of socialism in China and the future of China. Here the important question is whether the course of Chinese reassessment will guide China's path to the future, or whether it has simply been a symptom of a collapsing communist society that ultimately will have little impact on the society constructed in the future.[2]

COMPETING PERSPECTIVES AND THE POST-MAO REASSESSMENT

This book has traced the origin and dynamics of post-Mao rethinking on socialism in four phases of development from 1976 to 1992: epistemological, moderate, radical, and comprehensive. The rethinking of Chinese socialism has deepened incrementally from an examination of mistakes in Chinese theory and practice to that of problems inherent in socialism as it was originally conceived. This overall evolution has been affected both by the process of empirical reforms and by political contention among competing groups, whose views also evolved in the course of analyzing past and continuing problems of Chinese society.

In each phase, serious contention over reassessment was evident among three leading groups, two of these within the party and a broad coalition of societal forces outside it. Four alignments of these groups emerged in the discussion: (1) the whatever group, the practice group, and social/intellectual critics during the epistemological phase of reassessment in 1976–79; (2) the conservers, adjusters, and reformers, and social/intellectual critics during the early phase of moderate reassessment in 1979–81 and the adjusters, reformers, and social/intellectual critics in the later phase of moderate reassessment in 1981–83; (3) the conservative reformers, radical reformers, and social/intellectual critics during the radical reassessment of 1983–86; and (4) the conservative reformers, radical reformers, and social/intellectual critics during the comprehensive reassessment of 1987–89 and the conservative comeback from 1989 to 1992. For analytical purposes, the grouping of reform theorists and intellectuals poses some difficulty here, for in many areas they have been the intellectual spokespersons of the radical reform leadership and thus belong to the group of radical reformers. But in other areas they have gone beyond at least officially sanctioned socialism and thus been categorized by the regime as "liberal" critics. Except for the whatever group, which differed from all others in denying any need for reform, contention among all remaining groups was characterized by a disagreement over the nature and severity of the problems of Chinese socialism and the remedies they proposed.

Three dominant views stand out here. For adjusters and conservative reformers, past errors pertain mainly to ultra-leftist excesses in Chinese theory and practice, to an unrealistic adoption of the Soviet sectoral model, and partially to the Soviet economic model. In this view reform entails correcting the above mistakes and perfecting socialism in basic conformity with the vision of the founding fathers. For radical reformers, past errors are due not entirely to a mistaken understanding and application of socialism but also to the nature and designs of the original theory. In this view reform entails not only correcting erroneous conception and application, but also making revisions and adaptations in the original theory. For "liberal" intellectual and social analysts, problems in Chinese theory and practice are ultimately linked to those in the original designs of socialism. Reform must entail fundamental changes in the conceptual and institutional bases of the Chinese system. The consistency and coherence of each view suggests that the contention among these groups has stemmed fundamentally from a clash over a basic assessment of socialism, rather than just from an intra-elite rivalry over power. To put it in another way, value clash and intra-elite rivalry are at least intertwined and help reinforce each other.

The disputes among the contending groups have greatly affected the way the Chinese reassessment has evolved. A sequence to the conflict has been uncovered in this research that reveals a complex relationship between the political and intellectual levels of post-Mao reassessment: (1) Intrasystem reassessment encouraged by the reform leadership has always gained support from many reform theorists and intellectuals, but also always spurred independent reassessment, some by social forces on the Right. (2) The latter in turn has always led to a reassertion of official orthodoxy by political forces on the Left. (3) The conservative backlash would be circumscribed by a return to the reform line. Thus the campaign to emancipate the mind in 1978 was modified by the crackdown on the Democracy Wall movement in early 1979. The subsequent relapse into leftism in spring 1979 was "righted" by a moderate reassessment in 1979–83, which was then followed by a campaign against bourgeois liberal tendencies in 1981 and one against spiritual pollution in late 1983. The conservative insurgence, in turn, paved the way for a radical reassessment in 1984–86, which was again followed by an antiliberal campaign in late 1986. The latter was only to stimulate the comprehensive reassessment of 1987–mid-1989, which culminated in a crackdown on "counterrevolutionary rioters" and yet another campaign against bourgeois liberalization in the remainder of 1989 and 1990.

In this cycle of relaxation, deviance, and reideologization, the official reform view has remained the dominant line. Its attempt to reorient socialism, on the one hand, and constrain its direction, on the other, has resulted in a "middle course" in the post-Mao Chinese reassessment of socialism. This middle course is marked by "two zones of demarcation" that set apart the Left and Right.[3] For the purpose of this study, one zone is the dialectical and historical materialist approach to socialism, which allows reinterpretation and adaptation, and the other is the Four Fundamental Principles, which define the ultimate parameters of reformulation. Importantly, the first direction has mainly applied to the economic realm, while the second has been significant to the political and ideological realm. This middle course has been manifest in each phase of reassessment and has been at the root of the ideological cycling in post-Mao political developments.

The middle course has stemmed from the post-Mao regime's need for reassessment and the inherent contradictions therein. If the first direction of this course has been entailed by policy exegesis and a genuine desire to rectify past theory and practice, the second direction has been dictated by the contention among elites, on the one hand, and the state and society, on the other. At the elite level, reassessment has led to opposition from those who have appealed to the "consummatory" nature of official doctrine to express misgivings over real or perceived cognitive dissonance. At the level of the state versus society, reassessment has pushed the rethinking process to its logical conclusion: the questioning of the very sanctity of socialism. The unleashing of the "liberal" reassessment of societal groups has necessitated a policy of concession to the Left and reaction against the Right. In this light, the periodic political campaigns against ideological deviance may be seen as efforts to keep the reassessment of the socialist system within the middle course and off the rightist track.

Consequently, the middle course of reassessment has both shaped and been shaped by the political contention within the state and that between the state and the society. In the intrastate contention, the more reformist leadership has prevailed over the more conservative in the economic realm, where repudiation of past theory and practice did not directly threaten the foundation of the system. Thus the pragmatists prevailed over the whatever group, adjusters over conservers, and radical reformers over conservative reformers. Here the more reformist leadership has welcomed and even relied on the intellectual support of reform theorists. In the state-societal contention, the more conservative leadership has prevailed over the more reformist in the political and ideological realm, where repudiation of established theory and practice would threaten the foundation of the system. Thus the first two of the post-Mao political campaigns were indirectly prompted by the whatever group, while the last three were directly brought about by conservative reformers. Here the reformist leadership has distanced itself from reform theorists and intellectuals, treating them as part of the "liberal" forces outside the party.

The different effects of elite contention on the Chinese reassessment must be accounted for primarily by the nature of political contention between the state and society. In periods of official encouragement, when reform leaders normally tolerated reform theorists and relied on some of them for intellectual support, they did not always want to appear to be tolerant of "liberal" critics: Tolerance rendered them ideologically vulnerable. Moreover, they never sanctioned any reassessment that would question or reject the socialist system itself. Most importantly, coping with antisystem analyses was a matter of political control and legitimacy. At issue here is thus a fundamental conflict between the state and society. Hence reform leaders have always yielded to conservative pressures for assaults on bourgeois liberalism. Further, because official relaxation always seemed to have nourished "liberal" analyses, conservative leaders were able to blur the line between "liberal" critics and reform theorists among the societal forces, and to extend their attack from the former to the latter. In attacking the latter, they also sought to undermine the ideological standing of reform leaders. In this way, conservative leaders helped to safeguard the second direction of the middle course.

Deng Xiaoping has played a pivotal role in the pursuit of the middle course of reassessment because of his quest for economic modernization and his concern with the political environment of economic development. Deng's role can be seen in several aspects. First, Deng has himself launched or sanctioned post-Mao efforts to rethink Chinese socialism. He was directly behind such key post-Mao formulations as the dialectical materialist approach, "let some get rich first," diverse models of socialism, socialism with Chinese characteristics, and the production criterion. He gave personal approval for notions that heralded major landmarks of economic reform: a planned commodity economy in 1984, the primary stage of socialism in 1987, a new order of socialist commodity economy in 1988, and a socialist market economic order in 1992. His active sponsorship of new formulations and reform-minded officials contributed crucially to the initiation and sustainment of reassessment in each period. Second, Deng must be held politically responsible for the political campaigns against intellectual deviance in post-Mao China. He set limits on the Emancipation of the Mind campaign with the four principles and gave final approval for each of the five political campaigns in the post-Mao period. He supported the rethinking of socialist theory and practice only where such efforts facilitated economic reform and necessary political reform. Where such efforts threatened political "stability and order," viewed by him as the precondition for economic development, he stood with conservative leaders. This approach was shaped by his valuation of economic efficiency and an instrumental view of ideology geared to this purpose.

In short, the post-Mao reassessment of socialism has not been a haphazardly articulated post facto justification of policies already recommended or executed by political leaders. It has been rigorously and consistently pursued by competing groups at both the state and societal levels who have fundamental differences over the reappraisal of Chinese socialism. The evolving contention among political elites and between elites and society has resulted in a syncretic reformulation and the preservation of the "consummatory" framework of socialism. The process of the Chinese reassessment has confirmed an observation of a Sovietologist that "the readiness to renounce ideology in the name of truth—under pressure from scientific fact—is now admissible where it does not threaten the stability of the system but only where it contributes to this stability."[4] Conversely, where renouncing ideology threatens the stability of the system, truth must give way to ideology.

The significance of a middle course in the Chinese reassessment is highlighted by the different process of reappraisal in the Soviet Union under Gorbachev. In the latter case, although three contending views were also present and cut across elite and societal lines, there was no periodic cycling of relaxation, deviance, and reideologization. The interplay of elite conflicts did not affect the reassessment of intellectual and other societal forces or make victims of them. The competing schools of reassessment did not congeal into a conflict between the state and society. Gorbachev's dependence on the intelligentsia for support of his cause resulted in a process and outcome favorable to the latter: intellectual and political pluralism. Contrasted with the Soviet case, the impact of a middle course on the evolution of the Chinese reassessment has been remarkable: Its presence has helped to save the increasingly precarious fabric of socialist ethos from a total breakdown in China, while its absence has helped to erode it completely in the USSR.

Here the role of reassessment in the two countries has been one of maintaining or jettisoning official ideological hegemony or a syncretic route to ideological change. If the deideologization of political discourse is directly linked to the concurrent meltdown of central political institutions in the Soviet case, China's middle course has contributed to the regime's hegemony over the direction of political and policy discourse, which in turn helped contribute to systemic maintenance and stability in China. The latter condition has apparently safeguarded China's smoother and more successful economic transition.

CORE THEMES OF THE POST-MAO REASSESSMENT

While different impetuses and emphases differed with each phase of the post-Mao reassessment, the issues raised in all phases have certain basic continuities. They all concerned the appropriate forms of socialism and the feasibility of socialism for China. These issues included the nature and stage of Chinese society, the model and method of its socialist development, the place of nonsocialist elements in society, the sources of economic maladies and political abuses under socialism, the motive force and goals of socialist society, and the incongruence between socialist theory and Chinese reality. The range of Chinese judgments on these questions may be characterized by two basic themes.

One theme reflects the reassessment from the official analytical framework. In this perspective, the key to mistaken Chinese theory and practice in the past, and to their remedy in the post-Mao period, has to do fundamentally with the neglect or the recognition of the primacy of material forces in understanding and attaining socialism. This judgment has in turn led to three conclusions. One pertains to the relationship between socialism and Chinese socialism, the second to the relationship between socialism and capitalism, and the third to the relationship between socialism as a theory and Chinese reality.

According to the first conclusion, shared by both conservative and radical reformers, a basic mistake in the past Chinese socialist experience has been to underestimate the unique difficulties of building socialism in an underdeveloped country.[5] This fallacy does not place enough emphasis on the material constraints upon China's socialist development and does not draw a distinction between *what should be* and *what could actually be* the type of socialism in China. This mistake is partly attributed to domestic and international pressures on the revolutionary movement. But, more crucially, it is blamed on a subjective and dogmatic approach to building socialism that neglected the scientific basis of socialism in theory and the peculiarity of Chinese society in practice.

The result of this mistake is that *policy priorities* appropriate to the task of building socialism in China have been seriously misjudged at least from Mao's Great Leap to Hua's new Leap Forward. Attention was paid not to the overcoming of material constraints on socialist construction but to the elevation of economic and political institutions to stages that exceeded the existing state of social development. In the political and economic sphere, emphasis was on ensuring the normative socialist character of the state and the economy without regard for the peculiar constraints of the material base on them, such as a strong "feudal" legacy and weak bourgeois heritage in politics, economics, and ideology. This emphasis impeded the realization of socialism by inhibiting policies necessary to overcome China's material constraints, thereby aggravating the lag of the material base on which scientific socialism must be built. In this view, the post-Mao shift away from class struggle and from the Maoist, Soviet, and classic Marxist models of socialist economy has marked a return to a correct approach to socialist theory and practice. This summary of the official view, nonetheless, must be qualified. For conservative reformers among the Chinese leadership, the primacy of material forces is mainly meant to repudiate the Maoist model, the Soviet sectoral model, and partially the

Soviet-type economic system. It does not mean that material forces are the sole determinant of policy priorities. And it must be placed in given contexts of production relations and superstructure.

According to the second conclusion arising from the assertion of the primacy of material forces, accepted by radical reformers and to a lesser extent by conservative reformers, another basic mistake in China's past socialist experience has been to overestimate the role of socialist production relations and superstructure in building socialism.[6] This fallacy places too much emphasis on the character of production relations and superstructure in socialist development and draws too sharp a distinction between *what is* and *what is not* socialism. This mistake is attributed to a subjective and dogmatic understanding of and approach to socialism and capitalism, particularly a neglect of the sequential and horizontal relationship between them and a neglect of the nonclass basis of certain economic and political forms.

The result of this mistake is that *political methods* appropriate to the task of socialist development in China have been misjudged in the past. Emphasis was on the promotion of socialist institutions and the exclusion of all capitalist practices and ideas per se to ensure proletarian interests, with little regard for their actual efficacy. These methods have done harm to Chinese socialism by restraining practices conducive to safeguarding the actual interests of the working people. Certain elements of the market economy and political democracy are the products of material conditions common to large-scale socialized production and can therefore play a useful role under economies with different class character. In this view, the post-Mao use of traditionally nonsocialist practices has meant a greater range of effective methods for socialist development. This range, however, is considerably smaller for conservative reformers than it is for radical reformers.

According to the third conclusion drawn from the assertion of the primacy of material forces, made by "liberal" critics, the discrepancy between socialism and Chinese reality simply shows that socialism does not fit Chinese society. This discrepancy is fundamentally responsible for the misjudgment of policy priorities and political methods of national development after the revolution. Socialist institutions have impeded the growth of the material base, because of their incompatibility with China's level of production forces. Moreover, because of changes in the domestic and international environment, historical circumstances could no longer constitute a valid justification of the socialist path of national development. In this view, China should abandon that path and adopt more compatible social arrangements.

The second major theme in the post-Mao reassessment reflects the view from outside the official analytical framework. It is important to reiterate that not all those who have gone beyond the official framework reject socialism per se. Some—of whom Su Shaozhi and Wang Ruoshui are primary examples—simply reject official socialism or official utilization of socialism. Su continues to espouse his vision of socialism even after his exile overseas since mid-1989.[7] And so does Wang. In the unofficial perspective on the post-Mao rethinking, the key to the problems of Chinese socialism and their fundamental remedy lies essentially in the neglect or the recognition of the value of the person. That is, socialism in China, with its characteristic class orientation, has led to the deemphasis of the person that is at the root of the maladies of the political and economic system. Although attributed partly to the influences of tradition and revolutionary circumstances, this class orientation is mainly blamed on its theoretical origin. Whether or not the "starting point" of Marxism is the abstract person or the class-defined person, the role assigned to the class in the liberation of the individual has helped to justify group-oriented goals and means that are often falsely defined. In the words of Wang Ruoshui, "in classical Marxism, the individual is supposed to reach full self-realization through the collective; but in the Chinese system, those charged with determining the collective interest have, at all levels, abandoned this pursuit in favor of pure self-interest."[8]

The class orientation of socialism has contributed to the neglect of the person, first of all, by superseding the interests and rights of the person with those of the group. In the economic realm, social planning, ownership, and distribution have ignored the needs, initiatives, and interests of individuals. In the political realm, class-buttressed dictatorship has excluded segments of society from political life and disregarded the opinions and rights of citizens in general. The ultimate judgment here is that collective means and goals in the end have failed to serve the individual or the collective as a community of individuals. Thus, "liberal" criticism of central planning, state ownership, egalitarian distribution, class-based treatment of individuals, class-defined democracy, alienation, and the lack of democracy denounces fundamentally the disregard for the volition and integrity of the person. On the other hand, "liberal" advocacy of the market, individual ownership, self-interests, human rights, universal human values, non–class-based democracy, and a diversity of truth asserts the intrinsic rights and worth of the person.

The class orientation of socialism has also contributed to the suppression of the person because it helps to buttress the absolute authority of the state as the rightful representative of class interests. In the economic realm, the state has been the direct decision maker, manager, and allocator. In the political realm, the state has maintained one school of thought, a single political party, and highly centralized power. It is the claim of the group, in the "liberal" analysis, that has accorded the state the political and moral authority to determine the interests and values of the society and the means of realizing them. The problem here, then, is not so much the nature of Marx's theory or its misapplication by Chinese leaders. Rather, it is the monopolistic position of Marxism, buttressed by group claims, that has allowed official abuse. Thus the "liberal" criticism of the command economy, the party's leadership, socialist democracy, ideological monopoly, the bureaucratic class, and totalism targets the authority of the state. The "liberal" proposal for a free economy, a multiparty and parliamentary system, a recognition of the legitimacy of diverse views, and a retreat of the state from society seeks to assert the autonomy of the person vis-à-vis the authority of the state.

The reassessment of Chinese socialism within the official framework, then, is a methodological one, and that from the unofficial framework is a normative one. The former is concerned with the problems of bridging socialist theory and Chinese reality, while the latter is concerned with socialism itself. The material emphasis of the former approach, symbolized in the practice criterion and the production criterion, is based on a mechanistic reading of Marxism. It deliberately makes use of selected parts of Marx's works, in particular, Marx's later works that emphasize historical materialism, without considering Engels's mechanistic interpretation of them or early Soviet influences in Chinese absorption of Marxism. The CCP chooses to ignore those early works of Marx that have a more humanistic approach, that is, those emphasized by Wang Ruoshui, or Marx's discussion of the Asiatic mode of production, which more directly addresses issues of an Asian context. As a result, the CCP cannot confront the fundamental questions raised by the "liberal" forces: whether China possesses the material requisites for the transition to socialism, whether difficulties in building socialism in China have some relation to its socalled feudal legacy, and ultimately whether genuine socialism can be built on such a social basis without serious distortion.

It is, however, not difficult to understand why the CCP opts for such a prejudicial application of Marxism. Political needs aside, the domestic and international pressures of modernization require that the normative goals of socialism be compromised, even if temporarily. This is best demonstrated in the definition of progress toward socialism in terms of GNP rankings in the world. As Su Shaozhi and his colleagues remark in their semiofficial work on the development of Marxism, under China's current material conditions socialism can only appeal to the people with the basic goal of enriching the country and its people, not yet the higher goals of social equality and the full development of the person.[9] But since a distinct national consciousness and path of development are a part of that catching up, socialism still serves a fundamental end rather than merely serving as an instrument of a ruling party.

The normative emphasis of the "liberal" reassessment, on the other hand, has a more problematic doctrinal and cultural basis. Although humanists like Wang Ruoshui have employed Marx's early works to assert the primacy of the individual, the relatively limited emphasis on Marx's early works in the history of the CCP—due both to the historical circumstances of the Chinese Revolution and the official monopoly on the interpretation of Marxism—has afforded their arguments little doctrinal legitimacy. Short of fundamental values on which to base their arguments, critics of socialism from the individualistic perspective also lack the "considered convictions" to which defenders of socialism could appeal, that is, Chinese rejection of the bourgeois value system on the basis of national experience. In his *A Theory of Justice*, John Rawls justifies his conception of the person as "a free, autonomous, and rational being" on the ground of "our considered convictions" that "we seem unwilling to give up."[10] His critics have pointed out that Rawls appeals to perfectionist principles here, namely, fundamental principles that maximize certain goals.[11] Therefore his conception of the person can be culturally, ideologically, and group bound.[12] Conversely, the problem of the Chinese "liberal" challenge to socialism has been the lack of perfectionist principles that are culturally and nationally accepted. By contrast, the group claim of the Chinese state seems more in line with the Confucian cultural tradition.

Although the reassessment of the CCP is not shared by the CPSU, the similarities and differences between the reassessment of the two parties have illuminated some generic problems of theory and practice in socialist movements. Most importantly, these include the gap between theory and application, between theory and realities of the host society, between the empirical conditions of Marx's times and those of the present, and, most of all, between socialism as an ideal of liberation for all and the tyranny of its collective and teleological orientation in practice. The Soviet reassessment suggests that the difficulties and failures in socialist practice are not solely due to the material constraints of an underdeveloped society. It also confirms the judgment of the Chinese "liberal" view about the tyranny of the monopolistic place of even the best-intended ideology.

On the other hand, the Soviet reassessment and the Soviet experience also testify to the limitations and the "class" bias of Chinese "liberals." The Soviet reassessment went in many ways as desired by Chinese intellectuals.[13] The resultant choice of reform model emphasized political reform favored by the intelligentsia. But the lag of economic reform and the eventual collapse of the CPSU, due partly to that sequence of reform, may not have served the interests of the masses as satisfactorily as the Chinese model of political behind economic reform. The plight of the Russian economy and of the masses after the collapse of the CPSU, in sharp contrast to the vibrancy of the Chinese economy and the increasing prosperity of Chinese citizens, has shown that China may not be better off, after all, with the dissolution of the CCP. Even China's corruption looks mild compared with the mafia-ridden economy of post-Soviet Russia, because of the capacity of China's stronger state to control the scope and nature of corruption. The CCP's emphasis on economic development and political stability has by now turned out to hold quite true for a society in transition, and a dramatic transition for that matter. So the CCP's group claim in this regard may have a point after all. Has the freedom of a few politicians to engage in open power rivalry and of a few intellectuals to engage in open discussions really signified the end of alienation and the restoration of human integrity in post-Communist Russia? The answer is still unclear, especially in the light of the one-third increase in mortality rate and the 50 percent reduction in birthrate among the common people, due essentially to a more difficult life and increasing desperation. Or will China have the last laugh because its transition to a politically more open society will be more solid and less painful in the long run?

THE REASSESSMENT OF SOCIALISM AND IMPLICATIONS FOR THE FUTURE

One major implication that the post-Mao reassessment seems to hold for both the fate of socialism in China and China's future is the decline of ideological monopoly and hence a singular view of social order and development. The emergence of a widely shared consensus over the tremendous harm of a single interpretation of a broadly shared ideology was a crucial step in the repudiation of Hua Guofeng's whateverism and the unfolding of the subsequent reassessment in the post-Mao era. The recognition of a pluralistic conception and interpretation of official doctrine has made it possible to articulate the practice criterion against the Maoist model, socialism with Chinese characteristics against the Soviet model, and the primary stage of socialism against the orthodox Marxist model of development. This internal differentiation within official doctrine has had important ramifications for the fostering of ideological pluralism in Chinese politics and Chinese thinking.

The legitimation of a pluralistic conception of socialism has made it more difficult to characterize opponents in political and ideological disputes as guilty of ideological deviation. Even though the seriousness of such accusations increased over the decade, they have not been taken as seriously. From the Antirightist movement of 1957 and especially after the purge of Peng Dehuai in the wake of the Great Leap, it had become routine in Chinese politics to accuse critics of the party and Chairman Mao of ideological deviation. In fact, ideological deviation became practically the worst political sin, as all political campaigns after the Great Leap were directed against rightist tendencies and almost all of Mao's opponents—from Peng to Liu Shaoqi—were persecuted on ideological grounds. Ideological tyranny became such that the post-Mao change of political course had to begin with the resolution of an ideological dispute. The reassessment of Chinese socialism as it developed after the truth debate has signified a significant moderation of ideological labeling. The post-Mao leadership has identified doctrinaire tendencies on the Left as the principal cause of troubles in the past and viewed them as more dangerous than the deviationist tendencies of the Right in terms of China's socialist development. Hence dogmatism has become a greater concern of the reform leadership than has deviation. The party has consistently urged the purge of those aspects of doctrine that were "outdated, utopian, or arbitrarily added"; encouraged efforts to "reconceptualize" socialism and "develop" Marxism; and called upon the public to "find new solutions to new problems." As a result, different interpretations and reformulations have legitimately been discussed in open forums. At least two distinct schools of reformers have coexisted within the party. The internal differentiation of official doctrine has widened the post-Mao ideological spectrum to an unprecedented breadth both within and outside the party.

Outside the party, doctrinal pluralization has provided greater room for expression for intellectuals and the public in general. While intellectuals were the frequent targets of ideological reeducation during the Mao era, now they have been given a central role in reformist discourse. The reform leadership has not only encouraged them to reinterpret theories to justify reform but also turned to them for intellectual support and even relied on some of them as their think tank. This new climate has allowed reform theorists and other intellectuals constantly to push the official parameters toward deeper reassessment, which has in turn often been incorporated into the official platform. This process has contributed to a gradual secularization of official doctrine. Reinterpretation can also go a long way in directions unintended by the party. Using the analytical tools of Marx, reform theorists and intellectuals have been able to draw sometimes devastating conclusions. The use of Marxism itself has certainly lent these analyses a degree of legitimacy that makes official rebuttal of them more difficult. Through intellectual contributions, post-Mao intellectuals have also gained political strength. Apart from their think tank role, individuals have also been directly promoted to political posts that can influence ideological and other matters. For his article on the truth criterion, Professor Hu Fuming was offered the deputy directorship of the Department of Propaganda in Jiangsu Province, which he declined. A less-known example is Lu Jidian, a college instructor who was promoted to head the Department of Propaganda in the city of Chongqing for his reformist writings.[14] On the conservative side, Wu Shuqing of People's University leaped from a mere associate professor during the antiliberal campaign in 1986 to the vice president of People's University and then to the president of Beijing University after Tiananmen. The restoration of the role of intellectuals as moral force of society certainly marks a reversal of Mao's anti-intellectualism that will have a long-term significance for China.

Pluralistic approaches to understanding socialism have further helped to mitigate the political costs of ideological deviation, or to "deescalate the stakes of ideological conflict" as Joseph predicts in his study of the Chinese critique of ultra-leftism.[15] This holds true even in light of Tiananmen. The postliberation history of the CCP has shown a gradual broadening of the scope and intensification of ideological struggle within the top leadership and in the political system as a whole. From the Antirightist movement of 1957, ideological deviance within and outside the party was increasingly addressed with coercive methods, from demotion to violent purges and persecution.[16] In the post-Mao reassessment, ideological differences within the party have increasingly come to be seen as divergent views of socialism within the party. Except in rare cases, ideological deviance outside the party has been treated as an improper attitude rather than as being counterrevolutionary in nature. As a result, there appears to be a significant mitigation of the costs to the "losers" in elite conflicts as well as in mass political campaigns, as Joseph predicts.[17] This, along with an increasing appreciation for the importance of institutionalizing politics, will again have a significant impact in the future.

The fate of political leaders and intellectual dissenters in the five political campaigns in post-Mao China has on balance shown the deescalation of the political costs of ideological deviance. After the student protests of 1986 and 1989, Hu Yaobang and Zhao Ziyang were respectively removed from post of the general secretary of the CCP. But the demotion of both leaders was couched in terms of a decision of an enlarged meeting of the Politburo—and in Hu's case, to accept his request for resignation for his mistakes. Hu was not subject to public censure for his alleged errors, and Zhao was only briefly criticized in public forums. Hu also retained his seat on the Central Committee and Zhao was not expelled from the party. Zhao was allowed to give a lengthy and assertive defense of himself at a post-Tiananmen party plenum. Hu continued to be commended for his role in promoting the Emancipation of the Mind, and Zhao received praise for his role in the economic reform. Neither was demoted to remote areas. The party's prolonged indecision or intense debates over Zhao's fate, even in the light of the dramatic unfolding of events in mid-1989, further suggest the moderation of the methods of ideological struggle. Local leaders, too, will not always cooperate with the center in censuring ousted leaders. Xiao Yang, mayor of Chongqing in 1989, refused to call protests in his city "turmoil" or to criticize Zhao Ziyang after the latter's fall. Yet he was promoted to replace Sichuan's governor, who actually did follow the party line to criticize Zhao publicly.

Political costs to individual dissidents have also been significantly moderated, as can be seen from the five post-Mao campaigns. Even in the two cases where arrests were made, that is, in the campaigns of 1979 and 1989, the methods were still more moderate than what might have been expected in the prereform period. For the most part, individuals targeted by the campaigns were subject to internal criticism and loss of political posts, not physical persecution or intense public invective. Wang Juntao and Chen Ziming were given relatively long sentences partly because of their defiant attitudes, and partly because of their long linkage to dissident movements since 1979. Most targeted individuals have reappeared in public forums, often to resume espousing the same views. Despite his 1979 controversial article and his being subject to repeated criticisms, Su Shaozhi headed the CASS Institute of Marxism-Leninism in much of the 1980s and remained a leading intellectual spokesperson for reform well into the late 1980s. Even after the crackdown of 1989–1990, many leading reform theorists and intellectuals, including Yu Guangyuan, Tong Dalin, Wang Ruoshui, Zhang Xiangyang, Sun Changjiang, and Li Yining, reemerged after Deng's southern tour of 1992 to advocate some of the very views criticized in the preceding campaign. Not surprisingly, one of them continued to dispute the status of the official ideology that had allowed leftists to monopolize power over its "annotation."[18] The increasing separation of the political and the intellectual, in turn, will contribute to the weakening of China's long-term tradition of combining politics and morality.

In addition to discrediting ideological monopoly, the reassessment of socialism has also had the effect of contributing to the decline of socialist goals in China and, in the longer run, to certain new but perhaps dubious value orientations. Not only has the "liberal" view but also the mainstream reassessment of radical reformers consistently suggested a deemphasis of the normative goals of socialism. In fact, the official materialist line has done the most to shift the ideological orientation of the country. Like the fostering of ideological pluralism, it has a profound impact on the fate of socialism in China and China's future political culture.

First, by prioritizing the methodology of Marxism over its world view, radical reformers have in effect substituted normative goals of socialism for economic ones. The reformist line of reassessment has explicitly redefined socialism in this direction. The goal of socialism, the superiority of the socialist system, and the desirability of all policies are now judged on the basis of the growth of production forces. The materialist conception of socialism is held in check only by conservative reformers, who still see the normative goals of socialism as at least as important as the economic ones. To the extent the conservative view represents mainly that of veteran revolutionaries and has remained on the defensive, the materialist view is likely to have greater ramifications for Chinese political values. This is especially so given the deeper cause of the substitution of normative goals with material ones, that is, the concern with national survival. As Zhao Ziyang noted in his Thirteenth Congress report, "In today's world, revolutionary new technologies develop rapidly, market competition intensifies daily, and world politics changes unpredictably. The challenge we face is severe. If we do not have a full understanding of this situation, if we do not make greater efforts, our country and people may be left further behind, and we will not have a place in the world that we deserve." Since the gap between China and industrialized countries will not be closed soon, the normative goals of socialism are not likely to reassert themselves for some time. By contrast, the catch-up psychology is more likely to determine ultimately national goals and policy priorities.

The reassessment of socialism has also contributed to the decline of socialist goals by leaving the realization of these goals to historical forces. The new orthodoxy of the production criterion and the primary stage of socialism have linked current policies to the transition to full socialism only in terms of building the necessary material basis. Under this logic, anything that contributes to the growth of production forces contributes to socialism. And with this growth, history will take its course. Although the retreat to a more rudimentary stage is meant to better prepare for the full transition to socialism, the latter is not really the immediate concern of the new orthodoxy. Rather, the role assigned to material forces serves as a reminder of the complexity of the task of building socialism and a check against any hasty march toward it. The emphasis on the unique difficulties of building socialism in an underdeveloped country, then, has contributed to a deemphasis on the conscious building of socialism.[19] Nor is any future regime likely to have much interest in a teleological design of society, socialist or otherwise.

On the other hand, the reassessment of socialism in China could also have an important impact on the orientation of Chinese political values—specifically, "a new skewing of Chinese political values," in Joseph's words.[20] The Chinese ideological spectrum has clearly shifted to the right in the post-Mao period. The so-called ultra-leftists have been silenced as a viable political voice. Conservative reformers, whose representatives were among the leading spokespersons of the Right in the party in the 1950s and 1960s, have now become the Left. What would otherwise have been the ultra-Right in the Mao era, the radical reformers, have been pushed to the middle by "liberal" forces who now occupy the place on the Right. Thus far the balance of power within the party and the challenge of the new Right outside it have inhibited a new official dogma "inclined toward intolerance of any sort of feedback or dissent that might be interpreted as reflecting even the slightest shading of Leftist sentiment."[21] But the direction of the post-Mao reassessment could induce a new skewing toward the right in two ways that would undermine both the socialist orientation of China and a long-term pluralizing trend discussed earlier.

First, the official elevation of production forces to the first principle has already produced a skewing toward economics. Two aspects of the post-Mao reassessment have contributed to this skewing. On the one hand, all past and present problems of China's socialist development have been reduced to the insufficient elevation of the level of production forces. On the other hand, the solution to these problems and the building of socialism in general have been consigned to the working out of production forces. On the basis of this assessment there has emerged a new dogma characterized by an intolerance of any feedback or dissent that appears to obstruct the development of production forces. The new dogma leads to an aversion toward both the Left, whose obstructiveness has been the assertion of the normative principles of socialism, and the Right, whose obstructiveness lies in the threat to political stability viewed as essential to economic development. This new orthodoxy of economic determinism may move the national agenda further away from the question of the "person," by dismissing the assertion of group interests on the Left and the claim of individual rights on the Right.

In an important way, the events of mid-1989 have already demonstrated the consequences of this new economic orthodoxy. The neglect of the negative effects of reform, that is, social inequality and economic corruption—typical concerns of the Left—contributed to the social basis of the mass protests of 1989. The neglect of issues of political reform, that is, political participation and citizen rights—typical concerns of the Right— led to the forceful crackdown of the protesters. It is not surprising that the unfolding of the events in mid-1989 has caused a backlash of the Left and a radicalization of the Right. Politically, the dogma of economic determinism has found expression in the concept of neo-authoritarianism. In this context, the role of socialism is likely to be reduced to the leadership of the party in an authoritarian, developmental state. But the running of this new variant of the East Asian model will perhaps be less smooth than its predecessors because of the frustrated Left and the radicalized Right. Both may help contribute to a stronger "society" than in the other East Asian developmental states during their early development. The Left will be more vocal in pushing backward toward socialist values, while the Right will push forward toward individualistic values. The Tiananmen protests already demonstrated this simultaneous pushing: The masses resentful of inequality and corruption, on the one hand, and the intellectual strata anxious for political change, on the other, combined to put serious pressure on the state in mid-1989.

The other current of the new skewing to the right that is likely to develop from the "liberal" assessment of socialism could be an orthodoxy of antisocialism and, in the longer run, and a detrimental effect on the pluralizing tendencies discussed earlier.[22] Several factors reinforce the likelihood of an ideological skewing against socialism. Established socialism has been held responsible for all of China's past and present problems since the liberation in the "liberal" reassessment. For the most part, the capitalist economic and political system is taken as the solution to these problems and the remedy for China as a whole. Most of all, this view is most influential among the younger generation of reformers—intellectuals and students—among whom memories of pre-1949 days are weak. The new dogma that is likely to emerge here would be an intolerance of any practices, values, or dissent that might reflect a slight flavor of socialism and an indiscriminate acceptance of the practices and values of its antithesis. In this context, there would be an ironical reversal of the anticapitalist orthodoxy that emerged in the 1950s and was pushed to the extremes in Mao's late years.[23] A call during the 1989 protests to "kill all Communist party members" is an extreme expression of this likely new dogma. It does not help much either that some of the leading spokespersons of liberal and radical reformers are now in exile in the West. Limited language skills and contacts with the larger society may actually reinforce their idealistic, sometimes simplistic understanding of Western democracy.

Has the post-Mao reassessment of socialism laid down any concepts and lessons that will be of lasting historical value, bridge China's past and future, and affect the society constructed in the future?[24] At least three concepts are likely to endure far beyond Chinese socialism: the value of the person, multilinearism in social development, and the diversity of truth. Su Shaozhi, for example, hopes that the post-Mao reassessment will lead to the construction of a new society based on democratic socialism.[25] Not everyone will embrace those concepts, but neither will they be able to deny their relevance completely. A few lessons will also be of lasting importance: the deviation from the original chosen path of development and social goals, the transformation of a party of class liberation into one of new class oppression, the independence of the new state from the social groups it purports to serve, and, most of all, the neglect of national conditions and the interests of the host society to which a new social order is applied. These lessons may be especially relevant to those liberal forces who are eager to borrow a new foreign model—this time, Western-type capitalism and democracy. But ironically, the above lessons are also most likely to be lost on the group that has most ardently criticized socialism.

As Joseph concludes from his analysis of the Chinese critique of ultra-leftism, to base the new social order entirely on a negative assessment of the old may eclipse the real lessons of the past.[26] And it may turn the long history of post-Mao debates into a record of vindicative blaming for the historical mistakes made in choosing the socialist path. If the real lessons of the post-Mao reassessment are not learned, the liberal forces may not be any more successful than the CCP in choosing and implementing a new national path. If the post-Soviet experience is any guide, overnight transition to Western-type democracy and capitalism will not resolve most problems of the old society.

On balance, the Chinese nation will be better off as a result of the post-Mao reassessment of its socialist experience. At the very least it has involved soul-searching, although it will take some time to see if there will be true learning. Those who are interested in understanding the difficulties of applying socialism in specific societies and the complexities of transforming them to new ones will also have much to learn from the Chinese reassessment of socialism.

Notes

CHAPTER ONE

1. "Only Socialism Can Develop China" *Renmin ribao* (hereafter *RMRB*), July 22, 1989.

2. Wang Renzhi, "On Opposing Bourgeois Liberalization," *RMRB*, February 2, 1990.

3. For example, Wang Chongjie, "Drastic Change in the Soviet Political Situation," *Neican xuanbian* 38 (1991): 18–20; Guan Xuelin, "A Continuing Series of Blunders in Economic Reforms—Summary 18 of the Situation in the Soviet Union during Gorbachev's Six Years of Reign," *Neican xuanbian* 24 (1991): 20–22; Zhang Heping, "How Has Gorbachev Proposed and Promoted a Line of 'Humanistic and Democratic Socialism' and Put the Soviet Union on a Road to Peaceful Evolution?" (Summary of documents by the Marxism-Leninism Office, Sichuan Institute of Foreign Affairs, 1992): 1–20; Jiang Zhaoyong, "A Crisis-ridden Soviet Union," *Sulian dong'ou xingshi cankao ziliao* (Reference materials on the current situation in the Soviet Union and East Europe), Chongqing Research Association of Employees' Ideological and Political Work (January 1990): 38–52.

4. Telephone interview with Guo Luoji, New York City, April 1994.

5. Interview with Yan Jiaqi, Brown University, Providence, Rhode Island, December 9, 1989.

6. Ibid.

7. Arif Dirlik and Maurice Meisner, "Politics, Scholarship, and Chinese Socialism," in *Marxism and the Chinese Experience*, ed. Dirlik and Meisner, 6.

8. Paul Cohen, "The Post-Mao Reforms in Historical Perspective," *Journal of Asian Studies* 47, 3 (August 1988): 518–40.

9. Lucien Pye, *The Dynamics of Chinese Politics* and *The Mandarin and the Cadre: China's Political Cultures*.

10. Pye, "On Chinese Pragmatism in the 80's," *The China Quarterly* 106 (July 1986): 207–34.

11. Michael D. Lampton, ed., *Policy Implementation in Post-Mao China*; Kenneth Lieberthal and Michel Oksenberg, *Policy Making in China*.

12. Dirlik and Meisner, in their *Marxism and the Chinese Experience*, suggest that such an evaluation is implicit in the use of the term "second revolution" to describe post-Mao reforms. The usage originates in Harry Harding, *China's Second Revolution: Reform after Mao*.

13. Helena Richer, "Ideology Soviet Style," *Crossroads* (Jerusalem) (Autumn 1978): 27–46.

14. Z. K. Brzezinski, *Ideology and Power in Soviet Politics*, 79.

15. Helmut Dahm, "The Function and Efficacy of Ideology," *Studies in Soviet Thought* 21, 2 (May 1980): 109–11.

16. Pye, *The Mandarin and the Cadre*, especially chap. 3, and "On Chinese Pragmatism."

17. Tang Tsou, *The Cultural Revolution and Post-Mao Reform, a Historical Perspective*, 6–8.

18. Deng is cited to this effect in "Tightly Grasp Our Treasured Tool," *RMRB*, October 15, 1992.

19. Barrington Moore, *Soviet Politics: The Dilemma of Power, the Role of Ideas in Social Change*, 421–22.

20. Martin Seliger, *Ideology and Politics*, 233.

21. Dirlik, "Post-socialism? Reflections on 'Socialism with Chinese Characteristics,'" in *Marxism and the Chinese Experience*, ed. Dirlik and Meisner, 369.

22. Ibid.

23. Li Honglin, *Sizhong zhuyi zai Zhongguo* (Four kinds of isms in China).

24. Joseph Fewsmith, "The Dengist Reforms in Historical Perspective," in *Contemporary Chinese Politics in Historical Perspective*, ed. Brantly Womack, 23.

25. The phrase "on its own terms" is from Jonathan Spence, *The Search for Modern China*, 746.

26. William A. Joseph, *The Critique of Ultra-Leftism in China, 1959–1981*; Dorothy J. Solinger, ed., *Three Visions of Chinese Socialism*; Solinger, *Chinese Business under Socialism: The Politics of Domestic Commerce 1949–1980*; Stuart Schram, "'Economics in Command?' Ideology and Policy since the Third Plenum 1978–84," *The China Quarterly* 99 (September 1984): 417–61; Schram, *Ideology and Policy since the Third Plenum, 1978–1984*; Bill Brugger, *Chinese Marxism in Flux, 1978–84*; and Brugger with David Kelly, *Chinese Marxism in the Post-Mao Era*.

27. Franz Michael et al., *China and the Crisis of Marxism-Leninism*; Mark Selden, *The Political Economy of Chinese Development*; and Solinger, *China's Transition from Socialism: Statist Legacies and Market Reform*.

28. Meisner, "The Deradicalization of Chinese Socialism," in *Marxism and the Chinese Experience*, ed. Dirlik and Meisner.

29. Dirlik, "Post-socialism?".

30. Lieberthal and Oksenberg, eds., *Policy Making in China*.

31. Cited in ibid., chap. 1.

32. Andrew Nathan, "A Factionalism Model of CCP Politics," *The China Quarterly* 53 (January–March 1973): 34–66; Pye, *The Dynamics of Chinese Politics*; and Roderick MacFarquhar, *The Origins of the Cultural Revolution*.

33. Joseph, *The Critique of Ultra-Leftism*, 4.

34. Joseph V. Femia, "Ideological Obstacles to the Political Evolution of Communist Systems," *Studies in Soviet Thought* 34, 4 (November 1987): 217.

35. Vladmir Shlapentokh, *Soviet Public Opinion and Ideology, Mythology and Pragmatism in Interaction*, 10–11.

36. Yan Jiaqi, talk at Brown University, Providence, Rhode Island, December 9, 1989. Telephone interviews with Ruan Ming, April 1994, and Chen Yizi, May 1994, both in the United States.

37. Interviews with Ruan Ming, Yan Jiaqi, and Chen Yizi. Telephone interviews with Su Shaozhi, Guo Luoji, Zhao Wei, and Hu Ping, March, April, and

May 1994, all in the United States. Interview with Wu Guoguang, New York, April 1991.

38. Interviews with Ruan Ming and Yan Jiaqi.

39. See, for example, Lampton, ed., *Policy Implementation*; Lieberthal and Oksenberg, eds., *Policy Making* in China; Pye, *The Dynamics of Chinese Politics*; Pye, "On Chinese Pragmatism"; and Pye, *The Mandarin and the Cadre*.

40. The following discussions are based on Seven M. Goldstein, "Reforming the Socialist System: Some Lessons of the Chinese Experience," *Studies in Comparative Communism* 21, 2 (Summer 1988): 233.

41. Hanson C. K. Leung, "The Role of Leadership in Adaptation to Change: Lessons of Economic Reform in the USSR and China," *Studies in Comparative Communism* 18, 4 (Winter 1985): 227–46, especially 230; and Goldstein, "Reforming the Socialist System," 233.

42. Goldstein, "Reforming the Socialist System," 233.

43. Pye, "On Chinese Pragmatism" and *The Mandarin and the Cadre*, chap. 7.

44. Stephen Haggard, *Pathways from the Periphery: The Politics of Growth in the Newly Industrializing Countries*, 47.

45. Interviews with Ruan Ming, Yan Jiaqi, Su Shaozhi, Chen Yizi, Guo Luoji, and Wu Guoguang.

46. Arnold Buchholz, "A Sortie into Soviet Ideology," *Studies in Soviet Thought* 36, 2 (July/August 1988): 111–16, and *"Perestroika* and Ideology: Fundamental Questions as to the Maintenance of and Change in the Soviet System," *Studies in Soviet Thought* 36, 3 (October 1988): 149–68.

47. James Scanlan, "Ideology and Reform," in *Gorbachev's Reforms, U.S. and Japanese Assessments*, ed. Peter Juviler and Hiroshi Kimura; and Archie Brown, "Ideology and Political Culture," in *Politics, Society and Nationality inside Gorbachev's Russia*, ed. Seweryn Bialer, 1–40.

48. See Solinger, ed., *Three Visions*; and Solinger, *Chinese Business under Socialism*. See also Jack Gray, "The Two Lines," in *Authority, Participation and Cultural Change*, ed. Stuart Schram.

49. Goldstein, "Reforming the Socialist System," 234. See also Dorothy Solinger, "Economic Reform via Reformulation in China: Where Do Rightist Ideas Come From?" *Asian Survey* 29, 9 (September 1981): 947–60.

50. Schram, "China since the Thirteenth Congress," *The China Quarterly* 114 (June 1988): 179.

51. Samuel Huntington and Jorge Dominguez, "Political Development," in *Handbook of Political Science*, ed. Fred Greenstein and Nelson Polsby, 5:3; and Jorge I. Dominguez, "Revolutionary Values and Developmental Performance: China, Cuba and the Soviet Union," in *Value and Development: Appraisal of the Asian Experience*, ed. Harold Lasswell, Daniel Lerner, and John Montgomery, 21.

52. For some examples of the early Chinese response, see Benjamin Schwartz, *In Search of Wealth and Power: Yen Fu and the West*; Joseph Levenson, *Liang Chi-chao and the Mind of Modern China*; Lin Yusheng, *The May Fourth Movement*; and Lin, *The Crisis of Chinese Consciousness: Radical Anti-traditionalism in the May Fourth Era*.

53. Huntington and Dominguez, "Political Development," 20–21.

54. Ibid.

55. John Schull, "What Is Ideology? Theoretical Problems and Lessons from Soviet-Type Societies," *Political Studies* 40 (1992): 40–41.

56. For the importance that Confucian and post-Confucian elites attached to the way one thinks, see Lin, *The Crisis of Chinese Consciousness*.

57. He Jiacheng et al., "On the Discussion of the Primary Stage of Socialism of Our Country," *RMRB*, June 15, 1987.

58. Zhao Fusan, "The Trends of the Spiritual Civilization on Mainland China," *RMRB*, July 10, 1985.

59. Su Shaozhi, review of Bill Brugger and David Kelly, *Chinese Marxism in the Post-Mao Era*, in *The Australian Journal of Chinese Affairs*, 1 (23) (1993): 168–169.

60. For example, Zhu Fu'en, "Cultural Reconstruction and Development of Marxism in China," *Xuexi yu tansuo* 6 (June 1987), in *Xinhua wenzhai* 2 (February 1988): 154–57; and Ren Ping, "Cultural Reconstruction and Marxism," *RMRB*, August 28, 1988.

61. Tsou, *The Cultural Revolution*, xv.

62. Pye, "Chinese Pragmatism," 223–26.

63. I am grateful to Joseph Fewsmith for sharpening my thought on these questions.

64. Mel Gurtov, ed., *The Transformation of Socialism*, offers a collection of individual studies of Chinese and Soviet reforms, although most are not comparative in nature.

CHAPTER TWO

1. CCP Central Committee Documents Research Department, *Guanyu jianguo yilai dang de ruogan wenti de jueyi zhuyiben* (Notes to the resolution on CCP history), 456–61.

2. Brantly Womack, "Politics and Epistemology in Post-Mao China," *The China Quarterly* 80 (December 1979): 768–95; Schram, *Ideology and Policy*; and Michael Sullivan, "CCP Ideology since the Third Plenum," in *Chinese Marxism in Flux*, ed, Brugger, 67–97.

3. Su Shaozhi and Zhang Xiangyang, eds., *Sanzhong quanhui yilai Makesizhuyi zai Zhongguo de fazhan* (The development of Marxism in China since the Third Plenum), 31.

4. "Study Well the Documents and Grasp Well the Key Link," *RMRB*, February 7, 1977; also in *Jiefangjun bao* (hereafter *JFJB*) and *Hongqi* (hereafter *HQ*).

5. See Hua Guofeng's report in *Zhongguo gongchandang di shiyijie dahui cailiao ji* (Collected Materials of the Eleventh Congress of the Chinese Communist Party), 6, 16–19.

6. Ibid.; see also Hua's speech at the second All-National Conference on Learning from Dazhai, December 25, 1977, in *RMRB*, December 28, 1977.

7. In April 1976 crowds of Beijing workers and residents gathered in front of the Tiananmen in memory of Zhou Enlai. The memorial turned into indirect attacks on the Gang of Four and Mao when memorial poems that appeared in the

square criticized radical policies and the Gang of Four in person. The police were ordered to put down the gatherings and arrested many activists and poem writers. The party labeled the mass movement "counterrevolutionary," and Deng was forced to step down just a year after his rehabilitation.

8. Zeng Tao, "The Great Debate of 1978," *Xuexi yuekan* 12 (December 1988).

9. For the evolution of this critique of the Gang, see Joseph, *The Critique of Ultra-Leftism*, chap. 5.

10. Hua, speech at the All-National Conference on Learning from Dazhai.

11. Hue Jiwei, "In Accordance with Books, Authority or Practice?" *Guangming ribao* (hereafter *GMRB*), May 7, 1988.

12. Wu Jiang, "Facts Surrounding the Debate on the Practice Criterion," in *Guanyu zhenli biaozhun wenti taolun wenji* (Collected articles from the debate on the truth criterion), ed. Theoretical Research Department, Central Party School, 165.

13. Deng Xiaoping, *Deng Xiaoping wenxuan* (Selected works of Deng Xiaoping), 34.

14. Ibid., 39.

15. Ibid., 35–36, 39–40, 42.

16. Chen Mingxian et al., *Xin Zhongguo sishinian yanjiu* (A study of forty years of new China), 462.

17. Wang Zhaozheng and Huang Zheng, *Cong sanzhong quanhui dao shi'er da* (From the Third Plenum to the Twelveth Congress), 31.

18. Wu Jiang and Sun Changjiang, "Hu Yaobang and the Debate on the Criterion of Truth," *GMRB*, April 24, 1989. See also Hu Jiwei, "Authority or Practice?"

19. Hu Jiwei, "Authority or Practice?"

20. The policy documents are, respectively, "Report on Conscientiously Implement the Party's Policy and Alleviate Unreasonable Burdens for Peasants" and "Investigation Report on How Cadres in Xunyi Country Gave Compulsory Orders, Violated Laws and Disciplines," cited in Chen et al., *Xin Zhongguo*, 459.

21. *RMRB*, February 26, 1978.

22. During the same period, Deng sent Zhao Zhiyang to Sichuan Province to experiment with rural reform. The appointments were made to prepare Zhao and Wan with the experience for wider reforms as national leaders.

23. Wan Li, "Conscientiously Implement the Party's Rural Economic Policies," *RMRB*, March 17, 1978.

24. "Editorial: Simultaneously Grasp the Three Revolutionary Movements," *RMRB*, April 22, 1978.

25. Deng, *Deng Xiaoping wenxuan*, 98–99.

26. Cited in Zeng Tao, "The Great Debate."

27. Interview with Guo Luoji. See also Wu and Sun, "Hu Yaobang." For circumstances surrounding the publication of the article, see Michael Schoenhals, "The 1978 Truth Criterion Controversy," *The China Quarterly* 126 (June 1991): 251–68.

28. Special Commentator, "Practice Is the Sole Criterion of Truth," *GMRB*, May 11, 1978.

29. Interview with Guo Luoji.

30. See the full text of Wu Lengxi's telephone call to Hu Jiwei in Ruan Ming, *Zhenli biaozhun zhi zhan* (The battle over the truth criterion), ms., 78–80, quoted in Schoenhals, "The 1978 Truth Criterion Controversy," 261–62. The text is also reproduced in Tao Kai, Zhang Yide, and Dai Qing, "Removing Modern Superstition: The Beginning and End of the Truth Criterion Debate," *Zhongshan* 3 (March 1988).

31. Ruan Ming, *Zhenli biaozhun zhi zhan*, 80.

32. Wang and Huang, *Cong sanzhong quanhui*, 31; Chen et al., *Xin Zhongguo*, 467.

33. Ruan Ming, *Zhenli biaozhun zhi zhan*, 80–81.

34. Zeng Tao, "The Great Debate."

35. Deng, *Deng Xiaoping wenxuan*, 175. Deng's speech appeared in *RMRB*, June 6, 1978, 1.

36. *RMRB*, June 4, 1978.

37. Deng, *Deng Xiaoping wenxuan*, 108–13.

38. I am grateful to Joseph Fewsmith for suggesting this point.

39. I am grateful to Joseph Fewsmith for suggesting this point.

40. Hua, speech on June 7, 1978, in *RMRB*, July 12, 1978.

41. Zeng Tao, "The Great Debate."

42. Wu and Sun, "Hu Yaobang."

43. Special Commentator, "A Most Basic Principle of Marxism," *JFJB*, June 23, 1978.

44. Wu and Sun, "Hu Yaobang."

45. A majority of provincial leaders had spoken out by early November, before the work conference opened on November 10. See *RMRB*, July 25–November 5, 1978. Leaders from several provinces did so during the period of the November work conference. See *RMRB*, November 16–December 6, 1978. Among the last to express support for the debate was the leadership from Hunan, Mao's home-town, where Hua was provincial governor for some years. See *RMRB*, December 6, 1978.

46. Deng, *Deng Xiaoping wenxuan*, 133.

47. Deng's speech during a meeting with Jilin's provincial committee, in ibid., 121–23.

48. "Struggle for the Complete Victory of the Exposure and Criticism of the Gang of Four," *RMRB*, October 4, 1978.

49. Hu Qiaomu, "Act According to Economic Laws, Speed up the Realization of the Four Modernizations," *RMRB*, October 6, 1978.

50. Chen et al., *Xin Zhongguo*, 466; Wang and Huang, *Cong sanzhong quanhui*, 4, 47.

51. See Merle Goldman, "Hu Yaobang's Intellectual Network and the Theory Conference of 1979," *The China Quarterly* 126 (June 1991): 219–42.

52. Wu and Sun, "Hu Yaobang."

53. Special Commentator, "Distinguish Two Ideological Lines, Uphold the Four Fundamental Principles," *GMRB*, May 11, 1979. For an overview of the offensive in the second half of 1979 to "make up for missed lessons" of the crite-rion of truth, see Frank Ching, "The Current Political Scene in China," *The China Quarterly* 80 (December 1979): esp. 701–6.

54. Special Commentator, "Deepen the Discussion of the Criterion of Truth," *HQ* 7 (July 1979): 47–48, and "Conscientiously Make up the Lesson of the Criterion of Truth," *HQ* 9 (September 1979): 2–4.

55. Interview with Guo Luoji.

56. Wang and Huang, *Cong sanzhong quanhui*, 13.

57. Schram, *Ideology and Policy*, 1–2.

58. Deng, *Deng Xiaoping wenxuan*, 39–41.

59. Song Zhenting, "On Upholding the Flag of Mao Zedong Thought," *RMRB*, October 27, 1978.

60. "Refuting the So-called 'Every Word Is Truth' of Lin Biao," *RMRB*, August 29, 1978; Deng, *Deng Xiaoping wenxuan*, 41.

61. Deng, *Deng Xiaoping wenxuan*, 157–58, 109–13.

62. Franz Schurmann, *Ideology and Organization*, chap. 1.

63. Special Commentator, "On the Question of 'Abstract Affirmation and Concrete Negation," *RMRB*, September 22, 1978. See also Special Commentator, "The Scientific Attitude of Marxism," *GMRB*, September 19, 1978; Song Zhenting, "Mao Zedong Thought"; and Deng, *Deng Xiaoping wenxuan*, 110–11.

64. Special Commentator, "Fundamental Principle"; Special Commentator, "Scientific Attitude"; Special Commentator, "'Abstract Affirmation.'"

65. Deng, *Deng Xiaoping wenxuan*, 109–11; Song Zhenting, "Mao Zedong Thought"; Yu Lianghua, "'Seeking Truth from Facts Is the Essence of Mao Zedong Thought," in *Shijian shi jianyan zhenli de weiyi biaozhun* (Practice is the sole criterion of truth), ed. Xinhuashe, 39–41.

66. Xing Fensi, "On the Question of the Criterion of Truth," *RMRB*, June 16, 1978, and *GMRB*, December 14, 1978.

67. Special Commentator, "'Abstract Affirmation'"; and Special Commentator, "The Correct Approach to Marxism," *RMRB*, October 30, 1979.

68. Zhang Dingcheng, "Rectification at the Central Party School in Yenan," *RMRB*, September 20, 1977; Deng, *Deng Xiaoping wenxuan*, 109; Special Commentator, "Fundamental Principle"; Special Commentator, "'Abstract Affirmation.'"

69. Special Commentator, "Fundamental Principle"; and Special Commentator, "Correct Approach."

70. Wang and Huang, *Cong sanzhong quanhui*, 31.

71. Cited in Xing Fensi, "The Criterion of Truth."

72. Special Commentator, "Fundamental Principle"; and Xing Fensi, "The Criterion of Truth."

73. Li Honglin, "Science and Superstition," *RMRB*, October 1978; and Li Fan, "The Guiding Role of Theory On Practice," in *Shijian*, ed. Xinhuashe, 19–21.

74. Special Commentator, "Correct Approach."

75. Deng, *Deng Xiaoping wenxuan*, 121.

76. Special Commentator, "Fundamental Principle."

77. Li Fan, "What Is to Uphold the Flag of Mao Zedong Thought," in *Shijian*, ed. Xinhuashe, 36–39.

78. Li Honglin, "Science and Superstition."

79. Hu Yaobang, "Opening Speech at the Conference on Theoretical Work" (January 18, 1979), *Sanzhong quanhui yilai zhongyao wenxian xuanbian* (Selected important documents since the Third Plenum), ed. CCP Central Committee, Documents Research Department, 52–53.

80. Zeng Tao, "The Great Debate"; and Hu Jiwei, "Report on a Series of Struggles in the Top Echelon of the CCP," *Cheng ming* 34 (August 1, 1980), in *Foreign Broadcast Information Service—China* (hereafter *FBIS-CHI*), August 15, 1980, U1–17.

81. Special Commentator, "Correct Approach."

82. Special Commentator, "Fundamental Principle."

83. Ibid.

84. Hu Yaobang, "Opening Speech," 59; and Deng, *Deng Xiaoping wenxuan*, 165.

85. See "Study the Resolution on CCP History," *RMRB*, July 28, 1981, 5, and Feng Wenbin, "Conscientiously Carry Out the Third Plenum Line, Firmly March Forward along the Path of Scientific Socialism," *HQ* 10 (May 1981): esp. 7.

86. Karl Marx, "Preface to the Critique of Political Economy," in *Marx-Engels Reader*, ed. Robert C. Tucker, 4–5.

87. Mao Zedong, *Mao Zedong xuanji* (Selected works of Mao Zedong), 5:375–77.

88. Jie Wen, "On the Class Struggle and the Principal Contradiction in Socialist Society," *HQ* 20 (October 1981): 6, 26–31.

89. Special Commentator, "How Do Marxists Look at Material Interests," *RMRB*, September 12, 1978; Ren Zhongyi, "The Emancipation of the Mind Is a Great Historical Trend," *HQ* 12 (December 1978): 25–33.

90. Hu Qiaomu, "On Some Concepts Regarding Class Struggle in the Socialist Period," in *Wenxian xuanbian*, 36–40.

91. Ibid., p. 55.

92. Deng, *Deng Xiaoping wenxuan*, 155, 168.

93. Zhang Tie et al., "A Brief Discourse on the Principal Contradiction in Our Society at the Present," *Shehui kexue jikan* 5 (May 1979): 16–18; Jiang Niandong, Li Shaogen, and Yang Peishan, "Has the Exploiting Class Been Eliminated as a Class in Our Country?" *HQ* 2 (February 1980): 35–39; Zhang Tiexiao, "On the Question of the Stage of Our Society and Class Struggle," *Qunzhong luntai* 1 (January 1980): 15–18; Kong Jieping and Liu Xiangcheng, "On the Principal Contradiction of Our Country at the Present Stage," *Wen shi zhe* 5 (May 1981): 84–88.

94. See the articles cited in note 93; also Xu Yuanjun, "How to Understand the Principal Contradiction in Our Country at the Current Stage," *Fengdou* 5 (May 1981): 13–15; Zhang Tengxiao, "Deeply Understand the Change of the Principal Contradiction under Socialism in Our Country," *Fengdou* 7 (July 1981): 22; Feng Wenbin, "Path of Scientific Socialism," 2–8; and Jie Wen, "Class Struggle."

95. *Resolution on CCP History (1949–1981)*, 44–45.

96. Shi Zhongquan, "On 'Bourgeois Rights,'" *HQ* 11 (June 1985): 12–17.

97. *Resolution on CCP History*, 44–45.

98. Joseph Stalin, *Economic Problems of Socialism in the USSR*. Stalin's basic law of socialist society will be discussed in chapter 3.

99. Deng, *Deng Xiaoping wenxuan*, 168.

100. Su Shaozhi, "On the Principal Contradictions Facing Our Society Today," *Xueshu yuekan* 7 (July 1979).

101. See chapter 7 for a treatment of this matter.

102. Chen et al., *Xin Zhongguo*, 530–34.

103. Deng, *Deng Xiaoping wenxuan*, 83, 176.

104. Ibid., 123.

105. Xu Dixin, "We Must Recognize and Conscientiously Use Objective Economic Laws," *GMRB*, July 21, 1978; Liu Jia'en, "The Triumph of Socialism Must Be Premised on the Development of Production Forces," *GMRB*, February 17, 1979.

106. See articles cited in note 105.

107. Xue Muqiao, "On the System of Collective Ownership under Socialism," *Jingji yanjiu* 10 (1978); and Xu Dixin, "Objective Economic Laws."

108. Wu Shengkui, "Production Forces Play a Decisive Role in Historical Development," *HQ* 1 (January 1979): 77–80; Special Commentator, "Use Economic Laws, Raise Management Methods," *HQ* 8 (August 1978): 74–79; Special Commentator, "Scientific Attitude"; Hu Qiaomu, "Economic Laws"; and "Practice Is the Essence of the Philosophical Thinking of Mao," *RMRB*, December 26, 1978.

109. Tsou, *The Cultural Revolution*, 156.

110. Xu Dixin, "Objective Economic Laws."

111. Hu Qiaomu, "Economic Laws" (emphasis added).

112. Special Commentator, "Scientific Attitude."

113. Joseph, *The Critique of Ultra-Leftism*, 73–75.

114. Xing Fensi, "Does Truth Have a Class Nature?" *RMRB*, November 28, 1978.

115. "We Must Understand Clearly the Purpose of Socialist Production," *RMRB*, October 29, 1979.

116. Special Commentator, "Scientific Attitude."

117. Hu Qiaomu, "Economic Laws."

CHAPTER THREE

1. Morris Bornstein lists nine characteristics of the Soviet economic model in "Economic Reform in East Europe," in *East European Economies Post Helsinki*, 102–34, esp. 103–5. Robert Dernberger enumerates ten basic features of the Chinese variation of the Soviet-type economy in "Economic Policy and Performance," in *China's Economy Looks toward the Year 2000*, vol. 1: *The Four Modernizations*, 15–48, esp. 21–24.

2. Dernberger, "Economic Policy," 23–24.

3. Karl Marx, "The Critique of the Gotha Program," in *Basic Writings on Politics and Philosophy, Karl Marx and Friedrich Engels*, 117–19.

4. Xue Muqiao, *Current Economic Problems of China*, 3–11.

5. These policy changes were documented in "The CCP Central Committee Decision on the Acceleration of Agricultural Development," in *Wenxian xuanbian*, 165–89.

6. Wang and Huang, *Cong sanzhong quanhui*, 71.

7. Chen Yun, "The Problem of the Plan and the Market," in *Wenxian xuanbian*, 67; and Chen Yun and Li Xiannian, "Letter to the Politburo Bureau on Financial and Economic Work," in ibid., 70, 72–75.

8. Li Xiannian, "Speech at the CCP Work Conference," in ibid., 115–19.

9. Deng, *Deng Xiaoping wenxuan*, 149–50.

10. The eight characters refer to "adjustment, reform, rectification, and consolidation." First implemented in the early 1960s in the wake of the Great Leap, the "eight-character policy" has become the quintessential program of the conservative reformers. See Li Xiannian, "Speech at the Work conference of the Central Committee," in *Wenxian xuanbian*, 104–39; and Hua Guofeng, *Diwujie renda er'chongquanhui zhengfu gongzhuo baogao* (Government work report to the second session of the Fifth NPC), 11–28.

11. Chen Yun, "The Problem of the Plan and the Market," in *Wenxian xuanbian*, 65–68.

12. For the distinction between "administrative decentralization" and "economic decentralization" in the reform of a Soviet-type economy, see Bornstein, "Economic Reform in East Europe," 109–10.

13. Deng Lijun, *Shangpin jingji de guilü he jihua* (The law of a commodity economy and planning), quoted in *RMRB*, October 15, 1979.

14. Fang Weizhong, "The Problems of the Current Economic System and Some Ideas on Reform," *Caimao zhanxian* 8 (August 1978), reprinted in *RMRB*, September 21, 1979.

15. Li Xiannian, "Speech at the CCP Central Committee Work Conference," *Wenxian xuanbian*, 134.

16. I am grateful to Joseph Fewsmith for suggesting this point.

17. See summary discussion in Guo Daimo and Yang Zhaoming, "Different Viewpoints in Discussions on the Reform of the Economic Management System," *RMRB*, September 21, 1979.

18. Dong Fureng, "On the Form of Socialist Ownership in Our Country," *Jingji yanjiu* 1 (January 1979). For disputes surrounding the article, see "Discussion on the Problem of State Ownership," *GMRB*, January 5, 1980.

19. Xue Muqiao, "Problems of Economic Management and Structural Reform," *HQ* 8 (August 1979), 16–24. See also, Xue "How to Carry out Planned Management of National Economy," *RMRB*, June 15, 1979.

20. Yu Guangyuan, "Discussing the 'Theory of the Purpose of Socialist Economy,'" *Jingji yanjiu* 11 (November 1979).

21. Liu Guoguang, "On the Relation between the Socialist Commodity Economy and the Market"; and Sun Shangqing et al., "Some Theoretical Problems Concerning the Integration of the Planned and Market Nature of Socialist Economy," both cited in *RMRB*, May 5, 1979; original articles published in *Jingji yanjiu* 5 (May 1979).

22. See Zhao Ziyang's discussion with economists in Chengdu, *RMRB*, March 13, 1979.

23. See Zhao Ziyang, comments on ultra-leftist influences in economic work, *RMRB*, November 10, 1979.

24. This term is from Dorothy Solinger, "The Fifth National People's Congress and the Process of Policy Making," 1242.

25. *FBIS-CHI*, June 28, 1979, esp. U4.

26. Some of these views may be found in a very conservatively toned editorial of *Renmin ribao* published during the April conference, on April 19, 1979. Others may be found in reformers' critique of those views, in Contributing Commentator, "Study [Ye Jianying's] Speech, Eliminate Ultra-leftist Thinking in the Economic Domain," *JFJB*, October 20, 1979, and *RMRB*, October 26, 1979; and Contributing Commentator, "Rectify Ideological Line, Eliminate Ultra-leftist Thinking," *Wen hui bao*, August 4, 1979, and *RMRB*, August 11, 1979.

27. On April 19 and 24, 1979, *RMRB* published an editorial and a special commentator's article calling for more forceful ideological work and "struggle between two roads." But in an editorial on April 11, the same paper repudiated class struggle, and in another editorial on May 5, it defended reformers' version of the socialist road.

28. The impact was especially felt by rural cadres. See the case of Anhui, in Wu Xiang and Xu Zhongying, "Why Do Peasants Like the Production Responsibility System So Much?" *RMRB*, November 14, 1979, and a similar case in Jiangxi, in *RMRB*, May 16, 1979.

29. For example, Special Commentator, "We Must Be Genuinely Clear about the Purpose of Socialist Production," *RMRB*, October 20, 1979; "Editorial: We Must Be Clear about the Purpose of Socialist Production," *RMRB*, October 20, 1979; Li Ping, "Why Is It Necessary to Discuss the Question of the Purpose of Socialist Production?" *RMRB*, November 24, 1979. At least five symposiums were held by economic officials and researchers in the capital in late 1979, as reported in *RMRB*, September 22, November 8, and November 24, 1979.

30. Yu Guangyuan, "Discussing the Question of the "Theory of the Purpose of Socialist Economy," *RMRB*, October 22, 1979.

31. Xue Muqiao, *Woguo guomin jingji de tiaozheng he gaige* (The readjustment and reform of our national economy), 33.

32. According to both Marx and Lenin, capitalist production in its fervent pursuit of profits would result in chronic "production for production's sake" in disregard of the consumption needs of the masses. Cited in Wu Jiang, "Study Again the Basic Economic Laws of Socialism," *HQ* 12 (June 1980): 12.

33. Ibid., 15.

34. For a comprehensive discussion of Marx's original thesis, see Lin Zili, *Xuexi Makesi de zai shengchan lilun* (Studying Marx's theory of reproduction). For a more orthodox interpretation, see Deng Liqun, "The Basic Principles of Marx's Theory of Reproduction Must Be Upheld," *HQ* 5, 6, and 7 (March–April 1982).

35. Zhou Shulian and Wu Jinglian, "Placing Priority on the Development of Light Industry," *RMRB*, August 31, 1979; and Wu Jiang, "The Basic Economic Laws," 16–17. See also the summary of recent symposiums by Zhou Mi, "Problems Of Economic Arrangements Demanding Research," *GMRB*, September 22,

1979; and Zhao Ziyang, comments on ultra-leftist influences in economic work, *RMRB*, November 10, 1979.

36. Zhou and Wu, "Placing Priority"; "Problems of Economic Arrangements"; and Du Yi and Zhou Caiyang, "Is Starting from Heavy Industry the Law of Socialist Industrialization?" *GMRB*, March 15, 1980.

37. Wu Jiang, "The Basic Economic Laws," p. 16.

38. Special Commentator, "The Purpose of Socialist Production."

39. *Cheng ming* 34 (August 1980): 5–8, in *FBIS-CHI*, August 6, 1980, esp. U4–5. For the disciplinary action against Kang Shi'en, see *RMRB*, August 27, 1980, 2.

40. "Decision on the Acceleration of Agricultural Development."

41. Speech at the enlarged session of the Standing Committee of the Provincial Committee of Sichuan on January 31, 1979, cited in Chen et al., *Xin Zhongguo*, 479.

42. Chen Yusan, "Reports from the Fengyang Countryside," *RMRB*, March 23, 1981.

43. For a summary of the origin and issues of the debate, see Wu Xiang, "The Open Road and the Log Bridge," *RMRB*, November 5, 1980.

44. See Hua's speech on April 29, in *RMRB*, May 8, 1980.

45. Wang and Huang, *Cong sanzhong quanhui*, 97–98.

46. Secret efforts at *Baochan daohu* during the collectivization drive in the 1950s were put down by a debate between "two lines." Its implementation in some regions of Anhui after the Great Leap, acquiesced to by moderate leaders such as Chen Yun, was banned as "restoration of capitalism" in 1962. Still less individually oriented practices were attacked as "revisionism" during the Cultural Revolution.

47. For excerpts from this speech on rural policy, see Deng, *Deng Xiaoping wenxuan*, 275–77. The portion of Deng's speech concerning socialism across countries appears on pp. 278–79. One of Nikita Khrushchev's main three revisions in Stalinism at the Twentieth Party Congress in 1956 concerned the legitimacy of divergent paths of socialism across countries. Since Khrushchev was denounced in China as a "revisionist" who had restored capitalism in the Soviet Union, Deng's assumption of this posture was very daring at this time. See the polemics over Soviet revisionism in Donald Zagoria, *The Sino-Soviet Conflict*.

48. Wang and Huang, *Cong sanzhong quanhui*, 98.

49. That is, "what the Party has not thought about localities may think about; what the Party has not instructed localities may do as they see fit; what the Party has decided but does not fit local conditions localities may try other methods; and what the Party has decided wrongly localities may debate." See editorial note to Hu Yaobang's speech, "Be a Thorough Materialist," *RMRB*, December 7, 1980.

50. Xue Muqiao, "Nine Years' Reform and Ideological Breakthroughs," preface to Gao Shangquan, *Jiunian lai Zhongguo jingji tizhi gaige* (Nine years of economic structural reform in China).

51. "On Further Strengthening and Improving the Production Responsibility System in Agriculture," in *Wenxian xuanbian*, 506–7.

52. "The CCP Central Committee Comments on Relaying the Self-Critical Report of Shanxi Province on the Lessons of the Movement to Learn from Dazhai," *Wenxian xuanbian*, 514–15. Hu Yaobang, "Be a Thorough Materialist."

53. Contributing Commentator, "Continue to Emancipate the Mind, Correctly Understand Current Policies," *JFJB*, October 26, 1980; Contributing Commentator, "Unification of Theory and Practice," *JFJB*, December 22, 1980; Contributing Commentator, "Pay Attention to Developing Production Forces," *RMRB*, October 22, 1980.

54. Chen et al., *Xin Zhongguo*, 480–82. See also "Minutes of the All-National Conference on Rural Work" (December 1981), *Wenxian xuanbian*, 994–1010.

55. Stalin, *Economic Problems*.

56. For the distinction between "systemic change" and "policy change" in the reform of a Soviet-type economy, see Bornstein, "Economic Reform in East Europe," 108–9.

57. *RMRB*, December 2, 1981, and January 26, 1982.

58. For why limited reform tends to produce disruptive results, see Nina Halpern, "China's Industrial Economic Reforms: The Question of Strategy," *Asian Survey* 25, 10 (October 1985): 998–1012; and Leung, "The Role of Leadership."

59. Wang Jiyie and Wu Kaitai, "Resolutely Implement the Strategic Policies of Readjustment," *RMRB*, December 23, 1980. "Editorial: Comprehensively and Resolutely Carry Out Readjustment Policy," *RMRB*, November 2, 1980.

60. Wu Jinglian and Zhou Sulian, "Correctly Handle the Relation between Readjustment and Reform," *RMRB*, December 5, 1980.

61. Dong Fureng, "Develop a Socialist Economy Beneficial to the People," *RMRB*, January 29, 1981.

62. Fang Weizhong, "An Unshakable Fundamental Principle," *HQ* 9 (May 1982): 13–19, esp. 14.

63. *RMRB*, January 26, 1982.

64. See Zhou Taihe, speech at the opening session of the symposium, *RMRB*, May 16, 1982; and Xue Muqiao, "Discussions on the Theory of Reforming the System of Economic Management," speech at the opening session, in Xue Muqiao, *Woguo guomin jingji*, 103–16.

65. Xue, "Discussions on the Theory," 111.

66. Fang Weizhong, "Fundamental Principle," 13–19.

67. Xue Xin and Ma Piao, "Upholding the Socialist Road Requires the Planned Economy," *GMRB*, May 9, 1982.

68. See a collection of articles written between mid-1981 and mid-1982 in defense of the plan, in *Jihua jingji yu shichang tiaojie wenji* (Collected essays on the planned economy and market regulation), ed. Hongqi Editorial Board.

69. Cited in Xue Muqiao, "Discussions on the Theory," 106; and Fang Weizhong, "Fundamental Principle," 104–20, esp. 105.

70. Cited in Xue Muqiao, "Discussions on the Theory," 106.

71. Ibid.; Yu Guangyuan, "Carry Out Discussions on the Theoretical Problems of the Economic Structural Reform," *RMRB*, June 11, 1982; Liu Guoguang, "Upholding the Basic Direction of Reforming the Economic System," *RMRB*, September 6, 1982.

72. Xue Xin and Ma Piao, "Upholding the Socialist Road"; Jing Ping, "Comments on the Discussion of Planned Regulation and Market Regulation," *HQ* 22 (November 1982): 20–22; and Fang Weizhong, "Fundamental Principle," 105.

73. Hu Yaobang, "Comprehensively Create a New Situation in Socialist Construction," political report to the Twelfth Congress, in *Shiyijie sanzhong quanhui yilai zhongyao wenxian xuandu* (Selected readings of important documents since the Third Plenum of the Eleventh Congress), ed. CCP Central Committee, Documents Research Department, 485.

74. For a discussion of competing policy packages and political compromises surrounding the Twelfth Congress, see Carol Lee Hamrin, "Competing 'Policy Packages' in Post-Mao China," *Asian Survey* 24, 5 (May 1984): 487–518.

75. Hu Yaobang, report to the Twelfth Congress, 523.

76. See Zhao Ziyang, "Opinions on Three Problems in the Economic Structural Reform," presented to the Central Committee on September 9, 1984, in *Shi'er da yilai zhongyao wenxian xuanbian* (Selected important documents since the Twelfth Congress), ed. CCP Central Committee, Documents Research Department, 533–38.

77. Bo Yibo, "Some Questions Concerning the Planned and Proportionate Development of the National Economy," *HQ* 19 (October 1983); He Jianzhang, "The Inevitability of the Socialist Planned Economy," *HQ* 3 (February 1984); and Fang Weizhong, "Building a Planned Management System and Science with Chinese Characteristics," *HQ* 9 (May 1984).

78. *Ching ming*, November 1, 1984, 6–9, in *FBIS-CHI*, November 6, 1984, and *Ching ming*, December 1, 1984, 6–9, in *FBIS-CHI*, December 3, 1984.

79. Research Group on Comparative Economic Systems, CASS, "The Problem of the Target Model in the Reform of the Chinese Economic System," *Zhongguo shehui kexue* 4 (1984).

80. Jin Wen, "Determined Reform Requires Further Emancipation of the Mind," *JFJB*, July 10, 1984; and Liu Guoguang, "Several Problems in Current Economic Reform and Readjustment," *Xinhua wenzhai* 6 (June 1984): 46–48.

81. Contributing Commentator, "On Reconceptualization" and "Deepen Theoretical Understanding of Reform," *HQ* 12 (June 1984): 2–8, 38–40.

82. Collected in Deng Xiaoping, *Jianshe you Zhongguo teshe de shehuizhuyi* (Building socialism with Chinese charateristics), 52.

83. See *Shi'er da yilai*, 533–38.

84. *Ching ming*, November 1, 1984, 6–9, in *FBIS-CHI*, November 6, 1984; and *Ching ming*, December 1, 1984, 6–9, in *FBIS-CHI*, December 3, 1984.

85. "Resolution of the CCP Central Committee on the Economic Structural Reform" (1984), in *Wenxian xuandu*, 766–95.

86. Deng, *Shehuizhuyi*, 78.

87. For these problems see Harding, *China's Second Revolution*, 73.

88. Chen Yun, speech at the National Congress of the CCP on September 23, 1985, *Wenxian xuanbian*, 975–76.

89. See conservative rebuttals of these views in Fan Maofa, Xun Dazhi, and Liu Xiaping, "The Joint Stock System Is Not the Direction for Enterprises Owned by the Whole People," *Jingji yanjiu* 1 (January 1986): 17–23.

90. See Li Yining, *Beijing ribao*, May 19, 1986; *Shijie jingji daobao* (hereafter *Daobao*), November 8, 1986; and "Proposal for the Reform of the Ownership System of Our Country," *RMRB*, September 26, 1986.

91. Tong Dalin, "Stockfication Will Be a New Basis of Socialist Enterprises," *RMRB*, August 18, 1986.

92. Zhou Shulian, *Zhongguo de jingji gaige he qiye gaige* (Economic reform and enterprise reform in China), 141–44.

93. Shi Shangsong, "Methods and Stages of Economic Structural Reforms," *Jingji shehuitizhi bijiao* 2 (February 1986); Wu Jinglian, "Discussing Again the Maintenance of a Good Environment for Economic Reform," *Jingi yanjiu* 5 (May 1985); and Wu Jinglian, "Some Thoughts on the Choice of Reform Strategies," *Jingji yanjiu* 2 (February 1987): 3–14.

94. For example, Chen Yun, written speech at the Third Plenum of the Twelfth Congress, October 20, 1984, 293–94; written speech at the national conference on swapping work experience in the rectification of the party style, June 29, 1984, in ibid., 301–2; speech at the work conference on rectifying party style on June 29, 1985; at the national conference of the CCP on September 23, 1985; and at the Sixth Plenum of the Central Disciplinary Commission on September 24, 1985. Also Li Xiannian, closing speech at the national conference of the CCP on September 23, 1985, in *Jianchi sixian jiben yuanzhe, fandui zichan jieji ziyou hua* (Uphold the Four Fundamental Principles, Oppose Bourgeois Liberalization), ed. CCP Central Committee, Documents Research Department, 301–2, 316–19, 320–21, 322–25.

95. "Resolution on the Economic Structural Reform," 784–86.

96. Feng Keping, *Shehui bao*, September 9, 1986; reprinted under the title "'Unselfishness' Is Not a Communist Slogan," *RMRB*, November 3, 1986.

97. These conservative attacks were enumerated by Zhao Ziyang at the conference of cadres from the fields of propaganda, theory, media, and party schools on May 13, 1987, in *RMRB*, July 10, 1987.

98. Contributing Editor, "The Spirit of Displaying Public Concern and Unselfishness Should Not Be Distorted," *RMRB*, January 16, 1987.

99. Wu Shuqing, "Stockfication Is Not the Direction of the Reform of Large and Medium-size Enterprises Owned by the State," *RMRB*, March 16, 1986.

100. Stanley Rosen, "China in 1987, the Year of the 13th Congress," *Asian Survey* 28, 1 (January 1988): 37.

101. For detailed treatment of the notion, see chapter 7.

102. For how the double-track price system could be manipulated for profiteering and racketeering, see *RMRB*, July 14 and 25, September 3, 1988; and *Gongren ribao*, August 24, 1988. For cadre profiteering, see *Shehui kexue* 12 (1988): 31–32; *Shichang bao*, May 29, 1989; *Xinwen bao*, June 13, 1989; *Qingnian bao*, June 30, 1989; *Wenzhai zhoubao*, July, 7, 1989; *Meizhou wenzhai bao*, July 19, 1989. For common means of abuse, see *Gongren ribao*, May 2, 1989; *Jingji ribao*, June 12, 1989; *Wenzhai zhoubao*, June 23 and July 17, 1989. See also Jean Oi, "Market Reforms and Corruption in Rural China," *Studies in Comparative Communism* 22, 2–3 (Summer 1989): 221–33.

103. Luo Haiguang, "On the Sources of the Corrupt Phenomenon in the Party," *RMRB*, June 18, 1988.

104. Chen Shenshen, "Establishing a Fair and Competitive Market," *Daobao*, August 8, 1988.

105. He Jianzhang, "The Commodity Economy Is an Insurmountable Stage of the Socialist Economic Development," *RMRB*, May 23, 1986; and Wu Shuqing, "Social Division of Labor Is the Basis of the Existence and Development of the Commodity Economy," *HQ* 18 (September 1987): 43–46.

106. Lowell Dittmer, "China in 1988: The Continuing Dilemma of Socialist Reform," *Asian Survey* 29, 1 (January 1989), esp. 22–23. Also Dittmer, "China in 1989: Crisis of Incomplete Reform," *Asian Survey* 30, 1 (January 1990): 25–47.

107. See Dittmer's articles cited in note 106.

108. See public opinion polls conducted shortly before the outbreak of the 1989 mass protests, in *Ban yue tan* 11 (May 1989); *Jingjixue zhoubao*, May 28, 1989; *RMRB*, November 1, October 28, and March 4, 1988. See also Yan Sun, "The Chinese Protests of 1991: The Issue of Corruption," in *Asian Survey* 31, 8 (August 1991): 762–82.

109. Dittmer, "China in 1988," 24.

110. *Ching pao*, January 18, 1989, 28–32, in *FBIS-CHI*, January 27, 1989, 22–27; quote on p. 24.

111. Jiang Yiwei, "Several Problems Concerning the Joint Stock System," *Jingji wenti* 1 (1988), in *Xinhua wenzhai* 3 (1988): 38–40. Li Yining, "The Joint Stock System Is the Best Form to Clarify the Property Relations of Enterprises," *HQ* 1 (1988): 21–24.

112. Yan Jiaqi, *Daobao*, November 11 and December 4, 1988; and Chen Yizi, Wang Xiaojiang, and Li Jun, "The Deeper Problems and Choice of Strategies Faced by China's Reform," *Zhongguo: Fazhan yu gaige* 4 (1988), in *Xinhua wenzhai* 6 (June 1989): 63–66.

113. Chen Yizi, *Zhongguo: Shinian gaige yu bajiunian minyun* (China: Ten years' reform and the 1989 democratic movement), 2.

114. Cited in Qiu Yang, "On 'China-Hope: Manifesto of Private Ownership,'" *Qiushi* (hereafter *QS*) 22 (1989): 19–24; Fu Jing, "On the Anti-People Nature of the 'Manifesto of Private Ownership,'" *GMRB*, July 25, 1989; Zhong Han, "Upholding Socialist Public Ownership," *GMRB*, August 26, 1989.

115. Wu Jiaxiang and Zheng Pengrong, "On the Choice of Gradually Implementing the Joint Stock System," *RMRB*, December 2, 1988; Wang Zilin, "The Difficulty and Hope of Reform: the Personalification of State Property," *RMRB*, July 28, 1988.

116. Li Ming, "On the Way Out at Present for the Reform of Our Country," in *Sanzhong quanhui yilai zhengzhi tizhi gaige yu shijian* (The theory and practice of political structural reform since the Third Plenum), ed. Li Shengping, 158–62; Zhang Zhiqing, "The Market Economy and the Way Out for China's Reform," *Jingji kexue* 2 (1989).

117. John K. Fairbank, *The United States and China*, 298.

118. For example, Pan Shi, "Two Questions in Rethinking the Ownership of the Means of Production," *Shehui kexue zhanxian* 4 (1987).

119. *Gongren ribao*, May 5, 1989.

120. For wealth of official merchants, see *Wen hui bao* (Hong Kong), February

16, 1989. For urban private entrepreneurs' shady practices, see *Xiaofei shibao*, April 29, 1989; *Zhongguo xiaofei shibao*, June 5, 1989; *Wenzhai zhoubao*, January 6, 1989; and *RMRB*, March 7 and April 25, 1989.

121. *RMRB*, July 14 and 25, and September 3, 1988.

122. Zhang Zhiqing, "The Market Economy."

123. Cited in "A Great Practice, a Brilliant Document," *RMRB*, October 24, 1992.

124. Ibid.

125. Edward Friedman discusses three broad "socialist projects" in "Maoism, Titoism, Stalinism: Some Origins and Consequences of the Maoist Theory of the Socialist Transition," in *The Transition to Socialism in China*, ed. Mark Selden and Victor Lippit. See also Hamrin, "Competing 'Policy Packages,'" esp. 517–18.

CHAPTER FOUR

1. Peter Schran, "On the Organization of Production under Socialism," in *Marxism and the Chinese Experience*, ed. Dirlik and Meisner, 59.

2. Karl Marx, *Capital*, 1:90–91, in *Marxist Social Thought*, ed. Robert Freeman, 299–300.

3. Marx, "Critique of the Gotha Program," 117.

4. Ibid., 118–19.

5. Vladimir I. Lenin, *Liening quanji* (Complete works of Lenin), 1:225.

6. Ibid., 29:111.

7. Lenin, *Liening shougao* (Manuscripts of Lenin), vol. 8, cited in *Makesizhuyi*, ed. Su and Zhang, 141.

8. Lenin, *Liening xuanji* (Selected works of Lenin), vol. 3, cited in *Makesizhuyi*, ed. Su and Zhang, 141.

9. Lenin, *Liening quanji*, vol. 3, cited in *Makesizhuyi*, ed. Su and Zhang, 142.

10. Stalin, *Economic Problems*, 12–18.

11. Ibid., 12–22.

12. Mao Zedong, "The Minutes of a Talk on Reading Stalin's 'Economic Problems of Socialism in the Soviet Union,'" cited in *Makesi zhuyi*, ed. Su and Zhang, 144.

13. Shi Zhongquan, "On 'the Bourgeois Right,'" in *Guanyu jianguo yilai dang de ruogan wenti de jueyi zhuyi ben* (Notes to the resolution on CCP history), rev. ed., reprinted in *HQ* 11 (June 1986): 12–17; and Su and Zhang, eds., *Makesizhuyi*, 142–45.

14. Deng Liqun, *Shangpin jingji de guilü he jihua*; Sun Yefang, *Shehuizhuyi jingji de yixi wenti* (Some theoretical problems of socialist economy); and Xue Muqiao, *Current Economic Problems*, chaps. 9 and 11.

15. You Lin, "Planned Production as the Principal Part, Free Production as the Supplementary Part," *Jingji yanjiu* 9 (September 1981); and Xue Muqiao, *Current Economic Problems*, chap. 11.

16. Xue Muqiao, "Again on the Reform of Economic Structures and the Management System," in Xue Muqiao, *Woguo guomin jingji*, 4–24; and He Wei, "On the Question of the Planned Economy and the Commodity Economy," *RMRB*, June 6, 1982.

17. Du Runsheng, "The Output Related Contract System and New Developments in Rural Cooperative Economy," *RMRB*, March 7, 1983.

18. Xue Muqiao, *Current Economic Problems*, chap. 11; and "Again on the Reform," 5.

19. Chen Yun, "The Problem of the Plan and the Market," in *Wenxian xuanbian*, 65.

20. For example, Zhuo Jiong, "Also on the Planned Economy and the Commodity Economy," *GMRB*, August 9, 1982; Jia Kecheng, "The Socialist Economy Is Both Planned and Commodity Economy," *GMRB*, June 12, 1982.

21. Xue Xin and Ma Piao, "Upholding the Socialist Road Requires the Planned Economy," *GMRB*, May 9, 1982; Contributing Commentator, "Constructing a System of Planned Management with Greater Conformity to Our Country's Conditions," *RMRB*, September 21, 1982; Wang Jiye, "Several Points of Understanding on the Planned Economy," *RMRB*, June 22, 1982; He Wei, "On the Question"; and He Rongfei, "The Commodity Economy Does Not Reflect the Nature of Socialist Economy," *GMRB*, May 29, 1982.

22. For example, Fang Weizhong, "An Unshakable Fundamental Principle," *HQ* 9 (May 1982): 13–19

23. I am grateful to Joseph Fewsmith for these points.

24. Yu Guangyuan, "The Basic Attitude toward Socialist Ownership," *RMRB*, July 7, 1980; and Xue Muqiao, "Building Socialism with Chinese Characteristics," *HQ* 19 (September 1982): 27–28.

25. Yu Guangyuan, "The Basic Attitude"; Duan Shixian, "The State of Production Forces Should Be the Basic Starting Point of Everything," *HQ* 24 (December 1980): 5–10; Du Runsheng, "The Output Related Contract System"; and Gao Hongfan, "Theoretical Abstraction of the Profound Changes in the Countryside—Reading (Du Runsheng's) *Economic Reform in Rural China*," *RMRB*, January 30, 1986.

26. Duan Shixian, "The State of Production Forces."

27. Ibid.; Wu Shuqing, "How to Look at the Co-existence of Multiple Economic Forms in Our Country's Current Stage," *HQ* 8 (April 1982): 34–35; and Yu Guangyuan, "The Basic Attitude."

28. Dong Fureng, "On the Question of the Form of Our Socialist Ownership," *Jingji yanjiu* 1 (1979). For reformist discussions in the early 1980s and a conservative critique, see You Lin, "Introducing and Commenting on Discussions of the Reform of the Management System of State Enterprises," *GMRB*, April 3 1982.

29. Dong Fureng, "Socialist Ownership"; and Jiang Yiwei, "The Theory of Enterprise Independence," *Zhongguo shehui kexue* 1 (January 1981).

30. Wang Mingsheng, "Reforming State Enterprise," *HQ* 8 (August 1980): 14; and Yun Xiliang, "Some Issues Concerning the Whole People's Ownership," *HQ* 12 (December 1980): 22–28.

31. See critiques of Dong Fureng's article in Jiang Xuemo, "On the Nature and Form of Our Socialist Whole People's Ownership," *Xueshu yuekan* 10 (1979); and Li Yunfu, "On the State Ownership of Our Country," *Xueshu yukan* 10 (1979). See also You Lin, "System of State Enterprises"; and Fang Weizhong, "Fundamental Principle."

32. Shi Zhongquan, "On 'Bourgeois Rights,'" *HQ* 11 (June 1985): 12–17. For criticisms of past violation of distribution according to labor, see a series of discussions in *HQ* 3 (March 1979): 66–74; and He Rongfei, "Will Becoming Rich Necessarily Turn (People) Revisionist?" *HQ* 3 (February 1980): 45–48.

33. Fang Weizhong, "Fundamental Principle," 105.

34. Wang Rongchang, "The Theoretical Basis of Introducing 'Independent Management and Self-accounting' in State Enterprises," *GMRB*, May 20, 1984; Ma Bin, "On the Theoretical Basis of the Relative Independence of Enterprises Owned by the Whole People," *GMRB*, October 14, 1984; Chen Wentong, "On the Relative Separation of Ownership and Management Rights," *GMRB*, October 15, 1984; Zhu Guanghua, "The Theoretical Significance of the Appropriate Separation of Ownership and Management Rights," *HQ* 17 (August 1985): 44–46; and Chen Guijia, "Enterprises Owned by the Whole People Are Relative Independent Commodity Producers and Managers," *HQ* 20 (October 1987): 46.

35. Stalin, *Sidalin xuanji* (Selected works of Stalin), 578.

36. Central Party School, *Jianshe you Zhongguo teshe de shehuizhuyi de kexue lilun* (The scientific theory of building socialism with Chinese characteristics), 159–62.

37. Ibid.; and Ma Bin, "The Theoretical Basis."

38. Central Party School, *Kexue lilun*, 162–63.

39. Wu Shuqing, "The System of Planning and the Socialist Commodity Production," *GMRB*, April 22, 1984. See also Fang Weizhong, "Building a Planned Management System and Science with Chinese Characteristics," *HQ* 9 (May 1984): 26–30; He Jianzhang, "The Inevitability of the Socialist Planned Economy," *HQ* 3 (February 1984): 26–29.

40. Wu Shuqing, "The System of Planning."

41. Ibid.

42. Ibid.; and Fang Weizhong, "Planned Management System," 26–30.

43. See Li Ye, "Summary of the Discussion of Our Country's Ownership Question," *Xuexi yu yanjiu* 9 (1986).

44. Ibid.

45. Su and Zhang, eds., *Makesizhuyi*, 150–51; Shi Bao, "The Important Topic of Urban Reform," *GMRB*, September 9, 1984.

46. General Office of the State Council, *Geti jingji diaocha yu yanjiu* (Investigation and study of the individual economy).

47. Wang Rongchang, "The Theoretical Basis"; and "Theoretical Research Must Catch Up with Urban Reform," *GMRB*, July 29, 1984.

48. Chen Wentong, "On the Relative Separation"; and "Urban Reform."

49. Liu Guangdi, in *Nongchun yu chengshi gaige de fansi* (Reflections on rural and urban reforms), ed. Central Party School and State Commission on Economic Structural Reform, 159; Li Zhongfan, in ibid., 152.

50. Yu Zhanming, "Sixteen Forms of the Contract Management Responsibility System," *Jingji ribao*, August 3, 1987.

51. Hong Yi, "Summary of the Symposium on Lease Management in Industrial Enterprises," *RMRB*, June 12, 1986.

52. Li Yining, "Proposal on the Ownership Reform of Our Country," *RMRB*, September 26, 1986; Ning Qing, "Summary of the Symposium on the Deepening

of Reform and the Development of Enterprises," *Jingjixue dongtai* (July 1987); Tong Dalin, "The Stockification Is a New Foundation of the Socialist Enterprise," *RMRB*, August 18, 1986.

53. Xu Maokui, "Contract Management and Lease Management Are Important Topics in the Economic Structural Reform," *Jingjixue dongtai* 8 (August 1987).

54. For reports on industrial experiments of this method, see Central Party School and State Commission on Economic Structural Reform, eds., *Fansi*. See also Gu Shutang and Chai Xiaozhen, *Shehuizhuyi jingji lilun he jingji zhidu yanjiu* (A study of socialist economic theory and economic practice); and Zhou Shulian, *Zhongguo de jingji gaige he qiye gaige*.

55. Jian Shaohua, "The Power of Expanded Production Cannot Be Fully Transferred to the Enterprise," *GMRB*, November 23, 1985; Wu Wei and Liu Chengrui, "The System of Planning and the System of the Whole People's Ownership," *GMRB*, April 15, 1985; Tao Zengji, "Market Regulation of Investment Does Not Work in Our Country," *Jingji ribao*, October 19, 1985.

56. Wu Shuqing, "Stockfication Is Not the Direction of the Reform of Large and Medium Size State Enterprises," *RMRB*, March 16, 1987.

57. Fan Maofa, Xun Dazhi, and Liu Xiaping, "The Joint Stock System Is Not the Direction for Enterprises Owned by the Whole People," *Jingji yanjiu* 1 (January 1986): 17–23. See also Ding Bangshi, "Share Ownership—More Harm than Benefit," *Jingji ribao*, September 19, 1985.

58. Fan Maofa et al., "The Joint Stock System," 20–21; and Wu Shuqing, "Stockfication."

59. See *Jingji ribao*, January 1986; Yang Qixian, "The Nature and Function of the Stock System under Socialist Conditions," *RMRB*, July 3, 1987; Zuo Mu, "Problems of the Reform of China's Ownership Structure," *Jingji yanjiu* 1 (January 1986): 6–10; and Wu Shuqing, "Stockfication."

60. Wu Jinglian, "Some Thoughts on the Choice of Reform Strategies," *Jingji yanjiu* 2 (February 1987): 3–14.

61. Commentator, "Common Prosperity Is Not 'Concurrent Prosperity,'" *GMRB*, July 22, 1984; Wang Furu, "How to Look at Reform Correctly," *Lilun jiaoyu* 2 (February 1986): 1–3, 23, 43; Du Runsheng, speech at the central conference on agricultural work, *RMRB*, January 27, 1986; and Zhao Guoquan, "Five Aspects of Contradiction in Developing the Commodity Economy," *RMRB*, December 1, 1986.

62. Zheng Bijian and Luo Jingbo, "Deepening the Scientific Understanding of Socialism," *RMRB*, November 2, 1984; Liu Qingchun, "Tentative Discussion on Two Basic Characteristics of the Marxist Concept of Equality," *GMRB*, March 9, 1987.

63. Zhang Yongxun, "Continue to Resolve the Problem of Understanding 'Let Some People Get Rich First,'" *GMRB*, August 9, 1984; Fang Gongwen, "Correctly Understand Some Phenomena in the Current Economic Structural Reform," *GMRB*, November 16, 1985; Yan Wenguang, "Briefly Discussing Inequality under Socialism and Its Significance," *Hebei ribao*, February 26, 1986; Dong Jichang, "Correctly Understand and Treat Farmers Who Have Got Rich First," *HQ* 10 (May 1984): 34–37.

64. Fang Gongwen, "Some Phenomena"; Wang Furu, "How to Look at Reform."

65. "Equity Achieved at the Expense of Efficiency Is Not Fair," *Daobao*, August 3, 1986; Lan Qiuliang and Chen Lixian, "Discussing the Socialist Principle of Equity," *RMRB*, March 3, 1986; Shang Xuanli, "Opening to the Outside, Enlivening the Domestic Economy, and Conceptual Reform," *RMRB*, July 29, 1986.

66. Du Runsheng, speech at the central conference on agricultural work.

67. Huang Xiaojing and Yang Xiao, "From Employment Security to Labor Market" and "Equality Achieved at the Expense of Efficiency."

68. *Daobao*, May 9, 1988, 1.

69. Du Runsheng, speech at the central conference on agricultural work; Li Mingsan, "Why Common Prosperity Does Not Mean Concurrent Prosperity," *HQ* 15 (July 1984): 46–47; Zhang Luxiong, "Will [the Policy of] Letting Some People Get Rich First Cause Social Polarization," *HQ* 17 (August 1984): 38–39; and Zheng Bijian and Luo Jingbo, "Scientific Understanding."

70. Shang Xuanli, "Opening to the Outside," Zhao Guoquan, "Five Aspects of Contradiction."

71. Yuan Zhiming, "The Emotional Person and the Rational Person," review of *A Philosophical Exploration of Our Country's Economic Reform* by Hu Ping, in *Dushu* 4 (April 1986), reprinted as "Egalitarianism and Morality," *RMRB*, April 30, 1986.

72. Contributing Editor, "The Spirit of Displaying Public Concern and Unselfishness Should Not Be Distorted," *RMRB*, January 16, 1987.

73. Gong Jinguo, "Developing the Marxist Theory of Planned Economy in Practice," *HQ* 10 (May 1987): 41–45; Su and Zhang, eds., *Makesizhuyi*, 149.

74. Zhao Ziyang, political report to the Thirteenth Congress, "Advance Along the Path of Socialism with Chinese Characteristics," *RMRB*, November 4, 1987; Su and Zhang, eds., *Makesizhuyi*, 148–54; Gong Jinguo, "Developing the Marxist Theory"; Yu Guangyuan, "The Socialist Commodity Economy Is the Foundation and Center of the New Economic Structure," *Jingji yanjiu* 1 (1988): 3–8; He Jianzhang, "The Commodity Economy Is an Insurmountable Stage of the Socialist Economic Development," *RMRB*, May 23, 1986.

75. Su and Zhang, eds., *Makesizhuyi*, 148–54; Central Party School, *Kexue lilun*, 168–70; He Jianzhang, "The Commodity Economy"; Wu Shuqing, "Social Division of Labor Is the Basis of the Existence and Development of the Commodity Economy," *HQ* 18 (September 1987): 43–46; and Huang Zhenqi, "The Planned Regulation and the Market Regulation," *HQ* (April 1988): 43–46.

76. Ibid.

77. Xue Muqiao, "To Constantly Push the Science of Marxism Forward," *RMRB*, March 20, 1987.

78. Su and Zhang, eds., *Makesizhuyi*, 154.

79. Gao Shangquan, "Effectively Achieving the Inherent Unity of the Plan and the Market," *RMRB*, November 16, 1987; Jiang Yiwei, "On the Socialist Commodity Economy and the Capitalist Commodity Economy," *Jingji ribao*, January 26, 1990.

80. Zhao Ziyang, report to the Thirteenth Congress; Gao Shangquan, "The

Plan and the Market"; Jiang Yiwei, "The Socialist Commodity"; Yu Guangyuan, "The Socialist Commodity Economy"; and He Jianzhang, "The Commodity Economy."

81. Xue Muqiao, "The Science of Marxism"

82. Xiao Shaoji, "Several Problems of the Commodity Economy that Require Emphatic Study at Present," *Beijing shehui kexue* 3 (1986); Zhao Lukuan and Yang Tiren, "Some Opinion on Certain Controversial Problems in the Reflection on the Decade of Reform," *Daobao*, December 5, 1988; Zhang Weiguo, "Conversation with Yan Jiaqi," *Daobao*, November 7, 1988.

83. Ding Ningning, "What the Market Cannot Do?" *QS* 2 (1988).

84. Wu Shuqing, "Stockfication."

85. Zhang Zhiqing, "The Market Economy and the Way Out for China's Reforms," *Jingji kexue* 2 (1989): 72.

86. Chen Wentong, "Labor Is Not a Commodity in the Socialist Mode of Production," *GMRB*, June 18, 1986; Feng Chonglin, "Disputing Several Viewpoints Regarding the Theory of Labor as Commodity," *Zhongguo shehui kexue* 1 (1987); Ding Xuexun, "Labor Is Not a Commodity under Socialist Conditions," *GMRB*, July 29, 1986.

87. He Wei and Han Zhiguo, "On the All-Dimensional Opening of the Socialist Market in Our Country," *Zhongguo shehui kexue* 2 (1986); Han Zhiguo, "Labor Is Still a Commodity under Socialist Conditions," *GMRB*, August 2, 1986; and Zhuo Tongwu, "A Preliminary Discussion of the Question of Labor as Commodity under Socialist Conditions," *GMRB*, July 19, 1986.

88. Hu Peizhao, "A Brief Discussion of Exploitation," *Zhongguo jingji wenti* 1 (1988).

89. Yu Guangyuan, "The Fate of State Ownership in the Reform," *Jingji yanjiu* 3 (1988); Wang Zilin, "The Difficulty and Hope"; Xue Muqiao, "The Evolution of the Ownership of the Means of Production in Our Country," in Xue Muqiao, *Gaige yu lilunshang de tupo* (Reform and breakthroughs in theory), 80–106; and "Conscientiously Taking Good Care of Socialist State Property," in ibid., 107–11; Li Yining, "The Joint Stock System," 21–24.

90. Yu Guangyuan, "The Fate of State Ownership."

91. "[Summary of Discussion] on the Question of the Theory of Property Relations and the Joint Stock System in the Reform of the State Ownership," *Xinhua wenzhai* 4 (April 1989): 52–53.

92. Wang Zilin, "The Difficulty and Hope"; Li Yining, "The Joint Stock System"; Xue Muqiao, "The Evolution"; and Zuo Mu, "On Several Problems of Theory and Policy Concerning the Joint Stock System," *HQ* 1 (January 1988): 25–28.

93. *Daobao*, September 15, 1988. See also Zheng Bifeng and Jia Chunfeng, *Shehuizhuyi chujijieduan lunwenxuan* (Selected essays on the primary stage of socialism).

94. *Daobao*, April 4, 1989.

95. *FBIS-CHI*, February 2, 1989.

96. Fan Gang, "Reform, Inflation, and the Inherent Contradiction of the State Ownership," *Jingjixue zhoubao*, January 22, 1989; Zhong Dong, "Does Socialism Need Private Ownership?" *Guangzhou yanjiu* 5 (May 1988), in *Xin-*

hua wenzhai 7 (July 1988): 13–16; Gao Youqian, "A Sociological Perspective of the Ownership Question," *Jingjixue zhoubao*, August 14, 1988; and Wang Dingkun and Wang Yuanjing, "Redefining Public Ownership," *Dongbei chaijing shifan daxue yanjiusheng xuebao* 3 (1988), in *Xinhua wenzhai* 1 (January 1989): 48–50.

97. Zhong Dong, "Private Ownership."

98. Ibid.; Zhang Zhiqing, "The Market Economy"; Fan Gang, "Reform, Inflation"; and Gao Youqian, " A Sociological Perspective."

99. Yong Jian and Fan Hengsan, "On the Opening of Ownership," *Kaifang shidai* 1 (January 1989), in *Xinhua wenzhai* 4 (April 1989): 36–39.

100. Tian Yuan and Zhu Yong, "On the Reform of the System of Property Rights," *Zhongguo: Fazhan yu gaige* 12 (1988): 3–13.

101. Wu Jiaxiang, "Several Options for Property Rights Reform," in *Zhongguo: Fazhan yu gaige* 4 (1988): 45–57.

102. Lin Huiyong, "[We] Must Rectify a Misunderstanding of the Marxist Theory of Ownership," *Zhongguo jingji wenti* 2 (1989).

103. Marx, *Capital*, 1:832.

104. Lin Huiyong, "The Marxist Theory of Ownership"; and Yang Jianbai, "On Social Individual Ownership," *Zhongguo shehui kexue* 3 (1988).

105. Wang Dingkun and Wang Yuanjing, "Redefining Public Ownership"; Lin Huiyong, "The Marxist Theory of Ownership"; and Zhang Ziqing, "The Market Reform."

106. Zhang Ziqing, "The Market Reform."

107. Cao Siyuan, *Daobao*, September 21, 1987.

108. Cited in Yu Guangyuan, "The Fate of State Ownership"; and Ding Ningning, "On the 'Enterprise Ownership' of the Means of Production," *Dangzheng luntai* 1 (1988).

109. Li Guangyuan, "Public Ownership, the Contract System, and the Laborer," *QS* 7 (April 1989): 25–29; Su Xing, "A Tentative Discussion of the Socialist Economy of the Whole People's Ownership," *QS* 20 (October 1989): 25–29.

110. Li Guangyuan, "Public Ownership."

111. Su Xing, "The Whole People's Ownership."

112. Li Guangyuan, "Public Ownership"; Su Xing, "The Whole People's Ownership"; Gao Di, "The Contract Responsibility System Is the Road to Deepening Reforms," *RMRB*, June 13, 1988; and Hu Yongming, "Investigation into the Mutual Relation of the State Economy and the Commodity Economy," *Xuexi yu cankao* 1 (1988).

113. Ai Feng, "The Debate on Social Equality," *RMRB*, July 11 and 12, 1988.

114. Ai Yun, "Summary of Discussion on the Question of Socialist Distribution," *Jianghai xuekan* 3 (1988), in *Xinhua wenzhai* 9 (September 1988): 52–54; Zhang Weida, "The Transformation of the Form of Distribution According to Labor," *Zhongguo shehui kexue* 2 (1988), in *Xinhua wenzhai* 6 (June 1988): 44–45; and Xiao Mei, "Distribution According to Labor under the Condition of Socialist Commodity Economy," *HQ* 3 (February 1988): 44–46.

115. Ai Yun, "Summary."

116. Ibid. See also Central Party School, *Kexue lilun*, 172–73; and Zhang Guisheng, "Correctly Understand Income Derived from Nonlabor Sources," *RMRB*, July 11, 1988.

117. Ai Yun, "Summary"; Xiao Mei, "Distribution According to Labor"; Liu Guoguang, "Socialism Is Not Egalitarianism," *Beijing Review* 30, 39 (September 28, 1987): 16–18; and Liu Guoguang, "Developing Marxist Economic Theory in the Reform Practice," *RMRB*, August 3, 1987.

118. Liu Guoguang, "Socialism Is Not Egalitarianism," 17.

119. Wang Jiuying, "A Brief Analysis of the Causes of Inequalities in Social Distribution in Our Country," *GMRB*, October 15, 1988; Chen Shenshen, "Establishing a New Economic Order," *Daobao*, August 8, 1988; Hu Zhenmin, "The Major Principle to Follow in Reforming 'Official Departmentalism,'" *RMRB*, October 13, 1988; and Hu Shoujun, "Aspects of the Power Economy," *Daobao*, August 13, 1988.

120. Jia Fuyu, "The Path to Competition—the Equality of Opportunity," *RMRB*, August 16, 1988; Li Honglin, "On Competition," *RMRB*, May 17, 1988; Jiang Yiwei, "Views on Establishing the New Socialist Commodity Economic Order," *RMRB*, August 26, 1988.

121. Zhong Dong, "The Private Ownership"; Gao Youqian, "A Sociological Perspective"; Lin Huiyong, "The Marxist Theory of Ownership"; Wang Dingkun and Wang Yuanjing, "Redefining the Public Ownership"; and Cao Siyuan, "Characteristics of Public Ownership in the Primary Stage of Socialism," *Daobao*, September 21, 1987.

122. Liu Yaojing, "Ten Value Changes in the Decade of Reform," *Gongren ribao*, December 9, 1988; and Mao Yushi, "The Sense of Morality: From the Negation of Individual Interests to Its Affirmation," *Daobao*, February 29, 1988.

123. Hu Peizhao, "A Brief Discussion of Exploitation."

124. Wang Runsheng, "Social Equality: Some Reflection on Cultural Reconstruction," *Zhongguo qingnian bao*, March 25, 1988.

125. Zhang Weiguo, "Conversation with Yan Jiaji"; Li Ming, "On the Way Out at Present for the Reform of Our Country," in *Zhengzhi tizhi gaige*, ed. Li Shengping, 158–59; Gao Youqian, "A Sociological Perspective"; and Zhang Ziqing, "The Market Economy."

126. Zhang Dehua, "Commenting on Several Views that Negate Distribution According to Labor," *QS* 5 (1990): 29–32; Wang Zhiliang, "Economic Reform Must Adhere to Socialist Direction," *GMRB*, September 9, 1989; and Mao Chuanbing et al., "Summary of the Symposium on Socialist Spiritual Civilization," *GMRB*, March 10, 1986.

127. See speakers at the theory symposium in memory of the Third Plenum of the Eleventh Congress, in "Counterattack on Ideological Front Charged," *FBIS-CHI*, January 27, 1989, 26; and He Ganqiang, "Defending '[Asking] Socialist or Capitalist,'" *GMRB*, August 7, 1989.

128. Li Guangyuan, "Public Ownership," 25; and Su Xing, "The Whole People's Ownership," 27.

129. Wu Ke, "Bourgeois Liberalization Is the Hotbed of Corruption," *QS* 18 (September 1989): 13–15; Wu Jianguo, "On the Sources of Corruption," *QS* 21 (November 1989): 20–28; Xu Lijun, "How Do They Oppose the Four Basic

Principles," *GMRB*, July 22, 1989; Luo Guojie, "What Kind of Moral Principles Do We Need?" *GMRB*, July 5, 1989; Wu Jianguo, "Fully Realize the Harm of Bourgeois Liberalization, Correctly Understand the Intrinsic Unity of the Two Basic Points," *GMRB*, July 6, 1989; and Luo Guojie, "Upholding the Normative Direction of Collectivism," *GMRB*, August 28, 1989.

130. See articles cited in note 129.

131. Sun Yongren, "The Socialist Sense of Value Has Taken Roots in the People," *RMRB*, October 9, 1989.

132. Yuan Enzhen, Tao Youzhi, and Gu Guangqing, "Privatization Is Not the Direction of Chinese Economic Reform," *Shanghai shehui kexue* 7 (July 1989); Su Xing, "The Whole People's Ownership"; Wang Zhengping, "A Brief Analysis of [the Thesis] Socialism Is the 'Reconstruction of the Individual Ownership,'" *GMRB*, September 13, 1989; Qiu Yang, "Commenting 'China's Hope—the Manifesto of Private Property,'" *QS* 22 (1989): 19–24.

133. Jiang Zemin, report to the Fourteenth National Party Congress, October 12, 1992, *RMRB*, October 21, 1992.

134. "Discussions of the Development of the Non-State Economy in Beijing," *Liaowang* (overseas edition) 48 (November 30, 1992): 5.

135. Wang Jue, Pang Yongjie, and Dong Guoying, *Gaige yu fazhan de lilun sikao* (Theoretical reflection on reform and development), 211–14.

CHAPTER FIVE

1. Chen et al., *Xin Zhongguo*, 467; and Zeng Tao, "The Great Debate of 1978," *Xuexi yuekan* 12 (December 1988), in *Xinhua wenzhai* 2 (February 1989): 149–51.

2. Chen Yun, speech at the first plenum of the Central Disciplinary Committee, January 4, 1979, in *Jianchi sixian jiben yuanzhe*, 4–8.

3. Ibid.

4. Deng, *Deng Xiaoping wenxuan*, 134–42.

5. "The Truth about the Tiananmen Incident," *RMRB*, November 21 and 22, 1978; "Long Live the People," *RMRB*, December 21, 1978; and "Ensure Full Democracy Inside the Party," *RMRB*, January 11, 1979.

6. From 1979 to 1981 the people's court at different levels reversed over 300,000 verdicts given during the Cultural Revolution, involving 326,000 victims. Gradually, former industrialists, mutineers from enemy forces, and victims of the 1957 Antirightist movement were also rehabilitated. By the end of 1985 the verdicts of more than 2,900,000 victims were reversed. See Li Shengping, "The Theory and Practice of Political Reform since the 3rd Plenum," in *Zhengzhi tizhi gaige*, 21.

7. Ma Peiwen, "From Drastic Shift of Political Line to Major Breakthrough in Theory—Reflection on the Theoretical Work Conference of Ten Years Ago," in *Meng xin de shike*, ed. Hu Jiwei et al.; and Wei Shiqing, "History Will Not Forget This Meeting," *Huaqiao ribao* (New York), February 1, 1990.

8. Su Shaozhi, review of *Chinese Marxism*, 169.

9. For speeches of those theorists, see Yan Jiaqi, *Wode sixiang zizhuan* (An autobiography of my thinking), 31–35. See also Goldman, "Hu Yaobang's Intel-

lectual Network," esp. 232–34. Li Honglin's views were later collected in Li Honglin, *Lilun fengyun* (Winds of theory).

10. Guo Luoji, "To Emancipate the Mind, Theory Must Be Thorough," *HQ* 3 (March 1979): 33–41.

11. Li Yizhe was a collective pen name for three members of the Red Flag faction in Guangzhou during the Cultural Revolution. It stands for *Li* Zhengtian, Chen *Yi*yang, and Wang Xi*zhe*.

12. Kjeld Brodsgaard, "Democracy Movement in China, 1978–79," *Asian Survey* 21, 7 (July 1981): 768–69. For an example of "social democrats," see Chen Erjin, "On the Democratic Revolution of the Proletariat," *Siwu luntan* (May Fourth forum) 10 (June 1979). For the "abolitionist" group, see Wei Jingsheng, "Democracy or New Dictatorship?" *Tansuo* (Exploration) 3 (March 25, 1979).

13. Yan Jiaji wrote "The Secret of Modern Religion" under the pseudonym Bu Shuming, in *Beijing zhi chun* (Beijing spring) 1 (1979) and "Democratic Self-Management and the Theory of the Withering of the State" under the pseudonym Wen Qun, in ibid. 6 (1979). The latter was a speech he made at the theoretical work conference. Cited in Andrew Nathan, "Chinese Democracy in 1989: Continuity and Change," *Problems of Communism* 37 (September/October 1989): 18.

14. See official complaints about theoretical workers, in Special Commentator, "Revolutionaries Must Look Forward," *RMRB*, April 1, 1979; and Ke Weiran, "Theoretical Workers Must Make Contributions to the Four Modernizations," *HQ* 5 (May 1979): 25–28.

15. Hu Qiaomu, "The *Current Ideological Front*," 161.

16. Deng, *Deng Xiaoping wenxuan*, 152, 165–66.

17. Ibid., 216–217.

18. Hua Song, "Remove the Disturbances of Anarchism," *HQ* 2 (January 1980): 23–26; Teng Wensheng, "Uphold the Unity of Democracy and Centralism," *HQ* 3 (February 1980): 27–31, 48. For a critique see Wang Xizhe, "The Direction of Democracy," in *Chi zhih nien tai* (Hong Kong) (May 1980).

19. Contributing Commentator, "Improve the Party's Work Style Is a Fundamental Requirement for the Realization of the Modernizations," *RMRB*, July 1, 1979; "The Crisis of Confidence," *Wen hui bao*, January 13, 1980; and Lei Zheng, "Confidence and Trust," *RMRB*, March 13, 1980.

20. Mao Zedong, "On New Democracy," *Selected Works of Mao Zedong*, collected volume, 623–70.

21. Deng, *Deng Xiaoping wenxuan*, 203–37.

22. Ibid., 280–302.

23. Li Shengping, "The Theory and Practice of Political Reform" and *GMRB*, September 26, 1988. For treatment in the English language, see David S. G. Goodman, "The Chinese Political Order after Mao: 'Socialist Democracy' and the Exercise of State Power," *Political Studies* 2 (1985): 218–35; and Harding, *China's Second Revolution*, 74–75, 174–87, 204–14.

24. Richard Baum, "Socialist Modernization and Legal Reform: The Rebirth of Socialist Legality," *Studies in Comparative Communism* 19, 2 (Summer 1986): 69–103.

25. Li Honglin, "The Leader and the People," *RMRB*, September 19, 1980.

26. Zhang Xianyang and Wang Guixiu, "On the Nature of the Line of Lin Bao and the Gang of Four," *RMRB*, February 28, 1979.

27. This was in Wang's speech at the 1979 theory conference, which was to be an appendix to the resolution on CCP history but was eventually deemed too radical. Reprinted in *Ching pao* (March 1989).

28. Cited in Lin Boye and Shen Zhe, "On the So-called Opposition to the Bureaucratic Class," *HQ* 5 (March 1981): 12–18.

29. Wang Xizhe and Xu Wenli, "The Political Views of the New Generation of Politicians," in *Chi zhih nien tai* (Hong Kong) 133 (February 1981).

30. "Uphold and Safeguard the Four Fundamental Principles," *JFJB*, April 17, 1981; Special Commentator, "The People's Dictatorship Is in Essence the Dictatorship of the Proletariat," *GMRB*, April 21, 1981; Special Commentator, "Upholding the People's Dictatorship Is an Unshakeable Principle," *GMRB*, April 23, 1981; and Special Commentator, "Carry Out the Third Plenum Line, Uphold the Four Fundamental Principles," *RMRB*, April 24, 1981.

31. Huang Kecheng, "On the Evaluation of Chairman Mao and Attitudes toward Comrade Mao Zedong," *JFJB*, April 10, 1981, and *RMRB*, April 11, 1981.

32. Schram, "Ideology and Policy," 359; Tsou, "Political Change and Reform: The Middle Course," in *China: The 80's Era*, ed. Norton Ginsburg and Bernard Lalor, 34–35.

33. Deng, *Deng Xiaoping wenxuan*, 34–37. Hu Yaobang, speech at the Symposium on Script Writing, February 12 and 13, 1980, in *Wenjian xuanbian*, 319–59.

34. See Wang Renzhi, "On Opposing Bourgeois Liberalization," *RMRB*, February 2, 1990.

35. Deng, *Deng Xiaoping wenxuan*, 46–47; Hu Yaobang, speech at the "Symposium on Problems of the Ideological Front," *Wenxian xuanbian*, 825–35; and Hu Qiaomu, "*The Current Ideological Front*," in *Jianchi sixiang jiben yuanzhe*, 158–80.

36. See "Summary of the Major Views in the Discussion of Deng Xiaoping's Thinking on Political Structural Reform," *Kexue shehuizhuyi yanjiu* 2 (February 1988): 73–77.

37. For the evolution of the intellectual discussion of the topic, see Li Lanke, "The Discussion of 'Marxism and Humanism' in Recent Years," *RMRB*, January 11, 1983. For treatment in the English language see Bill Brugger, "Alienation Revisited," *Australian Journal of Chinese Affairs* 12 (July 1984): 143–52; and Schram, *Ideology and Policy*, esp. 43–45.

38. Schram, *Ideology and Policy*, 44.

39. Wang Ruoshui, "On the Question of Alienation," *Xinwen zhanxian* 8 (August 1980) and "The Person Is the Starting Point of Marxism," in *Ren shi makesizhuyi de chufadian* (The Person Is the Starting Point of Marxism) (Beijing: Renmin chubanshe, 1981); Ru Xin, "Is Humanism Revisionism? A Reconception of Humanism," *RMRB*, August 15, 1980.

40. "Abstractly" refers to Ludwig Feuerbach's objection to the subordination of humans to superhuman forces in the spiritual realm. Marx, however, objected

not only to the subordination of humans in the spiritual realm but also to that in all actual human relations that affected the being of the person. See Wang Ruoshui, "A Defense of Humanism," *Wen hui bao*, January 17, 1983.

41. Zhou Yuanbing, "Human Nature and Humanism," *Jiefang ribao*, January 14, 1981; Lu Meilin, "Marxism and Humanism," *Wenyi yanjiu* 3 (1981); Xue Dezhen and Yang Zhao, "Marx's Theory of Man and Feuerbach's Humanism," *Xueshu yuekan* 12 (1980); and Ma Zhemin, "Dissection of 'Philosophy of Man,'" *Xuexi yu yanjiu* 1 (1982). All appear in Institute of Philosophy, Chinese Academy of Social Science, *Renxing, rendaozhuyi taolun ji* (Collection of discussions on the questions of human nature and humanism). Closer to the official view are Wang Ruisheng, "The Fundamental Principles of Materialist View of History Will Last Forever," *RMRB*, April 29, 1983; and Chen Hui, "Great Transformation of Marx on the View of History," *HQ* 6 (March 1983): 30–36.

42. Wang Ruoshui, "A Defense of Humanism."

43. Zhang Kuiliang, Bi Zhiguo, and Wang Yalin, "On Problems of the Person's Value in Socialist Society," *Xuexi yu tansuo* 1 (January–February 1981): 67–80.

44. Wang Ruoshui, "The Question of Alienation." The article thus drew sharp criticism during the crackdown. See Ke Wen, "An Article of Serious Mistakes," *Xuexi yu tansuo* 6 (November–December1983), in *Xinhua wenzhai* 2 (February 1984): 26–29.

45. Zhou Yang, "We Must First Uphold and Second Develop (Marxism)," *RMRB*, June 23, 1982 (emphasis added).

46. Lin Mohan, "On Humanism and Other [Issues]," *GMRB*, December 25, 1983.

47. Wang Ruoshui, "The Question of Alienation."

48. Zhou Yang, "Exploring Several Theoretical Problems of Marxism," *RMRB*, March 18, 1983.

49. Yu Qiuli, speech at the enlarged meeting of the Party Committee of the PLA General Political Department, *RMRB*, December 24, 1983.

50. For power conflict as an explanation, see Lo Ping, "Repercussions of the Fierce Struggle between Hu Yaobang and Deng Liqun," *Ching pao*, April 1, 1984, in *FBIS-CHI*, April 6, 1984, W1–8.

51. For general moral and ideological degeneration as an explanation of the campaign, see Thomas Gold, "Just in Time!" *Asian Survey* 24, 9 (September 1984): 947–74.

52. Hu Qiaomu, "On Humanism and the Question of Alienation," *HQ* 2 (January 1984): 20–29.

53. Li Yongchun, "The Formation and Deepening of the Party's Thinking on Political Structural Reform in the Two Historical Transformations," in *Shiyi jie sanzhong quanhui yilai zhengzhi tizhi gaige de lilun yu shijian* (The theory and practice of political structural reform since the Third Plenum), ed. Li Yongchun and Luo Jian, 35.

54. Wang Zhaozheng, *Cong shi'er da dao shisan da* (From the Twelfth Congress to the Thirteenth Congress), 60–61.

55. See Deng, *Shehuizhuyi*, 132–48; Wang Zhaoguo, "To Carry out Reform Well Is the First Historic Task of Young and Middle-aged Cadres," *HQ* 17 (Sep-

tember 1986): 6–15; Wan Li, "Democratic and Scientific Decision Making Is an Important Topic of Political Reform," *RMRB*, August 15, 1986.

56. Interview with Yan Jiaji.

57. Interview with Chen Yizi and Yan Jiaqi.

58. Interview with Yan Jiaji, Chen Yizi, and Ruan Ming.

59. Zhu Houze, "Some Reflections on the Problems of Ideology and Culture," *RMRB*, August 11, 1986.

60. Contributing Commentator, "Political Problems Can Be Discussed," *RMRB*, August 30, 1986.

61. Harding, *China's Second Revolution*, 192.

62. Interview with Yan Jiaji and Su Shaozhi.

63. Li Yongchun, "The Formation and Deepening of the Party's Thinking," 34–37; Wu Guoguang, "Political Structural Reform Is the Guarantee to Economic Structural Reform," in *Deng Xiaoping zhengzhi tizhi gaige sixian yanjiu*, ed. Chi Fulin and Huang Hai, 202–97.

64. See sources cited in note 63.

65. Ibid.

66. Wang Huning, "Towards a Highly Efficient and Democratic Political System," *GMRB*, July 21, 1986.

67. Su Shaozhi and Wang Yizhou, "Several Problems Concerning Political Structural Reform," *Baike zhishi* 1 (January 1987): 2–5.

68. For example, Jiang Siyi, "Eliminating the Evil Legacy of Feudalism Is An Important Task," *RMRB*, August 1, 1986; and Tian Jujian, "Feudal Remnants Must Be Analyzed in Depth," *RMRB*, September 13, 1986.

69. Su Shaozhi, "Political Structural Reform and the Opposition to Feudal Influences," *RMRB*, August 14, 1986.

70. Ibid.; Su Shaozhi, "Feudal Remnants Block China's Path," *China Daily*, July 22, 1986; and Tian, "Feudal Remnants."

71. See sources cited in note 70.

72. Zhou Houze, "Some Reflection."

73. The leader was cited without reference to name in Zhang Zhonghou, "Build a Modern Sense of Democracy and Law," *RMRB*, August 8, 1986.

74. Su Shaozhi, remarks at the *Hongqi* symposium on "Building Socialist Spiritual Civilization and Theoretical Work," in *HQ* 14 (July 1986): 27; Liu Shiding, "Political Structural Reform Must Be Coordinated with Economic Structural Reform," *Minzhu yu fazhi* 8 (August 1986): 20–21; and Zhang Zhonghou, "Democracy and Law."

75. For Fang's views during the period, see "Conversation of Fang Lizhi with Wen Hui, Ming Lei," *Zheng ming* (Hong Kong) 117 (July 1987): 17–36; and "Excerpts of Fang Lizhi's Counterrevolutionary Statements," in CCP Central Committee Commission on Discipline Inspection, *Fang Lizhi de zhenmianmu* (The true nature of Fang Lizhi), 90–101. For Wang Ruowang's statements in 1985–86, see Yu Sheng, "Party Discipline Does Not Allow Opposition to the Four Fundamental Principles," *Jiefang ribao*, January 16, 1987; Zhang Zhenlu, "Seeing the Essence of Bourgeois Liberalization from Wang Ruowang's Speeches," *RMRB*, January 20, 1987; and Le Baoyun, "Wang Ruowang the Man and His Deeds," *RMRB*, January 10, 1990.

76. "Resolution of the Central Committee of the Chinese Communist Party on the Guiding Principles for Building a Socialist Society with an Advanced Culture and Ideology," *RMRB*, September 28, 1986. For political debates surrounding the drafting of the document, see *Ching ming* 109 (November 1986), in *FBIS-CHI*, November 18, K1–9.

77. See "Resolutely Oppose Bourgeois Liberalization," *HQ* 3 (February 1987): 23–26.

78. Deng Xiaoping, *Deng Xiaoping tongzhi zhongyao tanhua* (February–July 1987), 10.

79. Interview with Yan Jiaji.

80. "Resolutely Oppose Bourgeios Liberalization," 22–26; Deng, *Shehuizhuyi*, 149–160; and Deng, *Zhongyao tanhua*, 1–29.

81. Zhao Ziyang, "Speech at the Meeting of Cadres from the Propaganda and Theoretical Circles, the Media, and Party Schools (May 13, 1987)," *RMRB*, July 10, 1987.

82. See sources cited in note 81.

83. Deng, *Zhongyao tanhua*, 32–41.

84. Zhao Ziyang, speech at the preparatory meeting of the Seventh Plenum of the Twelfth Congress, October 14, 1987, in *RMRB*, October 27 and November 26, 1987.

85. Interview with Yan Jiaji and Chen Yizi.

86. Sun Liping, "Political Modernization and the Political Structural Reform of Our Country," in *Zhengzhi tizhi gaige*, ed. Li Shengping, 53–71; Li Ming, "On the Way Out for at Present for the Reform of Our Country," in *Zhengzhi tizhi gaige*, ed. Li Shengping, 149–62. Also Hu Jiwei and Chang Dalin, "An Exploration of the Theory of Chinese Democracy," *RMRB*, November 30, 1988; Wang Guixiu, "Promoting the Construction of Socialist Political Democracy," *RMRB*, December 9, 1988; and Hu Jiwei, "Disorder Is Always Created by Iron Control," *Daobao*, January 18, 1989.

87. Li Ming, "On the Way Out," 149–62.

88. Ibid.; and Hu Jiwei, "There Is No Real Stability without the Freedom of the Media," *Daobao*, May 8, 1989.

89. Yan Jiaqi, "From 'Non-Procedural Politics' to 'Procedural Politics,'" *Tianjin shehui kexue* 4 (April 1988).

90. Tang Tsou, "Twentieth Century Chinese Politics and Western Political Science," *PS* 20, 6 (Spring 1987): 327–33. The author visited China in the summer of 1986.

91. "Summary of the Symposium on 'Neo-authoritarianism,'" *GMRB*, March 24, 1989; "The Discussion of 'Neo-authoritarianism' (a series of four articles)," *Xinhua wenzhai* 4 (April 1989): 1–7. For a summary analysis in the English language, see Barry Sautman, "Sirens of the Strongman: Neo-Authoritarianism in Recent Chinese Political Theory," *The China Quarterly* 125 (March 1991): 72–102.

92. Wu Jiaxiang, cited in "The Symposium on 'Neo-authoritarianism'"; and Chen Yizi, Wang Xiaojiang, and Li Jun, "The Deeper Problems and Choice of Strategies Faced by China's Reform," *Zhongguo: Fazhan yu gaige* 4 (1988).

93. Li Ming, "On the Way Out," 157–62; and Hu Jiwei, "Iron Control."

94. Yan Jiaqi and Wen Yuankai, "Dialogue on Current Affairs," *Jingjixue zhoubao*, December 4 and 11, 1988.

95. Ibid.; Cao Siyuan, "The Safe Passage for Political Structural Reform," *Daobao*, November 21, 1988; and Su Shaozhi and Wang Yizhou, "Crisis and Reflection," *Daobao*, October 24, 1988.

96. For Wang Zhen's attack, see He Yuan-cheng, "Counterattack on the Ideological Front Charged," *Ching pao*, January 18, 1989; in *FBIS-CHI*, January 27, 1989, 22–27

97. Ibid., 23, 24; and Lo Ping, "Li Xiannian Urges Changing the General Secretary," *Cheng ming*, April 1, in *FBIS-CHI*, April 3, 1989, 39, 40. The quote appears on p. 40.

98. *RMRB*, February 17 and April 3, 1989.

99. Wu Shuqing, "Reform and Opening Must Adhere to the Socialist Direction," *RMRB*, November 17, 1989; Wang Renzhi, "Bourgeois Liberalization."

100. Zhong Shuo, "Forever Uphold the People's Democratic Dictatorship," *RMRB*, October 11, 1989.

101. Deng Liqun, "Correctly Recognize the Contradictions of Socialist Society, Take Initiative in Dealing with Them," *RMRB*, October 23, 1991.

102. Jiang Zemin, "Speech at the Convention Commemorating the Seventieth Anniversary of the Founding of the CCP," *RMRB*, July 2, 1991.

103. See two major documents on "party construction": CCP Central Committee Documents Research Department, ed., *Xinshiji tang de jianshe wenxian xuanbian* (Selected documents on party construction in the new era); and CCP Central Committee Organizational Department, ed., *Zai shehuizhuyi gongchanzhuyi qizhixia* (Under the banner of socialism and communism).

104. Wu Wei and Fang Mingying, *Zhongguo shehuizhuyi minzhu zhengzhi lungang* (The principles of Chinese socialist democracy).

105. Baum, "Modernization and Legal Reform."

CHAPTER SIX

1. Marx, *Capital*, ed. Frederick Engels, 3:791.

2. Germaine Hoston, *The State, Identity, and the National Question in China and Japan*.

3. Marx, "Critique of the Gotha Programme," in *Marx-Engels Reader*, ed. Robert C. Tucker, 395.

4. John M. Maguire, *Marx's Theory of Politics*, 13, cited in Hoston, *The State*, 54.

5. Hoston, *The State*, 56–57.

6. Ibid., 61-62.

7. Marx, *On the Jewish Question*, 33, cited in ibid. 50.

8. Vladimir I. Lenin, *State and Revolution*.

9. Lenin, *Liening quanji* (Complete works of Lenin), 26:3.

10. Lenin, *Liening xuanji* (Selected works of Lenin), 4: 404–57; 32:166; and *Sugong jueyi huiji* (Collection of the resolutions of the CPSU), 2:51, cited in Cui Pengting and Lan Weiqing, "Lenin's Theory and Practice in Creating the Political System of the Soviet State," in *Zhengzhi tizhi gaige*, ed. Li and Luo, 266–68.

11. *Sugong jueyi huiji*, 2:52; cited in Cui and Lan, "Lenin's Theory and Practice," p. 268.

12. Lenin, *Liening quanji*, 33: 148–221 and 4:653–704; Lenin, *Liening wengao* (Manuscripts of Lenin), 4:222–342; *Sugong jueyi huiji*, 2:54–71 and 1:565; all cited in Cui and Lan, "Lenin's Theory and Practice," 269–75.

13. Lenin, *Liening xuanji*, 4:687–700; and Lenin, *Liening quanji*, 36:615–19., cited in Cui and Lan, "Lenin's Theory and Practice," 274–80.

14. Mao Zedong, "On the People's Dictatorship," in Mao Zedong, *Mao Zedong xuanji* (Selected works of Mao Zedong), collected volume, 1351–71.

15. Mao, "On the Correct Handling of the Contradictions among the People," in *Mao Zedong xuanji*, 5:363–402.

16. *Resolution on CCP History*, 30; Central Party School, *Kexue lilun*, 82–85.

17. Zou Xun, "The Democratic System Must Be Institutionalized and Legalized," *RMRB*, April 27, 1979; Li Honglin, "What Kind of Democracy Do We Want?" *GMRB*, March 11, 1979; and Lu Zhichao, "Democracy Is Both a Means and an End," *Zhexue yanjiu* 12 (1980).

18. Yan Jiaqi, "Socialist Countries Must Also Properly Resolve the Problem of the 'Political System,'" *GMRB*, December 8, 1980.

19. Feng Wenbin, "On the Question of Socialist Democracy," *RMRB*, November 24, 1980. See also Su and Zhang, eds., *Makesizhuyi*, 200.

20. *Resolution on CCP History*, 27–47; Feng Wenbin, "Socialist Democracy"; and Yan Jiaqi, "Socialist Countries."

21. Feng Wenbin, "Socialist Democracy"; and Yan Jiaqi, "Socialist Countries."

22. "Prospect and Retrospect: China's Socialist Legal System," *Beijing Review* 2 (January 12, 1979): 27–28; and Su and Zhang, eds., *Makesizhuyi*, 200.

23. "Prospect and Retrospect," 27–28.

24. Wu Jialin, "Several Problems Concerning Socialist democracy," *RMRB*, May 22, 1979.

25. Ibid.; Zhang Xiangyang and Wang Guixiu, "The Proletarian Democracy and the Bourgeois Democracy," *RMRB*, September 6, 1979; and Xinhua News Agency Special Commentator, "Upholding the Correct Direction of Socialist Democracy," *GMRB*, January 21, 1980.

26. Cited in Deng, *Deng Xiaoping wenxuan*, 160.

27. Li Honglin, "What Kind of Democracy?"; and Wu Jialin, "Socialist Democracy."

28. *Ma'en xuanji* (Selected works of Marx and Engels), 1:477; 2:335–439; 25:432; and 4:508; cited in Chu and Lan, "Lenin's Theory and Practice," 257–62.

29. Zhang and Wang, "Proletarian Democracy"; Wu Jialin, "Socialist Democracy"; and Jiang Jianxin and Yin Jinbao, "Does Democracy Require a Western Multiparty System?" *Xinhua ribao*, December 8, 1981.

30. Deng, *Deng Xiaoping wenxuan*, 287–94.

31. Special Commentator, "On the Division of Work between the Party and the State," *RMRB*, December 18, 1980; and Special Commentator, "Power Should Not Be Overcentralized in Individuals," *HQ* 17 (September 1980): 5–8.

32. See articles cited in note 31; and Teng Wensheng and Jia Chunfeng, "Power Must Not Be Overcentralized," *RMRB*, November 14, 1980.

33. Ibid.

34. Liu Junzhi and Niu Xinfang, "The Party Must Lead the People to Be Masters," *HQ* 24 (December 1980): 9–12; and Jing Dong, "The Party Must Not Substitute the State," *HQ* 21 (October 1980): 5–8.

35. Xiong Fu, "On the Position and Function of the Party in State Affairs," *HQ* 9 (May 1981): 2–9.

36. Liu and Niu, "The Party Must Lead," 11.

37. Teng Wensheng, "Uphold the Unity of Democracy and Centralism," *HQ* 6 (March 1980): 27–32; Special Commentator, "Power Should Not Be," 7–8; Teng and Jia, "Power Must Not Be"; and Wu Jialin, "Socialist Democracy."

38. See articles cited in note 37; and Lu Zhichao, "A Means and an End."

39. Special Commentator, "Power Should Not Be," 5–6; and Xiong Fu, "On the Position and Function," 3.

40. It is unclear if the Li Yizhe group had been influenced by Milovan Djilas's book *The New Class* on this point.

41. Hua Song, "Removing the Disturbances of Anarchism," *HQ* 2 (January 1980): 23–27.

42. Wu Junce and Luo Ruirong, "A Matter of Principle Concerning Socialist Democracy," *Xueshu yanjiu* 3 (1981).

43. Xiong Fu, "On the Position and Function," 7–9.

44. Lin Boye and Shen Zhe, "On the So-called Opposition to the Bureaucratic Class," *HQ* 5 (March 1981): 12–18.

45. Du Feijin and Xu Cailiao, "The Commodity Economy and Democratization," *RMRB*, October 11, 1986; Wang Hesheng, "Socialist Commodity Economy and Socialist Democracy," *Shehui kexue* 9 (1987): 19–21; Zhou Zuohan, "Developing the Commodity Economy and Political Democratization," *Hunan shifan daxue shehui kexue bao* 6 (1986): 34–38; also Lin Shunong and Zhang Shouying, "Socialist Democratic Politics and the Commodity Economy," *HQ* 10 (May 1988): 31.

46. See articles cited in note 45.

47. Ibid.; and Wei Xinwen, "Perfecting the Mechanisms of Checks and Balances Is the Essential Means to Improving the Party and State Relations," in *Dangzheng fenkai lilun tantao* (Exploring the theory of separating the party and the state), ed. Nie Gaomin et al., 220.

48. Wang Hesheng, "Socialist Democracy," 19; Zhou Zhuohan, "The Commodity Economy and Socialist Democracy," 35; and Lin and Zhang, "Socialist Democratic Politics," 28.

49. Du and Xu, "The Commodity Economy"; and Ling and Zhang, "Socialist Democratic Politics," 28.

50. Deng, *Deng Xiaoping wenxuan*, 294–98.

51. Su Shaozhi and Wang Yizhou, "Several Problems Concerning Political Structural Reform," *Baike zhishi* 1 (January 1987): 2–5; Jian Siyi, "To Eliminate the Harmful Tradition of Feudalism Is an Important Task," *RMRB* August 1, 1986; and Miao Changgen, "Eliminating the Influences of the Evil Tradition of Feudalism Is an Important Task of Political Structural Reform," in *Deng Xiaoping zhengzhi tizhi*, ed. Chi and Huang, 232–54.

52. Wang Xiaoqiang, "A Critique of Agrarian Socialism," *Nongye jingji wenti* 2 (February 1980), 9–20.

53. Tian Jujian, "Feudal Remnants"; and Liu Heren and Sun Liancheng, eds., *Zhengzhi tizhi gaige de jiben gouxiang* (A basic outline of political structural reform), 32.

54. Tian Jujian, "Feudal Remnants"; Jian Siyi, "The Harmful Tradition of Feudalism"; Bai Jinian, "Seriously Eliminate the Harmful Tradition of Feudalism in Political Life," *RMRB*, April 18, 1986; "Feudalism Clings Like Barnacles," *China Daily*, August 4, 1986; and Su Shaozhi, "Political Structural Reform and the Struggle against Feudal Influences," *RMRB*, August 16, 1986.

55. See articles cited in note 54.

56. Liu and Sun, eds., *Zhengzhi tizhi gaige*, 31–35; and Miao Changgen, "The Evil Tradition of Feudalism," 244–47.

57. G. William Skinner, "Marketing and Soical Structure in Rural China," *Journal of Asian Studies* 24, 1 (November 1964): 3–44 (part 1); 24, 2 (February 1965): 195–288 (part 2); 24, 3 (May 1965): 363–400 (part 3).

58. Deng, *Deng Xiaoping wenxuan*, 276–77.

59. Liu and Sun, eds., *Zhengzhi tizhi gaige*, 31–35; and Miao Changgen, "The Evil Tradition of Feudalism," 244–47.

60. Feng Shujun, "Political Structural Reform Must Eliminate the Fundamental Evil of the Overconcentration of Power," *GMRB*, September 22, 1986; Yang Chenxun, "Bureaucratism and the Highly Centralized Management System," *RMRB*, September 13, 1986; and Lin and Zhang, "Socialist Democratic Politics," 27.

61. See articles cited in note 60; and Li and Luo, eds., *Zhengzhi tizhi gaige*, 288–89.

62. Lieberthal and Oksenberg observe a fragmented structure of decision-making authority that requires complex coordination among many bureaucratic units nested in distinct chains of authority, and a diffuse policy process that is protracted, disjointed, and incremental. See their *Policy Making in China*, chaps. 2 and 3.

63. Deng, *Deng Xiaoping wenxuan*, 287–88.

64. Feng Shujun, "Political Structural Reform"; Li and Luo, eds., *Zhengzhi tizhi gaige*, 198–99; and Dai Qing, "On the Political Structural Reform of China—Interview with Yan Jiaqi," *GMRB*, June 30, 1986.

65. Lin and Zhang, "Socialist Democratic Politics," 27–30; Su Shaozhi, "Humble Opinions on the Political Structural Reform," *Dushu* 9 (September 1986); and Liu and Sun, eds., *Zhengzhi tizhi gaige*, 32.

66. Sui Qiren, "Opposing Feudalism with Capitalism Is a Retrogression," *Wen hui bao*, September 12, 1986; and Chen Shi, "Modernization Cannot Do without Political Construction," *Gongren ribao*, September 18, 1986.

67. Su and Wang, "Political Structural Reform."

68. Wang Zhenyao, "An Outline of the Study of the Party and State Relations," in *Dangzheng fenkai lilun tantao*, ed. Nie Gaomin et al., 124–125; and Liao Gailong, "Marxist Theory of the State and the Structural Reform of the Chinese Political System," in *Deng Xiaoping zhengzhi tizhi*, ed. Chi and Huang, 1–5.

69. Liu Shiding, "Political Structural Reform Must Be Coordinated with the Economic Structural Reform," *Minzhu yu fazhi* 8 (1986): 20–21.

70. "Summary of Views Concerning Political Structural Reform among Theoretical Circles," in *Zhengzhi tizhi gaige*, ed. Li and Luo, 296–98; Wang Zhenyao, "Party and State Relations," 124–25; and Liu and Sun, eds., *Zhengzhi tizhi gaige*, 117–18, 136.

71. For a distinction between the regulatory state and the developmental state, see Steve Chan, *East Asian Dynamism*, 47–50. The term "developmental state" is developed in Chalmers Johnson, *MITI and the Japanese Miracle*.

72. Yan's interview with Dai Qing in Dai Qing, "Political Sturctural Reform."

73. Ibid.; Feng Shujun, "Political Structural Reform"; Zhang Mingshu, "Summary of the Symposium on 'the Political Structural Reform and Economic Structural Reform,'" *RMRB*, November 3, 1986; and Li Honglin, "Modernization and Democracy," *Daobao*, June 2, 1986.

74. Yao Jianhua, "A Discussion of the Functions of the Party," in *Dangzheng fenkai*, ed. Nie Gaomin et al., 10–23; Wang Zhongtian, "A Discussion of the Governing Methods of the Party," in ibid., 24–29. See also Gao Jiansheng, "On the Party's Leaderhsip of the State," in ibid., 1–9; and Zhang Wei, "An Exploration into the Governing Methods of the Party in National Affairs," in ibid., 30–39.

75. See articles cited in note 74, especially Yao Jianhua, 20–22.

76. Yan Jiaqi, "From 'Non-Procedural Politics' to 'Procedural Politics,'" *Tianjin shehui kexue* 4 (April 1988); Su Shaozhi and Wang Yizhou, "The Two Historical Tasks of Reform," *RMRB*, March 7, 1988; and Su Shaozhi, "The Role of the Party in Current Reform," *Xuexi yu tansuo* 1 (January 1989).

77. Han Kang, Zhou Weimin, and Lu Zhongyuan, "Getting Out of the Difficult Situation: New Thinking on China's Political Structural Reform," in *Zhengzhi tizhi gaige*, ed. Li Shengping, 35; and Li Ming, "On the Way Out for at Present for the Reform of Our Country," in ibid., 149–61.

78. Tsou, "Twentieth Century Politics," 328–29.

79. Wang Yizhou, "Several Points of Study on the Socialist System," *Guangzhou yanqiu* 4 (April 1988).

80. Sun Liping, "Political Modernization and the Political Structural Reform of Our Country," in *Zhengzhi tizhi gaige*, ed. Li Shengping, 54–57.

81. Han Kang et al., "China's Political Structural Reform," in ibid., 32–35.

82. Su Shaozhi, "On the Role of the Party."

83. Yan Jiaqi, "'Non-Procedural Politics.'"

84. Yan Jiaqi, talk delivered at Brown University, December 9, 1989.

85. Yan Jiaqi, "'Non-Procedural Politics.'"

86. Li Ming, "On the Way Out," 152–55.

87. Ibid., 150–57.

88. Sun Liping, "Political Modernization," 61–65; Su and Wang, "The Two Historical Tasks"; Yan Jiaqi, "'Non-Procedural Politics'"; and "Report on the Conversation with Yan Jiaqi," *Daobao*, November 7 and 14, 1988.

89. Sun Liping, "Political Modernization," 56–58; Yan Jiaqi, "'Non-Procedural Politics'"; and Liu Junning, "The Institutionalization of the Democratic System," *RMRB*, February 22, 1988.

90. Ibid.

91. Ibid.; and Su and Zhang, eds., *Makesi zhuyi*, 201.

92. Luo Haiguang, "Exploring the Sources of Corrupt Phenomena in the Party," *RMRB*, June 18, 1988. See also Sun Liping, "Political Modernization," 62; and Su and Wang, "Crisis and Reflection," *Daobao*, October 24, 1988.

93. Yan Jiaqi and Wen Yuankai, "Dialogue on Current Affairs," *Jingji xue zhoubao*, December 4 and 11, 1988; Yan Jiaqi, "'Non-Procedural Politics'"; Cao Siyuan, "The Safe Passage for Political Structural Reform," *Daobao*, November 21, 1988; and Sun Liping, "Political Modernization," 62–65.

94. Zhang Kai, "The Power Structure of the State Must Possess Self-Regulating Mechanisms," *RMRB*, February 11, 1989; and Yan and Wen, "Dialogue on Current Affairs."

95. Yan and Wen, "Dialogue on Current Affairs.".

96. Sun Liping, "Political Modernization," 64.

97. Cited in Li Ming, "On the Way Out," 151–52.

98. "Conversation with Yan Jiaqi"; Yong Jian, "Whether or Not 'New Authoritarianism' Will Work in China?" *Daobao*, January 16, 1989; and Huang Wansheng, "Questions and Answers on the Criticism of the New Authoritarianism," *Wen hui bao*, February 22, 1989.

99. See articles cited in note 98; and Cao Siyuan, "The Safe Passage"; and Li Ming, "On the Way Out," 158–59.

100. Luo Jianhua and Gao Zhengang, "On the Spirit of Democracy," *GMRB*, March 24, 1989; Zhou Guanghui, "On Democracy and People—Reflection on the Value, Nature, and Spirit of Democracy," *Shidai pinglun* (inaugural issue, 1988); Li Nianke, "The Development of the Person and Social Progress," *Wen hui bao*, March 18, 1989.

101. Wang Yizhou, "The Socialist System"; Sun Yuecai, "The Question of Humanism and Alienation and the Contention of a Hundred Schools—Rereading Hu Qiaomu's 'On Humanism and Alienation,'" *Dangxiao luntai* 1 (January 1989); Bao Xiaolin and Li Jingrui, "The Mirror of Philosophy and History—Brief Reflection on the Development of Philosophy in the Past Ten Years," *GMRB*, December 12, 26, 1988.

102. Zhou Guanghui, "On Democracy and People."

103. Yu Guangyuan, "For the Victory of Reform and Opening and the Modernization Cause of Socialist Construction," *RMRB*, April 28, 1989.

104. Wang Yizhou, "The Socialist System."

105. Yan Jiaqi, "Democracy and Social Equity: A Comparative Analysis of the Role of the Government," *Guangzhou yanjiu* 7 (July 1988).

106. Su and Wang, "The Two Historical Tasks"; Wang Yizhou, "The Socialist System."

107. Yan Jiaqi, "Democracy and Social Equity."

108. Liu Zaifu, "Two Historical Breakthroughs: From the New Cultural Movement of the 'May Fourth' to the 'Modern Cultural Consciousness' of the New Era," *RMRB*, April 27, 1989.

109. Li Honglin, "What Kind of Marxism Do We Uphold?" *Makesizhuyi yanjiu*, 1 (January 1989).

110. Li Xinmin, "Skepticism, Equal Rights, and Pluralism," *GMRB*, January 25, 1988; and Chen Chengde, "The Question of Methodology in the Development of Philosophy," *GMRB*, October 31, 1988.

111. Hu Jiwei, "No Real Stability without the Freedom of the Media," *Daobao*, May 8, 1989; and "Interview with Xia Yan," in ibid., June 20, 1988.

112. Wang Penglin, "Bring about Change in the Theme [of Marxist Classics] and Develop Marxism," *RMRB*, January 19, 1989.

113. See, for example, Benjamin Schwartz, "Yen Fu and the West."

114. Deng Xiaoping, *Shehuizhuyi*, 132–41.

115. "Interview with Xia Yan"; and Li Nianke, "The Development of the Person."

116. Li Nianke, "The Development of the Person"; Li Ming, "On the Way Out," 158; and "Interview with Xia Yan."

117. Wang Guixiu, "Promoting the Political Construction of Socialist Democracy," *RMRB*, December 9, 1988; and Huang Wansheng, "Questions and Answers." For the "idealistic" and "instrumental" approaches, see Xueliang Ding, "The Difference between Idealistic Reformers and Instrumental Reformers," *Asian Survey* 28, 11 (November 1987): 1117–39.

118. For a critique of a teleological conception of political order, see John Rawls, *A Theory of Justice.*

CHAPTER SEVEN

1. Su Shaozhi and Feng Lanrui, "The Question of the Stages of Social Development," *Jingji yanjiu* 5 (May 1979): 14–19.

2. Interview with Su Shaozhi.

3. For example, Xue Muqiao used a variety of formulations of the same idea in his 1979 book, *Zhongguo shehuizhuyi jingji wenti yanjiu* (A study of the problems of the Chinese socialist economy). I would like to thank Joseph Fewsmith for bringing these points to my attention.

4. Su and Feng, "Stages of Social Development."

5. Su Shaozhi, "On the Principal Contradictions Facing Our Society Today," *Xueshu yuekan* 7 (July, 1979).

6. Lin Yuhua, "The General Character of the Transitional Period and Its Specific Pattern," *Shehui kexue* 1 (1980); and Ma Jihua, "Is Socialist Society a Transitional Period?" *Shehui kexue* 2 (1980).

7. Wang Dake et al., "On the Stage of Social Development at which Our Country Is Located," *Jiaoxue yu yanjiu* 1 (January 1980): 53–56.

8. Zhu Shuxian, "Also Discussing the Question of Stages of Social Development after the Seizure of Power by the Proletariat," *Jingji yanjiu* 8 (August, 1979).

9. Interview with Su Shaozhi.

10. See Special Commentator, "On the Socialist Nature of China's Current Stage," *GMRB*, May 14, 1981; Feng Wenbin, "Conscientiously Carry Out the Third Plenum Line, and Firmly March Forward along the Path of Scientific Socialism," *HQ* 10 (October 1981): 2–12; and Huang Wanzhuan, "Correctly Recog-

nize the Social Nature of the Current Stage of Our Country," *Beijing ribao*, May 11, 1981.

11. Hu Qiaomu, "The Current Ideological Front," in *Jianchi sixiang jiben yuanzhe*, 158–89; quote on 172–73.

12. Deng, *Shehuizhuyi*, 30.

13. Wang Renzhi, "On Opposing Bourgeois Liberalization," *RMRB*, February 2, 1990. Also cited in Shi Zhongquan, "Three Points of Discussion on the 'Primary Stage of Socialism,'" *Xuexi yu yanjiu* 8 (1987): 3–26.

14. Hu Qiaomu, "The Current Ideological Front," 173. See also Feng Wenbin, "The Third Plenum Line"; and Special Commentator, "China's Current Stage."

15. Di Mo, "The Theory and Practice of the Transitional Period," *Nanchong sifan xuebao* 2 (1979): 1–12.

16. Wang Xiaoxiang, "A Critique of Agrarian Socialism," *Nongye jingji wenti* 2 (February 1980): 9–20. I am grateful to Joseph Fewsmith for suggesting Wang Xiaoxiang's contribution.

17. Prior to this date, two major debates had occurred before the revolution, in the 1930s and 1940s, and two in the 1950s and 1960s. For a summary of the latter two debates and the latest debate, see Xian Renlong, "Summary Discussion of the Debates on the Question of the Asiatic Mode of Production since the Founding of Our Country," *Zhongguo lishi yanjiu* 3 (1981): 147–59.

18. Pang Zhuoheng et al, "Minutes of the Symposium on the 'Asiatic Mode of Production,'" *Zhongguoshi yanjiu* 3 (1981); Zhang Yaqing and Bai Jinfu, "Where Is the Root Problem of the Asiatic Mode of Production?" *Shijie lishi* 4 (1981); and Wu Dakun, "The Asiatic Mode of Production as Viewed by Political Economy in Its Broad Sense," *Zhongguoshi yanjiu* 3 (1981); all excerpted in *Xinhua wenzhai* 1 (January 1982): 82–98.

19. Wu Dakun, "Refuting Karl Wittfogel's 'Oriental Despotism,'" *Lishi yanjiu* 4 (1982): 28–36; Lin Ganquan, "The Asiatic Mode of Production and the Ancient Chinese Society," *Zhongguoshi yanjiu* 3 (1981), excerpted in *Xinhua wenzhai* 1 (January 1982): 92–95; and Editorial Group of Early World History, "The Asiatic Mode of Production and the State," *Lishi yanjiu* 3 (1982): 39–52.

20. Interview with Su Shaozhi. "Agrarian socialism" was criticized, among other things, in Special Commentator, "China's Current Stage."

21. The English translation is found in *Resolution on CCP History*, 74.

22. Hu Yaobang, "The Light of the Great Truth of Marxism Shine on Our Path Forward," speech at the CCP convention in memory of the centennial of Marx's death, in *Wenxian xuandu*, 2:645.

23. Su Shaozhi, "Develop Marxism in the Full-Scale Reform and Build Socialism with Chinese Characteristics," *GMRB*, March 11, 1983; and Su Shaozhi, "Developing Marxism under Contemporary Conditions," in *Marxism in China*, ed. Su Shaozhi et al., 35–39, 44–46.

24. Yu Guangyuan, "Developing Marxism as the Science of Soicalist Construction," *RMRB*, March 14, 1983; Fan Ruoyu, "The Principles of Scientific Socialism and the Building of Socialism with Chinese Characteristics," *HQ* 4 (February 1983): 7–11; and Lin Jingyao, "The Epistemology of Marx and the Socialist Modernization of China," *RMRB*, March 4, 1983.

25. Song Zhenting, "Finding Out Our Own Path," *Xuexi yu tansuo* 1 (1983); Hu Sheng, "Marxism and Reality of China," *Beijing Review* 26 (April 11, 1983): 14–18; Su Shaozhi, "Developing Marxism," 35–39, 44–46.

26. Su Shaozhi, "Developing Marxism," 37–38.

27. Song Zhenting, "Our Own Path"; Hu Sheng, "Marxism and Reality," 15–16; and Su Shaozhi, "Developing Marxism," 37–38.

28. Song Zhenting, "Our Own Path,"; Hu Sheng, "Marxism and Reality," 15–16; and Su Shaozhi, "Developing Marxism," 46.

29. Deng Xiaoping, *Shehuizhuyi*, 30.

30. Zhao Zhiyang, report to the first session of the Sixth NPC on June 7, in *RMRB*, June 7, 1983.

31. Hu Yaobang, "The Central Party Organs Must Serve as the Model for the Country," speech at the meeting of cadres from the Central Party organs on January 9, in *Shi'er da yilai*, 2:995–96; and Hu Qili, speech at the graduation ceremony of the Central Party School, *RMRB*, January 19, 1986.

32. Yan Jiaqi, "On Shifting the Focus of Theoretical Work," *GMRB*, February 14, 1986.

33. Wang Zhaoguo, speech at the graduation ceremony of the Central Party School, *RMRB*, July 13, 1986.

34. Zhu Houze, "Some Reflection on the Question of Ideology and Culture," *RMRB*, August 11, 1986.

35. Hu Sheng, "Several Questions Concerning the Strengthening of Social Science Research," *HQ* 9 (May 1986): 3–10; esp. 7.

36. "Summary of the Discussion of the 'Development and Adherence to Marxism,'" *Zhongguo shehui kexueyuan yanjiusheng xuebao* 3 (1986); and in *RMRB*, August 6, 1986; Li Keming, "Time Requires the Modernization of Marxist Philosophy—on the First Anniversary of *Modern Philosophy*," reprinted in *RMRB*, November 17, 1986; Wang Yongxiang, "How to Conceive the Present Status of Philosophy in Our Country," *GMRB*, March 3, 1986; Gao Zengde, "Break Away with Ossified Concepts, Uphold and Develop Marxism," *Shehui kexue* 1 (1986): 11–13; and Deng Weizhi, "Breakthroughs in the Study of Marxism," *RMRB*, March 14, 1986.

37. Su Shaozhi, "Several Theoretical Questions Concerning Marxism," in Su Shaozhi, *Mingzhu yu gaige*, unpublished manuscript, 1986. The book was already at the publishing house when it was banned during the campaign against bourgeois liberalization later that year. Excerpts of the book appear in *China Spring* (New York) 52 (October 1987).

38. Su Shaozhi "Several Theoretical Questions"; Su Shaozhi and Wang Yizhou, "The Reconception of Socialism," *Daobao*, November 24, 1986; Wang Zhuo, "Continue to Reform, Study Reform, and Overcome Difficult Problems," *Zhongzhou xuekan* 4 (1986); Xia Zhengkui, "Theoretical Reflection in the Tide of Reform," *Jianghan luntan* 11 (1986); Yu Guangyuan, "Marxism and Socialist Construction," *Makesizhuyi yanjiu* 1 (1986); and Zhao Yao, "The Reconception of Socialism," *Liaowang* 9 and 10 (1986).

39. Li Keming, "The Modernization of Marxist Philosophy"; "Summary of Discussions"; and Su Shaozhi, "A Humble Opinion on the Political Structural Reform," in Su Shaozhi, *Minzhu yu gaige*.

40. Bao Jialin, "Humans and Their Subjectivity—A Topic Worthy of Attention," *GMRB*, October 20, 1986.

41. Su Shaozhi, "A Humble Opinion."

42. "Conversation of Fang Lizhi with Wen Hui, Ming Lei," *Zheng ming* 117 (July 1987): 17–36; Fang Lizhi, cited in Zhou Longbin, "The Past and the Present of Wholesale Westernization," *HQ* 8 (April 1987); and Central Committee Disciplinary Commission, *Fang Lizhi*, 90–101. For Wang Ruowang's statements in 1985–86, see Yu Sheng, "Party Discipline Does Not Allow Opposition to the Four Fundamental Principles," *Jiefang ribao*, January 16, 1987; Zhang Zhenlu, "Seeing the Essence of Bourgeois Liberalization from Wang Ruowang's Speeches," *RMRB*, January 20, 1987; and Le Baoyun, "Wang Ruowang the Man and His Deeds," *RMRB*, January 10, 1990.

43. Peng Zhen, "[We] Must Have a Fine Command of the Philosophical Weapons of Marxism," speech at Zhejiang University on January 28, 1986, in *Jianchi sixiang jiben yuanzhe*, 334–41.

44. Deng Lijun, "The Four Basic Principles Is the Basis of All Policies," *Dang de jianshe* 5 (May 1986): 3–5.

45. "The Resolution of the Central Committee of the Communist Party on the Guidelines to the Building of the Socialist Spiritual Civilization," *RMRB*, September 29, 1986.

46. *Hongqi* symposium of theoretical workers from the capital, *HQ* 3 (February 1987): 23–27.

47. "Some Views of the Theoretical Circle on the Primary Stage of Socialism," *Daobao*, August 10, 1987.

48. Bao Tong, "The Puppy Horse of Socialism and the Old Horse of Capitalism," *RMRB*, January 6, 1987.

49. For Zhao Ziyang, see "Speech at the Gathering of Spring Festival Greeting" (January 29, 1987); "Proposal on the Draft of the Outline of the Thirteenth Congress Report" (March 21, 1987); and "Speech at the Meeting of Cadres from the Circles of Propaganda, Theory, the Media, and Party Schools" (May 13, 1987), all in *Shi'er da yilai*, 3:1260–67, 1307–9, 1397–1409. For Deng Xiaoping, see *Zhongyao tanhua*, 20–29.

50. For an account of the process of drafting the Thirteenth Congress report, see "The Fruit of Practice, the Collection of Wisdom," *RMRB*, November 5, 1987.

51. Zhang Kai, "Some Opinions of the Theoretical Circle on the Primary Stage of Socialism," *Daobao*, August 10, 1987; Ma Caojun and Zhang Ning, "Summary of the Discussion on the Primary Stage of Socialism," *Xuanzhuan shouce* 16 (1987): 11–14; "Summary of the 'Symposium on the Theory of the Primary Stage of Socialism,'" *Daobao*, July 20, 1987; Zhu Shu, "Summary of the Research on the Primary Stage of Socialism," *Huadong shiyou xueyuan xuebao* 4 (1987): 84–88; "Summary of the Symposium on the Primary Stage of Socialism," *GMRB*, August 10, 1987; and Yin Sheng, "Exploring the Theory of the Primary Stage, Deepening Structural Reform—Summary of the Discussion on the Question of the Primary Stage of Socialism," *Lilun xinxi bao*, September 28, 1987.

52. Central Party School, ed., *Kexue lilun*; and Wang Zhaozheng, ed., *Cong shi'er da dao shisan da*.

53. Chen Yan, "What Are They Promulgating?" critique of Hu Jiwei et al., eds., *Mengxing de shike*, in *RMRB*, April 4, 1990; and Ma Liming, "A Major Exposure of [His] Antisocialist and Anti-Marxist Nature," critique of Su Shaozhi, in *RMRB*, April 24, 1990.

54. Su and Zhang, eds., *Makesizhuyi*, 18–25.

55. Ibid., 43–44.

56. Ibid., 18–19; Sun Changjiang, "From the Practice Criterion to the Production Criterion," *RMRB*, May 9, 1988; "Summary of the Discussion on the Question of the Criterion of Production Forces," *RMRB*, August 22, 1988; Gong Yuzhi, "The New Starting Point of the Emancipation of the Mind," *Wen hui bao*, June 2, 1988; Wu Jiang, "On the Historical Stage of Socialist Construction," *RMRB*, May 5, 1988; and Yu Guangyuan, "In Memory of the Decennial of the Debate on the Criterion of truth," *RMRB*, May 8, 1988.

57. Sun Changjiang, "The Practice Criterion"; Su and Zhang, eds., *Makesizhuyi*, 19.

58. Su and Zhang, eds., *Makesizhuyi*, 20–22; and Gao Fang, "The Development of Scientific Socialism by the Party since the Third Plenum," *Zhongguo renmin daxue xuebao* 1 (1987): 64–75.

59. Su and Zhang eds., *Makesizhuyi*, 22–25, Chen Chengde, "The Question of Methodology in the Development of Marxism," *GMRB*, October 31, 1988; and Yu Guangyuan, "In Memory of the Decennial."

60. Su and Zhang eds., *Makesizhuyi*, 46–47.

61. Yu Guangyuan, "In Memory of the Decennial"; and "A Great Beginning," *RMRB*, December 16, 1988.

62. Su Shaozhi and Wang Yizhou, "Crisis and Reflection," *Daobao*, October 24, 1988; Wang Yizhou, "Several Points of Study on the Socialist System," *Guangzhou yanjiu* 4 (April 1988); and Wang Yizhou, "The Three Waves and Four Trends of the Reform of Socialist Countries," *Zhongguo qingnian bao*, May 27, 1988.

63. Bao Xiaolin and Li Jingrui, "The Mirror of Philosophy and History," *GMRB*, December 12 and 26, 1988.

64. Chen Chengde, "The Question of Methodology."

65. Zhang Xiangyang, "Marxism: Reflection and Transcendence," *Wen wei po* (Hong Kong), January 25, 1989.

66. Gao Qinghai, "An Outline on the Study of Humans," *Jilin shehui kexue* 1 (1988); and Mao Chufu and Gao Tinghe, "The System of Philosophical Principles: A Possible Fate," *Tianjin shehui kexue* 5 (1988).

67. Bao and Li, "The Mirror of Philosophy and History"; Zhang Xiangyang, "Reflection and Transcendence"; Gao Qinghai, "The Study of Man"; and Chen Chengde, "The Question of Methodology."

68. Zhang Shigu, "Exploring the New Frontier of the Study of Socialism," *GMRB*, January 4, 1988; "Symposium on the 'Nonessential Additions' to the Basic Characteristics of Socialism," *Lilun yu shijian* 16 (1987): 12–19; and Editorial Commentator, "Cleanse Additions to Socialism," *Wen hui bao*, September 4, 1987.

69. Wu Jianguo, "A Historical Leap in the Reconception o Socialism," *HQ* (January 1988): 11–15; He Jiancheng et al., "Exploring the Question of the

Primary Stage of Socialism of Our Country," *RMRB*, June 19, 1987; Xiao Liang, "Several Theoretical Problems Concerning the Primary Stage of Socialism," *Jingji ribao*, August 4, 1987; Liu Yefu, "Have a Good Command of the Theory of the Primary Stage of Socialism, Effectively Carry Out the Party's Basic Line," *Zhonggong Zhejiang sheng tangxiao xuebao* 1 (January 1988): 2–10.

70. See articles cited in note 69; also Su and Zhang, eds., *Makesizhuyi*, 105–8; and Central Party School, ed., *Kexuelilun*, 126–128.

71. Su and Zhang, eds., *Makesizhuyi*, 98–100.

72. Ibid.,106–108.

73. Central Party School, ed., *Kexue lilun* 127; Wu Jiang, "On the Historical Stage."

74. Su and Zhang eds., *Makesizhuyi*, 102–3.

75. Ibid. See also Xue Muqiao, *Woguo guomin jingji*, 6–8.

76. Deng Xiaoping, *Shehuizhuyi*, 103–4.

77. Ibid., 51–53, 115–16.

78. Su and Zhang, eds., *Makesizhuyi*, 11.

79. Zhao Zhiyang, political report to the Thirteenth Congress.

80. Su and Zhang, eds., *Makesizhuyi*, 108–12.

81. Xu Yaotong, "Existing Socialism: A Path to Industrialization and Modernization—Interview with Researcher Hong Yingsan," *Shehui zhuyi yanjiu* 4 (1988): 29–32. This view is also cited in Su and Zhang, eds., *Makesizhuyi*, 110–11.

82. Su and Zhang, eds., *Makesizhuyi*, 111; and Zhang Kuiliang, "Marx's Puzzlement and Exploration in His Late Years," *GMRB*, May 29, 1989.

83. Cited in Zhang Wei, "The Replacement of Capitalism by Socialism Is an Objective Law of History," *QS* 22 (1990): 45–46.

84. Wang Yizhou, "The Socialist System."

85. For the symposium at Beijing University, see *Jingbao yuekan* (Hong Kong) 2 (February 1989). Jin Guangtao's speech appeared in an issue of *Lianhe bao* (Taiwan) under the title "China Walks toward the Twenty-first Century" in January 1989.

86. Fang Lizhi, "China's Disappointment and Hope," *Lianhe bao*, January 1, 1989.

87. "Saving Education Demands Immediate Attention," *Ziran bianzhengfa bao*, March 4, 1989.

88. Perry Link, "The Chinese Intellectuals and the Revolt," *New York Review of Books*, June 29, 1989, 38.

89. Su and Zhang, eds., *Makesizhuyi*, 12–17. See also "Summary of the Symposium on the Reconception of Capitalism," *GMRB*, June 20, 1988.

90. Deng Xiaoping, *Shehuizhuyi*, 94–97.

91. Central Party School, ed., *Kexue lilun*, 284–305; and Su and Zhang, eds., *Makesizhuyi*, 341–50.

92. Tong Dalin, *Dangdai zibenzhuyi yinlun* (Introduction to contemporary capitalism), 12, 36.

93. *Jingjixue zhoubao*, April 23, 1989.

94. Xu Jiatun, "Rethinking Capitalism and Conscientiously Building Socialism," *QS* 5 (March 1988): 2–6; "Summary Report of Developments of Research on the Reconception of Socialism and Capitalism," *Xinhua wenzhai* 4 (April

1989), 52; and Lu Congming, "The Characteristics of Contemporary Capitalism," *RMRB*, November 26, 1988.

95. Yu Guangyuan, "In the Course of Reconceptualizing Socialism," *RMRB*, July 22, 1988; and "How to Look at the Moribund Nature of Capitalism," *RMRB*, April 3, 1989.

96. Xu Jiatun, "Rethinking Capitalism," 3.

97. Li Zheng, "Observing the Convergence Phenomenon under the Two Systems from the Criterion of Production Forces," *GMRB*, September 12, 1988; Jiang Fuxing, "The Convergence of the Socialist and Capitalist Society," *Nanjing shelian* 4 (1988), in *RMRB*, March 7, 1989.

98. Arif Dirlik, "Spiritual Solutions to Material Problems: The 'Socialist Ethics and Courtesy Month' in China," *South Atlantic Quarterly* 81, 4 (Autumn 1982): 359–75.

99. Su and Zhang, eds., *Makesizhuyi*, 222.

100. "The Resolution on Socialist Spiritual Civilization."

101. Su Shaozhi, speech at the theory symposium in memory of the Third Plenum of the Eleventh Congress, December 21, 1988, excerpted in *Daobao*, December 26, 1988; see also Su's contribution in Hu Jiwei et al., eds., *Mengxing de shike*.

102. Li Honglin, contribution in *Mengxing de shike*, ed. Hu Jiwei et al.

103. Mao and Gao, "The System of Philosophical Principles."

104. See Ruan Ming and Wang Ruoshui, in *Mengxing de shike*, ed. Hu Jiwei et al.

105. Wu Dakun, "The Impact of the Asiatic Mode of Production on China," *Shehui kexue bao*, June 8, 1989.

106. Jiang Jianqiang, "Five Distortions in the Sinification of Marxism," *Shehui kexue bao*, July 14, 1988.

107. Wang Ruoshui, "Realism and the Theory of Reflection," *GMRB*, July 12, 1988.

108. Jin Guantao, *Ren de zhexue* (The philosophy of the person), criticized in Zhang Weixiang, "Why Is It Wrong to Replace the Theory of Reflection with the Theory of Choice?" *QS* 15 (1990): 46–47.

109. Wang Zhenwu, "The Methodological Significance of the Choice Theory," *Zhexue yanjiu* 11 (1988).

CHAPTER EIGHT

1. Xueliang Ding, "Idealistic Reformers and Instrumental Reformers," esp. 1120–21.

2. Wang Renzhi, "On Opposing Bourgeois Liberalization," *RMRB*, February 2, 1990.

3. Deng, *Deng Xiaoping wenxuan*, 152–53, 216–17.

4. "Editorial: The Leadership of the Party Is the Fundamental Guarantee to the Realization of the Four Modernizations," *RMRB*, April 7, 1979; Commentator, "The Socialist System Can Guarantee the Full Realization of the People's Rights," *GMRB*, October 28, 1979; Xinhuashe Special Commentator, "Uphold the Correct Direction of Socialist Democracy," *RMRB*, January 21, 1980; "Editorial: Democracy Must Be Realized under Stability and Unity," *RMRB*,

February 9, 1981; Special Commentator, "The People's Democratic Dictatorship Is in Essence the Dictatorship of the Proletariat," *RMRB*, April 21, 1981; and Special Commentator, "Upholding the People's Democratic Dictatorship Is an Unshakable Political Principle," *GMRB*, April 23, 1981.

5. Hu Qiaomu, "Problems on the Ideological Front," *Jianchi sixiang jiben yuanzhe*, 171–72, 179; Deng, *Shehuizhuyi*, 29–30; and Wang Renzhi, "Bourgeois Liberalization."

6. Hu Qiaomu, "Problems on the Ideological Front," 181.

7. Ibid., 160–175. See also Hu Yaobang, speech at the CDP symposium on script writing, February 12 and 13, 1980, in *Wenxian xuanbian*, 1:319–59; and speech at the CDP symposium on problems of the ideological front, in ibid., 2:825–35.

8. Deng, *Deng Xiaoping wenxuan*, 346.

9. Hu Yaobang, speech at the symposium on script writing, 839.

10. Hu Qiaomu, "Problems on the Ideological Front," 160-61, 172–76, 181.

11. Deng, *Shehuizhuyi*, 29.

12. Ibid., 29–30; Wang Renzhi, "Bourgeois Liberalization."

13. Deng, *Shehuizhuyi*, 26–37. Deng Liqun, speech at the CDP symposium of theoretical workers, *RMRB*, November 10, 1983. For authoritative but less official criticisms, see Xing Fensi, "Alienation and Spiritual Pollution," *RMRB*, November 5, 1983; and Lu Zhichao, "Proceeding from Reality or from Vaccum," *RMRB*, January 10, 1984.

14. Zhang Haipeng, "Also on Foreign Invasions and the 'Opening' of China in Modern History," *HQ* 6 (March 1986): 32–36, quote on 32.

15. Zhou Longbin, "The Past and Present of the Theory of 'Wholesale Westernization,'" *HQ* 8 (April 1987): 28–32, quote on 28.

16. Deng Xiaoping, *Zhongyao tanhua*, 5.

17. Wang Renzhi, "Bourgeois Liberalization"; Wu Shuqing, "Reform and Opening Must Adhere to the Socialist Direction," *RMRB*, November 17, 1989; and Xiao Chen, "The Problem of One-sidedness in the Theoretical Promulgation in Recent Years," *Beijing ribao*, September 18, 1989.

18. Wang Renzhi, "Bourgeois Liberalization."

19. Chen Liang, "To Take Over the Propaganda and Opinion Forums with Socialist Ideas," *Liaowang* 33 (August 14, 1989).

20. Wan Yi, "Ideological Sources of the Turmoil," *Beijing qingnian bao*, July 7, 1989.

21. Hu Qiaomu, "Problems of the Ideological Front," 178.

22. Deng, *Deng Xiaoping wenxuan*, 243.

23. Hu Qiaomu, "Problems of the Ideological Front," 178.

24. Deng Liqun, speeches on November 9 and 28 and December 7, 1983, in *RMRB*, November 10, November 29, and December 10, 1983; and Zhao Ziyang, speech at the Spring Festival gathering and greeting, *RMRB*, January 1987.

25. Wang Renzhi, "Bourgeois Liberalization"; Wu Shuqing, "Reform and Opening"; and Wei Hanxin and Li Weixin, "Correctly Understand and Command the Dialectic Relation between the 'Two Basic Points,'" *RMRB*, December 4, 1989.

26. Deng, *Deng Xiaoping wenxuan*, 162–63.

27. Hu Qiaomu, "Problems of the Ideological Front," 171–73.

28. Contributing Commentator, "Resolutely Oppose Bourgeois Liberalization," *HQ*, 3 (February 1987): 24–25; and Su Shuanbi, "A Brief Discussion of the Academic Question and the Political Question in the Contention of a Hundred School," *Xinhua wenzhai* 1 (January 1990): 12–15.

29. Shao Tiezhen and Guo Dehong, "Why Is Marxism Universal Truth," *HQ* 7 (April 1981): 25–30.

30. Hu Qiaomu, "Problems of the Ideological Front," 151, 181.

31. Gong Yuzhi, "New Starting Point of the Emancipation of the Mind," *Wen hui bao*, June 2, 1988.

32. Deng, *Deng Xiaoping wenxuan*, 243.

33. Deng, *Shehuizhuyi*, 35; Hu Qiaomu, "Problems of the Ideological Front," 172.

34. Contributing Commentator, "Resolutely Oppose Bourgeois Liberalization," 24–25; and Xiao Chen, "The Problem of One-sidedness."

35. Lo Ping, "Inside Story of Deng Xiaoping and Hu Yaobang's Launching of the 'Great Criticism,' *Ching ming*, October 1, 1981, in *FBIS-CHI*, October 21, 1981, esp. W10–11.

36. For Zhao's criticism of conservative linkage of political liberalization to economic reform, see Zhao, speech at the conference of ideological, theoretical, media, and party school officials, May 13, 1987, in *RMRB*, July 10, 1987.

37. Zhang Zhen, "Marxism Is the Theoretical Guide to Our Thinking," *QS* 18 (September 1989): 2–8; and Han Shuying, "Varieties of Strange Talks to Negate Marxism in Recent Years," *GMRB*, July 20, 1989.

38. Han Shuying, "Varieties of Strange Talks"; and Zhang Jianxin, "Commenting on the Plurality of Truth," *QS* 8 (April 1990): 20–28.

39. "Marxism Must Lead the Way," *China Daily*, January 12, 1987; Contributing Commentator, "Resolutely Oppose to Bourgeois Liberalization"; Chen Yan, "What Are They Propagating," *RMRB*, April 5, 1990; Su Shuanbi, "A Brief Discussion," 12–15.

40. He Xin, "China's Democracy, Socialism, and Their Future," *Beijing qingnian bao*, June 1, 5, and 8, 1990; reprinted in *GMRB*.

41. Hu Sheng, "Why Cannot China Take the Capitalist Road," *RMRB*, March 5, 1987.

42. Ibid.; and Chen Junsheng, "Uphold the Four Fundamental Principles in Reform and Opening," *RMRB*, January 12, 1987.

43. Hu Qiaomu, "Commemorating the Great Pioneer of the Chinese Communist Movement Li Dazhao," *RMRB*, November 6, 1989; Hou Zhongbin, "China Must Take the Socialist Road," *QS* 20 (October 1989): 6–11; Zhao Dayi, "Marxism Is the Guiding Thought to Save China," *RMRB*, October 2, 1989; Jin Chongji, "Why Did They Choose Socialism?" *RMRB*, August 23, 1989; and Hou Qie'an, "Li Dazhao and Marxism," *QS* 21 (November 11, 1989): 15–19.

44. Liu Danian, "On Historical Choice," *QS* 24 (December 24, 1989): 23–26; Hu Sheng, "The Capitalist Road"; Hu Qiaomu, "How Did China Choose Socialism in the '50s?" *RMRB* October 5, 1989.

45. Liu Danian, "On Historical Choice," 24.

46. Hu Sheng, "The Capitalist Road."

47. Deng, *Deng Xiaoping wenxuan*, 153; Hu Yaobang, speech at the symposium on script writing, *Wenxian xuanbian*, 324–25.

48. Bao Tong, "Socialism the Young Horse and Capitalism the Old Horse, etc." *RMRB*, January 6, 1987; and Chen Junsheng, "Reform and Opening."

49. Gao Di, "China's Being Poor?" *RMRB*, January 5, 1990; Lu Zhichao, "On the Fundamental Conflict between the Four Fundamental Principles and Bourgeois Liberalization," *RMRB*, November 1, 1989; He Xin, "The Economic Situation of the World and Economic Problems of China,'" *RMRB*, December 11, 1990; and Wen Di, "Socialism Can Save China," *RMRB*, January 15, 16, 18, and 19, 1990. For Deng Xiaoping, see *RMRB*, October 15, 1992, 3.

50. Chen Junsheng, "Reform and Opening."

51. He Xin, "The Economic Situation."

52. Ibid.; Chen Junsheng, "Reform and Opening"; Wen Di, "Socialism Can Save China"; and Lu Zhichao, "The Fundamental Conflict."

53. Hu Yaobang, speech at the symposium on script writing, 333–37; and Hu Qiaomu, "Problems of the Ideological Front," 175.

54. Zhu Gelin, "Has the Nature of Capitalism Changed?" *QS* 20 (1990): 35–42.

55. Xian Da, "Why Do We Say the Theory of 'Socialist Alienation' Is Wrong?" *HQ* 22 (November 1983): 45–46.

56. Xiong Fu, "Response to a Challenge from Bourgeois Liberalization," *RMRB*, August 16, 1987.

57. Wan Yi, "Ideological Sources."

58. Hu Yaobang, speech at the symposium on script writing, 334–35; Hu Qiaomu, "Problems of the Ideological Front," 175.

59. Ibid.

60. Wu Shuqing, "Reform and Opening"; and Wu Jianguo, "On the Roots of Corrupt Phenomena," *QS* 21 (November 1989): 20–28.

61. Hu Yaobang, speech at the symposium on script writing, 325; Deng, *Deng Xiaoping wenxuan*, 214–15; Hu Qiaomu, "On Humanism and the Question of Alienation," *HQ* 2 (January 1984): 20–26.

62. Xiong Fu, "Response to the Challenge."

63. Hu Qiaomu, "Problems of the Ideological Front," 886–87.

64. Hu Qiaomu, "Humanism and the Question of Alienation," 20–29.

65. Wu Jianguo, "The Roots of Corrupt Phenomena," 20–28; and Wu Shuqing, "Reform and Opening."

66. Xinhuashe Special Commentator, "Uphold the Correct Direction of Socialist Democracy," *GMRB*, January 21, 1980; and Yu Xinyan, "The Fundamental Difference between Socialist and Bourgeois Democracy," *Beijing ribao*, October 22, 1989.

67. Contributing Commentator, "Uphold the People's Dictatorship," *HQ* 2 (January 1987): 8; Li Jian, "What Kind of Democracy Does that Small Group of People Want?" *QS* 16 (August 1989): 14–21; Zheng Kangsheng, "Adopt a Correct View of Democracy," *Beijing ribao*, August 3, 1989; and Yu Ming, "Analyzing the Western Democracy Promulgated by Fang Lizhi," *RMRB*, November 8, 1989.

68. Yu Xinyan, "The Fundamental Difference."

69. Deng, *Deng Xiaoping wenxuan*, 231. See also Lin He, "How to Look at the Bourgeois 'Separation of Powers'?" *RMRB*, February 2, 1987.

70. Yu Xinyan, "The Fundamental Difference."

71. Ibid., and Zheng Kangsheng, "A Correct View of Democracy."

72. See articles cited in notes 70 and 71.

73. Deng, *Deng Xiaoping wenxuan*, 160–2, 220–21.

74. Hu Qiaomu, "Problems of the Ideological Front," 174; Wang Ruisheng, "Is There Abstract Human Nature?" *HQ* 22 (November 1983): 42–43; Ke Wen, "An Article with Serious Mistakes," *Xuexi yu tansuo* 6 (December 1983); and Hu Qiaomu, "Humanism and the Question of Alienation," 26.

75. Wang Renzhi, "Bourgeois Liberalization."

76. Xiao Wen, "Is There No Distinction between Western and Eastern Democracy?" *RMRB*, February 21, 1990.

77. Zhou Longbin, "The Past and Present," 30. Wen Ping, "From National Nihilism to National Betrayal—on the Bourgeois Liberalization Theories of Liu Xiaobo," *RMRB*, November 7, 1989.

78. Shi Qiao, "Why Is It Wrong to Promulgate Abstract Humanism?" *HQ* 22 (November 1983): 43–44.

79. Contributing Commentator, "The Socialist System Can Guarantee the Full Realization of the People's Rights," *GMRB*, October 26, 1979; and Xiao Wen, "Western and Eastern Democracy?"

80. Zheng Kangsheng, "A Correct View of Democracy."

81. Cited in Zhang Jianxin, "The Plurality of Truth," 27–28.

82. Zhang Zhen, "Marxism-Leninism," 7.

83. Li Jian, "What Kind of Democracy?" quote on 18.

84. Yu Xinyan, "The Fundamental Difference"; Zhang Zhen, "Marxism-Leninism," 7–8; Zhang Jianxin, "The Plurality of Truth," 27–28; and Li Jian, "What Kind of Democracy?" 14–21.

85. Hu Sheng, "The Capitalist Road."

86. Deng, *Zhongyao tanhua*, pp. 10–13.

87. Xiao Wen, "Western and Estern Democracy?"

88. Zhang Jianxin, "The Plurality of Truth."

89. Hu Qiaomu, "Problems of the Ideological Front," 181.

90. Nathan, "Chinese Democracy in 1989," 24.

CHAPTER NINE

1. These issues were first raised in "The Novosibirsk Report" (1984), a research project on the problems and the necessity of reform of the Soviet economy headed by Tayana Zaslavskaya. The then unpublished report was circulated among top official circles.

2. Mikhail S. Gorbachev, report at the CPSU Central Committee Plenum on January 27, 1987, *Pravda*, January 28, 1987.

3. James Scanlan, "Ideology and Reform," 50–51. For the concept of "developed socialism," see Alfred Evans, Jr., "'Developed Socialism' in Soviet Ideology," in *Soviet Studies* 39, 3 (July 1977): 409–28.

4. Yuri Andropov, "Ucheniye Karl Marx i Nekotorye Vonrosy Sotsialisti-cheskolo stroiteltva v CCCP," *Kommunist* 3 (1983): 9–23; and "Gorbachev Key-notes Ideological Conference," *The Current Digest of the Soviet Press* (hereafter *CDSP*) 36, 50 (1985): 2.

5. For the evolution and decline of "developed socialism," see Alfred Evans, Jr., "The Decline of Developed Socialism? Some Trends in Recent Soviet Ideol-ogy," *Soviet Studies* 38, 1 (January 1987): 1–23.

6. Gorbachev, speech at the all-union conference of the heads of social sciences faculties, *Pravda*, October 2, 1986.

7. Gorbachev, *Zhivoe tvorchestvo naroda* (Creating a lively climate) (Moscow: Izdatek'stvo politicheskoi literatury, 1985), 13.

8. Gorbachev, speech at the all-union conference of the heads of social sciences faculties.

9. "The Living Spirit of Marxism," *Pravda*, October 21, 1986.

10. Gorbachev, speech at the all-union conference of the heads of social sci-ences faculties.

11. Gorbachev, report at the CPSU Central Committee plenum, April 23, 1985, in Gorbachev, *Speeches and Writings*, 136–38; and political report to the Twenty-seventh Congress, in ibid., 36–37, 60–66.

12. During Gorbachev's first year in office, from April 1985 to February 1986, over 140 leading members of central and republic party and state organs were discharged and replaced. At the Twenty-seventh Congress, 44 percent of the 307 Central Committee members and 69 percent of the 170 alternate members were new entrants.

13. Gorbachev, report at the CPSU Central Committee plenum, January 27, 1987, *Pravda*, January 28, 1987.

14. Gorbachev, report at the CPSU plenum, February 17, 1988, *Pravda*, Feb-ruary 18, 1988; and talk at the meeting with media executives, May 7, 1988, in *Pravda*, May 8, 1988.

15. The Law on State Enterprises adopted at the plenum formally transformed the centralized structure of the economy by making enterprises the most impor-tant component of the economy with freedom to make most economic decisions. See *Pravda*, July 29, 1987.

16. Gorbachev, report at the CPSU Central Committee Plenum, January 27, 1987.

17. For official criticism and dismissal of Yeltsin, see *Pravda*, November 13, 1987.

18. Gorbachev, speech at the ceremonial meeting of the CPSU on the seventi-eth anniversary of the October Revolution, *Pravda*, November 3, 1987; speech at the meeting with media representatives on January 12, *Pravda*, January 13, 1988; and speech at the CPSU Central Committee Plenum, February 17, 1988.

19. For a comparison of Chinese and Soviet reforms, see Lowell Dittmer, "So-viet Reform and the Prospect of Sino-Soviet Convergence," *Studies in Compara-tive Communism* 22, 2/3 (Summer/Autumn 1989): 123–38.

20. Gorbachev, political report to the Nineteenth All-Union Conference of the CPSU, *Pravda*, July 19, 1988.

21. Ibid.

22. Gorbachev, "Socialist Thought and Revolutionary Restructuring," *Pravda*, November 26, 1989.

23. Gorbachev's report at the CPSU Central Committee Plenum on February 5, 1990, in *CDSP* 42, 6 (1990): 2–5.

24. Ye. K. Ligachev, statement for *Pravda*'s "Debate Page," *Pravda*, May 12, 1990, in *CDSP* 42, 19 (1990): 4.

25. See the draft Democratic Platform, *Pravda*, March 3, 1990, in *CDSP* 42, 19 (1990): 1–3.

26. Gorbachev, speech at the CPSU Central Committee, *Pravda*, March 12, 1990, in *CDSP* 42, 11 (1990): 16; speech to Communists of the Capital's Frunze Borough, *Pravda*, May 14, 1990, in *CDSP* 42, 19 (1990): 1–2.

27. "Toward a Humane, Democratic Socialism (Program Statement of the Twenty-eighth CPSU Congress)" *Pravda*, July 15, 1990; in *CDSP* 42, 37 (1990): 15–17.

28. Gorbachev, report at the CPSU Central Committee Plenum on July 25, 1990, *Pravda*, July 26, 1990, in *CDSP* 42, 30 (1990): 2–6.

29. Deng, *Deng Xiaoping wenxuan*, 137–39, 165–66.

30. Quoted in Herbert Ellision, "*Perestroika* and the New Economic Policy (1921–1928): The Uses of History," in *Transformation of Socialism*, ed. Gurtov, 21.

31. Gorbachev, speech observing the seventieth anniversary of the October Revolution.

32. B. P. Kurashvil, "Models of Socialism," *Soviet Sociology* (July–Aug. 1990): 33–52.

33. Gorbachev, report at the CPSU the Central Committee Plenum, July 25, 1990, 2–3.

34. Cited in "Toward Confrontation or Unity," *Pravda*, September 17, 1989, in *CDSP* 41, 42 (1990): 1.

35. Ellison, "*Perestroika*," 26.

36. Ibid., 21.

37. Kurashvil, "Models of Socialism," 38–41.

38. Vasily Selyunin, "Sources," *Novy mir* 5 (May 1988), in *CDSP* 40, 40 (1988): 14–17; A. Tsipko, "The Roots of Stalinism," *Nauka and zhizn* 11 (November 1988), in *CDSP* 41, 10 (1989): 1–5.

39. Gorbachev, speech at the CPSU Central Committee Plenum on February 17, 1988; speech at the meeting with media representative on May 7, 1988.

40. Gorbachev, speech at the CPSU Central Committee plenum on February 17, 1988.

41. Gorbachev, report to the CPSU Central Committee Plenum on January 6, 1989, in *CDSP* 41, 1 (1989): 1.

42. "Questions of Theory—Debate Rostrum: Toward a Contemporary Concept of Socialism," *Pravda*, July 14, 1989, in *CDSP* 41, 31 (1989): 4; Gorbachev, political report to the Twenty-eighth CPSU Congress, in *CDSP* 42, 27 (1990): 2; and "Prospects for Democratization" (roundtable on democratization), *Soviet Sociology* (March–April 1991), esp. 35.

43. Tayana Zaslavskaya, *The Second Socialist Revolution*, 9–10. See also "Prospects for Democratization," esp. 35, and "Alienation under Socialism," *Soviet Sociology* (November-December 1990): 58–78.

44. "Alienation under Socialism," 71.

45. "Toward a Humane, Democratic Socialism," 16.

46. Gorbachev, speech at the CPSU Central Committee Plenum on February 5, 1990, 4.

47. "Alienation under Socialism," 70–73.

48. Gorbachev, remarks at the meeting with world cultural figures, *Tass* (Moscow), October 20, 1986.

49. Gorbachev, "Common Responsibility for the Fortunes of Peace," *Pravda*, November 30, 1989.

50. Gorbachev, speech on the results of the discussion of the political report to the Twenty-eighth Congress, *Pravda*, July 11, 1990.

51. Gorbachev, report at the CPSU the Central Committee Plenum, July 25, 1990, 4.

52. Gorbachev, report at the CPSU Central Committee Plenum, February 6, 1990, *Pravda*, February 6, 1990, in *CDSP* 42, 6 (1990): 4.

53. Gorbachev, "Common Responsibility"; and speech on the results of the discussion of the political report to the Twenty-eighth Congress.

54. Gorbachev, "Socialist Thought"; and "Debate Rostrum," 5–6.

55. Gorbachev, report at the CPSU Central Committee Plenum on February 6, 1990, 3.

56. Gorbachev, speech on the results of the discussion of the political report to the Twenty-eighth Congress.

57. Gorbachev, political report to the Twenty-eighth Congress, 5; "Toward a Humane, Democratic Socialism," 17.

58. Gorbachev, political report to the Twenty-eighth Congress, 5.

59. Gorbachev, report at the CPSU Central Committee plenum, *Pravda*, March 12, 1990, in *CDSP* 42, 11 (1990): 11.

60. Gorbachev, report at the plenum of the CPSU Central Committee, February 6, 1990.

61. Guan Xuelin, "A Continuing Series of Blunders in Economic Reforms—Summary 18 of the Situation in the Soviet Union during Gorbachev's Six Years of Reign," *Neican xuanbian* 24 (1991): 20–22.

CHAPTER TEN

1. For example, symposiums held by the journal *Gaige* (Reform) on March 14, 1992, and by the editorial board of *Lishi chaoliu* (Historical trends) on June 15, 1992, both in Beijing.

2. I am grateful to Joseph Fewsmith for suggesting these points.

3. The term is from Tsou, "Political Change and Reform: The Middle Course."

4. Dahm, "The Function and Efficacy of Ideology," 110–11.

5. This conclusion is conceptually similar to Joseph's finding from the Chinese critique of ultra-lefitism. See Joseph, *The Critique of Ultra-leftism*, 228–29, for a comparison.

6. This conclusion is conceptually similar to Joseph's finding from the Chinese critique of ultra-lefitism. See ibid.

7. See Su Shaozhi, *Maliezhuyi xinlun* (A new theory of Marxism); and *Marxism and Chinese Reform.*

8. Quoted in Link, "The Chinese Intellectual and the Revolt," 39.

9. Su and Zhang, eds., *Makesizhuyi*, 11.

10. Rawls, *A Theory of Justice*, 318.

11. For Rawls' perfectionism, see Vinit Haksar, "Autonomy, Justice and Contratarianism," *British Journal of Political Science* 3 (1973): 501; Wayne Proudfoot, "Rawls on Self-Respect and Social Union," *Chinese Philosophy* 5 (1978): 264; and Vinit Haksar, *Equality, Liberty, and Perfectionism*, esp. 53.

12. See Milton Fisk, "History and Reason in Rawls' Moral Theory," in *Reading Rawls*, ed. Norman Daniels, 54; and Kai Nielsen, "The Choice between Perfectionism and Rawlsian Contratarianism," *Interpretation* 6 (1977): 133.

13. I am grateful to Joseph Fewsmith for suggesting this point.

14. Interview with Lu Jidian, Chongqing, June 1989.

15. Joseph, *The Critique of Ultra-leftism*, 235–36.

16. See Frederick Teiwes, *Politics and Purge in China: Rectification and the Decline of Party Norms, 1949–1965.*

17. Joseph, *The Critique of Ultra-leftism*, 236.

18. *Shijie ribao* (New York), March 15 and June 15, 1992.

19. The preceding discussion is based on Meisner, "De-radicalization and Chinese Socialism," in *Marxism and the Chinese Experience*, ed. Dirlik and Meisner, 356–57.

20. Joseph, *The Critique of Ultra-leftism*, 243.

21. Joseph describes the likelihood of such a new dogma. See ibid.

22. See Joseph's prediction of a likely orthodoxy of antileftism, in ibid., 243.

23. See Joseph's observation of a possible reversal of the notion of the "Left is better than Right," in ibid., 243.

24. I am grateful to Joseph Fewsmith for suggesting these points.

25. Interview with Su Shaozhi, June 1994.

26. Joseph, *The Critique of Ultra-leftism*, 244.

References

CHINESE LANGUAGE SOURCES

Periodicals

Baike zhishi (Encyclopedic knowledge), Beijing, 1979–.

Ban yue tan (Fortnightly talk), Beijing, 1980– (originally *Shishi shouce*, 1950s–1980).

Beijing qingnian bao (Beijing youth daily), Beijing, 1949–.

Beijing ribao (Beijing daily), Beijing, 1952–.

Beijing shehui kexue (Beijing Social Sciences), Beijing, 1986–.

Caimao zhanxian (Finance and trade front).

Dangde jianshe (Party construction), Sichuan, 1985– (originally *Zhibu shenghuo*, ?–1985).

Dangxiao luntan (Party School forum), Beijing, 1988–.

Dangzheng luntan (Forum on the party and the government), Shanghai, 1978–.

Dushu (Reading), Beijing, 1979–.

Fengdou (Striving), Ha'erbin, Heilongjiang, 1958–.

Gongren ribao (Workers' daily), Beijing, 1949–.

Guangming ribao (Enlightenment daily), Beijing, 1949–.

Guangzhou yanqiu (Guangzhou research), Guangzhou, 1982–.

Guangzhou yuekan (Guangzhou monthly), Guangzhou.

Hebei ribao (Hebei daily), Shijiazhuang, Hebei, 1949–.

Hongqi (Red flag), Beijing, 1958–1989 (renamed *Qiushi*, 1989–).

Hunan shifan daxue shehui kexue bao (Hunan Teachers' University journal of social sciences), Changsha, Hunan, 1956–.

Huadong shiyou xueyuan xuebao (Journal of the Northeastern Institute of Petroleum), Shandong, 1984–.

Jilin shehui kexue (Jilin social sciences), Changchun, Jilin, 1978–.

Jianghan luntan (Jianghan forum), Wuchang, Hubei, 1979–.

Jiaoxue yu yanjiu (Teaching and research), Beijing, 1953–.

Jiefangjun bao (Liberation Army daily), Beijing, 1956–.

Jiefang ribao (Liberation daily), Shanghai, 1941–.

Jindao yuekan (Jindao monthly), Hainan, mid–1980s–?.

Jingjixue dongtai (Trends in economics), Beijing, 1960–.

Jingji kexue (Economic sciences), Beijing, 1979–.

Jingji ribao (Economic daily), Beijing, 1983–.

Jingji shehui tizhi bijiao (Comparative economic and social systems), Beijing, 1986–.

Jingji wenti (Economic problems), Taiyuan, Shanxi, 1979–.

Jingji yanjiu (Economics research), Beijing, 1955–.

Jingjixue zhoubao (Economics weekly news), Beijing, 1980–1989.

Jingjixue zhoukan (Economics weekly), Beijing, ?–1989.

Kaifang shidai (Times of opening), Guangzhou.
Kexue shehuizhuyi yanjiu (Research in scientific socialism), Beijing, 1980–.
Liaowang (Outlook weekly), Beijing, 1981–.
Lilun dongtai (Theoretical trends), Beijing, 1991–.
Lilun jiaoyu (Theoretical education), Taiyuan, Shanxi, 1984–.
Lilun yu shijian (Theory and practice), Shengyang, Liaoning, 1977–.
Lilun xinxi bao (Theory information news), Beijing, 1980s–?
Lishi yanjiu (Historical research), Beijing, 1974–.
Longye jingji wenti (Problems of agrarian economy), Beijing, 1980–.
Makesizhuyi yanjiu (Research in Marxism), Beijing, 1983–.
Meizhou wenzhai bao (Weekly digest news), Fuzhou, Fujian, 1980–.
Minzhu yu fazhi (Democracy and rule of law), Shanghai, 1979–.
Nanchong sifan xuebao (Journal of Nanchong Teachers College), Nanchong, Sichuan, 1980–.
Neican xuanbian (Selected internal references), Beijing, 1986–.
Qingnian bao (Youth news), Shanghai, 1949–.
Qiushi (Seeking truth), Beijing, 1988–.
Qiushi xuekan (Journal of seeking truth), Ha'erbin, Heilongjiang, 1974–.
Qunzhong luntai (Mass opinion forum), Beijing, 1985–.
Renmin ribao (People's daily), Beijing, 1948–.
Shanghai shehuikexue (Shanghai social sciences), Shanghai, 1979–.
Shehui bao (Social news), Shanghai, 1981–.
Shehuikexue (Social sciences), Shanghai, 1979–.
Shehuikexue xuebao (Journal of social sciences).
Shehuikexue jikan (Social science quarterly), Shanghai, 1985–.
Shehuikexue zhanxian (Social sciences front), Changchun, Jilin, 1978–.
Shehuizhuyi yanjiu (Research in socialism), Wuhan, Hubei, 1978–.
Shichang bao (Market News), Beijing, 1979–.
Shidai pinglun (Times commentary), Changchun, Jilin, 1988–.
Shijie jingji daobao (World economic herald), Shanghai, 1980–1989.
Shijie lishi (World history), Beijing, 1978–.
Tianjin shehui kexue (Tianjin social sciences), Tianjin, 1981–.
Wen hui bao (Wen hui daily), Shanghai, 1938–.
Wen shi zhe (Culture, history, and philosophy), Jinan, Shandong, 1951–.
Wenyi yanjiu (Literary study), Beijing, 1979–.
Wenzhai zhoubao (Weekly digest), Chengdu, Sichuan, 1984–.
Xiaofei shibao (Consumer news), Beijing, 1985–.
Xinhua ribao (Xinhua daily), Nanjing, 1949–.
Xinhua wenzhai (Xinhua digest of articles), Beijing, 1979–.
Xinwen bao (News paper), Shanghai, 1990–.
Xinwen zhanxian (Journalistic front), Beijing, 1957–.
Xuanchuan shouce (Propaganda pamphlet), Beijing, 1984–.
Xueshu yanjiu (Academic research), Guangzhou, 1957–.
Xueshu yuekan (Research monthly), Shanghai, 1957–.
Xuexi yuekan (Study monthly), Wuhan, Hubei, 1986–.
Xuexi yu sikao (Study and reflection), Hangzhou, 1984–.

Xuexi yu tansuo (Study and exploration), Ha'erbin, Heilongjiang, 1979–.

Xuexi yu yanjiu (Study and research), Beijing, 1980–.

Yunnan shehui kexue (Yunnan social sciences), Kunming, Yunnan, 1981–.

Zhexue dongtai (Trends in philosophy), Beijing, 1979–.

Zhexue yanjiu (Studies in philosophy), Beijing, 1977–.

Zhongguo: Fazhan yu gaige (China: Development and reform), Changsha, Hunan, 1985–.

Zhongguo jingji wenti (Chinese economic problems), Fujian, 1959–.

Zhongguo kexueyuan yanjiusheng xuebao (Journal of the Chinese Academy of Social Sciences graduate students), Beijing, 1981– (originally *Xuexi yusikao*).

Zhongguo qingnian bao (Chinese youth daily), Beijing, 1951–.

Zhongguo renmin daxue baokan zazhi shuoyin (Chinese People's University digest of newspapers and journals), Beijing, 1958–.

Zhongguo renmin daxue xuebao (Journal of Chinese People's University), Beijing, 1987–.

Zhongguo shehui kexue (Chinese social sciences), Beijing, 1980–.

Zhongguo shi yanjiu (Chinese history studies), Beijing, 1979–.

Zhongguo xiaofei shibao (Chinese consumer times), Beijing, 1985– (renamed *Xiaofei shibao* in 1988).

Zhonggong zhejiangsheng tangxiao xuebao (Journal of the Party School of the Chinese Communist party of Zhejiang Province), Hangzhou, Zhejiang, 1985–.

Zhongshan, Nanjing, 1974–.

Zhongzhou xuekan (Zhongzhou research journal), Zhengzhou, Henan, 1979–.

Ziran bianzhengfa bao (Journal of dialectics of nature), Beijing.

Books

CCP Central Committee Commission on Discipline Inspection, ed. *Fang Lizhi de zhenmianmu* (The true nature of Fang Lizhi). Beijing: Falu chubanshe, 1989.

CCP Central Committee Documents Research Department, ed. *Sanzhong chuanhui yilai zhongyao wenxian xuanbian* (Selected important documents since the Third Plenum). Vols. 1 and 2. Beijing: Renmin chubanshe, 1982.

———. *Guanyu jianguo yilai dang de ruogan wenti de jueyi zhuyiben* (Notes on the resolution on CCP history). Beijing: Renmin chubanshe, 1983.

———. *Guanyu jianguo yilai dang de ruogan wenti de jueyi zhuyiben* (Notes on the resolution on CCP history). Revised edition. Beijing: Renmin chubanshe, 1986.

———. *Jianchi sixiang jiben yuanzhe, fandui zichan jieji ziyou hua* (Uphold the Four Fundamental Principles, oppose bourgeois liberalization). Beijing: Renmin chubanshe, 1987.

———. *Shi'er da yilai zhongyao wenxian xuanbian* (Selected important documents since the Twelfth Congress). Vols. 1 and 2. Beijing: Renmin chubanshe, 1988.

———. *Shisan da yilai zhongyao wenxian xuanbian* (Selected important documents since the Thirteenth Congress). Vols. 1 and 2. Beijing: Renmin chubanshe, 1991.

CCP Central Committee Documents Research Department, ed.. *Shiyijie sanzhong chuanhui yilai zhongyao wenxian xuandu* (Selected readings of important documents since the Third Plenum). Vols. 1 and 2. Beijing: Renmin chubanshe, 1987.

———. *Xinshiqi tang de jianshe wenxian xuanbian* (Selected documents on party construction in the new era). Beijing: Renmin chubanshe, 1991.

CCP Central Committee Organizational Department, ed. *Zai shehuizhuyi gongchanzhuyi qizhixia* (Under the banner of socialism and communism). Beijing: Hongqi chubanshe, 1991.

Central Party School. *Jianshe you zhongguo teshe de shehuizhuyi de kexue lilun* (The scientific theory of building socialism with Chinese characteristics). Beijing: Zhonggong zhongyang dangxiao chubanshe, 1989.

Central Party School Department of Theoretical Research. *Guanyu zhenli biaozhun wenti taolun wenji* (Collected articles from the debate on the truth criterion). Beijing: Zhonggong zhongyang dangxiao chubanshe, 1982.

Central Party School and State Commission on Economic Structural Reform, eds. *Nongchun yu chengshi gaige de fansi* (Reflections on rural and urban reforms). Beijing: Jingjikexue chubanshe, 1987.

Chen Mingxian et al. *Xin Zhongguo sishi nian yanjiu* (A study of forty years of new China). Beijing: Beijing Ligongdaxue chubanshe, 1989.

Chen Yizi. *Zhongguo: Shinian gaige yu bajiunian minyun* (China: Ten years' reform and the 1989 Democratic movement). Taipei: Linking Corp., 1990.

Chen Yun. *Chen Yun wengao (1956–1985)* (Manuscripts of Chen Yun). Beijing: Renmin chubanshe, 1986.

Chi Fulin and Huang Hai, eds. *Deng Xiaoping zhengzhi tizhi gaige sixiang yanjiu* (Studies of Deng Xiaoping's thought on political structural reform). Beijing: Chunqiu chubanshe, 1987.

Deng Lijun. *Shangpin jingji de guilü he jihua* (The law of a commodity economy and planning). Beijing: Renmin chubanshe, 1979.

Deng Xiaoping. *Deng Xiaoping tongzhi zhongyao tanhua, February–July 1987* (Important speeches of Comrade Deng Xiaoping). Beijing: Renmin chubanshe, 1987.

———. *Deng Xiaoping wenxuan* (Selected works of Deng Xiaoping). Beijing: Renmin chubanshe, 1983.

———. *Jianshe you Zhongguo teshe de shehuizhuyi* (Building socialism with Chinese characteristics). Beijing: Renmin chubanshe, 1984.

Gao Shangquan, *Jiunian lai zhongguo jingji tizhi gaige* (Nine years of economic structural reform in China). Beijing: Renmin chubanshe, 1987.

General Office of the State Council, *Geti jingji diaocha yu yanjiu* (Investigation and study of the individual economy). Beijing: Jingjikexue chubanshe, 1986.

Gu Shutang and Chai Xiaozhen. *Shehuizhuyi jingji lilun he jingji zhidu yanjiu* (A study of socialist economic theory and economic system). Shanxi: Shanxi renmin chubanshe, 1986.

Hongqi Editorial Board, ed. *Jihua jingji yu shichang tiaojie wenji* (Collected essays on the planned economy and market regulation). Beijing: Hongqi chubanshe, 1982.

Hu Jiwei et al., eds. *Mengxing de shike* (Sudden awakening). Beijing: Zhongwai wenhua chubangongsi, 1989.

Hua Guofeng. *Diwujie renda er'chongquanhui zhengfu gongzhuo baogao* (Government work report to the Second Session of the Fifth NPC). Beijing: Renmin chubanshe, 1979.

———. *Zhongguo gongchandang dishiyijie dahui cailiao ji* (Collected materials of the Eleventh Congress of the Chinese Communist party). Beijing, Renmin chubanshe, 1977.

Institute of Philosophy, Chinese Academy of Social Sciences, ed. *Renxing, rendaozhuyi taolun ji* (Collection of discussions on the question of human nature and humanism). Beijing: Renmin chubanshe, 1982.

Jin, Guantao. *Ren de zhexue* (The philosophy of the person). Chengdu: Sichuan renmin chubanshe, 1988.

Lenin, Vladimir I. *Liening quanji* (Complete works of Lenin). Vol. 1. Beijing: Renmin chubanshe, 1955.

———. *Liening quanji* (Complete works of Lenin). Vol. 8. Beijing: Renmin chubanshe, 1959.

———. *Liening quanji* (Complete works of Lenin). Vol. 26. Beijing: Renmin chubanshe, 1956.

———. *Liening quanji* (Complete works of Lenin). Vol. 29. Beijing: Renmin chubanshe, 1956.

———. *Liening quanji* (Complete works of Lenin). Vol. 32. Beijing: Renmin chubanshe, 1958.

Li Honglin. *Lilun fengyun* (Winds of theory) Beijing: Dushu shenghuo xinzhi, 1985.

———. *Sizhong zhuyi zai Zhongguo* (Four kinds of isms in China). Beijing: Dushu shenghuo xinzhi, 1987.

Li Shengping, ed. *Sanzhong quanhui yilai zhengzhi tizhi gaige yu shijian* (The theory and practice of political structural reform since the Third Plenum). Beijing: Guangming ribao chubanshe, 1989.

Li Yongchun and Luo Jian, eds. *Shiyijie sanzhong quanhui yilai zhengzhi tizhi gaige de lilun yu shijian* (The theory and practice of political structural reform since the Third Plenum). Beijing: Chunqiu chubanshe, 1987.

Lin Zili. *Xuexi Makesi de zai shengzhan lilun* (Studying Marx's theory of reproduction). Beijing: Renmin chubanshe, 1981.

Liu Heren and Sun Liancheng, eds. *Zhengzhi tizhi gaige de jiben gouxiang* (A basic outline of political structural reform). Beijing: Guangming ribao chubanshe, 1986.

Mao Zedong. *Mao Zedong xuanji* (Selected works of Mao Zedong). Collected volume. Beijing: Renmin chubanshe, 1970.

———. *Mao Zedong xuanji* (Selected works of Mao Zedong). Vol. 5. Beijing: Renmin chubanshe, 1977.

Nie Gaomin, Li Yizhou, and Wang Zhongtian, eds. *Dangzheng fenkai lilun tantao* (Exploring the theory of separating the party and the state). Beijing: Chunqiu chubanshe, 1987.

Ren shi Makesizhuyi de chufadian (The person is the starting point of Marxism). Beijing: Renmin chubanshe,1981.

Ruan Ming. "Zhenli biaozhun zhi zhan" (The battle over the truth criterion). Unpublished manuscript.

Stalin, Joseph. *Sidalin quanji* (Complete works of Stalin). Vols. 1 and 2, Beijing: Renmin chubanshe, 1979.

―――. *Sidalin xuanji* (Selected works of Stalin). Beijing: Renmin chubanshe, 1979.

Su Shaozhi. *Maliezhuyi xinlun* (A new theory of Marxism). Taipei: Shidai zazhishe, 1992.

―――. "Minzhu yu gaige" (Democracy and reform). Unpublished manuscript, 1986.

Su Shaozhi and Zhang Xiangyang, eds. *Sanzhong quanhui yilai Makesizhuyi zai Zhongguo de fazhan* (The development of Marxism in China since the Third Plenum). Beijing: Renmin chubanshe, 1989.

Sun Yefang. *Shehuizhuyi jingji de yixi wenti* (Some theoretical problems of socialist economy). Beijing: Renmin chubanshe, 1979.

Tong Dalin. *Dangdai zibenzhuyi yinlun* (Introduction to contemporary capitalism). Beijing: Kexue chubanshe, 1988.

Wang Jue, Pang Yongjie, and Dong Guoying, eds. *Gaige yu fazhan de lilun sikao* (Theoretical reflection on reform and development). Beijing: Zhonggong zhongyang dangxiao chubanshe, 1991.

Wang Zhaozheng and Huang Zheng. *Cong sanzhong quanhui dao shi'er da* (From the Third Plenum to the Twelfth Congress). Beijing: Zhonggong zhongyang dangxiao chubanshe, 1984.

―――. *Cong shi'er da dao shisan da* (From the Twelfth Congress to the Thirteenth Congress). Beijing: Zhongyang dangxiao chubanshe, 1989.

Wu Wei and Fang Mingying. *Zhongguo shehuizhuyi minzhu zhengzhi lungang* (The principles of Chinese socialist democracy). Beijing: Zhongyang dangxiao chubanshe, 1991.

Xinhuashe, ed. *Shijian si jianyan zhenli de weiyi biaozhun* (Practice is the sole criterion of truth). Beijing: Renmin chubanshe, 1979.

Xue Muqiao. *Anzhao keguan jingji guilu guanli jingji* (Manage the economy according to objective economic laws). Beijing: Renmin chubanshe, 1986.

―――. *Dangqian wuoguo jingji ruogan wenti* (Current problems of our country's economy). Beijing: Renmin chubanshe, 1979.

―――. *Gaige yu lilunshang de tupo* (Reform and breakthroughs in theory). Beijing: Renmin chubanshe, 1989.

―――. *Woguo guomin jingji de tiaozheng he gaige* (The readjustment and reform of our national economy). Beijing: Renmin chubanshe, 1982.

―――. *Zhongguo shehuizhuyi jingji wenti yanjiu* (A study of the problems of the Chinese socialist economy). Beijing: Renmin chubanshe, 1979.

Yan Jiaqi. *Wode sixiang zizhuan* (An autobiography of my thought). Hong Kong: Joint Publishing Co., 1988.

Zheng Bifeng and Jia Chunfeng. *Shehuizhuyi chujijieduan lunwenxuan* (Selected essays on the primary stage of socialism). Beijing: Zhongguo qingnian chubanshe, 1988.

Zhongguo gongchandang dishiyijie dahui cailiao ji (Collected materials of the Eleventh Congress of the Chinese Communist party). Beijing: Renmin chubanshe, 1977.

Zhou Shulian. *Zhongguo de jingji gaige he qiye gaige* (Economic reform and enterprise reform in China). Beijing: Jingji guanli chubanshe, 1989.

ENGLISH LANGUAGE SOURCES

Apter, David. *The Politics of Modernization.* Chicago: University of Chicago Press, 1965.

Baum, Richard. "Socialist Modernization and Legal Reform: The Rebirth of Socialist Legality," *Studies in Comparative Communism* 19, 2 (Summer 1986): 69–103.

Bornstein, Morris. "Economic Reform in East Europe," in *East European Economies Post Helsinki.* Committee Print, Joint Economic Committee, 95th Congress, 1st session. Washington, D.C.: GPO, 1977.

Brodsgaard, Kjeld. "Democracy Movement in China, 1978–79," *Asian Survey* 21, 7 (July 1981): 747–74.

Brown, Archie. "Ideology and Political Culture," in *Politics, Society, and Nationality inside Gorbachev's Russia,* ed. Seweryn Bialer. Boulder: Westview Press, 1989.

Brugger, Bill. "Alienation Revisited," *Australia Journal of Chinese Affairs* 12 (July 1984): 143–52.

———, ed. *Chinese Marxism in Flux 1978–84.* Armonk, N.Y.: M. E. Sharpe, 1985.

Brugger, Bill, and David Kelly, *Chinese Marxism in the Post-Mao Era* (Stanford: Stanford University Press, 1990).

Brzezinski, Z. K. *Ideology and Power in Soviet Politics.* New York: Praeger, 1967.

Buchholz, Arnold. "*Perestroika* and Ideology: Fundamental Questions as to the Maintenance of and Change in the Soviet System," *Studies in Soviet Thought* 36, 3 (October 1988): 149–68.

———. "A Sortie into Soviet Ideology," *Studies in Soviet Thought* 36, 2 (July/August 1988): 111–16.

Chan, Steve. *East Asian Dynamism.* Boulder: Westview Press, 1990.

Ching, Frank. "The Current Political Scene in China," *The China Quarterly* 80 (December 1979): 691–715.

Cohen, Paul. "The Post-Mao Reforms in Historical Perspective," *Journal of Asian Studies* 47, 3 (August 1988): 518–40.

Dahm, Helmut. "The Function and Efficacy of Ideology," *Studies in Soviet Thought* 21, 2 (May 1980): 109–18.

Daniels, Norman, ed. *Reading Rawls.* New York: Basic Books, 1974.

Dernberger, Robert. "Economic Policy and Performance," in *China's Economy Looks toward the Year 2000.* Vol. 1: *The Four Modernizations.* Committee Print, Joint Economic Committee, 99th Congress, 2d session. Washington, D.C.: GPO, 1986.

Ding, Xueliang. "The Difference between Idealistic Reformers and Instrumental Reformers," *Asian Survey* 28, 11 (November 1987): 1117–39.

Dirlik, Arif. "Socialism and Capitalism in Chinese Socialist Thinking," *Studies in Comparative Communism* 21, 2 (Summer 1988): 133–52.

———. "Spiritual Solutions to Material Problems: The 'Socialist Ethics and Courtesy Month' in China," *South Atlantic Quarterly* 81, 4 (Autumn 1982): 359–75.

Dirlik, Arif, and Maurice Meisner, eds. *Marxism and the Chinese Experience.* Armonk, N.Y.: M. E. Sharpe, 1989.

Dittmer, Lowell. "China in 1988: The Continuing Dilemma of Socialist Reform," *Asian Survey* 29, 1 (January 1989): 12–28.

———. "China in 1989: Crisis of Incomplete Reform," *Asian Survey* 30, 1 (January 1990): 25–47.

———. "Soviet Reform and the Prospect of Sino-Soviet Convergence," *Studies in Comparative Communism* 22, 2/3 (Summer/Autumn 1989): 123–38.

Djilas, Milovan. *The New Class.* New York: Frederick A. Praeger, 1957.

Dominguez, Jorge I. "Revolutionary Values and Developmental Performance: China, Cuba and the Soviet Union," in *Value and Development: Appraisal of the Asian Experience,* ed. Harold Lasswell, Daniel Lerner, and John D. Montgomery. Cambridge, Mass.: MIT Press, 1976.

Eisenstadt, S. N. *Modernization: Protest and Change.* Englewood Cliffs, N.J.: Prentice-Hall, 1966.

Ellison, Herbert. "Perestroika and the New Economic Policy (1921–1928): The Uses of History," in *Transformation of Socialism,* ed. Mel Gurtov. Boulder: Westview Press, 1990.

Evans, Alfred, Jr. "The Decline of Developed Socialism? Some Trends in Recent Soviet Ideology," *Soviet Studies* 38, 1 (January 1987): 1–23.

———. "Developed Socialism in Soviet Ideology," *Soviet Studies* 39, 3 (July 1977): 409–28.

Fairbank, John K. *The United States and China.* Cambridge: Harvard Univeristy Press, 1948.

Femia, Joseph V. "Ideological Obstacles to the Political Evolution of Communist Systems," *Studies in Soviet Thought* 34, 4 (November 1987): 215–32.

Fewsmith, Joseph. "The Dengist Reforms in Historical Perspective," in *Contemporary Chinese Politics in Historical Perspective,* ed. Brantly Womack. Cambridge: Cambridge University Press, 1991.

Fisk, Milton. "History and Reason in Rawls' Moral Theory." In *Reading Rawls,* ed. Norman Daniels. New York: Basic Books, 1974.

Friedman, Edward. "Maoism, Titoism, Stalinism: Some Origins and Consequences of the Maoist Theory of the Socialist Transition," in *The Transition to Socialism in China,* ed. Mark Selden and Victor Lippit. Armonk, N.Y.: M. E. Sharpe, 1982.

Friedman, Robert. *Marxist Social Thought.* New York: Harcourt, Brace & World, 1959.

Gold, Thomas. "Just In Time!" *Asian Survey* 24, 9 (September 1984): 947–74.

Goldman, Merle. "Hu Yaobang's Intellectual Network and the Theory Conference of 1979," *The China Quarterly* 126 (June 1991): 219–42.

Goldstein, Steven M. "Reforming the Socialist System: Some Lessons of the Chinese Experience," *Studies in Comparative Communism* 21, 2 (Summer 1988): 221–37.

Goodman, David S. G. "The Chinese Political Order after Mao: 'Socialist Democracy' and the Exercise of State Power," *Political Studies* 2 (1985): 218–35.

Gorbachev, Mikhail S. *Speeches and Writings.* New York: Pergamon, 1987.

Gray, Jack. "The Two Lines," in *Authority, Participation and Cultural Change*, ed. Stuart Schram. Cambridge: Oxford University Press, 1973.

Gurtov, Mel, ed. *Transformation of Socialism.* Boulder: Westview Press, 1990.

Haggard, Stephen. *Pathways from the Periphery: The Politics of Growth in the Newly Industrializing Countries.* Ithaca: Cornell University Press, 1991.

Haksar, Vinit. *Equality, Liberty, and Perfectionism.* Oxford: Oxford University Press, 1979.

———. "Review Article: Autonomy, Justice and Contractarianism," *British Journal of Political Science* 3, 4 (October 1973): 487–509.

Halpern, Nina. "China's Industrial Economic Reforms: The Question of Strategy," *Asian Survey* 25, 10 (October 1985): 998–1012.

Hamrin, Carol Lee. "Competing 'Policy Packages' in Post-Mao China," *Asian Survey* 24, 5 (May 1984): 487–518.

Hamilton, Malcolm B. "The Elements of Ideology," *Political Studies* 35 (1987): 18–38.

Harding, Harding. *China's Second Revolution: Reform after Mao.* Washington, D.C.: Brookings Institution, 1987.

Hoston, Germaine. *Marxism and the Crisis of Development in Japan.* Princeton: Princeton University Press, 1986.

———. *The State, Identity, and the National Question in China and Japan.* Princeton: Princeton University Press, 1994.

Huntington, Samuel, and Jorge Dominguez. "Political Development." In *Handbook of Political Science*, ed. Fred Greenstein and Nelson Polsby. Reading, Mass.: Addison-Wesley, 1972.

Johnson, Chalmers. *MITI and the Japanese Miracle.* Stanford: Stanford University Press, 1982.

Joseph, William, A. *The Critique of Ultra-Leftism in China, 1959–1981.* Stanford: Stanford University Press, 1984.

Lampton, Michael D., ed. *Policy Implementation in Post-Mao China.* Berkeley: University of California Press, 1987.

Lenin, Vladimir I. *State and Revolution.* Beijing: Foreign Language Press, 1967.

Leung, Hanson, C. K. "The Role of Leadership in Adaptation to Change: Lessons of Economic Reform in the USSR and China," *Studies in Comparative Communism* 18, 4 (Winter 1985): 227–46.

Levenson, Joseph. *Liang Chi-chao and the Mind of Modern China.* Cambridge: Harvard University Press, 1985.

Lieberthal, Kenneth, and Michel Oksenberg. *Policy Making in China.* Princeton: Princeton University Press, 1988.

Lin, Yusheng. *The Crisis of Chinese Consciousness: Radical Anti-traditionalism in the May Fourth Era.* Madison: University of Wisconsin Press, 1979.

Lin Yusheng. *The May Fourth Movement*. Cambridge: Harvard University Press, 1965.

Link, Perry. "The Chinese Intellectuals and the Revolt," *The New York Review of Books*, June 29, 1989, 38–41.

MacFarquhar, Roderick. *The Origins of the Cultural Revolution*. 2 vols. New York: Columbia University Press, 1974, 1983.

Maguire, John M. *Marx's Theory of Politics*. Cambridge: Cambridge University Press, 1978.

Mao Zedong. *Selected Works of Mao Zedong*. Vol. 3. Beijing: Foreign Language Press, 1965.

Marx, Karl. *Capital*, ed. Frederick Engels. Vol. 3. New York: International Publishers Co., 1967.

———. *Capital,*. Vol. 1. In *Marxist Social Thought*, ed. Robert Freeman. New York: Harcourt, Brace & World, 1968.

———. The Critique of the Gotha Program. In *Basic Writings on Politics and Philosophy, Karl Marx and Friedrich Engels*, ed. Lewis S. Feuer. New York: Anchor Books, 1959.

———. "Critique of the Gotha Programme," in *Marx-Engels Reader*, ed. Robert C. Tucker. New York: W. W. Norton, 1974.

———. "Preface to the Critique of Political Economy," in *Marx-Engels Reader*, ed. Robert C. Tucker. New York: W. W. Norton, 1974.

Michael, Franz, et al. *China and the Crisis of Marxism-Leninism*. Boulder: Westview Press, 1990.

Moore, Barrington. *Soviet Politics: The Dilemma of Power, the Role of Ideas in Social Change*. New York: Harper Torchbooks, 1965.

Nathan, Andrew. "Chinese Democracy in 1989: Continuity and Change," *Problems of Communism* 37 (September/October 1989): 1–19.

———. "A Factional Model of Chinese Politics," *The China Quarterly* 53 (January–March 1973): 34–66.

———. "Policy Oscillations in the People's Republic of China: A Critique," *The China Quarterly* 68 (1976): 20–50.

Nielsen, Kai. "The Choice between Perfectionism and Rawlsian Contractarianism," *Interpretation* 6, 2 (May 1977): 132–39.

Oi, Jean. "Market Reforms and Corruption in Rural China," *Studies in Comparative Communism* 22, 2/3 (Summer 1989): 221–33.

Pye, Lucien. *The Dynamics of Chinese Politics*. Cambridge, Mass.: Oelgeschlager, Gunn and Hain, 1981.

———. *The Mandarin and the Cadre: China's Political Cultures*. Ann Arbor: Center for Chinese Studies, University of Michigan, 1988.

———. "On Chinese Pragmatism in the 80's," *The China Quarterly* 106 (July 1986): 207–34.

Rawls, John. *A Theory of Justice*. Cambridge: Harvard University Press, 1975.

Resolution on CCP History (1949–1981). Beijing: Foreign Language Press, 1981.

Richer, Helena. "Ideology Soviet Style," *Crossroads* (Jerusalem) (Autumn 1978): 27–46.

Rosen, Stanley. "China in 1986: A Year of Consolidation," *Asian Survey* 27, 1 (January 1987): 35–55.

————. "China in 1987, the Year of the Thirteenth Congress," *Asian Survey* 28, 1 (January 1988): 35–51.

Rozman, Gilbert. *The Chinese Debate about Soviet Socialism, 1978–1985.* Princeton: Princeton University Press, 1987.

Sautman, Barry. "Sirens of the Strongman: Neo-Authoritarianism in Recent Chinese Political Theory," *The China Quarterly* 125 (March 1991): 72–102.

Scanlan, James. "Ideology and Reform," in *Gorbachev's Reforms, U.S. and Japanese Assessments*, ed. Peter Juviler and Hiroshi Kimura. New York: Aldine de Gruyter, 1988.

Schoenhals, Michael. "The 1978 Truth Criterion Controversy," *The China Quarterly* 126 (June 1991): 251–68.

Schram, Stuart. "China since the Thirteenth Congress," *The China Quarterly* 114 (June 1988): 177–97.

————. "'Economics in Command?' Ideology and Policy since the Third Plenum 1978–84," *The China Quarterly* 99 (September 1984): 417–61.

————. *Ideology and Policy since the Third Plenum, 1978–1984.* London: Contemporary China Institute, School of Oriental and African Studies, 1984.

Schull, Joseph. "What Is Ideology? Theoretical Problems and Lessons from Soviet-Type Societies," *Political Studies* 40 (1992): 728–41.

Schurmann, Franz. *Ideology and Organization.* London: Cambridge University Press, 1968.

Schwartz, Benjamin. *In Search of Wealth and Power: Yen Fu and the West.* Cambridge: Harvard University Press, 1964.

Selden, Mark. *The Political Economy of Chinese Development.* Armonk, N.Y.: M. E. Sharpe, 1993.

Seliger, Martin. *Ideology and Politics.* London: Allen and Unwin, 1976.

————. *Marxist Conception of Ideology.* Cambridge: Cambridge University Press, 1977.

Shlapentokh, Vladimir. *Soviet Public Opinion and Ideology, Mythology and Pragmatism in Interaction.* New York: Praeger, 1986.

Skinner, G. William. "Marketing and Soical Structure in Rural China," *Journal of Asian Studies* 24, 1 (November 1964): 3–44 (part 1); 24, 2 (February 1965): 195–288 (part 2); 24, 3 (May 1965): 363–400 (part 3).

Solinger, Dorothy J. *China's Transition from Socialism: Statist Legacies and Market Reform.* Stanford: Stanford University Press, 1993.

————. *Chinese Business under Socialism: The Politics of Domestic Commerce 1949–1980.* Berkeley: University of California Press, 1984.

————. "Economic Reform via Reformulation in China: Where Do Rightist Ideas Come From?" *Asian Survey* 29, 9 (September 1981): 947–60.

————. "The Fifth National People's Congress and the Process of Policy Making: Reform, Readjustment, and the Opposition," *Asian Survey* 22 (December 1982): 1238–75.

————, ed. *Three Visions of Chinese Socialism.* Boulder: Westview, 1984.

Spence, Jonathan. *The Search for Modern China.* New York: W. W. Norton, 1990.

Stalin, Joseph. *Economic Problems of Socialism in the USSR.* New York: International Publishers, 1952.

Su Shaozhi. *Marxism and Chinese Reform.* Norttingham: Spokesman, 1993
———. *Marxism in China.* Norttingham: Spokesman, 1983.
———. Review of *Chinese Marxism in the Post-Mao Era,* by Bill Brugger and David Kelly, in *The Australian Journal of Chinese Affairs* 1, 23 (1993): 168–69.
Sullivan, Michael. "CCP Ideology since the Third Plenum," in *Chinese Marxism in Flux 1978–1984,* ed. Bill Brugger. Armonk, N.Y.: M. E. Sharpe, 1985.
Sun, Yan. "The Chinese Protests of 1991: The Issue of Corruption," *Asian Survey* 31, 8 (August 1991): 762–82.
Tasas, Ray. *Ideology in a Socialist State, Poland 1956–1983.* Cambridge: Cambridge University Press, 1984.
Teiwes, Frederick. *Politics and Purge in China: Rectification and the Decline of Party Norms, 1949–1965.* White Plains, N.Y.: M .E. Sharpe, 1979.
Tsou, Tang. *The Cultural Revolution and Post-Mao Reform, a Historical Perspective.* Chicago: University of Chicago Press, 1986.
———. "Political Change and Reform: The Middle Course," in *China: The 80's Era,* ed. Norton Ginsburg and Bernard Lalor. Boulder: Westview Press, 1984.
———. "Twentieth Century Chinese Politics and Western Political Science," *PS* (Spring 1987): 327–33.
Womack, Brantly. *Contemporary Chinese Politics in Historical Perspective.* Cambridge: Cambridge University Press, 1991.
———. "Politics and Epistemology in Post-Mao China," *The China Quarterly* 80 (December 1979): 768–95.
Xue, Muqiao. *Current Economic Problems of China.* Boulder: Westview, 1982.
Zagoria, Donald. *The Sino-Soviet Conflict.* Princeton: Princeton University Press, 1962.
Zaslavskaya, Tatyana. *The Second Socialist Revolution.* Bloomington: Indiana University Press, 1990.

Index

over plan vs., 56, 63–67, 69, 75, 76, 81, 82, 91, 97, 117; and corruption, 78, 80, 81, 144; and democracy, 144; differences under socialism and capitalism, 107; and distribution, 103, 115–17; distribution ethic of, 103, 104, 117; integration of plan and, 62, 66, 68, 75, 92, 117; labor, 108; origin and function of, 86, 106, 107; and political system, 172; supplementary role of, 56, 64, 66, 91, 101, 120, 255; traditional resistance to, 166; transition to, 146, 148; under socialism, 87, 89, 95, 98, 105, 108, 120. *See also* Commodity economy; Market economy

Market economy, 53, 66, 69, 76, 83, 103, 113, 118, 242, 265. *See also* Commodity economy

Marx, Karl: on base and superstructure, 164; on capitalism, 48, 58, 86, 87, 101; centenary of, 131, 132, 187; on class struggle, 42; on commodity economy, 52, 53, 86, 95; and conception of humans, 131, 132, 303n, 304n; and development of the person, 178, 179, 203, 208; on distribution, 44, 87, 89, 94, 117; early works of, 267, 268; on expanded production, 59; on exploitation, 208; and five modes of production, 187; original theories of, 74, 84, 152; on product economy, 52, 53, 56, 76, 86, 89–91, 106, 107; on revolution, 153, 198; and social justice, 178; on socialist society, 65, 86, 188, 189, 190, 198; in Soviet discussion, 239, 249, 252; on the state, 153, 154, 157, 180, 181; view of ownership, 86, 90, 108–10, 112

Marxism, 13, 29, 37, 40, 69, 72, 83, 95, 223; applicability and feasibility of, 212, 213; application of, 188, 189, 216; bifurcation of, 35–37, 39, 50, 198, 221, 222; and Chinese reassessment, 272; defense of, 224, 235; development of, 136, 139, 183, 187–94, 197–200, 217, 270; feudalization of, 210, 211; "liberal" attitudes toward, 217, 219, 224, 236; methodology of, 192, 197, 198, 200, 244, 272; monopolistic status of, 210, 229, 267, 268; normative view of, questioned, 179, 199, 100; as source of value, 222; upholding of, 191, 194, 199, 217, 223; upholding vs. development of, 5–7, 16

Marxism-Leninism, 14, 22, 28, 121, 221, 246; dialectic materialist approach to, 35, 36, 38; dogmatic approach to, 40, 50, 147; guiding role of, 252

Masses: relationship with leaders, 123, 124; relationship with party, 150, 162

May Fourth Movement, 17, 177, 178, 196, 205

Medvedev, V. A., 244

Meisner, Maurice, 8, 13

Mengxin de shike (The moment of sudden awakening), 147, 210

Metaphysical idealist line, 37, 38, 40, 50

Modernization: Chinese road of, 55, 56, 84; as common course, 208; cultural, 191; economic, 127, 138, 151, 224; economic and political, 138; heavy industrial, 54; process of, 267

Moore, Barrington, 10

Multiparty system, 145, 147, 159, 160, 182, 231, 234, 244

Nathan, Andrew, 236

National People's Congress, 26, 34, 43, 57, 60, 62, 64, 67, 72, 157, 180.

Natural economy, 106, 107, 164, 165

"Neo-authoritarianism" (*xinquanwei zhuyi*), 145, 146, 176, 274

New Democracy, 186, 195

New Economic Policy, 87

"New Order of the Socialist Commodity Economy," 76, 105

"New thinking" (Gorbachev), 3, 4, 237, 239, 257

Nie Rongzhen, 25

Nineteenth All Union Conference of CPSU (1988), 240, 242

NPC. *See* National People's Congress

Objective laws, 26, 32, 50, 103

—content of: basic law of socialist economy, 49, 54, 58; law of planned and proportionate development, 48, 49, 58, 60; law of prior development of the producer sector, 58, 59; law of value, 48, 88, 91

October Revolution, 3, 4, 87, 248

Oksenberg, Michel, 13, 169

Opium War, 206, 218

Ownership: collective, 90, 92, 93; common, 86, 94, 102; cooperative, 52, 96, 90, 95, 106, 109, 120; enterprise, 93, 98; exclusivity of, 111, 112; individual, 64,

About the Author

YAN SUN is Assistant Professor of Political Science at Queens College of the City University of New York.